Sardar Sarovar

Work on the main canal south of the Mahi River, Gujarat.

Sardar Sarovar

Report of the Independent Review

Chairman *Bradford Morse*
Deputy Chairman *Thomas Berger*

Senior Advisors
ENVIRONMENT Donald Gamble
RESETTLEMENT Hugh Brody

Published for THE INDEPENDENT REVIEW *by*
Resource Futures International (RFI) INC

Copyright © 1992 by Bradford Morse and Thomas R. Berger

Editors: Heather Jarman, Brian Scrivener
Design © Robin Ward
Photographs © Ulli Steltzer
Maps © Maps Unlimited
Typeset in Baskerville by
The Typeworks, Vancouver Canada
Printed and Bound in Canada by M.O.M., Ottawa

Front Cover: Construction on the Sardar Sarovar dam.
Back Cover: A Bhil ferryman crossing the Narmada River
from Gujarat to Maharashtra.

CANADIAN CATALOGUING IN PUBLICATION DATA

Independent Review of the Sardar Sarovar Project.
Sardar Sarovar
Chairman, Bradford Morse; deputy chairman,
Thomas R. Berger.
Includes bibliographical references.
ISBN 0-9696325-0-9
1. Sardar Sarovar (Narmada) Project—Social
aspects.   2. Sardar Sarovar (Narmada) Project—
Environmental aspects.   3. Water resources
development—Economic aspects—India—Narmada
River Watershed.   4. Water resources development
—Environmental aspects—India—Narmada River
Watershed.   5. Human settlements—India—Gujarat
(State).   6. Dams—Social aspects—India—Gujarat
(State).   I. Morse, Bradford F., 1921–
II. Berger, Thomas R.
III. Resource Futures International. IV. title.
HN690.G84I53 1992   333.3′1′5475
C92-091509-4

RESOURCE FUTURES INTERNATIONAL (RFI) INC.
Suite 406, One Nicholas Street,
Ottawa, Canada K1N 7B7

Contents

ACKNOWLEDGMENTS

OUR review was immensely strengthened by the efforts of many individuals and organizations in India and elsewhere. We would like to express our gratitude to all those who so kindly provided support and assistance.

Our work depended on the extraordinary cooperation of the officers and staff of the World Bank, both in Washington and Delhi. In India, we had the invaluable advantage of open and full participation by the Union Government Ministries of Water Resources and Environment and Forests, the Narmada Control Authority, officials of all three state governments and, especially, the Sardar Sarovar Narmada Nigam Limited under the chairmanship of Dr. C. C. Patel. We thank them all.

We want to thank the non-government organizations in India—especially Arch Vahini, Narmada Bachao Andolan, and the Anand Niketan Ashram—for their information and practical assistance. We are also grateful to the hundreds of people who made submissions and otherwise helped us to understand the many dimensions of the Sardar Sarovar Projects. And we want to thank the people of the Narmada valley for their warm hospitality during our visits.

Resource Futures International provided our review with an institutional home and, under the direction of Mr. Gamble and Mr. Brody, engaged the experts we needed to complete our task. We relied especially on a number of these specialists in the preparation of our report. We want to acknowledge the help in particular of Dr. Ruwani Jayewardene, Mr. Charles Howard, Dr. D. R. Bhumbla, Mr. Abdul Salam, Dr. Felix Padel, Ms. Amita Baviskar, Dr. Anthony Gaston, Dr. Gautam Appa, Mr. R. Sridharan, and Dr. Peter Sly.

We would also like to express our thanks to Heather Jarman for her untiring help in preparation of successive drafts of this report.

The photographs in our report are by Ulli Steltzer. We thank her for making them available to us.

It needs to be said that this Independent Review is, to the best of our knowledge, without precedent. The World Bank must be given full credit for a innovative and bold approach to a difficult problem.

INDEPENDENT REVIEW

Chairman
Bradford Morse

Deputy Chairman
Thomas R. Berger

June 18, 1992

Lewis T. Preston
President
The World Bank
1818 H Street, N.W.
Washington, DC 20433
USA

Dear Mr. President:

On September 1, 1991 we began our Independent Review of the Sardar Sarovar dam and irrigation projects in India. Since then we have spent much time in India: we conferred with ministers and officials of the Government of India and of the Governments of Gujarat, Maharashtra, and Madhya Pradesh; we met with non-government organizations and concerned citizens; we received hundreds of submissions. We travelled throughout the Narmada valley, to villages and relocation sites, to the dam site, the upstream area, the command area, and downstream. We also visited Kutchch and other drought-prone areas of Gujarat.

We have talked to whomever we thought could help us in the task assigned to us, that is, to conduct an assessment of the measures being taken to resettle and rehabilitate the population displaced or otherwise affected by the Sardar Sarovar Projects, and of the measures being taken to ameliorate the environmental impact of the Projects.

The World Bank has made an important contribution to the advancement of human and environmental concerns by developing policies for the resettlement and rehabilitation of people displaced or otherwise affected by Bank-supported projects and for the mitigation of the environmental effects of such

Suite 400, One Nicholas Street, Ottawa, Canada, K1N 7B7 Fax: (613) 563-4758 Phone: (613) 230-0162 projects. Similarly the Government of India has developed a comprehensive environmental regime to reduce the environmental impact of public works projects. In spite of these positive factors, however, we believe that the situation is very serious. We have discovered fundamental failures in the implementation of the Sardar Sarovar Projects.

We think the Sardar Sarovar Projects as they stand are flawed, that resettlement and rehabilitation of all those displaced by the Projects is not possible under prevailing circumstances, and that the environmental impacts of the Projects have not been properly considered or adequately addressed. Moreover, we believe that the Bank shares responsibility with the borrower for the situation that has developed.

The Sardar Sarovar Projects are intended to bring drinking water to Kutchch and other drought-prone regions of Gujarat, and to irrigate a vast area of that state as well as two districts of Rajasthan. This requires a large reservoir on the Narmada River and an extensive canal and irrigation system.

The Sardar Sarovar dam, under construction on the Narmada River, at Navagam and Kevadia, will impound water to a full reservoir level of 455 feet. It will submerge 37,000 hectares of land in three states: Gujarat, Maharashtra, and Madhya Pradesh.

The Sardar Sarovar dam, along with planned developments farther upstream, is designed to divert 9.5 million acre feet of water from the Narmada River into a canal and irrigation system. The canal itself is the biggest in the world in terms of its capacity, and will extend 450 kilometers to the border with Rajasthan. The main canal is 250 meters wide at its head and 100 meters wide at the Rajasthan border. The aggregate length of the distribution network is 75,000 kilometers. It will require approximately 80,000 hectares of land, more than twice as much land as the submergence area.

The Sardar Sarovar Projects constitute one of the largest water resources projects ever undertaken; their impact extends over an immense area and affects a very large number of people, especially tribals. At least 100,000 people, in 245 villages, live in the area affected by submergence. In Gujarat and Maharashtra almost all are tribals. A great many of them are encroachers, that is, they have no formal title to their land. There are thousands of tribal people in the submergence area of Madhya Pradesh as well, many of whom are encroachers. In Madhya Pradesh there are also many caste villages where the inhabitants are engaged in conventional agriculture.

In addition to the 100,000 people living in the villages in the submergence area, there are likely to be 140,000 farmers who will be affected by the canal and irrigation system. Finally, there are the people living downstream, below the dam, numbering thousands more, whose lives will be significantly affected.

In 1985 the Bank entered into credit and loan agreements with the Government of India and the Governments of Gujarat, Madhya Pradesh, and Maharashtra relating to the construction of the dam and the canal. Under these agreements the Bank has treated only the people whose villages will be affected by submergence as "project-affected" persons entitled to be resettled and rehabilitated. Our first task has been to consider the measures being taken for the resettlement and rehabilitation of these people. But our Terms of Reference refer to persons "displaced/affected by the reservoir and infrastructure." We were also asked by President Conable to consider, under our Terms of Reference, the status of resettlement and compensation for "canal-affected persons."

On the environmental side, our Terms of Reference require us to consider measures being taken to ameliorate the impact of "all aspects of the Projects." To do this we have reviewed the extent to which there has been compliance with the Bank's and India's requirements for the Projects. We have also considered hydrology and water management issues and their relationship to environmental impact upstream, downstream, and in the command area. Without an understanding of these matters it is impossible to appreciate what the environmental impact of the Projects may be, and thus to determine what ameliorative measures are appropriate.

The idea of damming the Narmada goes back many years, but its realization has been complicated by the fact that the river passes through three states, which could not agree upon division of project costs and benefits. In 1969 the dispute was referred to the Narmada Water Disputes Tribunal, established under India's *Interstate Water Disputes Act, 1956*. In 1979 the Tribunal handed down its award. The Tribunal, by agreement of the states, for the purpose of distribution of benefits accepted the figure of 28 million acre feet as the flow of the Narmada. It went on to apportion 9 million acre feet of water to Gujarat—the water to be diverted into the canal for use in that state (another.5 million acre feet was to be delivered to Rajasthan). The hydroelectric benefits were divided among the three riparian states. The assumptions upon which the Tribunal's award were based included a second dam project, Narmada Sagar, which was to be built, concurrently with Sardar Sarovar, upstream in Madhya Pradesh, as part of a basin-wide storage system.

In 1985 the World Bank made credits and loans, totalling US $450 million, to India and the states of Gujarat, Maharashtra, and Madhya Pradesh, to help finance the construction of the Sardar Sarovar dam and canal. A second application has been made for US $350 million to complete the canal. And there is now before the Bank an application for an additional US $90 million for an associated project, the Narmada Basin Development Project.

The Narmada Water Disputes Tribunal laid down conditions regarding resettlement and rehabilitation of those who would be displaced by submergence in Madhya Pradesh and Maharashtra, described in the award as the "oustees." The Government of India imposed certain environmental conditions. The Bank's credit and loan agreements contain requirements relating to both. There is a dispute within India and worldwide over the question of whether India and the states have lived up to these conditions and requirements.

Our Terms of Reference require us, in making our assessment, to consider all of the Bank's existing operational directives and guidelines, bearing in mind that the credit and loan agreements were approved in 1985. Under Bank policy at that time resettlement and rehabilitation and environmental impact had to be appraised at the threshold of a project. Yet there was no proper appraisal made of the Sardar Sarovar Projects; no adequate appraisals of resettlement and rehabilitation, or of environmental impact, were made prior to approval. The Projects proceeded on the basis of an extremely limited understanding of both human and environmental impact, with inadequate plans in place and inadequate mitigative measures under way.

It is noteworthy that the Bank has seen fit to establish our review. The Bank has provided us with all necessary documents, has engaged in the frankest discussions with us, and has given us the latitude we needed to do our job. We think it unlikely that any other international aid organization has ever established a review with a mandate as sweeping as ours in connection with a project, no matter how controversial. The Bank's willingness to do so is a tribute to its determination to understand what has gone wrong with the Projects. Similarly, we have had the cooperation of the Government of India, of the Governments of Gujarat, Maharashtra, and Madhya Pradesh, of nongovernment organizations, and of people affected by the Projects.

In the past, when high dams have been built, people living in the submergence area have often been evicted without proper compensation, often without due process. This has happened in developed countries as well as developing countries. Compensation, in such cases, did not usually include anything more than cash, and the cash was more often than not inadequate, rarely if ever sufficient to buy replacement land.

Since World War II, developed and developing countries have built high dams in rural, forest, and frontier regions. Usually, this has resulted in incursions on the lands of indigenous and tribal people. It was the special situation of these people that first gave rise to measures to protect persons subject to involuntary resettlement.

The earliest international recognition came in 1957. In that year the International Labor Organization (ILO) passed Convention 107; it required that indigenous or tribal oustee families be "provided with lands of quality at least equal to that of the lands previously occupied by them, suitable to provide for their present needs and future development." India ratified Convention 107 on September 29, 1958.

In 1979, in India itself, the Narmada Water Disputes Tribunal stipulated that landed oustees in Maharashtra and Madhya Pradesh were to receive land for land, in fact, a minimum of two hectares (five acres) of land. Moreover, the Tribunal held that major sons of landed families (i.e., those aged 18 and over) were to be treated as separate families. Landless oustees, under the award, were to receive only a house lot.

India and the three states, Gujarat, Maharashtra, and Madhya Pradesh, take the position that under the Tribunal award, land for land was only intended for the benefit of landowners holding formal title, i.e., having what is known in India as revenue land. They say that the Tribunal did not intend that tribal people cultivating encroached land in the forest, to which they have no formal title, should receive any land on resettlement.

In 1980, the World Bank, for the first time, adopted a general resettlement policy. Indeed, the Bank made clear that there must be not only resettlement but also rehabilitation. It therefore provided that, on resettlement, displaced persons should "regain at least their previous standard of living." Such persons were to include those displaced by dams and canals. Moreover, in 1982, the Bank developed a policy specifically designed for tribal people. It provided that their customary usage of land should be respected, and required that they should only be displaced when the borrower can implement "measures that will effectively safeguard the integrity and well-being of the tribal people."

In 1985, when the credit and loan agreements were signed between the Bank and the three states, no one knew the scale of the displacement that would result from the Sardar Sarovar Projects, nor did anyone have anything like a true picture of the peoples who were to be displaced, nor had the people themselves been consulted. In fact, resettlement policies for Sardar Sarovar, both those of the states and to a great extent those of the Bank, have been based on the measures set out in the 1979 Tribunal award. But the award sought mainly to adjudicate an interstate dispute. It did not, and should not have been expected to, design policies that would meet the needs of the affected people of the Projects as a whole. It did not even mention the Gujarat oustees, nor did it concern itself with the people potentially affected by the canal and irrigation system, nor did it take into account the cultural attributes of the oustee population; in the award there is no discussion of tribal peoples, or of encroachers, or of the real meaning of "landlessness."

In 1985, when the credit and loan agreements were signed, no basis for designing, implementing, and assessing resettlement and rehabilitation was in place. The numbers of people to be affected were not known; the range of likely impacts had never been considered; the canal had been overlooked. Nor had there been any consultation with those at risk. Nor were there benchmark data with which to assess success or failure. As a result, there was no adequate resettlement plan, with the result that human costs could not be included as part of the equation. Policies to mitigate those costs could not be designed in accord with people's actual needs.

When the Bank signed the agreements for the Sardar Sarovar dam, it adopted the definition of landed oustee as set out in the Tribunal's award, which did not include encroachers. Moreover, it did not address the question whether major sons were to receive land. This created the possibility of dispossession for the majority of tribal oustees.

At the same time the Bank, in the agreements for the canal, made no separate provision for those persons displaced or otherwise affected by the canal. Oustees were defined as those affected by submergence and project infrastructure, even though, in 1980, the Bank had acknowledged that resettlement is necessary in the case of persons displaced by canals and irrigation systems.

In 1990, the Bank announced a comprehensive resettlement policy applying to oustees generally, and in 1991 a specific resettlement policy relating to tribals. These policy statements reiterated and elaborated the principles laid down a decade earlier.

These Bank policies reflect the global adoption of new concepts of human rights. They constitute a recognition that large-scale projects, especially in rural, forested, and frontier areas, may displace people just as do war and natural calamities. They focus on people who are being displaced by the advance of development, and require that in any project the human rights of the oustees must be respected. According to ILO 107, these are rights not to be impaired on grounds of national sovereignty or national interest. These considerations may justify undertaking a project but, according to ILO 107, they do not justify the nullification of these human rights if a project goes ahead. The governments of the three states claim that they are prepared to implement the award of the Tribunal and to live by the Bank credit and loan agreements. There is disagreement, however, over interpretation. Gujarat, which has 4,700 oustee families, adopted a policy in 1988 which offers two hectares of land to all landed oustees. It also offers two hectares of land to those designated as landless; tribals and others who may be cultivating encroached land therefore receive two hectares of land. Under Gujarat's policy, in keeping with the Tribunal's award, major sons also receive two hectares.

The Government of Gujarat and the Governments of Madhya Pradesh and Maharashtra contend that Gujarat's policy goes beyond the requirements set out in the Tribunal award and the Bank agreements. Maharashtra, which may have as many as 3,000 families to be resettled, and Madhya Pradesh, with as many as 23,000 families to be resettled, are prepared to offer two hectares of land to landed oustees. But they are not willing to provide two hectares for major sons. Neither Madhya Pradesh nor Maharashtra acknowledges any rights of encroachers to adequate land on resettlement.

This disparity in state policies has resulted in a dispute over the meaning of the Tribunal award and the requirements of the Bank credit and loan agreements. The dispute may seem technical but upon its outcome depends the chances of thousands of oustees to land on resettlement.

The first aspect of the dispute relates to major sons. It is said that Madhya Pradesh and Maharashtra are obliged under the Tribunal award to provide two hectares for major sons of families displaced from revenue lands. The states say they are not. Yet the direction by the Tribunal that every major son be treated as a separate family stands without qualification, express or implied. What other purpose would this provision serve except to enable each major son to claim the same entitlement as the family to which he belongs? In our view the failure of Madhya Pradesh and Maharashtra to provide a minimum of two hectares of land to each major son in any landed family constitutes non-compliance with the Tribunal award.

Of course, even if the Tribunal's award were to be adopted, as regards major sons, by Madhya Pradesh and Maharashtra, it would still benefit only the major sons of landed families, for the Tribunal did not acknowledge any right in encroachers to be treated as landed.

This brings us to the second aspect of the disagreement, relating to encroachers. As noted above, Madhya Pradesh and Maharashtra say that encroachers must be treated as landless oustees with no entitlement to adequate land for cultivation on resettlement. The dispute here is whether tribal people, holding their land by customary usage, are entitled to be treated as landed oustees. Madhya Pradesh and Maharashtra say they are not, that they are illegal occupiers.

The result is that, in Madhya Pradesh and Maharashtra, thousands of tribal families, who are classified as landless but who are in fact cultivating land, may not receive any or adequate land on resettlement. Both states have provided that encroachers who can prove that they were cultivating encroached land prior to a certain date (in Maharashtra, 1978; in Madhya Pradesh, 1987) will be entitled to have their interests recorded. But these arrangements depend on documented proof which does not often exist. We estimate that, under the states' view, at least 60 per cent of tribal oustees engaged in cultivating land in Madhya Pradesh and Maharashtra will not receive adequate land on resettlement.

There are more than 60 million tribal people in India, many of them dependent on land they and their forebears have cultivated for generations. In 1987 the United Nations World Commission on Environment and Development (the Brundtland Commission) addressed the need for respect for indigenous and tribal land and resource rights. It said:

The starting point for a just and humane policy for such groups is the recognition and protection of their traditional rights to land and other resources that sustain their way of life—rights they may define in terms that do not fit into standard legal systems.

Central to the Bank's credit and loan agreements with India and the three states is the objective requiring that *all* oustees, including those described as landless, be enabled as a result of resettlement and rehabilitation measures taken on their behalf, to "*improve or at least regain* the standard of living they were enjoying prior to their displacement" [emphasis added]. How can this be guaranteed in the case of oustees for whom cultivation is their one skill and at the heart of their social, economic, and cultural lives, except by providing them, on resettlement, with land to cultivate? In 1984 the Narmada Control Authority, established to oversee the Projects, declared that: "For tribals, there is no rehabilitation more effective than providing land as the source of livelihood." We have concluded that it is in fact the only way to ensure that they improve or at least regain their standard of living. The result of classifying encroachers as landless oustees means that people who are in fact cultivating land they regard as their own will become landless laborers. This is not rehabilitation. It does not leave them at least as well off as before.

The tribal people in Madhya Pradesh and Maharashtra are aware of the issue, and what it will mean for them if they are resettled as landless laborers. When we visited Bamni, a tribal village in Maharashtra, the people told us, "We are farmers, not laborers." In our view Maharashtra and Madhya Pradesh, in failing to provide adequate land on resettlement for rehabilitation of encroachers, have not complied with the Bank credit and loan agreements.

The states point out that under the award and the Bank agreements all oustees have the right to resettle in Gujarat, where landed and landless oustees alike are to receive two hectares of irrigable land. Madhya Pradesh and Maharashtra contemplate that a very large number of oustees will therefore resettle in Gujarat. In fact, under Madhya Pradesh's plan for resettlement, its resettlement sites are to provide only 10 per cent of the land needed for its oustees.

But many oustees do not wish to go to Gujarat, for reasons which have to do with language, culture, and other ties to their region. It would, for many of them, be a long cultural journey. Under both the Tribunal award and under the Bank credit and loan agreements, oustees have the right to be resettled in their own state. It is true that in the last eighteen months Gujarat has achieved a measure of success in implementing resettlement, but Gujarat has thus far resettled something like 3,000 families. To resettle and then rehabilitate so many more oustees—perhaps 15,000 families—from Maharashtra and Madhya Pradesh would be an enormous task for Gujarat, and would impose a severe strain on its resources, which are not unlimited. Moreover, it is not just a question of resettlement; it also entails rehabilitation. The states may be able to effect the physical removal of thousands of families to land in Gujarat, but we do not think that it will be possible for Gujarat to rehabilitate them all.

It is important, we think, not to leave the matter there. The fact is that in Madhya Pradesh virtually no steps have been taken towards resettlement and rehabilitation. Even if Madhya Pradesh were to alter its policies, would it be reasonable to expect that Madhya Pradesh could implement a policy conforming to the Tribunal award and Bank agreements, if it were prepared to adopt one, within the time remaining before inundation? Could the implementation of resettlement and rehabilitation be done in time? We have reluctantly concluded that the answer must be "No."

In Maharashtra there are 33 submergence villages divided between two *talukas* or districts—Akkalkuwa and Akrani. Because of cultural links between Akkalkuwa and adjacent districts of Gujarat, a Maharashtra-to-Gujarat migration has always been part of the resettlement and rehabilitation plan for some Akkalkuwa villages. So far, some 400 Akkalkuwa families have relocated in Gujarat.

Maharashtra oustees, however, have the right to relocate within their own state. To this end, after its release was agreed by the Ministry of Environment and Forests in 1990, 2,700 hectares of forest land near Taloda were made available for resettlement.

Resettlement and rehabilitation in Maharashtra are beset by serious difficulties. As noted earlier, Maharashtra's policy fails to provide adequate land to encroachers (and major sons). The significance of this failure is revealed by the fact that none of the 24 Akrani villages are deemed by the Maharashtra plan to have any revenue land. The villagers of all 24 communities can only qualify for encroacher status, with one-acre land benefits.

Also, the number of oustee families in Maharashtra is much larger than originally anticipated; the Tribunal estimated 450 families; by 1988 the figure had grown to 2,000; it is now judged to be approximately 3,000. The Taloda forest land is not large enough to provide the land to which this number of oustees is entitled, even if the tribal people in the 24 Akrani villages are treated as landless. Additional forest land is unlikely to be released—the Taloda case is seen as unique.

This raises questions about the right of choice provided for in the Tribunal award and by the Bank agreements. That right ensures that displaced families, though obliged to leave their homes, ought not to be compelled to leave their home state. It is true that the bare right of choice remains. But the disparity in benefits means that they must choose between migrating to Gujarat or giving up their standard of living.

The only resettlement policy applicable to all three states is the Bank's. But

Bank policy has not been respected. The Projects were not appraised in accordance with Bank requirements. Basic information had not been gathered and adequate plans for resettlement and rehabilitation were not in place.

Notwithstanding Gujarat's success in providing land for submergence oustees, it has not provided land on resettlement for those oustees displaced in 1960-61, when the lands of six villages at Kevadia were expropriated to establish the construction site for the dam. To be sure, some of these villagers have received a measure of cash compensation. But since 1985 these people have been covered by the Bank agreements. Their entitlement to land should have been acknowledged seven years ago, yet the Bank has failed to secure an acknowledgment by Gujarat of their entitlement under the Bank agreements, let alone conveyance of appropriate lands.

Indeed, it is only recently that the Bank has urged—though it has never insisted—that India and the states comply with the 1979 Tribunal award regarding major sons, and develop policies to match the overarching objective of the Bank agreements in order to ensure land for encroachers.

Nor is it only that the Bank has failed to enforce the award and agreements. It has, in the case of the canal, failed to obtain a covenant in its agreement with Gujarat to require compliance with Bank policy. What about those villagers living in the path of the canal? Construction of the canal and irrigation system will affect as many as 140,000 families, of whom perhaps 13,000—no one knows how many—will lose much or all of their land. People losing land to the canal and irrigation system are offered compensation under the *Land Acquisition Act* of 1894. The number of such persons is a matter of competing estimates. But this much is clear: acquisition of land under the *Land Acquisition Act* has often meant that farmers losing land have been compensated at rates substantially lower than replacement costs.

The responsibility in this regard appears to us to rest with the Bank. It did not include resettlement benefits for canal oustees in the 1985 credit and loan agreements, even though such had been a part of Bank policy for five years.

Evolving respect for human rights has established new norms for resettlement and rehabilitation. The Bank's policies have been influential in establishing these norms, and India has adopted many of them. It ratified ILO 107 in 1958. India and the three riparian states signed the 1985 credit and loan agreements with the Bank. At the end of the day, however, the failure of India and the states to enforce the relevant provisions of the Tribunal award and the Bank agreements, and the Bank's failure to enshrine its policies in the agreements, mean that involuntary resettlement resulting from the Sardar Sarovar Projects offends recognized norms of human rights—human rights that India and the Bank have been in the forefront to secure.

In 1972, after the Stockholm Conference, a new consciousness of environmental issues emerged. In India, as elsewhere, in the 1970s and 1980s this was reflected in new environmental laws, guidelines, and practices. We have already noted the absence in India of a national policy in the field of resettlement and rehabilitation (the matter is regarded as a state responsibility). In the environmental field, however, the Government of India has developed a comprehensive structure of policies for environmental protection and assessment of environmental impact.

In 1983 environmental clearance for the Sardar Sarovar Projects was not forthcoming from India's Ministry of Environment and Forests because of a lack of information on environmental impact. In 1985 the Bank approved the credit and loan for the Projects. An appropriate environmental assessment was not made. In the Bank's 1985 Staff Appraisal Report no mention is made of the controversy that was holding up environmental clearance in India. The Bank required an environmental workplan by December 1985. It was not done. The date was extended to 1989. The workplan is still not available.

It was not until 1987 that a conditional environmental clearance for the Projects was given by India's Ministry of Environment and Forests. It was provided in the clearance that, instead of environmental impact studies being done before approval of the Projects, they were to be done *pari passu*, that is, concurrently with construction—an approach that we believe undermines the very basis for environmental planning. There was, however, an explicit schedule providing for the completion of the environmental impact studies by 1989. Most of the studies were not completed by 1989. Many have still not been completed. Without proper data and studies, proper assessments of environmental impact cannot be made and effective ameliorative measures cannot be developed.

The history of the environmental aspects of Sardar Sarovar is a history of non-compliance. There is no comprehensive impact statement. The nature and magnitude of environmental problems and solutions remain elusive. This feeds the controversy surrounding the Projects. As with the resettlement and rehabilitation issues, this has placed our review in a difficult position. To complete our work, we have had to assemble basic ecological information to establish the likely effects of the Projects upstream, downstream, and in the command area. This work should have been done by others before the Projects were approved.

The design and operation of a multi-purpose project like the Sardar Sarovar Projects depends on the hydrology of the river. Understanding impacts, therefore, begins with an understanding of the hydrology and the nature of the changes that will be caused by the engineering works.

During the proceedings before the Narmada Water Disputes Tribunal, the states agreed on a figure of 28 million acre feet as the average annual streamflow to be expected three years out of four. The Tribunal accepted this figure as a basis for the apportionment of the benefits of the Projects. It also provided a benchmark for design of the dam and canal.

We found discrepancies in basic hydrological information related to these works. We therefore examined the streamflow data and did our own analysis. We found that there is good reason to believe that the Projects will not perform as planned. The problems relate to the sequence and timing of streamflows and the capacity of the dam and canal to store and divert water. The effects of Sardar Sarovar upstream, downstream, and in the command area, therefore, will be different from what has been assumed to date whether or not the upstream Narmada Sagar Projects are built as planned. A realistic operational analysis upon which to base an environmental assessment is lacking. This alarmed us and it should alarm others, especially for a megaproject with such far-reaching implications as Sardar Sarovar.

For the area upstream of the dam there are piecemeal studies that suggest that the impact on biodiversity will be minimal. But there has been no attempt properly to assess the cumulative effects of the impacts arising from the Narmada Sagar Projects. Although the Narmada Sagar Projects are not within our Terms of Reference, the resulting cumulative impacts will almost certainly be serious. The Bank has placed itself in a difficult position by agreeing to proceed with Sardar Sarovar Projects before the environmental implications of directly related projects upstream are understood.

Programs in the upstream region for compensatory afforestation and catchment area treatment are under way. We believe that these programs, however successful in the short term, are likely to fail because of the lack of participation by local people. It is our view that achieving the necessary cooperation is not likely to be possible within the construction schedule imposed by Sardar Sarovar.

The backwater effect of sedimentation upstream of the dam is also an issue which has been ignored. Our analysis indicates this effect could mean a rapid, continuing, and cumulative rise in water level in the river above the reservoir. This can cause flooding to extensive areas of densely populated farmland. The human and environmental impacts could well be severe.

The construction of a dam on a free-flowing river has obvious implications for the downstream ecosystem, all the more so when proposed developments upstream will divert most of the river flows. But we found that no assessment of downstream impact has been done. Some of the basic information is only now being gathered. The implications of the Sardar Sarovar Projects for the geomorphology of the lower reaches of the river and its estuary and for the fishery and the people living in the region are unknown. We were able to assemble enough information to indicate that the impacts will be serious. It is likely, for example, that the hilsa fishery, the largest on the west coast, on which thousands of people depend, will suffer severe losses or be eliminated completely. The mitigative measures currently proposed are inadequate.

The shortcomings we have found in environmental assessment also extend into the command area. Although properly integrated studies are lacking, we have found that there are likely to be serious problems with waterlogging and salinity. Assumptions used in design of the canal and irrigation network, and on the development of mitigative measures, are questionable. We can only conclude that, when taken together, the problems that will arise in the command area will be quite similar to those identified by the Bank in many other irrigation projects in its 1991 *India Irrigation Sector Review.*

The priority water use is domestic consumption. We were surprised therefore to find that the plans for the delivery of water to the people in the villages and other centers in the drought-prone regions of Gujarat were only in the earliest stages of development. Apart from guidelines and intentions, we had little to review. We could not make any proper assessment as required by our Terms of Reference.

We have been conscious throughout our review of the close connection between the Projects' engineering design and the human and environmental impacts. This can be most clearly observed in the field of public health.

Large-scale irrigation projects such as the Sardar Sarovar Projects are known to carry health risks. From the first phases of construction, through creation of canals and ponds, to establishment of the reservoir itself, there are inevitable dangers of a large-scale increase in water-borne diseases. These have been documented since the 1930s, and World Bank-assisted projects have witnessed some of the problems that can occur.

Yet, as recently as January 1992, we find that the Bank's consultant says that the Sardar Sarovar Projects appear to have been "planned, designed and executed without incorporation of Health Safeguards." He describes various parts of the Projects as "death traps" and as "taking Malaria to the doorsteps of the villagers" and as creating "ideal breeding sites" for malarial mosquitoes. He reported a total collapse of vector control measures. The incidence of malaria has risen sharply in villages near the dam; local clinics have recorded deaths from malaria. The failure to anticipate and prevent malarial hazards is a part of the failure to implement measures to mitigate the impacts of the Projects.

The Bank is now proposing a Narmada Basin Development Project, and is considering providing a US $90 million credit for this purpose. The connections between this project and Sardar Sarovar are many. Although the Basin Development Project appears to address many of the problems raised during our review, and we recognize that some parts have merit, we have concluded that it will not succeed in meeting the stated objective as "a comprehensive program to tackle the growth and sustainability needs of the basin." Furthermore, the staff appraisal report for the proposed Basin project fails to acknowledge the linkages that also exist with the Narmada Sagar Projects. The Bank may be moving incrementally towards involvement in another major development project without prior consideration of the possible social and environmental consequences.

In spite of non-compliance with Bank resettlement and environmental requirements, the Sardar Sarovar Projects are proceeding—in the words of Chief Minister Patel of Gujarat—as "an article of faith." It seems clear that engineering and economic imperatives have driven the Projects to the exclusion of human and environmental concerns. Social and environmental trade-offs have been made that seem insupportable today.

The Bank has followed what it describes as an incremental strategy in an attempt to secure compliance with its resettlement policies. India has done much the same in its adoption of the *pari passu* principle with regard to environmental issues. These approaches, however, have failed to achieve their objectives. Moreover, they signify that these crucial matters—resettlement and environment—are of only secondary importance.

We are well aware of the scale of the development task facing India, of the importance India places on irrigation in increasing production in the agricultural sector, and of the longstanding partnership between India and the Bank in this endeavor. But our Terms of Reference are specific. They require us to consider the Bank's policies, India's environmental regime, and the credit and loan agreements. These emerge from the context of Bank-India relations just as surely as does the longstanding partnership in the enhancement of agricultural production between the Bank and India. If there was no intention of following Bank policy or India's regulatory regime, it would have been appropriate to acknowledge this. In any event the incremental strategy has been counter-productive.

The Bank, in crafting our Terms of Reference, invited specific recommendations which "should include, as appropriate, any recommendations for improvement of project implementation. . . ." If essential data were available, if impacts were known, if basic steps had been taken, it would be possible to know what recommendations to make. But we cannot put together a list of recommendations to improve resettlement and rehabilitation or to ameliorate environmental impact, when in so many areas no adequate measures are being taken on the ground or are even under consideration.

Important assumptions upon which the Projects are based are now questionable or are known to be unfounded. Environmental and social trade-offs have been made, and continue to be made, without a full understanding of the consequences. As a result, benefits tend to be overstated, while social and environmental costs are frequently understated. Assertions have been substituted for analysis.

Every decision as to the Sardar Sarovar Projects has always been, and will continue to be, a decision for India and the states involved. Together, they have spent a great deal of money. The foundations of the dam are in, the dam wall is going up, the turbines have been ordered and the canal is completed to the Mahi River. No one wants to see this money wasted. But we caution that it may be more wasteful to proceed without full knowledge of the human and environmental costs.

We have decided that it would be irresponsible for us to try to patch together a series of recommendations on implementation when the flaws in the Projects are as obvious as they appear to us. As a result, we think that the wisest course would be for the Bank to step back from the Projects and consider them afresh. The failure of the Bank's incremental strategy should be acknowledged.

Whatever decisions the Bank makes about its role in the Projects, it must bear in mind the critical importance of consultation with the people of the valley and along the route of the canal. Such consultation would be in accord with the Brundtland Report, which said that in the case of tribal people, "they must be given a decisive voice in the formulation of resource policy in their areas." The same must be achieved for non-tribals as well. As Prime Minister Rajiv Gandhi said to the United Nations on the adoption by the General Assembly of the Brundtland Report, "The search for the right answers must go on relentlessly. It is a worldwide endeavour to which India pledges its unstinting support."

Our job has been to make an assessment. We have done so. We have, in the course of our work, made many friends in India. We wish to assure them that our sole desire has been to find the truth and report it. We hope that our assessment may advance the search for constructive and creative solutions.

Yours sincerely,

Bradford Morse, Chairman

Thomas R. Berger, Deputy Chairman

The Sardar Sarovar Projects Area

© Maps Unlimited

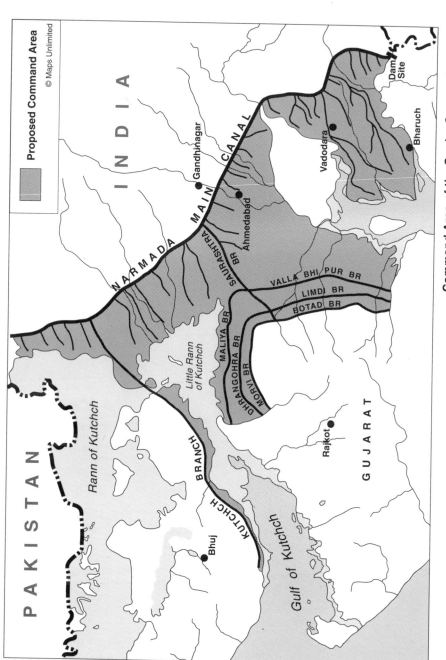

Command Area of the Sardar Sarovar Projects

Proposed Command Area

© Maps Unlimited

PAKISTAN

INDIA

Rann of Kutchch

Little Rann
of Kutchch

Gulf of Kutchch

GUJARAT

NARMADA MAIN CANAL

SAURASHTRA BR

KUTCHCH BRANCH

MALIYA BR

DHRANGOHRA BR

MORVI BR

VALLA BHI PUR BR

LIMDI BR

BOTAD BR

Gandhinagar

Ahmedabad

Vadodara

Bharuch

Dam
Site

Rajkot

Bhuj

THE PROJECTS

The Sardar Sarovar dam: the main dam wall is 1,210 meters long and reaches a maximum of 163 meters above the deepest foundations. The planned final height can be seen at the base of the two towers on the horizon.

Chapter 1
THE
SARDAR
SAROVAR
PROJECTS

AFTER Independence, Prime Minister Jawaharlal Nehru ordained high dams as India's "secular temples." India, in seeking to realize Nehru's vision, has become the world's greatest dam builder. Many of these dams have been financed in part by the World Bank.

It may be surprising, therefore, that the main stem of the Narmada River, India's fifth longest river, has never been dammed. This is not because there has been any dearth of proposals to dam the Narmada. But the river flows through three states. It rises in central India, in the state of Madhya Pradesh, and passes through Maharashtra and Gujarat, on its way to the Gulf of Cambay and the Arabian Sea. Proponents of dam construction on the river believe that construction should have begun long ago. But building of high dams on the Narmada had to await agreement among the three states as to the distribution of costs and benefits.

As a result, the Sardar Sarovar Projects, as well as the dams proposed further upstream, languished for two decades. Two thousand villagers in the vicinity of Kevadia in Gujarat had been removed from their homes in 1960-61 to make land available for infrastructure for the Sardar Sarovar dam and canal. But construction of the dam itself did not begin in earnest until 1987. Now the dam is rising, regarded as a symbol of progress by the Government of Gujarat and by many others, but, to most of the people living in the area to be submerged, feared as a threat to their land, their livelihoods, and their cultures.

Sardar Sarovar consists of several components. There is the dam, together with a riverbed powerhouse and transmission lines. There is also the main canal, a canalhead powerhouse, and irrigation network.[1] Together they are known as the Sardar Sarovar Projects.

In 1965 India appointed a committee to develop a master plan for the Narmada basin. It made recommendations for the dam and canal in Gujarat and for 12 major projects in Madhya Pradesh as well as for the allocation of water among the states. Gujarat endorsed the report, but Madhya Pradesh and Maharashtra rejected it. In 1969 the Government of India established the Narmada Water Disputes Tribunal under the *Interstate Water Disputes Act, 1956* to resolve finally the differences among the states. The Tribunal handed down its decision in 1979. That award established many of the fundamental design parameters for the series of dams on the lower Narmada River—the Narmada Sagar Projects, as well as the Sardar Sarovar Projects. These parameters include dam height, regulation of flows, canal levels and gradients, etc. They are among the most basic factors that determine environmental and resettlement impacts (see Chapter 11).

In the course of proceedings before the Tribunal, the states negotiated an agreed figure of 28 million acre feet (MAF) as the utilizable quantity of water from the Narmada with 75 per cent dependability (i.e., in three years out of four, on average). This figure was accepted by the Tribunal as a basis for the apportionment of the benefits of the Projects. It also provided a benchmark for design of the dam and the canal.

The height of Sardar Sarovar dam was fixed at 455 feet, creating a reservoir that will submerge approximately 37,000 hectares of land in three states: Gujarat, Maharashtra, and Madhya Pradesh. The dam itself is being built in a hilly region, inhabited by tribal people, that encompasses contiguous areas of all three states. Their villages extend well into the reservoir area. Virtually all of the affected people in Gujarat are tribals. This is also the case in Maharashtra. In Madhya Pradesh approximately 40 per cent of the people in the submergence area are tribals. In all three states, the tribal people are engaged in a mixed economy, cultivating land and grazing animals in or about the forests, collecting forest products, and fishing. The remainder of the submergence area in Madhya Pradesh extends upstream to include the caste villages of the Nimad plain, where irrigated arable agriculture forms the mainstay of the economy. The land here is some of the most fertile in India. Of the 245 villages to be submerged, 19 lie in Gujarat, 33 in Maharashtra, and 193 in Madhya Pradesh. In total, at least 100,000 people will be affected by submergence.[2]

---

[1] Bank agreements refer to these structures as the "Water Delivery and Drainage Project."

[2] The calculation of numbers affected varies widely. Government officals in India acknowledge that at least 90,000 persons live in the 245 villages affected by submergence. Most other estimates are greater. We think 100,000 a conservative figure.

The Tribunal's 1979 award set out the benefits and procedures for resettlement of those persons in Madhya Pradesh and Maharashtra to be displaced by submergence in the reservoir area, and apportioned the cost of their resettlement to the Government of Gujarat. The Tribunal did not deal with resettlement of people in Gujarat to be affected by the Projects.

The Tribunal ruled that the electrical power and energy benefits produced by the Projects will be shared among the riparian states (16 per cent to Gujarat, 57 per cent to Madhya Pradesh, and 27 per cent to Maharashtra). The Tribunal also determined the amount of water allotted for use by Gujarat and Rajasthan (9.5 MAF), which would be made up in part by regulated releases by Madhya Pradesh from the Narmada Sagar Projects. The Sardar Sarovar dam will divert this water into the canal and irrigation system, serving 1.8 million hectares in Gujarat, as well as the Barmore and Jallore districts of Rajasthan. The canal network will require approximately 80,000 hectares for construction, more than twice as much land as the reservoir. The canal itself will be the biggest in the world in terms of its capacity.

The Tribunal's award also established the Narmada Control Authority, an interstate administrative agency chaired by the Secretary of the Department of Water Resources, to secure compliance with the award.

In 1985 the World Bank entered into credit and loan agreements for $450 million[3] with India and the states of Gujarat, Maharashtra, and Madhya Pradesh to assist in the construction of the Sardar Sarovar dam and canal. Consideration of Narmada Sagar Projects was deferred, even though the Tribunal award and the project designs assumed simultaneous construction schedules. Forest and other environmental clearances covering much of the reservoir had to be obtained from the Government of India. These were secured in 1987, and construction began in earnest.

For many years Sardar Sarovar has been the dream of political leaders and planning officials in Gujarat. Its proponents say that it will bring enormous benefits to millions at a cost of displacing comparatively few people. Supporters of the dam say that it will provide drinking water to over 40 million people and irrigation to 1.8 million hectares of land in that state, not to mention hydroelectric power. They ask that these benefits be weighed against the numbers of people who may be adversely affected. They point out that the majority of the persons to be displaced are tribal people whose lands are said to consist of steep, rocky ground and degraded forests. The land which will be lost, they say, is of marginal value. The juxtaposition of these numbers, of beneficiaries on the one hand and of the persons to be displaced on the other, is said to be

---

[3] At the time of the Bank's appraisal this contributed 18 per cent of the cost of the dam and power project and about 30 per cent of the water delivery project.

sufficient justification for the Projects.

The Chief Minister of Gujarat, Chiman Patel, predicts that if the Sardar Sarovar Projects do not go forward, if water for drinking and for irrigation is not made available to the drought-prone areas in Kutchch, Saurashtra, and northern Gujarat, the result will be the involuntary resettlement of hundreds of thousands of Gujarati citizens who will be forced by drought to migrate from their homes.

On the other side, it is argued that the benefits which have been described may never materialize: that adequate drinking water will never reach Kutchch and other drought-prone areas, and that the irrigation benefits have been vastly overestimated. It is also argued that adequate measures are not being taken to resettle families displaced by the Projects, and that rehabilitation as planned cannot succeed. It is also contended that the environmental impact will be far greater than predicted. It is also alleged that the numbers of people to be affected by the Projects have been significantly underestimated, that those affected include not only the people in the submergence area, but also those already displaced by the construction of infrastructure at Kevadia, those to be displaced by the canal, as well as others affected downstream. People may also be adversely affected by compensatory afforestation, secondary displacement, public health hazards, and the Bank's newly proposed Narmada Basin Development Project. It is argued that when these people are added to those living in the submergence area, the numbers swell to 300,000 or more. It is also pointed out that the Sardar Sarovar Projects are linked to the construction of the Narmada Sagar Projects upstream, and that will have even greater environmental and social impacts.

The Sardar Sarovar Projects have come under scrutiny at a time of worldwide awakening to the consequences of large-scale projects in rural and remote areas, especially those inhabited by indigenous or tribal people. Sardar Sarovar has therefore become—in India and in many other countries—a symbol. To some it represents economic development which will bring enormous benefits to millions; others regard it as an imposition upon the land which will impoverish—culturally and economically—hundreds of thousands of people and irrevocably alter, if not destroy, the natural environment which the Narmada River supports.

The foundation of the dam has been completed, and work on the dam wall is well under way. Construction of the main canal, begun in 1987, already extends to the Mahi River—to provide water to an area representing approximately one-quarter of the total area to be irrigated in Gujarat. A substantial investment has already been made.

Relocation of the people living behind the dam has also begun. Virtually all of those already relocated are tribal people living in Gujarat, some 4,000 families numbering about 20,000 persons. The majority of those still to be relocated and resettled live in Maharashtra and Madhya Pradesh. In Maharashtra, resettlement has been immersed in controversy; in Madhya Pradesh, there have been virtually no steps taken to enable resettlement to proceed.

The Narmada Water Disputes Tribunal laid down conditions regarding resettlement. The Government of India imposed certain environmental requirements. The Bank's credit and loan agreements contain requirements touching on both. At the threshold of our task the issue is whether India and the states have lived up to these conditions and requirements. But our review was established because the Sardar Sarovar Projects have become a subject of controversy within India and throughout the world, especially with regard to the measures being taken to resettle and rehabilitate displaced and other affected persons, and to ameliorate the environmental impact of the Projects.

The conflict between development and the rights of indigenous and rural people is not a uniquely Indian phenomenon. In every continent, in developed and developing countries, high dams and other large-scale projects have inundated millions of hectares of land, raising serious questions about human and environmental impacts. Often the areas affected are tribal lands and land belonging to rural peasants. Sardar Sarovar has sharpened the focus of worldwide concern, in part because of the scale of the Projects, and in considerable part because people on the margins of development, whose ancestral lands are to be taken from them for what many believe to be the greater good of the majority, are beginning to speak out on their own behalf.

The Independent Review at work: Hugh Brody meeting with Madhya Pradesh oustees at their relocation site in Gujarat.

Chapter 2
THE
INDEPENDENT
REVIEW

OUR review is the result of a specific controversy over the question whether India and the three state governments have complied with India's own policies, especially the 1979 award of the Narmada Water Disputes Tribunal, relating to resettlement and rehabilitation and amelioration of environmental impact, and the Bank's conditions, set out in the 1985 credit and loan agreements, touching on both subjects.

But our Terms of Reference from the President of the Bank cover much broader issues.[1] They require our review to make:

> an assessment of the implementation of the ongoing Sardar Sarovar projects . . . as regards:
> (a) the resettlement and rehabilitation (R&R) of the population displaced/affected by the construction of the SSP infrastructure and by the storage reservoir; and
> (b) the amelioration of the environmental impact of all aspects of the projects.

Our Terms of Reference also provide:

> The assessment shall take account of all covenants and understandings reached between Government of India (GOI) and IBRD/IDA in the loan/credit documents and other relevant agreements as well as:

[1] See Appendix A.

(a) the decisions of the Narmada Water Disputes Tribunal, which sanctioned the projects;

(b) the environmental clearance decision of the GOI Ministry of Environment and Forests including subsequent decisions regarding release of forest lands for resettlement;

(c) union and state laws and directives relevant to the implementation of R&R in the three affected states Gujarat, Madhya Pradesh and Maharashtra.

The assessment shall make reference to existing Bank operational directives and guidelines with respect to project-related R&R and environmental assessments and safeguards, keeping in mind that several of these directives were promulgated and/or amended after these loans/credits were approved in 1985.

Since our Terms of Reference apply to the construction of the dam, the power facility, and the reservoir, and to those people "displaced/affected" thereby, our review must consider not only the people in the villages of the submergence area, but also the situation of people of the six villages affected by the early (1960-61) construction of infrastructure at Kevadia. Moreover, we were asked by President Conable to consider, under our Terms of Reference, the status of resettlement and compensation for "canal-affected persons."

The dispute within India regarding resettlement and rehabilitation has largely focused on agricultural oustees, i.e., those who will lose land to which they hold legal title. But the Tribunal award and the Bank credit and loan agreements have identified a whole class of landless oustees who will lose their means of livelihood and who must be provided for. Then there is the question of encroachers, that is, persons cultivating land to which they hold no formal title, who are treated as landless. We have included all of them in our review.

In approaching our task, we have taken the position that our assessment is not simply a question of determining compliance or non-compliance with the Tribunal award and the loan agreements. Compliance or non-compliance is not a *pro forma* question. The conditions laid down by the Bank relating to resettlement and rehabilitation and the amelioration of environmental impact are conditions intended to address underlying issues.

Failure to comply with India's or the Bank's conditions may raise the question whether compliance is possible. It is important to note that our review cannot proceed as if the terms and conditions required by the Tribunal and by the Bank are necessarily going to be fulfilled and all that remains to be done is to implement them. If they *cannot* be implemented, that must be considered, otherwise our review would be a charade.

Ensuring compliance is not simply a question of problem-solving, of looking at the implementation of policies adopted by the Bank, India, and the three states and working out ways of improving it. Implementation cannot be carried out if the assumptions that undergird the policies are themselves flawed. A consideration of implementation therefore requires a consideration of these assumptions.

Many questions arise. Are the stated environmental impacts accurately assessed? Is there sufficient data available to quantify those impacts? Will the proposed ameliorative measures be effective? Are the right issues being addressed in a timely way? Do the resettlement and rehabilitation plans take into account the characteristics of the people being displaced? Are they appropriate to such people? Are they capable of realization as stated?

We began our task in September 1991. This gave us the advantage of considering what had happened on the ground in the decade since the Tribunal award, and in the six years since the Bank's credit and loan agreements of 1985. It is now almost five years since the environmental clearances were granted by the Government of India in 1987. Much has been learned in the past decade.

We have had to contend with the fact that views are polarized. Wherever we went we found that opinion was sharply divided. Proponents conscientiously regard the Projects as "the lifeline of Gujarat." Opponents, equally conscientious, regard the Projects as a human and environmental catastrophe.

We have been struck by the firmness with which all sides hold to their views of the Projects, by the compelling case made for the need for water in drought-prone areas of Gujarat, by the genuine concerns expressed about the impact of the Projects on the affected people and on the environment, and by the goodwill and cooperation that all sides have extended to our review.

We made it clear wherever we went that we would conduct a truly independent review, that though our Terms of Reference are quite properly set by the President of the Bank, none of us work for the Bank nor have any of us ever worked for the Bank. We made it plain that we intended to travel wherever we thought it important to go, and to talk with whomever we thought it appropriate to speak. The independence of our review has been integral to our entire modus operandi, and has been welcomed on all sides. The Bank has provided all the necessary financial support, but we have designed and administered our own budget. Having retained editorial control of this report, we are fully and solely responsible for its content.

In the course of our review, we travelled throughout the Narmada valley, including the dam site, the submergence area, the catchment area, and the area downstream, and around the command area, including the route of the canal.

We visited Kutchch and Saurashtra where recurring drought conditions have meant that people in these districts suffer great hardship. The people there told us how eager they were to see the waters of the Narmada flow to their region.

Of course, there are many claims on the waters of the Narmada. Many of the people in the submergence area, who will be flooded out, told us of their long history of spiritual and economic dependence on the river. The concerns, too, of the villagers downstream, dependent on the fishery, were forcefully brought to our attention.

We have, therefore, together with the two senior members of the review team, Donald Gamble and Hugh Brody, met frequently with officials of the Government of India, including the Minister of Water Resources, his deputy, and other Union officials.

We have met with the Governments of the three states, as well as with the Narmada Control Authority, the Narmada Valley Development Authority, and the Sardar Sarovar Narmada Nigam Limited. All of the officials of Union and state governments and relevant agencies whom we met cooperated with us fully and provided us with whatever documents we requested. All dealt with us in good faith. The Bank's staff in Washington, D.C., and in India provided us with complete and unimpeded access to Bank files.

We can confidently say that we were made fully aware of the range of opinion about Sardar Sarovar, because we talked to all sides. The Chief Minister of Gujarat, members of the Gujarat legislature, Members of Parliament from Gujarat and the Gujarat business community emphasized the benefits the Projects are expected to bring to Gujarat. We talked to the Chief Minister of Madhya Pradesh and the Chief Minister of Maharashtra and to officials from both of these states, who also emphasized the benefits the Projects would bring. We spent time talking with and touring sites with the non-government organizations Arch Vahini and Anand Niketan Ashram, both of which have worked tirelessly to help with resettlement of oustees.

At the same time, many critics challenged fundamental assumptions upon which the Projects are based, while others proposed stopping the construction of the dam altogether. Opponents of the dam not only urged upon us what they regard as flaws in the Projects but also questioned the advisability of proceeding with them at all. We heard this side most often from Narmada Bachao Andolan, an Indian non-government organization, which also organized for us trips to villages and meetings with people of the valley.

We met with eminent persons on both sides of the issue in New Delhi, Bombay, Gandhinagar, Ahmedabad, Baroda, Bhopal, and Indore.

We visited 65 villages, tribal and peasant, throughout the Narmada valley and command area. At gatherings in those villages we heard from the inhabitants. Often people came from other villages, and in this way we heard from 60 additional villages. Twenty of the villages we visited were relocation sites. At these sites and at meetings with oustees at Kevadia, we heard from people who had come from another 30 relocation sites.

Often government officials accompanied us and provided translators, but in many places the non-government organizations have easier access than governments or World Bank representatives. With them we went to many villages where World Bank missions have not in the past been able to go. Representatives of Arch Vahini, Narmada Bachao Andolan, and Anand Niketan Ashram often accompanied us, in turn, to these places.

These local non-government organizations were happy to accompany us to the villages in which they were active. They and others were prepared, as well, to provide us with all of the research, surveys, etc., they had carried out. They were naturally eager to ensure we heard and understood their point of view, but they were also ready to answer our queries in the most straightforward and comprehensive way.

We found that, in the finest traditions of India and Indian democracy, there was uninhibited discussion, in the press and elsewhere, of the Projects, creating considerable intellectual ferment. We met academics, retired public servants, and scores of others, on all sides of the issue, who were eager to provide us with information and argument. Indeed, we challenged many to make formal, written submissions that we could consider carefully, which they did. We also felt it necessary to commission studies and to obtain expert advice on a number of issues.

Our knowledge, therefore, is based on what we were told during our meetings in India, what we were able to glean from research data and from government and Bank files, submissions written specially for our review, and what we were able to see for ourselves in tribal and peasant villages in the Narmada valley and in the relocation sites in Gujarat and Maharashtra. (There are as yet no relocation sites in Madhya Pradesh to which anyone has been resettled.)

We must acknowledge the enormous contribution to our work of our colleagues, Donald Gamble and Hugh Brody, without whose participation our review would not have been possible. Mr. Gamble gathered, organized, and analyzed the plethora of relevant data and documents on environmental questions. He conducted, on our behalf, scores of interviews. He engaged and supervised researchers, and performed a multitude of other critical tasks. Mr. Brody was in charge of our work on resettlement. He travelled, on our behalf, to many of the villages that we did not have time to visit. He met with hundreds, if not thousands, of affected people, frequently reaching remote villages by foot. He did extensive study on the cultures and lifestyles of tribal people, and reviewed the considerable literature on resettlement and rehabilitation. Mr. Gamble and Mr. Brody worked so closely with us that we regard the intelligence they gathered in their travels throughout the region as just as valuable as that which we obtained directly.

In the chapters that follow, we consider first the overarching principles of policy that apply generally to resettlement and rehabilitation (Chapter 3), and then deal at length with the resettlement and rehabilitation policy of each state and its progress of implementation. With respect to the environmental issues we describe the policy framework and then the progress of implementation.

It is hardly necessary to point out the relationship between the human and environmental issues. We found that any assessment of the present wellbeing of people in the submergence area depends on environmental factors, in particular, the condition of the forest, the productivity of the land, the fisheries, and water quality; indeed, almost every aspect of resettlement and rehabilitation depends on environmental assessment or predictions about environmental impacts.

This interdependency of environmental and human aspects has a direct bearing on our ability to provide a meaningful assessment of the adequacy of implementation of the Projects. Although the two issues will be considered separately, for the purposes of analysis, in the chapters which follow, the two objectives of our Terms of Reference are linked. Moreover, to make an assessment of the adequacy of measures taken in connection with resettlement and rehabilitation and environmental protection, it is necessary to consider them in the light of the Sardar Sarovar Projects as a whole, their history, design, and performance.

RESETTLEMENT AND REHABILITATION

Dance at Anjanvada, a tribal village in Madhya Pradesh, to celebrate payment of bride price—the money and goods that the groom's family must pay to the bride's family—in anticipation of a wedding.

Chapter 3
RESETTLEMENT AND HUMAN RIGHTS

IN an earlier era, involuntary resettlement was considered merely a necessary consequence of dam projects.

Of course, people may be displaced by political upheaval or natural calamity. At Independence, millions of persons in Punjab and Bengal had to be resettled. Earthquakes and floods may require resettlement of large numbers. From the point of view of the displaced, however, a dam that will submerge their land is not an inevitable natural calamity, but a man-made catastrophe.

In India, since Independence, the construction of high dams and the irrigation structures that usually go along with them has been the country's greatest cause of involuntary resettlement. Millions have been displaced to make way for such projects, their lives uprooted to serve the greater good.

It is not, however, simply a question of weighing the numbers on each side, not simply a question of statistical relativism, but a question of human rights. The development of international standards, of India's policies, and of the Bank's policies on resettlement reflect worldwide concern for the human rights of persons displaced by involuntary resettlement.

Our Terms of Reference require us, in making our assessment, to consider all of the Bank's existing operational directives and guidelines on resettlement and rehabilitation, bearing in mind that the credit and loan agreements for the Sardar Sarovar Projects were approved in 1985. In fact, India's policies on resettlement and the Bank's policies on resettlement have been developing side by side, though with some important differences.

In the past, when high dams have been built, the people who occupy land in the submergence area have often been evicted without proper compensation, often without due process. This has happened in developed as well as developing countries. Compensation, in such cases, did not usually include anything more than cash compensation, payable under conventional expropriation statutes, and the cash was more often than not inadequate, rarely if ever sufficient to buy replacement land. Other people affected by the loss of employment, access to fisheries, or other sources of livelihood, have usually been ignored.

Since World War II, developed and developing countries have built high dams in rural, forest, and frontier regions of the world. Usually, this has resulted in incursions on the lands of indigenous or tribal people. It was the special situation of indigenous or tribal people that first gave rise to measures to protect displaced persons.

There is, to begin with, International Labor Organization Convention 107 (ILO 107), adopted in 1957 as a "convention concerning the Protection and Integration of Indigenous and other Tribal and Semi-Tribal Populations in Independent Countries." India was one of the first countries to ratify ILO 107, doing so on September 29, 1958.

The Convention provides:

PART II, LAND
Article 11
The right of ownership, collective or individual, of the members of the populations concerned over the lands which these populations traditionally occupy shall be recognised.
Article 12
1. The populations concerned shall not be removed without their free consent from their habitual territories except in accordance with national laws and regulations for reasons relating to national security, or in the interest of national economic development or of the health of the said populations.
2. When in such cases removal of these populations is necessary as an exceptional measure, they shall be provided with *lands of quality at least equal to that of the lands previously occupied by them, suitable to provide for their present needs and future development.* In cases where chances of alternative employment exist and where the populations concerned prefer to have compensation in money or in kind, they shall be so compensated under appropriate guarantees.
3. Persons thus removed shall be fully compensated for any resulting loss or injury. [emphasis added]

There are three important things to notice about ILO 107. First, it affirms the right of tribal peoples to their traditional lands. Second, it stipulates the causes for which tribal peoples may be removed: national security, national economic development, and the health of the tribal population. Third, it provides that tribal peoples who are displaced shall be "provided with lands of quality at least equal to that of the lands previously occupied by them, suitable to provide for their present needs and future development." Undergirding the provisions of ILO 107 is the idea that resettlers should be at least as well off after resettlement as before. These themes recur in the development of Bank resettlement and rehabilitation policies and lie at the heart of the dispute over resettlement in the Sardar Sarovar Projects.

In India there are more than 60 million people designated as members of Scheduled Tribes, a designation found in India's Constitution. Although many of them have become assimilated into mainstream Indian culture, others maintain a traditional way of life distinct from the populations surrounding them (see Chapter 5). Along the Narmada, as elsewhere in India, many of the tribal people of the forest villages are said to be "encroaching" on government land, even though they may have been cultivating the land for generations pursuant to their customary usage, though without formal title.

In India, as in many other countries, tribal peoples are often displaced by construction of dams and other projects; this is so in the Sardar Sarovar Projects. But no special provision is made for them, or for any other group of persons to be displaced.

When Sardar Sarovar was mooted, India had no national resettlement policy; it has none today. The matter is treated as a state responsibility. In 1979, however, the Narmada Water Disputes Tribunal determined, for the first time, certainly in India, that landed oustees were to receive land for land.

The 1979 Tribunal award represented a break with the past. For the first time, persons to be dispossessed as a result of a large-scale development project were to receive benefits that amounted, it was declared at the time, to an opportunity for economic and social progress. Project-affected people of the submergence zone were to be given land to replace land they were losing, house sites, and short-term financial protection. The award provides not only cash compensation for property lost, but also monetary indemnification through rehabilitation grants and grants in aid, civic amenities in new or existing villages where those displaced are to relocate, house plots, and, most important of all, agricultural land of equal size for every displaced family losing more than 25 per cent of its holdings, subject to land ceiling laws, with a minimum of two hectares for each family. Also, the award provided that "major sons"[1] would also receive compensation benefits in their own right. This latter is a provision of the first importance.

The award of the Tribunal states:

> Clause xɪ: Directions Regarding Submergence, Land Acquisition and Rehabilitation of displaced persons.
>
> Sub-clause I: Definitions.
>
> ɪ(ɪ): "Land".—The expression "land" shall have the same meaning as defined in the Land Acquisition Act, 1894 (hereinafter referred to as the Act) which states "the expression 'land' includes benefits to arise out of land, and things attached to the earth or permanently fastened to anything attached to the earth".
>
> ɪ(2): "Oustee".—An "oustee" shall mean any person who since at least one year prior to the date of publication of the notification under Section 4 of the Act, has been ordinarily residing or cultivating land or carrying on any trade, occupation, or calling or working for gain in the area likely to be submerged permanently or temporarily.
>
> ɪ(3): "Family".—(*i*) A family shall include husband, wife and minor children and other persons dependent on the head of the family, e.g., widowed mother. (*ii*) *Every major son will be treated as a separate family.*
>
> . . .
>
> Sub-clause IV—Provision for Rehabilitation.
>
> ɪv(ɪ): According to the present estimates *the number of oustee families would be 6147 spread over 158 villages in Madhya Pradesh, 456 families spread over 27 villages in Maharashtra.* Gujarat shall establish rehabilitation villages in Gujarat in the irrigation command of the Sardar Sarovar Project on the norms hereinafter mentioned for rehabilitation of the families who are willing to migrate to Gujarat. *For oustee families who are unwilling to migrate to Gujarat, Gujarat shall pay to Madhya Pradesh and Maharashtra the cost, charges and expenses for establishment of such villages in their respective territories on the norms as hereinafter provided.*
>
> . . .
>
> ɪv(7): Allotment of Agricultural Lands—Every displaced family from whom more than 25 per cent of its land holding is acquired

---

[1] "Major sons" are sons who have reached the age of 18 by a date stipulated in each state's resettlement policy.

shall be entitled to and be allotted irrigable land to the extent of land acquired from it subject to the prescribed ceiling in the State concerned and a minimum of 2 hectares (5 acres) per family, the irrigation facilities being provided by the State in whose territory the allotted land is situated. This land shall be transferred to the oustee family if it agrees to take it. The price charged for it would be as mutually agreed between Gujarat and the concerned State. Of the price to be paid for the land a sum equal to 50 per cent of the compensation payable to the oustee family for the land acquired from it will be set off as an initial instalment of payment. The balance cost of the allotted land shall be recovered from the allottee in 20 yearly instalments free of interest. . . .[2] [emphasis added]

The 1979 Tribunal award focused on the oustees of Maharashtra and Madhya Pradesh. Its purpose was to protect oustees of these two states: the substantial benefits of the Sardar Sarovar Projects were seen to accrue principally to Gujarat, whereas most of those who stood to lose (some 85 per cent) lived outside that state. The award therefore stipulated that land for Maharashtra and Madhya Pradesh oustees be made available in Gujarat (this followed, naturally, also from the wish to offer land in the command area), and that Gujarat should pay the costs of relocation and rehabilitation for all oustees. But the award did not specify relocation and rehabilitation rights for the oustees of Gujarat itself.

A number of comments should be made about the 1979 Tribunal award. It did, indeed, provide for land-for-land for families in the agricultural sector. It made an attempt to estimate the number of oustee families in Madhya Pradesh and Maharashtra. The total came to 6,603. Today, the best estimate, for these two states together, exceeds 25,000. It provided that all oustees (not only landed oustees) should have the right to choose to resettle in Gujarat or in their own state.

The Tribunal also required that within two years of its award Madhya Pradesh and Maharashtra should have obtained the preferences of oustee families for resettlement in Gujarat or their own state, and that Gujarat should have acquired land for "rehabilitation villages."

Under the award, oustees were to become beneficiaries of the Sardar Sarovar Projects by virtue of being offered land and opportunities in the Pro-

[2] "Decision of the Narmada Water Disputes Tribunal as Modified by the Explanations and Guidance Given in its Further Report. Final Order and Decision of the Tribunal." New Delhi: Ministry of Agriculture and Irrigation (Department of Irrigation), December 7, 1979.

jects' command area. This measure sought to reduce, or even eliminate, the terrible divide that usually occurs with large-scale projects, between the beneficiaries and the losers. Relocation in the command area meant access to the irrigation the Projects sought to make available, and the possibility of a part in more widespread economic growth.

The Tribunal award does not, however, appear to have made any provision for encroachers; to this extent it ignored the customary usages of tribal people using encroached land for cultivation or grazing.

The states contend, therefore, that only those persons cultivating lands that would be acquired for the Projects under the *Land Acquisition Act, 1894,* are to be treated as landed oustees. Occupation by encroachers being illegal, there would be no need for the states to acquire their land under the Act; encroachers must therefore be classified as landless oustees, without entitlement to land under the award.

The language of the award has also given rise to a dispute as to major sons. Clause XI I(3)(ii) of the Tribunal award provides: "Every major son will be treated as a separate family"; and Clause XI IV(7) says: "Every displaced *family* from whom more than 25 per cent of its land holding is acquired shall be entitled to and be allotted irrigable land to the extent of land acquired from it . . ." [emphasis added].

It is said therefore that the plain meaning of the Tribunal award is that when a family loses its land the major sons, as well as the father, in the family will each receive two hectares of land. The direction by the Tribunal that every major son be treated as a separate family stands without qualification, express or implied. What other purpose would this provision serve except to enable each major son to claim the same entitlement as the family to which he belongs? The states say that the Tribunal only intended to make major sons eligible for non-farmland compensation, such as house lots.

We are aware that, pursuant to Attachment I, footnote I of the "Agreed Minutes" of negotiations between the Bank and India, the term "landed" means all those who, under the law, hold title to land or are in the process of acquiring title to land. But this does not advance the argument. It is the Tribunal's award that governs. Moreover, major sons do hold title to land jointly with their fathers.

We believe that the Tribunal award does require each state to provide a minimum of two hectares of land to each major son in any family that is displaced and entitled to land on resettlement; in our view the states' failure to do so constitutes non-compliance with the Tribunal award. We have not been advised of any holding to the contrary by the courts in India.

The point should be made, however, that it is only major sons of landed families who would be entitled to two hectares of land under the award. Neither encroachers nor major sons of encroacher families would qualify for two hectares of land.

Although the product of an independent panel, the Tribunal's award may be said to represent the state of India's resettlement policy in 1979. In the meantime the Bank was developing a policy of its own.

In February 1980, the World Bank published an operational manual statement on "Social Issues Associated with Involuntary Resettlement in Bank-Financed Projects."[3] The statement provided:

INTRODUCTION

1. Bank-assisted projects sometimes require that people living in the area be moved to another location, either permanently or for a long period. Such resettlement often causes hardship, disruption and constraint on further development unless appropriate preventive action is taken. This Statement describes the policy to be followed by Bank staff in projects that require involuntary resettlement, the procedures for preparing and appraising schemes for resettlement in such cases, and the conditions that are expected to be met by borrowers and resettlement agencies.

2. When the development projects require people to be relocated, the Bank's general policy is to help the borrower *to ensure that, after a reasonable transition period, the displaced people regain at least their previous standard of living and that so far as possible, they be economically and socially integrated into the host communities.* Planning and financing the resettlement should be an integral part of the project, *and the measures to be taken in this regard should be clarified before, and agreed upon during, loan negotiations.* [emphasis added]

The Bank's policy statement encompassed not only dams, but also canals and other projects that might result in involuntary resettlement. It provided:

3. Resettlement of people is sometimes necessary in order to execute projects that entail a major change of land use, such as: (a) the construction of *dams* for hydro-electric power, irrigation, or water supply which form man-made lakes; (b) the construction of new ports and towns; (c) the inception of mining operations; (d) the protection of grazing areas and of transhumance corridors; and (e) the construction of *canals, highways, transmission lines and the like.* Such projects contribute to the general welfare

---

[3] Operational Manual Statement No. 2.33, February 1980.

and may be critical for national or regional development, but measures must be taken to protect the life, welfare, and rights of those displaced. [emphasis added]

The Bank was concerned that where possible, resettlement should be avoided. The statement continues:

> 17. The Bank recognizes the human suffering and hardship caused by involuntary resettlement, and therefore tries to avoid or minimize such resettlement whenever feasible. All large construction projects such as dams, irrigation schemes, ports, new towns, airports, and highways should be examined by Bank staff at the time of identification and appraisal to determine whether people must be displaced, and, if displacement is unavoidable, to reduce it to a minimum compatible with the purpose of the project. The costs of the resettlement should be included in the project and taken into account in the rate of return analysis.

The statement stressed the need for a resettlement plan:

> 18. Where involuntary resettlement is unavoidable, relocation of those affected should be undertaken in conjunction with a well prepared resettlement plan. The content and detail required for such a plan will vary with circumstances. Where only a few people are to be relocated, appropriate compensation for assets (see para. 19 below), coupled with arrangements for removal to a new area and a relocation grant may suffice. In cases where the numbers of people to be moved are large, as when whole communities are involved, a more detailed plan is required. Such a plan would include compensation as one principal element but would also involve relocation and establishment in a new settlement area or, in the more likely cases, integration with existing communities in an already settled area.

The statement then proceeds to reiterate the objective set out in ILO 107:

> In such cases, the major objective is to ensure that settlers are afforded opportunities to become established and economically self-sustaining in the shortest possible period, at living standards that at least match those before resettlement.

In a quite far-reaching way, the Bank's statement acknowledges that oustees may lose not only land but also other tangible assets, such as crops and trees and, as well, intangible assets such as access to employment, fisheries, etc. It went on:

> 19. Government laws and regulations pertaining to compensation specify the procedures for taking property by the State and fixing the appropriate valuation for that property. Such laws are a partial means of reconciling the national interest to the interests of the groups and individuals immediately affected. Persons displaced by a large project are forced to relinquish rights to various immovable assets. These include housing, land (and improvement to both), access to economic activities (such as near-by jobs) and public services, as well as non-economic assets (such as shrines). In urban settings, relocation can cause special problems for traders, small businesses, and cottage industries through the disruption of commercial ties with suppliers, distributors and customers. In rural areas, lost assets can include fishing waters, irrigation works, standing crops, and trees. The laws and regulations governing compensation very often do not prevent serious hardships and suffering.

The statement then elaborates on this point in a very sensitive fashion:

> In particular, (i) compensation procedures typically relate to fair market values, whereas in practice the value of assets to their owners may well exceed such a valuation; (ii) certain types of intangible assets are excluded—ranging from proximity to clan and kinship groups and access to religious shrines and other places of cultural identification, to proximity to employment opportunities. The latter may be the most important of all to the poorest groups, whose asset base for legal compensation is typically meager; and (iii) the productive assets given up may be difficult to replace as in the case of land in densely populated areas. Finally, experience with the resettlement of large populations tends to show that payment of cash compensation *alone* is often a very inadequate strategy for dealing with the displaced; in some instances, the entire compensation has been used for immediate consumption purposes, leaving the displaced with nothing to replace their lost income-generating assets and op-

portunities. When only few people are involved, cash compensation may be adequate; but, even in that case, consideration should be given to the ability of displaced persons to find alternative homes and employment opportunities. Assistance in relocating also is often necessary.

The statement returns to the importance of a plan:

> 26. At the stage of loan negotiation, the borrower should satisfy the Bank that a *workable plan* for resettlement has been prepared in line with the criteria set forth above and that its implementation is accepted as part of the borrower's obligation to carry out the project. [emphasis added]

This statement of policy offers remarkably complete coverage of the main issues in involuntary resettlement. But it does not make any special reference to the needs of tribal peoples. In February 1982, however, the Bank did publish an operational manual statement dealing with tribal populations, entitled "Tribal People in Bank-Financed Projects."[4] It provides a detailed description of typical characteristics of tribal populations and goes on to note:

> 4. Experience has shown that, unless special measures are adopted, tribal people are more likely to be harmed than helped by development projects that are intended for beneficiaries other than themselves. Therefore, whenever tribal peoples may be affected, the design of projects should include measures or components necessary to safeguard their interests and, whenever feasible, to enhance their well-being. Sound project planning and design reduce the risk that tribal people will suffer from the project's consequences or disrupt its implementation.

The 1982 statement went so far as to acknowledge that there may be much to be learned from the traditional lifeways of tribal peoples:

> More positively, tribal people may offer opportunities to the wider society, especially by increasing the national society's knowledge of proven adaptation to and utilization of fragile and marginal environments.

[4] Operational Manual Statement No. 2.34, February 1992.

The Bank made it clear that its policy was onerous:

> 5. *As a general policy, the Bank will not assist development projects that knowingly involve encroachment on traditional territories being used or occupied by tribal people, unless adequate safeguards are provided.* In those cases where environmental and/or social changes promoted through development projects may create undesired effects for tribal people, the project should be designed so as to prevent or mitigate such effects. *The Bank will assist projects* only *when satisfied that the Borrower or relevant government agency supports and can implement measures that will effectively safeguard the integrity and well-being of the tribal people.* Measures at either extreme should be avoided; either those that perpetuate isolation from the national society and needed social services; or those promoting forced, accelerated acculturation unsuited to the future well-being of the affected tribal people. The Bank would not be prepared to assist with a project if it appears that the project sponsors had forcibly "cleared" the area of tribal people beforehand. [emphasis added]

The Bank admitted the dilemma that its championing of tribal interests created:

> 6. Some practical issues concerning tribal people are difficult to resolve. *For example, how can the government harmonize its interest in the development of a rich ore body or a major hydro potential with the need to safeguard the rights of tribal people in the project area?* These are matters for judgements guided by the principle that Bank assistance should help prevent or mitigate harm, and provide adequate time and conditions for acculturation. [emphasis added]

Yet the Bank reaffirmed the need to demarcate tribal areas and to protect tribal integrity:

> 7. Since successful acculturation is slow and gradual, development projects having tribal people in their zone of influence must provide time and conditions for acculturation. Such projects will require a tribal component or parallel program which includes: (a) *the recognition, demarcation and protection of tribal areas containing those resources required to sustain the tribal people's traditional*

means of livelihood; (b) appropriate social services that are consonant with the tribe's acculturation status, including, especially,
protection against diseases and the maintenance of health; (c)
*the maintenance, to the extent desired by the tribe, of its cultural integrity
and embodiments thereof*; . . . [emphasis added]

The Bank even specified the need for participation by tribal people in a way
that could only take place through effective public hearings:

(d) a forum for the participation of the tribal people in decisions
affecting them, and providing for adjudication and redress of
grievances.

The statement makes clear that proper implementation of its policy requires the acquisition of social science data bearing upon potential impacts of
resettlement and rehabilitation:

8. The design of an appropriate tribal component depends upon
detailed, contemporary knowledge of the peoples to be affected. Tribal societies are complex and information gathered on a particular society may not necessarily be ascribable even to neighboring
tribes. To the extent that project designers are unfamiliar with
the affected tribal peoples, pre-investment studies will be necessary, employing qualified indigenists and related disciplines.
The Bank, through its Office of Environmental Affairs, is prepared to assist in these endeavors. [emphasis added]

(The reference to the Bank's Office of Environmental Affairs is perhaps too
sanguine. It could not then have undertaken such studies, being without the
necessary staff or resources.)

Three years later, in the 1985 Bank credit and loan agreements relating to
the Sardar Sarovar Projects, India and the three states each agreed to adopt
and implement, within their respective state boundaries, resettlement and rehabilitation plans for the Sardar Sarovar dam and reservoir oustees, satisfactory to the Bank.

The agreements consist of a series of documents classified under two different Bank credit numbers, one for the "Dam and Power Project," the other for
the "Water Delivery and Drainage Project" (canal and irrigation system). It is
the Development Credit Agreement with the Government of India, under the
dam credit number, that lays down requirements for resettlement and rehabilitation.[5] It defines an "oustee" as:

(q) "Oustee" means any person, whether landed or landless, who since at least one year prior to the date of publication of the notification under Section 4 of the Borrower's [India's] Land Acquisition Act, 1894, as amended to the date of this Agreement, has been ordinarily residing, or cultivating land, or carrying on any trade, occupation, or calling or working for gain in Gujarat, Madhya Pradesh and Maharashtra, who would be displaced from his usual habitat due to the carrying out of the Project; . . .

This definition enlarges the scope of the term "oustee" beyond that of the Tribunal award by including oustees in Gujarat and encompassing all those displaced by the Project; it does not limit oustees to those affected by submergence.

The same credit agreement includes the following "principles and objectives":

The Oustees from the State of Gujarat, the State of Madhya Pradesh and the State of Maharashtra shall be relocated and rehabilitated pursuant to the provisions of the Decision [of the Narmada Water Disputes Tribunal] and to the following principles and objectives.

1. *The main objectives* of the Plan for Resettlement and Rehabilitation of the Oustees are to ensure that the Oustees shall, promptly after their displacement: (i) *improve or at least regain the standard of living they were enjoying prior to their displacement*; (ii) be relocated as village units, village sections or families in accordance with the Oustees' preference; (iii) be fully integrated in the community to which they are resettled, and (iv) be provided with appropriate compensation and adequate social and physical rehabilitation infrastructure, including community services and facilities.

2. The Plan for Resettlement and Rehabilitation of the Oustees shall ensure adequate participation by the Oustees.

3. Each landed Oustee shall be entitled to and allotted irrigable land *in the State in which he chooses to resettle*, of equal size to that which he owned prior to his resettlement, subject to the appli-

---

[5] Development Credit Agreement (Narmada River Development (Gujarat) Sardar Sarovar Dam and Power Project) between India and International Development Association, Credit Number 1552 IN, May 10, 1985.

cable land ceiling laws, acceptable to him; provided, however, that in those cases where the oustee owned less than 2 hectares of land, such Oustee shall be entitled to at least 2 hectares of irrigable land, acceptable to him. For the purposes of this paragraph, the term "State" means individually Gujarat, Madhya Pradesh and Maharashtra.

4. Each landless Oustee shall be rehabilitated in the agricultural or nonagricultural sectors, as the case may be, and shall be entitled to stable means of livelihood in accordance with the objectives set forth in paragraph 1 of this Schedule.

5. The level of compensation for land, irrigable and otherwise, to be paid to landed Oustees shall be based on the current market value of land of equivalent size, location and comparable quality in areas provided for and acceptable to each Oustee.

6. Where irrigable land is allocated to a landed Oustee in lieu of land previously owned by such oustee, 50% of the cash compensation to which such Oustee is entitled shall be applied towards the cost of the allocated land, subject to a maximum of the value of the land alloted, and the balance of the cost of such alloted land shall be treated by the State where the alloted land is located, as an interest-free loan repayable over 20 years. For the purposes of this paragraph, "State" means individually Gujarat, Madhya Pradesh and Maharashtra.

7. In no case shall cash payments be made in substitution for actual rehabilitation. Cash payments shall be restricted to such transactions as mandated by the Decision. [emphasis added]

The Development Credit Agreement with the Government of India defined "Sardar Sarovar Project" as including both the dam *and* canal.[6] The Bank also concluded project agreements with each of the three states for the dam and power project and with Gujarat for the canal (water delivery and drainage project). The project agreements for the dam refer to the principles and objectives of resettlement and rehabilitation set out in the Development Credit Agreement with India and covenant each state to carry them out. Since the definition of oustee embraced all persons displaced by the Projects, whether submerged or not, the Kevadia oustees were thereby covered. But the project agreement with the state of Gujarat for the canal made no reference to canal

---

[6] "(n) 'Sardar Sarovar Project' means the project whose salient features are described in Schedule 4 to this Agreement. . . ." Schedule 4 divides the Project into two parts. Part A is the dam and power project; Part B describes the main canal, subsidiary canals, and associated structures.

oustees or to the principles and provisions for resettlement and rehabilitation contained in the agreement with India. Yet in 1980 the Bank had acknowledged that resettlement of people is not only necessary in the case of dams, but also in the case of "canals... and the like."

This is not to say that canal oustees were left without any rights. They have the right to be compensated under the Indian *Land Acquisition Act, 1894*. But they were given no right to "land for land" or to any of the other advantages of the 1985 credit and loan agreements.

Furthermore, the agreements made no express reference to tribals, notwithstanding the elaborate Bank policy adopted in 1982.

The agreements did, however, provide that one of the objectives of resettlement and rehabilitation would be to enable *all oustees* to "improve or at least regain the standard of living they were enjoying prior to their displacement."

As can be seen, the credit and loan agreements make provision for each landed oustee to be allotted "irrigable land... of equal size to that which he owned prior to his resettlement...." However, the agreements contain a definition of oustee which goes beyond the issue of legal ownership and deals with the realities of use and occupation of land by tribal people. An oustee is "any person, whether landed or landless" who has been "ordinarily residing, or cultivating land...."

Both landed and landless oustees are therefore entitled to invoke the principles and objectives enshrined in the agreements. The all-embracing definition of oustees in the Bank agreements contemplates that, whether classified as landed or landless, oustees may have been engaged in cultivating land. Encroachers may be classified as landless, but in fact they are engaged in cultivating land pursuant to customary, though informal, usage.

The statement of principles and objectives in the 1985 credit and loan agreements provides that:

> 4. Each landless Oustee shall be rehabilitated in the agricultural or non-agricultural sectors, as the case may be, and shall be entitled to stable means of livelihood in accordance with the objectives set forth in paragraph 1 of this Schedule.

Paragraph 1 brings us back to the overarching principle of resettlement: any plan for resettlement must ensure that the oustees shall "improve or at least regain the standard of living they were enjoying prior to their displacement." This can only mean, in practice, that oustees engaged in cultivating land are entitled to adequate land on resettlement.

This is not a question of policy but a question of implementation. In 1984, the Narmada Control Authority declared that, "For tribals, there is no rehabilitation more effective than providing land as the source of livelihood."[7] Similarly, Bank officials have taken the position that, in the case of encroachers, the best means of complying with this overarching objective is to provide encroachers with adequate land. As Michael Baxter, Chief, Agricultural Unit, India, writing in 1991, put it, providing adequate land to encroachers is "... the soundest way to ensure that PAPS [oustees] improve or at least regain the standard of living they were enjoying prior to their displacement." We believe that, in Madhya Pradesh and Maharashtra, it is the only realistic way to implement the overarching objective of Bank policy.

Such an outcome is consistent with the provisions of ILO 107, which calls for provision to tribal people of "lands of quality at least equal to that of lands previously occupied by them."

The Bank felt that its resettlement policies had been successful and that they had been an important influence in the aid community. In 1986, Bank Vice-President S. Shahid Husain issued an Office Memorandum to "Recipients of Operations Policy Notes." In part, he said:

> The Bank has been the only international aid agency with a policy governing resettlement, and that policy has proven to be sound. The impact of the Bank's concern has not been limited to resettlement under Bank-financed projects; it has also had a substantial spill-over effect among borrowing governments, local agencies, and other international donors.

Our Terms of Reference require us also to consider Bank operational directives after 1985 to the present.

In June 1990, the World Bank issued an operational directive on involuntary resettlement.[8] The directive gathered together and restated the principles the Bank had adopted earlier:

> 2. Development projects that displace people involuntarily generally give rise to severe economic, social, and environmental problems: production systems are dismantled; productive assets and income sources are lost; people are relocated to environments where their productive skills may be less applicable and the competition for resources greater; community structures and

---

[7] *Sardar Sarovar Project, Land Acquisition and Rehabilitation of Oustees*, Narmada Control Authority, April 1984, p 66.
[8] Operational Directive 4.30: Involuntary Resettlement, June 29, 1990.

social networks are weakened; kin groups are dispersed; and cultural identity, traditional authority, and the potential for mutual help are diminished. Involuntary resettlement may cause severe long-term hardship, impoverishment, and environmental damage unless appropriate measures are carefully planned and carried out.

The Bank's objectives were reiterated:

3. The objective of the Bank's resettlement policy is to ensure that the population displaced by a project receives benefits from it. Involuntary resettlement is an integral part of project design and should be dealt with from the earliest stages of project preparation (para. 28), taking into account the following policy considerations:

(a) *Involuntary resettlement should be avoided or minimized where feasible, exploring all viable alternative project designs.* For example, realignment of roads or *reductions in dam height* may significantly reduce resettlement needs. [emphasis added]

(b) Where displacement is unavoidable, resettlement plans should be developed. All involuntary resettlement should be conceived and executed as *development programs*, with resettlers provided sufficient investment resources and opportunities to *share in project benefits.* Displaced persons should be (i) compensated for their losses at full replacement cost prior to the actual move; (ii) assisted with the move and supported during the transition period in the resettlement site; and (iii) assisted in their efforts to improve their former living standards, income earning capacity, and production levels, or at least to restore them. Particular attention should be paid to the needs of the poorest groups to be resettled. [emphasis in original]

. . .

(e) Land, housing, infrastructure, and other compensation should be provided to the adversely affected population, indigenous groups, ethnic minorities, and pastoralists who may have usufruct or customary rights to the land or other resources taken for the project. *The absence of legal title to land by such groups should not be a bar to compensation.* [emphasis added]

Once again, the fundamental necessity of informed, effective strategic planning prior to resettlement was emphasized:

4. Where large-scale population displacement is unavoidable, a detailed resettlement plan, timetable, and budget are required. *Resettlement plans should be built around a development strategy and package aimed at improving or at least restoring the economic base for those relocated*. Experience indicates that cash compensation alone is normally inadequate. Voluntary settlement may form part of a resettlement plan, provided measures to address the special circumstances of involuntary resettlers are included. *Preference should be given to land-based resettlement strategies for people dislocated from agricultural settings*. If suitable land is unavailable, nonland-based strategies built around opportunities for employment or self-employment may be used. [emphasis added]

This directive was quite specific about the extent and nature of socioeconomic data to be acquired:

11. Resettlement plans should be based on recent information about the scale and impact of resettlement on the displaced population. In addition to describing standard household characteristics, socioeconomic surveys should describe (a) the magnitude of displacement; (b) information on the full resource base of the affected population, including income derived from informal sector and nonfarm activities, and from common property; (c) the extent to which groups will experience total or partial loss of assets; (d) public infrastructure and social services that will be affected; (e) formal and informal institutions (such as community organizations, ritual groups, etc.) that can assist with designing and implementing the resettlement programs; and (f) attitudes on resettlement options. Socioeconomic surveys, recording the names of affected families, should be conducted as early as possible to prevent inflows of population ineligible for compensation.

The statement went so far as to insist upon fair consideration of customary land rights:

17. Resettlement plans should review the main land tenure and transfer systems, including common property and nontitle-based usufruct systems governed by locally recognized land allocation mechanisms. *The objective is to treat customary and formal rights as equally as possible in devising compensation rules and procedures.*

The plan should address the issues raised by the different tenure systems found in a project area, including (a) the compensation eligibility of land-dependent populations; (b) the valuation procedures applicable to different tenure types; and (c) the grievance procedures available for disputes over land acquisition. Plans should contain provisions for conducting land surveys and regularizing land tenure in the earliest stages of project development. Planning should also anticipate the approximate time needed to acquire and transfer land. [emphasis added]

This directive offered policy guidelines for including resettlement costs as an integral component of project-related financing or as a free-standing project in its own right:

26. Bank financing of resettlement can be provided as follows: (a) As a component of the main investment project causing displacement and requiring resettlement. (b) If large enough, as a free-standing resettlement project with appropriate cross-conditionalities, processed and implemented in parallel with the investment project that causes the displacement. The latter approach may better focus country and Bank attention on the effective resolution of resettlement issues. (c) As a sector investment loan. Where the specific resettlement needs of each subproject are not known in advance, the borrower would need to agree to resettlement policies, planning principles, institutional arrangements, and design criteria that meet Bank policy and requirements as a condition of the loan. An estimate should be provided of total population to be displaced and overall resettlement costs, as well as an evaluation of proposed resettlement sites. Subprojects in sector investment loans should be screened by the implementing agency to ensure consistency with this directive, and approved individually by the Bank. For countries with a series of operations requiring resettlement, efforts to improve the policy, institutional, and legal framework for resettlement should form part of the Bank's ongoing country and sector dialogue with the government. These efforts should be appropriately reflected in economic and sector work and in country strategy papers and briefs.

The development of Bank policy toward tribal peoples culminated in a World Bank Operational Directive issued in September 1991,[9] which specifically defined tribals as social groups with a social and cultural identity distinct from the dominant society that makes them vulnerable to being disadvantaged in the development process.

The Bank then offered a more elaborate definition:

> 5. Because of the varied and changing contexts in which indigenous peoples are found, no single definition can capture their diversity. Indigenous people are commonly among the poorest segments of a population. They engage in economic activities that range from shifting agriculture in or near forests to wage labour or even small-scale market-oriented activities. Indigenous peoples can be identified in particular geographical areas by the presence in varying degrees of the following characteristics:
>
> (a) a close attachment to ancestral territories and to the natural resources in these areas;
>
> (b) self-identification and identification by others as members of a distinct cultural group;
>
> (c) an indigenous language, often different from the national language;
>
> (d) presence of customary social and political institutions; and
>
> (e) primarily subsistence-oriented production.

The Bank then stated its policy objective related to treatment of tribals in Bank-sponsored projects:

> 6. The Bank's broad objective towards indigenous people, as for all the people in its member countries, is to ensure that the development process fosters *full respect for their dignity, human rights, and cultural uniqueness*. More specifically, the objective at the center of this directive is to ensure that *indigenous peoples do not suffer adverse effects* during the development process, particularly from Bank-financed projects, and that they receive culturally compatible social and economic benefits. [emphasis added]

The importance of planning to ensure that tribal peoples should not just escape impoverishment but also share in the perceived benefits of a project was made clear:

[9] Operational Directive 4.20: Indigenous Peoples, September 17, 1991.

9. Cases will occur, especially when dealing with the most isolated groups, where adverse impacts are unavoidable and adequate mitigation plans have not been developed. *In such situations, the Bank will not appraise projects until suitable plans are developed by the borrower and reviewed by the Bank.* In other cases, indigenous people may wish to be and can be incorporated into the development process. In sum, a full range of positive actions by the borrower must ensure that indigenous people benefit from the development investments. [emphasis added]

In sum, every effort must be taken to protect indigenous land rights:

15. . . . The project component for indigenous peoples development should include the following elements, as needed:
. . .
(c) *Land Tenure.* When local legislation needs strengthening, the Bank should offer to advise and assist the borrower in *establishing legal recognition of the customary or traditional land tenure systems of indigenous peoples.* Where the traditional lands of indigenous peoples have been brought by law into the domain of the state and where it is inappropriate to convert traditional rights into those of legal ownership, alternative arrangements should be implemented to grant long-term, renewable rights of custodianship and use to indigenous peoples. *These steps should be taken before the initiation of other planning steps that may be contingent on recognized land titles.* [emphasis added]

As required by our Terms of Reference, we have gone beyond 1985, the year of the credit and loan agreements in presenting this review of Bank policy. Directive 4.30 on involuntary resettlement generally and Directive 4.20 on resettlement of indigenous peoples in particular represent the culmination of a decade of policy development. At the very time when the Independent Review was being set up, the Bank had, in its 1990 and 1991 directives, set the highest standards of any aid or lending organization in the world for mitigating adverse consequences to human wellbeing caused by involuntary resettlement.

These policy changes reflect the worldwide development of concepts of human rights, for they constitute a recognition that large-scale projects, especially in rural, forest, and frontier areas may displace people just as do war and natural calamities. They focus on people who are being displaced by the advance of development, and require that in any project the human rights of the oustees must be respected. According to the ILO, these are rights not to be impaired on grounds of national sovereignty or national economic interest. Such considerations may justify a project; they do not justify the nullification of these basic human rights.

A fisherman returning from the river to his village in the submergence area of the Nimad, Madhya Pradesh. He sold his catch to buyers from Badwani.

Chapter 4
PROJECT
APPRAISAL

THE Bank's policies of 1980 and 1982 on involuntary resettlement enunciate its commitment to a program of resettlement and rehabilitation that will "protect the life, welfare, and rights of those displaced."[1] They also set forth the means by which the Bank is to ensure that it only supports projects that meet its resettlement and rehabilitation standards.

Implementation of these policies begins with systematic and thorough feasibility studies. These studies must include an assessment of the extent of displacement that could occur, and a detailed plan that shows how those displaced are to be resettled and assisted to maintain or restore their living standards. Under Bank policy, in the absence of assessments and plans of this kind, no project should proceed to the appraisal phase. This means that resettlement data and comprehensive plans are a condition for loans to any project that entails displacement. Where displacement is of tribal peoples, there must also be a full study of the nature of the societies to be affected. Implementation of the Bank's policies therefore begins with knowledge.

The need to assemble basic information before approving the project is spelled out in the Bank's 1980 Operational Manual Statement: "To be successful, the planning and implementation of resettlement usually necessitates a close scrutiny of the essential needs of the settlers" (p 1, §7). The 1982 Operational Manual Statement on tribal people is even more emphatic. It states: "The design of an appropriate tribal component depends upon detailed, contemporary knowledge of the peoples to be affected" (p 2, §8).

The process by which comprehensive data are gathered typically entails a great deal of collaboration with the people being studied. In order to know

---

[1] Operational Manual Statement No. 2.33, February 1980, p 1.

what the consequences of a project would be, it is essential to discuss it in detail with those to be impacted. This can be part of a consultative procedure; it can give the people an opportunity to make their own contribution to the description of the project, and to suggest measures that might help ameliorate its impacts. The absence of such consultation contributes to the estrangement from the project of the people who will be affected. This kind of collaboration and consultation is sorely missing from the history of Sardar Sarovar.

Policies have been designed, therefore, in a double vacuum—the data and the people's perspectives are both absent. When construction of intrastructure began in 1961 it would have been unreasonable to expect these kinds of enquiry or processes; but by the time the Bank was negotiating the loan agreement they had become a norm of development theory—including the theory being written by the Bank's own staff.

The essence of the Bank's resettlement policy lies in the requirement that the borrowing country gather detailed data and prepare a resettlement plan developed specifically for the project that the Bank is being asked to support. The resettlement plan should be prepared at the same time as plans for the "main" project (engineering design, etc.) so that the entire project proposal can be evaluated by the Bank's appraisal team and recommendations can be made to the Executive Board for or against approval. Based on a policy objective that requires at a minimum that the people displaced by the project at least recover their living standards after their relocation, the plan must show what their current standards are, how they will be relocated, where they will be resettled, and how they will be assisted after the move to ensure that living standards do not fall.

Few if any of these requirements were met during the Sardar Sarovar appraisal. No resettlement plan was prepared by the borrower, and none was appraised by the Bank. Although two missions pre-appraised the Project and two more completed the project appraisal in the 1982 to 1983 period, these missions limited themselves to the project's technical and economic aspects, failing to include social and cultural impacts upon the affected populace.

From the very beginning of the Sardar Sarovar Projects the Bank failed to implement its own policy. Anxiety about this within the Bank, on the part of those who were working on resettlement issues, resulted in a request being sent to India for full and detailed information. The only data forthcoming at that time, however, comprised a survey of 19 Gujarat villages—the 14 scheduled for submergence and the five rock-filled dyke villages near the dam site. This was based on the early stages of Professor Vidyut Joshi's work at the Centre for Social Studies, Surat. No adequate information was made available for submergence villages in Maharashtra or Madhya Pradesh. Nor was there any consideration of the impact on human populations of the canal and irrigation works.

Downstream effects did not come within the Bank's resettlement and rehabilitation policy, but a thorough socioeconomic impact assessment could not have ignored these, and Bank policy might well have been amended. This is a good example of how knowledge and policy must proceed together: to do otherwise places significant numbers of potentially affected people at social and economic risk.

The Bank's first in-depth attempt to evaluate the social impacts of the project came after the appraisal was completed and it was clear that the project would proceed. In 1983, Professor Thayer Scudder, an internationally known expert on resettlement from the California Institute of Technology, was engaged as consultant to the Bank and sent to India following the formal appraisal of the Project. He was accompanied by three members of Bank staff (a lawyer, an engineer, and an agricultural economist). The Bank's India Country Department opposed this mission, while Indian reaction to the announcement of Professor Scudder's forthcoming mission was defensive. Letters were sent to the Bank from the Government of India stating that "necessary steps are being taken to formulate a rehabilitation plan," and that no Bank mission "should be mounted specifically for this purpose." The Government of India also took the view that past experience had shown that India "could and did satisfy the Bank of the programmes of resettlement undertaken."[2] Despite these assurances, the mission went ahead. It resulted in a preliminary finding to the effect that crucial information was lacking.

The absence of information on resettlement was such that the Bank asked Professor Scudder to return to India in 1984 for a further three weeks on what was termed a "post appraisal" mission. This meant that the assessment of resettlement and rehabilitation implications of Sardar Sarovar—which was expected at the time to bear on the lives of at least 50,000 people, and in the event will affect at least 100,000—was based on five weeks of work by one person.[3]

Professor Scudder's findings were the following:
• The information available on the magnitude and implications of displacement was inadequate and there had been little effort to carry out a full investigation.

[2] Arjun Thapan, Under Secretary, Ministry of Finance, Government of India, to F. M. Patorni, Acting Chief, Agriculture Division, World Bank, New Delhi Office, August 19 and September 5, 1983.

[3] Professor Scudder indicates in his report on his 1983 mission that he spent five days in the submergence area, and was restricted in his contacts. He speaks of being "chaperoned." *The Relocation Component in Connection with the Sardar Sarovar (Narmada) Project*, November 1983. If the canal-affected people, whose prospects Scudder discussed, are included, the total number of those to be affected rises to well over 200,000.

- India's past record of reservoir-related relocation did not meet Bank standards, the reasons being: absence of a national policy and presence of an inappropriate legal instrument for property acquisition and compensation (the *Land Acquisition Act, 1894*); an inadequate institutional framework in each of the three states—they lacked the means and skills to implement resettlement; bureaucratic insensitivity and apathy towards the social and communal aspects of displacement and relocation; and a rigid orientation towards compensation to individuals rather than resettlement of whole communities.
- The Narmada Water Disputes Tribunal's 1979 provisions, though representing a major advance in India, did not meet the requirements of the World Bank policy guidelines on involuntary resettlement. There were serious shortcomings, for example, with regard to landless people and forest cultivators.
- The state governments were not serious about honoring the provisions of the Tribunal's award. Their plans and cost estimates were inadequate and unreliable.

For these reasons Professor Scudder concluded that resettlement of Sardar Sarovar oustees was likely to take place in a "very unfavorable environment."[4] Professor Scudder's primary criticism lies at the heart of many others: there was no adequate information. No one knew the scale of the displacement, nor did anyone have an accurate picture of the peoples who were to be displaced. As a result, there could be no appropriate resettlement plan. This means that Sardar Sarovar was appraised before the human costs could be added to the equation. It also means that provisions to mitigate those costs could not be designed in accordance with people's actual needs and wishes, or in the light of the facts as they might turn out. No one knew what the true impacts would be.

It is not possible to say whether or not the results of such studies would necessarily have altered the decision to fund the Sardar Sarovar Projects as they stood, though from what our review has discovered we think it is possible that, presented with thorough socioeconomic and environmental impact assessments, technological alternatives may have been considered, and resettlement and rehabilitation policy and practices could have been designed which were much more appropriate to the people affected. What needs to be understood fully here is that to make the decision to proceed with a project that is known to severely affect the lives of human beings, no matter how few will be adversely affected nor how many will benefit, in near total ignorance of the people and the impact, was at worst irresponsible and at best in contradiction to existing Bank policy.

---

[4] See Thayer Scudder, *The Relocation Component in Connection with the Sardar Sarovar (Narmada) Project*, November 1983. And "Addendum," August 1984.

Absence of data and lack of acceptable planning are themes that run through the record of events surrounding the Sardar Sarovar approvals. The Bank's letter to the three states explaining Scudder's forthcoming mission was emphatic on the point. It said: "We have not received a coherent set of descriptive data and attitudinal surveys concerning the population to be relocated, nor have we been provided with sufficiently detailed plans by the three State governments covering all successive plans of the rehabilitation process." This letter urged each state to collect and prepare "*all* available data on sociological, demographic, agricultural and physical" features of the resettlement aspects of the Projects, and required that these be made available by September 1983, when the mission was to be in the field. In an attachment to this letter the requirements were spelled out in some detail, and were to include surveys that would indicate "relocation-related desires, preferences, fears, etc., of the population."[5]

The absence of data reported by Professor Scudder can be seen as a failure on the part of the three states to meet the Bank's explicit requirements.[6] But, once this absence was made known through Scudder's report, it also indicates the failure of the Bank to follow through on its own position. At this point, the prospective borrower's lack of compliance with Bank policy was already conspicuous. Nevertheless, in the following year, 1984, the Bank pushed on towards negotiating the loan by extending the deadline for submission of the plan. The Aide-Memoire of Professor Scudder's post-appraisal mission begins: "In order to comply with Bank/IDA policy, [the Government of India, the Narmada Control Authority] and the States concerned would be required to provide at negotiation an overall detailed plan for the resettlement and rehabilitation of the oustees." Moreover, the Bank attenuated its requirements. It agreed to accept a plan for "Stage One oustees (350 foot elevation)" only, which it justified on the basis of "the extended implementation period of the SSP." In short, having recognized the governments' failure to conform to the Bank's requirements, the Bank relaxed these requirements.

The Aide-Memoire of August 21, 1984, goes on to require that Madhya Pradesh and Maharashtra provide "a detailed plan on the possibility that (a) all MP and Maharashtra oustees choose to resettle in their own states, and (b) 50 per cent choose to resettle in their own states." Although this may sound demanding on the surface, it implicitly acknowledges that the states had no information on preferences of oustees, and it ignores the fact that, under the

---

[5] See letter from William G. Rodger, Divisional Chief, Irrigation II Division, to states of Gujarat, Madhya Pradesh, and Maharashtra, July 5, 1983.

[6] It might be said that demands for detailed plans were unrealistic, and that plans made at so early a stage were likely to prove to be unreliable or ill-conceived. However, the primary issue here is data, without which *no* reliable planning can be done.

terms of the Tribunal's award, by 1981 both Madhya Pradesh and Maharashtra were to have informed Gujarat of precise numbers of families willing to relocate to Gujarat and those wanting to remain in their own states. This 1984 requirement remains unmet today.

In April 1984 the Narmada Control Authority produced a report entitled *Sardar Sarovar Project: Land Acquisition and Rehabilitation of Oustees*. This contains an outline rehabilitation plan, summarizes the policies on which it is based, and the organizational arrangements for carrying it out. A short chapter on each riparian state enumerates submergence villages, some characteristics of affected families, proposed organizational set up, progress to date, and possible plans for the future. A final chapter addresses the question of costs, and annexures include supporting documents and submergence, land acquisition, and resettlement schedules.

Some of the material presented shows that the Narmada Control Authority and the Indian states were aware of the special circumstances related to the resettlement and rehabilitation of tribals, the necessity of collecting household-by-household data about the oustee population, the desirability of consulting with oustees, and other factors consonant with Bank policy. On the other hand, there are statements in the report which should have acted as an early warning to the Bank. The outline of the rehabilitation plan begins with a discussion of how land will be allocated to landholding families. It states that in Madhya Pradesh there is almost no suitable agricultural land and that therefore oustees will either have to migrate to Gujarat or be resettled in other economic activities in Madhya Pradesh (pp 9, 21-2). In Gujarat it is feared that areas of land large enough for settlements of whole villages will not be available and that government land will have to be given in small plots and oustees dispersed wherever land is available (p 10). Whatever other good intentions are expressed in the report, these factors make compliance unlikely with either the conditions of the Tribunal's award or Bank policy on involuntary resettlement and tribal peoples.

If the Bank had wished to look at smaller details, it might have wondered how Madhya Pradesh arrived at its "latest indication" that "every oustee family of Madhya Pradesh would be willing to move over to Gujarat..." (p 18). The report says that the Madhya Pradesh Consultancy had, in April 1984, begun a door-to-door survey of 7,500 oustee families to make an assessment of their preferences for relocation. A copy of the questionnaire is included and indeed there is a question requiring the family to state exactly which village or town it would like to go to. However, the program of rehabilitation presented shows that the earliest date at which oustees will even see possible relocation sites is July 1984. How could families be expected to reply to the questionnaire prior to visiting potential sites? If willingness to move to Gujarat was not assessed on the basis of a household-by-household survey, how was it determined?

Much of the report appears to be an attempt to pull together scraps of data, policy, and planning in order to cover the failure to collect the necessary information or to prepare a rehabilitation plan. Its policy proposals adopt the Tribunal's award, its data are limited and provisional, and important elements of rehabilitation are promises rather than plans. It is hard to believe that the Bank accepted this as fulfilment of a borrower's obligation to assess resettlement and rehabilitation. Reliance on the Tribunal's award and a submergence schedule do not represent implementation of Bank policies.[7]

That the Bank's India Department continued to negotiate the 1985 credit and loan agreements on so slender a basis reveals its readiness to accept whatever India offered, and to disregard the World Bank's own requirements and expertise. The Bank's 1983 mission had explicitly identified the Tribunal's award as deficient in crucial respects as a basis for resettlement and rehabilitation policy. Professor Scudder and others had persistently pointed out the need for in-depth knowledge—not just a submergence schedule. In effect, in 1984 the Bank embarked on an approach to Sardar Sarovar that placed approval of the Project over compliance with Bank policy.

This substitute for resettlement studies and planning was accepted by the Bank's 1985 Staff Appraisal Report.[8] Although it mentioned that the first stages of construction had already caused displacement in Gujarat, and observed that 5,000 people had been adversely affected (p 55), it offered the assurance that "their position would be reassessed and appropriate rehabilitation conditions applied so that all oustees are subject to a uniform policy." This has still not been done. No investigation of these people has been carried out; no misgivings about Gujarat's use of the *Land Acquisition Act, 1894* and the fate of those being forcibly displaced appear to have shaped the terms of the credit and loan agreements. Despite its extensive and principled policy statements about involuntary resettlement, the Bank's pre-appraisal and appraisal missions do not seem to have given any weight to what was actually happening in a project it was about to fund. The process that led up to the signing of the 1985 credit and loan agreements with India and the three states was informed

---

[7] This is not meant to discount the importance of keying resettlement to the submergence schedule. As recently as February 1992, for example, a Bank supervision mission accepted proposals to move the major portion of Madhya Pradesh oustees only in the final year of reservoir filling. This lack of leeway for any schedule slippage, especially when it concerns the state where resettlement has been most problematic, creates the risk of a resettlement emergency operation, even though this might be defended on the grounds that the last year of submergence in Madhya Pradesh affects many people for whom impact is relatively limited.

[8] See the Staff Appraisal Report, Supplementary Data Volume, Part I, §6.04ff, pp 42 45.

neither by an overall impact assessment statement nor by a consideration of realities on the ground.

By this time warnings of the distress caused to families displaced by the Projects' construction were arriving at the Bank via another route. In August 1983, Arch Vahini, the non-government organization with closest links to Gujarat communities, detailed the problems and protested vigorously in a letter to William C. Rodger, Divisional Chief of the Irrigation Division of the Bank. Dr. Anil Patel, the leading member of Arch Vahini, also lobbied Professor Scudder, expressing his extreme anxiety about implementation problems. Scudder himself wrote to the Bank in early 1985 to pass on this growing apprehension.[9]

Apparently determined to press ahead with the loan, and in the absence of an in-depth socioeconomic impact assessment and project-specific resettlement plan, the Bank adopted the only convenient vehicle at hand, the Tribunal's award. Its adoption reflected a realization at the time that the award had broken new ground in insisting on a package that included land in the command area of the Projects as well as recognition of oustees' rights to make important choices of their own. But many of its defects had to be overlooked. The Tribunal had been convened to adjudicate an interstate dispute and apportion benefits and costs. In as much as some of these costs related to resettlement and rehabilitation, it set down provisions in the light of what was known in 1979. It was not intended, however, and should not have been expected, to establish policies and programs that would meet the needs of the affected people of the whole complex of Sardar Sarovar Projects. It did not even mention the Gujarat oustees, nor did it concern itself with the people potentially affected by the canal and associated irrigation works. It did not take into account the cultural attributes of the oustee population; there is no discussion of tribal peoples, encroachers, or the meaning of "landlessness." These are not criticisms of the award, but they are characteristics that make it an unsuitable document on which to base a resettlement and rehabilitation policy for the Projects.

The findings of the Tribunal's award may have been a useful starting point for policy discussions within the Bank. Its measures could have been checked against data, once these were accumulated. In the absence of full-scale project appraisal, however, reliance on the Tribunal's measures became a substitute for the processes the Bank had set out as a means to protect the rights of persons forcibly displaced by Bank-financed projects. Acceptance, at the same time, of submergence schedules in lieu of project-specific resettlement and rehabilitation plans was in violation of the spirit as well as the letter of Bank policy. By this device, data could be said to be on hand or in process. In reality,

[9] Thayer Scudder to Mr. Ronald P. Brigish, ASAD, World Bank, January 24, 1985.

they were neither. Meanwhile, the purposes for which the data were needed were to be short-cut by adoption of the Tribunal award as the legal and practical foundation of resettlement policies for all three states.

It might be argued that basic facts were known. For example, population of the submergence area could be calculated on the basis of census returns, and updated with the help of growth-rate statistics. Estimates of this kind were given at various points in the history of the Projects, but they have turned out to be grossly inaccurate, underestimating total oustee population by as much as 400 per cent. Even if such estimates were accurate, however, they would not constitute the kind of information that could provide a foundation for assessing impacts, devising policies, or effecting implementation. There was a need for a detailed understanding of how people lived—the nature of their resources, their relationship to them, their social and cultural interconnections—and a need for direct consultation with those to be affected. Both the Bank's guidelines and social science emphasize the value of these kinds of data.

In 1986 Dr. Michael Cernea, the Bank's expert on resettlement and rehabilitation and the first sociologist to be appointed (in 1976) to a key role in Bank policy appraisal, prepared a report on involuntary resettlement in Bank-assisted projects.[10] This is a review of projects funded by the Bank between 1979 and 1985, the period during which the 1980 and 1982 Operational Manual Statements came into force. One of the major problems Dr. Cernea identified was "the frequent low quality of preparation of resettlement components by the borrower" (p ii). He pointed out that "A recurrent weakness . . . has been an apparent disregard for Bank policy and norms." He continued with an example:

> A case in point was the Narmada Sardar Sarovar Irrigation and Power project. . . . During 1982-3, four Bank missions, two each for preappraisal and appraisal were mounted, but none of them appraised the resettlement component. Similarly, the borrowing agency did not prepare a resettlement plan. Thus the advance time vital for such planning was lost. It was only *after* full appraisal, during the issues review process, that this was recognized as a major issue. [emphasis in original] (p 11 §5.06)

Written about eighteen months after the loan agreement was signed and by an expert who was engaged with the issue at the time, this is a startling confir-

---

[10] Michael Cernea, "Involuntary Resettlement in Bank-Assisted Projects: a Review of the Application of Bank Policies and Procedures in FY79-85 Projects," Agriculture and Rural Development Department, World Bank, February 1986.

mation of what we heard from other sources. Sardar Sarovar Projects were funded despite minimal compliance with the Bank's own guidelines on the appraisal requirements for the resettlement component.[11]

As early as 1986, it was evident to Dr. Cernea that a fundamental problem that had arisen from the absence of proper project appraisal was: "The initial assumption that the rulings issued by the Narmada Water Disputes Tribunal would be sufficient to generate a resettlement action plan as part of the project was not confirmed" (p 11). The Bank found itself committed to a project that would displace some 100,000 people with a policy that had been defined in essence by the Tribunal. The vacuum left by the Bank's own lack of appraisal was filled by measures that would not be adequate. Thereafter everyone was left with the task of making the best of a bad job.

In 1985 the basis for designing, implementing, and assessing the overarching principle of at minimum retaining oustees' standard of living simply was not in place. The numbers of people to be affected were not known; the range of possible impacts had never been detailed; the effects of the canal had been ignored; the social organization of the peoples to be displaced was little understood in Gujarat, and not at all elsewhere. There was virtually no sociology with which to formulate a policy that might achieve the Bank's long-term objectives. Nor had there been any consultation with those at risk in virtue of which "adequate participation" could be said to be taking place. There were no benchmark data with which to assess success or failure. The resettlement and rehabilitation component of the Sardar Sarovar Projects had never adequately been appraised.

The absence of information and lack of plans continues as a refrain through the coming years. In 1986 and 1989 the Bank was under pressure from consultants and some of its own staff to suspend the Sardar Sarovar loan on the grounds that Bank policy was not being adhered to, and that the overarching principle of policy—that oustees should at least regain their previous standard of living—could therefore not be achieved.

As we shall see in the discussion below regarding each of the states, many of the weaknesses of implementation return to the original failure on the part of the Bank to insist upon a full project appraisal prior to 1985. Thereafter everyone was struggling. The Bank had the difficult task of pressing state govern-

---

[11] In June 1986, senior management at the Bank reviewed Cernea's report. It was noted at this meeting that "it is essential that we follow—and are seen to follow—our own guidelines," and that resettlement components of projects be prepared and supervised "with the same diligence and comprehensiveness applied to other components, such as engineering works. . . ." This indicates a responsiveness at high levels of the Bank to control problems. See Memorandum from Office of the Senior Vice-President, Operations, June 16, 1986.

ments into adopting policies that the Bank regarded as essential, but that the states argued went beyond the obligations set out by the Tribunal's award and the credit and loan agreements. Issues integral to people's wellbeing became items in legal and legalistic wrangles. Matters central to people's material and cultural existence were obscured by technical preoccupations. The actual economic conditions of the villages—especially in the case of the tribal peoples of the remoter communities—were systematically under-reported. Standards of measurement of factors like forest produce, the lenses through which people's lives were inspected, the elements of their lives that were accepted as relevant were all restricted by the terms of the accords and the absence of real information. Lack of data was supplemented by legally binding measures that had limited relevance.

The persistence of these problems and the seriousness of their outcome is revealed in the changing estimates of the overall scale of the displacement the Projects will entail, and the size of the tribal component within it. Resettlement planning is impossible without a reasonable estimate of the number of people that will be affected. The Bank's failure to prepare and appraise the resettlement component of the Sardar Sarovar Projects has led to radically disparate estimates because the required baseline surveys were never carried out. The Tribunal award gave the number as a total of 6,147 families for Madhya Pradesh and 456 families for Maharashtra. The Aide-Memoire following the April 1987 Mission gives the total for all three states as 12,000 families. The 1991 state data, given by the Nigam for Gujarat and by the resettlement plans of Maharashtra and Madhya Pradesh, indicate the total number of oustee families as approximately 27,000. If those being displaced by the canal are included, this rises by at least another 10,000. Thus a 1992 estimate puts the total at close to 40,000 families. Needless to say, the financial, organizational, and logistical problems of resettling the original estimate of 6,603 families are substantially increased when the number rises by six times to the current estimate of 40,000 families.

Opinions about how many of the displaced families are "tribal," and thus entitled to special protection because of heightened risk of impoverishment flow with equal disregard for an empirical basis. The Bank's 1985 Staff Appraisal Report stated that, "The majority of the oustees are tribal people belonging to a number of distinct ethnic groups."[12] The Aide-Memoire of the 1987 mission took the view on Gujarat oustees that only a small number of iso-

---

[12] Staff Appraisal Report, Supplementary Data Volume, Part I, p 42. If this was the opinion at the time of negotiating the credit and loan agreements, it is hard to understand why the Bank's 1982 policy on tribals had no effect on the outcome of negotiations.

lated villages qualified as tribal. On the other hand, the Maharashtra *Master Plan* of 1991 says that all Maharashtra oustees are tribals.[13] Yet in a 1992 letter to the Government of India, the Director of the Bank's India Country Department asked for "clarification on how tribals, who constitute about half of the Maharashtra oustees and about 24 villages in Madhya Pradesh, will be treated...."[14]

These kinds of discrepancies indicate the disarray that prevails at the level of basic information. If a socioeconomic study had been done between 1980 and 1985, when project appraisal was required (and it is to be recalled that the canal is included in the 1985 loan agreement definition of the Projects), numbers would have been known. Had the coordinated policy provisions requested by the Bank been clarified at appraisal, eligibility entitlements and procedures would have been understood from the outset. Moreover, if the attitudinal surveys and in-depth sociological studies had been done during project preparation, the needs of the affected populations would have been understood. Immense problems of policy and implementation could thereby have been avoided.

Under these circumstances many officials in India and the Bank struggled to make implementation work. They continue with this struggle. Sometimes they manage a degree of success. But the Bank's first and essential processes—the foundations for successful resettlement and rehabilitation, the basis for all calculations about the project—had been disregarded. The source of many of the problems that have dogged Sardar Sarovar stem from this failure. A good policy does not guarantee good implementation, but a poorly thought-out policy built on a shaky foundation is bound to frustrate implementation. It has created a plethora of difficulties for the most well-intentioned of officials, opportunities for successive evasions of appropriate implementation, and potential for abuses of human rights.

Virtually every aspect of implementation continues to entail improvisation and a patchwork of measures. Consultation with the peoples affected is limited in many of the villages; the initial failure to inform and consult has predictably come to fruition since 1988 in widespread opposition to the dam throughout Madhya Pradesh and much of Maharashtra. Government may be able to effect relocation; encouragement can always give way to force. But rehabilitation, the central objective of Bank policy, is unlikely to be achieved against this background of the Bank's own non-compliance that was created in the appraisal period, 1980 to 1985.

---

[13] *Sardar Sarovar Project: Master Plan for Resettlement & Rehabilitation of Project Affected Persons of Maharashtra State*, Dhule: Office of the Additional Collector, 1991, p 10.
[14] Vergin to Chitale, March 11, 1992.

Project appraisal is central to the prospects of successful resettlement and rehabilitation. Failure to achieve success in the resettlement and rehabilitation process has grave consequences. Project appraisal is the first step, and in many ways the foundation, in a process that begins with planning and ends with sustaining the livelihood, and even the lives, of many thousands of people. The seriousness of this can be measured by the Bank's experience of resettlement and rehabilitation in other projects.

If the resettlement problems of Sardar Sarovar constituted an aberrant case of fallen standards, measures to solve the situation could focus on the unique features of the Projects, such as the need for a coordinated three-state policy, institutional authority and skills appropriate for the resettlement tasks, insistence on proper identification and transfer of suitable land, and more in-depth supervision by the Bank. In fact, the problems besetting the Sardar Sarovar Projects are more the rule than the exception to resettlement operations supported by the Bank in India.

Curiously enough, although our independent investigation has been helped immeasurably by the many contributions from research and activist organizations in India and abroad, fieldwork in the project area, and specially commissioned studies by independent experts, in fact the richest source of material about the problems with resettlement activity in India are in the Bank's own internal documents. This finding is both heartening and perplexing: heartening because it shows the rich intellectual and informational resources available to the Bank; perplexing because there appears to be so little effort to develop a remedial strategy rather than to confront one resettlement problem after another.[15]

Since 1970, the World Bank has funded more than 400 hydro or irrigation projects around the world. Collectively, these have resulted in the dislocation of millions of people. Between 1978 and 1990, the Bank funded 32 projects in India which have entailed resettlement. A Bank India Department Working Group review of resettlement in 22 Indian projects asserted in 1988 that:

> Performance to date has not been good. In several key projects, despite legal covenants, the resettlement component has yet to be prepared, or is being implemented either inadequately or not at all. In some instances, the situation has deteriorated to the

---

[15] In fact, in 1989, at a time when the resettlement and rehabilitation problems of Sardar Sarovar had pushed the Bank to the edge of suspending the loan, Bank staff chose to adopt an incremental approach, hoping to secure implementation of policies through increasing pressure to win limited improvements. As we shall see, this technique has failed to secure its objectives in Maharashtra and Madhya Pradesh.

point where the Bank may have no other recourse but to exercise remedies under the Credit and Loan agreements.

Comparative analysis shows recurrent flaws in how the Bank approaches resettlement in India. These include the chronic failings in the Bank's appraisal of resettlement components. Projects are appraised and negotiated by the Bank despite the absence of resettlement plans, budgets, and timetables that meet the Bank's resettlement policy. All too often, decisions affecting the lives of thousands or even hundreds of thousands of peasant farmers and tribals are based on seriously deficient or flawed information and approved without requiring major conditions and actions for improvement despite a well documented record of the impoverishment caused by other resettlement operations in the same area.

Examples of appraisal and assessment failures are rife. The Upper Krishna I Project was closed in 1986 with a backlog of over 100,000 people still to be resettled. The Upper Krishna II Project included a careful and detailed resettlement plan, but between 1988 and 1991 appears not to have been supervised. When the first supervision mission did look at resettlement, it found altogether inadequate implementation. This was connected with large, India-wide factors, but the fact remains that Upper Krishna II, a project with 250,000 oustees, was not supervised during a critical phase of implementation.

But perhaps the most pertinent examples for this review are those occurring in the states where the Sardar Sarovar Projects will be built. These are, unfortunately, easy to find, although neither of the Sardar Sarovar appraisal reports saw fit to mention the distressing resettlement record for all three states in their descriptions of the Projects' context. Recurrent appraisal weaknesses include a failure to develop project-specific resettlement plans, lack of accurate, updated information, a failure to appraise the capability of the institutions expected to implement the resettlement, a lack of timetables, and a lack of acceptable legal frameworks. But clearly the single biggest appraisal failure is that despite these known weaknesses, projects were nonetheless sent to the Bank's management for approval.

The Gujarat Medium II Irrigation Project, which affects tribals similar to those who will be displaced by the Sardar Sarovar Projects, was approved in 1984 without project-specific resettlement plans and despite documented resettlement failures during the first Gujarat Medium Irrigation Project. Subsequent supervision reported the predictable widespread failure to rehabilitate the nearly 90,000 people displaced by these dams. The Maharashtra Composite Irrigation Project II, approved in 1986, also failed to appraise a resettlement action plan, and subsequent supervision found that displaced farmers were not being provided with replacement farms.

As early as 1984, Bank reports and letters to the Government of India noted the serious resettlement deficiencies in Madhya Pradesh, the state with nearly three-fourths of all future oustees from Sardar Sarovar.[16] The Madhya Pradesh Major Projects financed three large dams. No resettlement plans were appraised and none of the three projects produced satisfactory resettlement plans. Bank documentation reports that oustees' conditions deteriorated substantially after their displacement, but no serious quantification of how much worse off oustees were can be made from the available information. The Project Completion Report for the Madhya Pradesh Medium Irrigation Project found that:

> By far the most unsatisfactory aspect of the project implementation was R&R [resettlement and rehabilitation] of dam oustees. This may be considered due to the following:
>
> — very limited reference in the SAR [Staff Appraisal Report]
> — the absence of a senior IAS [Indian Administration Service] official at state level to be responsible
> — the lack of involvement by district administrations
> — the lack of a project R&R cell
> — the remote nature of MIP [Medium Irrigation Project] sites
> — the lack of clear state policy on R&R
> — the inability to proceed according to the MP Resettlement Act 1985 as rules to apply the Act had never been promulgated
>
> The last point is of particular importance, as GOMP [Government of Madhya Pradesh] had assured the Bank at Credit negotiations that the Act was being introduced and would be the vehicle for R&R activities under the project. In the event, it was never applied.[17]

The Upper Indravati Project, the Orissa Irrigation II Project, and the Subarnarekha Project were similarly appraised on the basis of general "policy principles" rather than project-specific plans, despite being projects that were

---

[16] See, for example, the March 28, 1984 letter, from the Acting Chief of the Bank's Agricultural Mission, to the Chief Secretary of the Government of Madhya Pradesh: "It is a matter of great concern to us that after nearly 3 years of implementation of the above-mentioned IDA assisted projects, the resettlement plans and organizational framework for implementing these plans for persons to be displaced from the future reservoir areas have still not been prepared by the Government of Madhya Pradesh."

[17] Project Completion Report, Madhya Pradesh Medium Irrigation Project (Cr. 1108-IN), December 28, 1990.

prepared and appraised well after the Bank's resettlement policy was issued. All three projects have resulted in widespread impoverishment of the oustees, tension between the Bank and the borrower, and substantial staff input in efforts to remedy situations that could and should have been avoided.

An equally serious generic problem is that even when the Bank has been aware of major resettlement problems in its India projects, it has failed to act firmly to address them. Violations of legal covenants are flagged[18] and then forgotten; conditions are imposed and when the borrower fails to meet them, the conditions are relaxed or their deadlines postponed. Our review of the documentation as well as our many interviews with government officials support the view that the result of this failure to act upon known problems is a widespread belief in India that the Bank is more concerned to accommodate the pressures emanating from its borrowers than to guarantee implementation of its policies.

In fact, in January 1992, the Bank wrote a letter to India in which it expressed its continuing dissatisfaction with various aspects of state policy.[19] It raised the possibility of submergence before resettlement, the problem of major sons receiving no benefits, the issue of encroachers, inadequacy of data vis-à-vis total numbers of oustees, and the problems that derive from interstate policy differences. In general, the letter raises the lack of compliance in these regards with policy requirements and the binding measures of the Tribunal's award. But it fails to spell out the appropriate basis for resettlement and rehabilitation, and allows the distinction between "landed" and "landless" to prevail (see Chapter 5 below).

The 1992 letter reveals the extent to which problems that were evident in the very early stages of Sardar Sarovar continue unresolved. Indeed, some of these problems reach right back to the lack of appraisal of resettlement and rehabilitation components. Discussion of the letter within the Bank included consideration of the possibility that the Bank threaten suspension of the loan. But attempts were made to soften the criticism. The view was expressed that to demand a major change in policy from either Maharashtra or Madhya Pradesh would be to ask too much, and would in any event be "strongly resisted" by Madhya Pradesh. Moreover, the argument was advanced that a demand by the Bank that major sons be recognized as oustees in their own right

---

[18] See, for example, supervision reports for the Subarnarekha Hydroelectric Project, Gujarat Medium II Project, Madhya Pradesh Major and Medium Irrigation Projects, and the Upper Indravati Hydroelectric Project. Similar failures to appraise and supervise adequately resettlement can be seen in the Bank's files on the Singrauli mining and thermal power complex.

[19] Heinz Vergin, Director, India Country Department, to Mr. M. S. Ahluwalia, Secretary, Department of Economic Affairs, Ministry of Finance, Government of India, January 17, 1992.

was something that could not be supported "by either the Award or Bank legal documents."[20]

Mr. Chitale, Secretary of Irrigation, Government of India, replied to the Bank's letter. He affirmed that all was well. He reiterated the position of the state governments. He said that there was full compliance with the Tribunal's award and Bank policy. The Bank's acknowledgment of Mr. Chitale's reply accepted all his assurances, noting that his "thoughtful response" had "gone a long way in clarifying the issues which we raised . . . on R&R." It went on: "We note with satisfaction that the Government of India has confirmed that progress on construction will be linked to progress in the implementation of R&R."[21] Apart from raising a concern about tribal peoples (expressed in a way that reveals a startling lack of understanding of the extent of tribal occupation of the submergence area), the Bank leaves the impression that all is well. Another confrontation has been avoided.

This exchange of letters illustrates the nature of the Bank's evident inability to turn a recognition of persistent fundamental difficulties into an effective demand for compliance. This has been the pattern since the first serious misgivings about resettlement policy and implementation expressed in the "post-appraisal" missions of 1983 and 1984. Again and again doubts about implementation have been caused by Madhya Pradesh. Yet the Bank somehow allowed the situation to continue; pressure was applied, but never enough. The tendency to press forward in a manner that avoids engagement with reality, evidenced by limited appraisal in 1983, is confirmed by readiness to accept reassurances in 1992.

Nevertheless, recent evidence shows that when the Bank takes serious steps to implement the resettlement policy substantial improvements are possible. In Andhra Pradesh, for example, where the displacement caused by the (non-Bank financed) Srisailam irrigation project in the 1980s was among the worst cases known, concerted Bank action for the Hyderabad Water Supply Project led to a full appraisal and apparently good implementation. Bank insistence on a full resettlement plan for the Maharashtra Composite Irrigation Project III similarly appears to have led to a net positive outcome, including some benefits that have gone to the poorly resettled farmers displaced by the Maharashtra Composite Irrigation II Project.[22]

Many factors contribute to the failure of resettlement and rehabilitation. Relations between those responsible for implementation of policy and those

---

[20] Office Memorandum to Jan Wijnand, January 14, 1992.

[21] See Heinz Vergin, Director, India Country Department, to Mr. M. A. Chitale, March 11, 1992.

[22] The Punjab Irrigation II Project, which was approved in 1991, is a Bank-assisted multi-dam project that is said to have been accompanied by successful resettlement and rehabilitation. How-

who are at risk are often uneasy or remote. The oustees are typically isolated rural peasant or tribal populations; these are people who have the lowest status in their societies. Often projects evolve against a background of very limited national support: development tends to take place in nations or regions without welfare systems. Also, an enduring habit has been for engineers to be given responsibility for all aspects of these projects, including the resettlement component. As a result of these kinds of factors, resettlement and rehabilitation have typically been done in an uninformed and *ad hoc* manner, and, as time goes on, as a form of crisis management. Again and again, in its policy documents the Bank insists upon consultation with the people at every stage of the process. Yet the Bank's reports and memoranda show the absence of people's participation. And where projects have achieved some success (as, for example, Arenal Hydroelectric Project in Costa Rica), Bank experts attribute this largely to the fact that people were consulted and participated in planning from the early stages.[23]

But a central and recurrent operational problem lies in the extent to which the number of people affected is underestimated, and the level of their income is undervalued.[24] Despite Bank policies, many projects have commenced without accurate data. Not only are the direct impacts of the project little understood, and plans made that do not take account of what is likely to happen, but also the broader dimensions of the difficulties go unappreciated. The needs of women and the elderly are left out of the calculation. The consequences for host communities—the villages where oustees will be relocated—are ignored, or evaluated much too late in the day. A range of secondary displacements go unconsidered. As a result, at each stage of project development, new emergencies arise. As these accumulate, those affected feel growing indignation, and political opposition begins to mount. The human costs of the projects are thus misrepresented from the beginning, and tend to be understated or avoided as they arise. By the time a project is under way, there are large interests that are best served by minimizing any apparent negative consequences. All of this is at issue when it comes to appraisal. These are factors that need to be included in a full and accurate assessment of a project's costs. Each element of implementation is at risk if the real human costs of a project are not fully anticipated.

All projects start with assessments of their engineering costs and financing

ever, the total number of oustees is estimated at only 300, and the Government of Punjab is considering dropping the dams that are likely to displace people.

[23] See William Partridge, *Successful Involuntary Resettlement: Lessons from the Costa Rican Arenal Hydroelectric Project,* 1991.

[24] See Scott Guggenheim, *The Financial Preparation of Resettlement in Bank Projects: A Policy and Operational Review,* World Bank Draft Document, 1990.

structures. These are minutely considered. But if the balance sheet fails to include the human distress caused by uprooting large numbers from their traditional homes and lands, the Bank's 1980 and 1982 policies are unlikely to be achieved. Lack of proper planning can lead to economic, political, and financial failure. As Bank experience has shown, those who may pay the most direct and extreme price for such failure are the oustees.

Our review of the Bank's failure to appraise Sardar Sarovar Projects highlights the origins of many of the problems that have appeared in the years since the Projects were approved. Failure to prepare and appraise the resettlement components of the Projects, despite both explicit policies and known negative experiences with other resettlement operations in India, is a major management oversight. The Sardar Sarovar Projects have evolved against this background. The failure of project appraisal in their case created, from the start, a real possibility that the Bank might find that once again its policy objectives—and the livelihood and wellbeing of large numbers of people—were at risk.

A *budva*, or shaman, at Anjavada, Madhya Pradesh. He is playing the *rantha*, an instrument made of bamboo and lizard skin stretched over a coconut shell. In the Bhilala creation myth, the playing of the *rantha* gives pleasure to spirits, causing them to become invisible.

Chapter 5

TRIBAL PEOPLE AND THE VALLEY

THE uppermost reaches of the Sardar Sarovar reservoir will flood land in the Khargone District of the Nimad region of Madhya Pradesh. Here the Narmada River flows through a wide valley, striking for its agricultural abundance and many irrigation pipelines leading from the river to a great variety of crops. Approximately 60 kilometers downstream of the beginnings of the Khargone submergence, the landscape changes: in Jhabua district of Madhya Pradesh, then in Maharashtra and Gujarat, the river cuts its way through the hills and canyons of the Vindhya and Satpura ranges. This is remote and difficult terrain: on both its north and south banks the Narmada is bounded by steep hills, fractured and worn by a network of tributaries into a myriad of escarpments and valleys, a landscape as forbidding as it is beautiful. This terrain predominates for the rest of the distance to the Sardar Sarovar dam site, where the hills abruptly come to an end, the valley again widens, and the Narmada continues its journey to the sea across the plains.

The cultural and economic histories and conditions of the peoples who live in these different landscapes are also distinct. The valley is occupied by a mixed population of Non-Scheduled Castes, Scheduled Castes and Scheduled Tribes. The proportion of each varies, and in some cases the groups are not easily distinguishable from each other. But throughout the region affected by Sardar Sarovar Projects, the people designated as Scheduled Tribes in the Indian Constitution are represented by the Bhils. These include the Tadvi, Vasava, Paura, Bhilala, Ratthwa, and Nayak—names the people themselves give to their distinctive tribal groups. They also refer to themselves as

Table 5.1 Estimated number of tribal people potentially affected by Sardar Sarovar Projects[1]

LOCATION	ESTIMATED NO. OF PEOPLE TO BE AFFECTED	TRIBAL PEOPLE %	ESTIMATED NO. OF TRIBALS TO BE AFFECTED
Gujarat	23,500*	90	21,150
Maharashtra	13,500+	95	12,825
Madhya Pradesh	115,000+	49	56,350
Canal	22,500+	10	2,250
Sanctuary	25,000	100	25,000
TOTAL	199,500	56	117,575

(Based on data from: *Nigam, +Maharashtra & Madhya Pradesh 1991 & 1992 resettlement plans, Arch Vahini & Rajpipla Social Services)

"*adivasi*"—the Hindi word used throughout India, meaning, literally, "original dwellers."[2]

The various groups do not speak a single language. Anthropologists have identified two distinct Bhil languages, though belonging to the same linguistic family. Many people also understand the official language of the state in which they live. Thus many Tadvi speak Gujarati, whereas some Vasava of Maharashtra speak Bhili and understand Marathi. Some Bhilala of Madhya Pradesh speak Bhilali and understand Hindi. It is important to note that relatively few Bhil women speak or understand non-tribal languages, as a consequence of infrequent contact with people outside their own tribal groups.

One or another group of Bhils is found in every region to be affected by Sardar Sarovar Projects. In addition to those in villages scheduled for submergence by the reservoir, there are Bhil and Nayak villages in the command

---

[1] These numbers are based on number of families multiplied by 5, the accepted figure for average family size in the area. Vulnerability of tribal people in Shoolpaneshwar Sanctuary is discussed in Chapter 16. Numbers at risk from the canal are more speculative. They are based on the number of farmers losing all or a substantial proportion of their land (see Chapter 9).

[2] In Madhya Pradesh the term "Bhil" is used to refer to the people who in Maharashtra and Gujarat are often known as Vasava. Also, the differences between Bhil and Bhilala tends to be obscured in most writings on the area. "Bhil" is widely, if rather inaccurately, used to refer to all the tribal people of the region. Paura and Ratthwa are often transliterated as "Pavra" and "Rathwa." The spellings used in this report have been chosen for their best approximation to English phonetics.

area, downstream of the dam site, and in the Shoolpaneshwar Wildlife Sanctuary. Also, compensatory afforestation throughout the catchment treatment area of the Narmada basin will directly impinge on encroachers and forest dwellers—most of whom are also tribals.

Although baseline data are lacking to calculate the exact number of tribals potentially affected by Sardar Sarovar, the figures shown in Table 5.1 indicate that, on the basis of membership in Scheduled Tribes, over 50 per cent of the potentially affected population is tribal.

Whether or not these people are truly tribal in terms of World Bank definitions is of great significance to the Bank, the people, and the three Indian states. Bank policy on involuntary resettlement makes special provision for tribal people. The 1982 Operational Manual Statement[3] urges that every effort be made to "safeguard the integrity and well-being" of tribal peoples, and at the minimum to "prevent or mitigate harm." Both the 1982 and 1991 policy directives emphasize the importance of detailed research into the social, economic, and cultural implications of projects that impinge on tribal peoples' lives and lands. If the people of the Narmada valley are not merely "backward Hindus"—a term that has been used to characterize the link between Scheduled Tribes and mainstream Indian society—then the Bank and governments are burdened with a greater responsibility. It is no wonder that the status of the peoples of the Narmada valley has been the subject of many arguments.

In April 1987, in response to mounting pressure to examine what was happening to implementation of resettlement policies for these Projects, the Bank sent its largest ever mission to the region. Included was a legal expert who was assigned the task of assessing the extent to which the people of the submergence villages constituted tribal or indigenous groups under the Bank's definition.

Officers at the Bank told us that the mission's interpretation of "tribal" was narrow, and inclined to attribute overriding significance to the possession of "modern" items. They interpreted the wearing of a factory-made shirt or the presence of images of Hindu gods in homes, for example, as an indication that a person or a family was "detribalized."[4] Nonetheless, the Bank's legal expert wrote in his memorandum of findings about the inhabitants of the ten Gujarat villages he investigated that: "The population of the villages of Gadher, Pandheria, Hanf[eshwar], Mankadkhada [sic], Kadada, Antras, Dhumna, Chharbara, Ferkada and Turkheda fall within the scope of the World Bank's policy on Tribal people (OMS 2.34)." He noted that the other nine submergence vil-

---

[3] Operational Manual Statement No. 2.34, February 1982.
[4] In some tribal houses, women pin up the picture of Ganesh that is printed on the paper used for wrapping a popular make of sari.

lages might contain similar tribal oustees and that the Government of Gujarat should conduct a survey of them.

The Aide-Memoire for this mission obscures these reported conclusions on tribal peoples. It covers the topic under the heading "Forest-dwelling oustees," where it speaks of eight Gujarat villages as being "forest-based," with two more "partly so." It makes no mention of the other nine villages, nor does it use the word "tribal" to describe the people. In effect, the Aide-Memoire minimizes the number of people whose circumstances might qualify them for the protection and benefits set out in the Bank's 1982 tribal policy.[5] The logic of the argument presented seems to be that there are some oustees whose way of life is "forest-based," that "the forest itself has disappeared," and that therefore it is reasonable to follow a policy that turns these people into "plains cultivators."

The mission's official conclusions—that there are few tribal villages and that the principal criterion is forest-based economies rather than tribal people's distinctive cultures—imply that the resettlement and rehabilitation needs of these people are less complex than might otherwise be the case. As we have seen, the 1982 Operational Manual Statement asks for special measures to be taken if a development project is known to encroach on the traditional territory of tribal people. It is worth quoting again the Bank's own words:

> Such projects will require a tribal component or parallel program which includes: (a) the recognition, demarcation and protection of tribal areas containing those resources required to sustain the tribal people's traditional means of livelihood; (b) appropriate social services that are consonant with the tribe's acculturation status, including, especially, protection against diseases and the maintenance of health; (c) the maintenance, to the extent desired by the tribe, of its cultural integrity and embodiments thereof; (d) a forum for the participation of the tribal people in decisions affecting them, and providing for adjudication and redress of grievances.[6]

But the 1985 credit and loan agreements between the Bank, India, and the three riparian states are silent on the subject of tribals.[7] They contain no men-

---

[5] This is a striking example of how important findings on the ground fail to reach management. Hence in 1992 the same issue continues to be a matter for speculation (see this chapter below), as if the work of the Bank's 1987 mission had never been done.

[6] Operational Manual Statement No. 2.34, p 1.

[7] The only exception is that the Agreed Minutes of negotiations note that among the

tion of the existence of tribal people within the Projects' area. Requirements laid down for resettlement and rehabilitation make no reference to special measures for tribals.

In December 1987, after the results of the mission were known, Mr. Nagendra Sharma, Acting Chief of Agriculture Operations, wrote to the Vice-Chairman of the Narmada Valley Development Authority: "... it was agreed that the communities in question [in Gujarat] are not now primarily dependent on forest products. . . . Therefore, the special treatment required is different from (and less than) what had been anticipated earlier."[8] Once the issue is narrowed to whether or not the forest is an adequate basis for the *economic* lives of the people, the implementation of policy does not have to deal with the problems that come with resettling cultures.

Some have argued a position that is anything but sympathetic to the protection of tribal culture. For example, Vidyut Joshi, now of the Gandhi Labour Institute in Ahmedabad, asserted with reference to tribal communities likely to be submerged by Sardar Sarovar that their displacement was part of the changes that other peoples have welcomed "in the name of progress, development or modernization." He went on to say:

> This being so, why should any one oppose when tribal culture changes? A culture based on lower level of technology and quality of life is bound to give way to a culture with superior technology and higher quality of life. This is what we call "development." What has happened to us is bound to happen to them because we both are part of the same society. I have extensively travelled in tribal areas for the last twenty years and I have observed their behaviour. I have formed an opinion that tribals want to change.[9]

Joshi carried out surveys of the tribal villages of Gujarat, and his work marks the first stage of monitoring and evaluation for Sardar Sarovar. Other individuals and organizations made submissions to our review that took fundamentally the same view.

---

maps received were those of tribal sub-plan areas adjacent to the reservoir, in the portion of the command area nearest to the dam, and in the vicinity of the relocation sites (Attachment 1, pp 2 and 3). The minutes do not say why these were required.

[8] Nagendra Sharma, Acting Chief, Agriculture Operations Division, Country Department IV, December 17, 1987.

[9] Vidyut Joshi, *Rehabilitation a Promise to Keep, a Case of SSP*, Ahmedabad, 1991, pp 68-9. Of course, even if people are eager to change, that does not mean that they are necessarily happy to relocate to a new environment.

This view minimizes the tribals' claim for special consideration. Others minimize their number, by arguing that many if not most of those in the submergence area who are designated as tribals have, in effect, already assimilated into mainstream Hindu India. In his letter of December 17, 1987, Mr. Sharma struggled with this aspect of the definition of tribals. He refers to the "special problem" of successfully implementing the resettlement policies in the case of "remote oustees." He goes on:

> We are not speaking of any recognized Indian legal category, such as "scheduled tribe," but of oustees, of whatever community, who, by nature of their physical, economic and cultural remoteness, require special treatment if they are to regain their pre-project livelihoods. In practice, this group is difficult to define; its definition tends to turn on low degree of integration into the larger community...reticence in contacts with outsiders and possible lack of self-esteem, and other criteria as well.

By avoiding all these criteria and drawing attention to decreased use of forest products (see above), Sharma's letter attempts to unite tribal with non-tribal oustees.

The place of tribal groups in Indian society has a long history and a particularly complex character. Over 700 different groups of people are identified, for administrative and census purposes, as Scheduled Tribes. Altogether they comprise approximately 60 million, living in a great variety of political and social circumstances. The Bhils alone number almost 4 million and are spread across an area that includes the deserts of Rajasthan, the plains of eastern and southern Gujarat, and the forests of Madhya Pradesh and Maharashtra.

The question that Indian anthropologists and others have asked about this vast panoply of tribal peoples in general, and about the Bhils in particular, is: to what extent are they properly designated "tribals" or have they in fact become castes within a dominant Hindu caste system?

Dr. Felix Padel, a British anthropologist who has worked intensively on the place of tribal groups within Indian society, in a submission to our review, considered some of the historical background to the issue:

> At first contact with tribal people in India, the British called them "wild tribes", "savage tribes", "forest tribes", "hill tribes"—terms taken from British contacts with the native peoples of Africa and America, but not so different from terms already used in India. "Forest tribes" translates the term used for them on the Emperor Asoka's edicts that threaten them with

dire punishment if they do not obey his rules. The derivation of many names for tribes . . . comes from the word for hill. . . . The census, started in 1871, distinguished the tribal population from Hindus and their religion, as "animism" from Hinduism.[10]

Dr. Padel told us that since the 1940s, there has been a tendency in some sections of Hindu society to claim that tribal peoples are just a poorly integrated part of the mainstream culture of India. Thus G. S. Ghurye, among the most prominent of Indian scholars who considered this question, called them "Backward Hindus"—a highly negative view of tribal culture. Ghurye, in order to oppose a British policy of divide and rule, argued that tribals could not be proved to be India's "aborigines."[11] His arguments have their place in India's nationalist movement. Ghurye sought to avoid an emphasis on tribals' indigenous status that could appear politically divisive. Dr. Padel, in a discussion of Ghurye, noted of the Bhils that they are

> like other tribal peoples of central India, a tribal society analogous to those of Africa or America, particularly in the sense of their connection with the *land*: their religion is based in their relationship with their natural environment, and their economy involves a close dependence on the forest and a high degree of self-sufficiency.[12]

The great difference historically from Africa and America, however, is that in India tribal cultures have always lived at the fringes of Hindu society. And although tribal religion has much in common with the animist or shamanic religions of tribal peoples elsewhere, its practices have never existed entirely apart from Hinduism. Tribals and nearby Hindus have often accepted each other's deities as different forms of their own deities. Thus, a paradox has arisen: the tribes *are* in some way castes (*jati* is the word often used for both), although they are formally outside the caste system.

Part of the difficulty here obviously lies in the great length of time during which "tribe" and "non-tribe" have coexisted on the Indian subcontinent. Ar-

[10] Felix Padel, "The Position of Tribal People in India," submission to the Independent Review, January 29, 1992, p 1.

[11] G. S. Ghurye stated in his book *The Scheduled Tribes* (1962): "Apart from the fact that terms like 'aborigines' and '*adivasis*' are question-begging and pregnant with mischief, the fact that the constitution of India speaks of these people as the Scheduled Tribes renders any other designation utterly wrong."

[12] Felix Padel, "The Position of Tribal People in India," submission to the Independent Review, January 29, 1992, Annex 1, p 4.

chaeological evidence indicates that it was at least 2,000 years ago when the Aryan "newcomers" began to invade from the north. It is in relation to them that the *adivasis*, the original-dwellers, constitute an aboriginal or tribal population. The *adivasis* resisted integration; they moved across large geographical areas as a result of economic, administrative, and military upheavals, in a web of change that is spread over centuries. As Amita Baviskar, an Indian anthropologist with field experience of villages in Madhya Pradesh, summarizes: "The notion of 'tribe' in the Indian context has been hard to pin down because of the porosity of the boundary between 'tribe' and 'non-tribe', both of which have existed side by side for centuries." Nevertheless, at Independence, the architects of the Indian Constitution felt able to identify, on the basis of census data, particular groups of people as "Scheduled Tribes."[13]

The isolation of many tribal groups made the creation of the Scheduled Tribe category much easier than might otherwise have been the case. For example, according to G. S. Aurora, an author with experience of tribal peoples in Madhya Pradesh, "In 1942, when all of British India was rocked by the struggles of the nationalists, only a few people in Alirajpur knew about it. The tribals were not even remotely aware of the nationalist movement."[14]

The Bhils and Bhilalas were classified as Scheduled Tribes in the 1950s. At that time they were to be given the benefits of government programs, but their rights to the forest remained unrecognized. Thus the reality of isolation played an immense part in tribal groups' continuing distinctive identity, while the material and cultural bases for their ways of life began to be eroded by the new and spreading administration.[15]

The boundary between *adivasi* and Hindu is thus rendered complex by long historical processes. But the remoteness of many regions where tribal groups continued to live (or to which they withdrew in order to maintain their ways of life) has meant that many groups maintain distinct tribal identities. The British classification that lies behind the modern official category of Scheduled Tribe may have been responsible for widening the divide between *adivasi* and Hindu populations and for securing the categories in popular and administrative thought, but the divide was already there.

Many tribal people in the submergence villages of all three states spoke to us about their land and way of life; they often referred to a timeless relationship with the earth, the forest, and the animals. They identified themselves

---

[13] After 1881, the decennial Indian census is remarkable for its attention to the social and cultural groups that make up the country.

[14] G. S. Aurora, *Tribe-Caste-Class Encounters: Some Aspects of Folk-Urban Relations in Alirajpur Tehsil*, Hyderabad: Administrative Staff College, 1972, p 210.

[15] See Amita Baviskar, "A History of Advasis in the SSP Submergence Zone (Tribal Areas of Madhya Pradesh and Maharashtra)," submission to the Independent Review, 1992, pp 30-5.

with their lands and with the river. They celebrated their use of the produce of their environment in order to establish their cultural heritage and their distinctive identities.

We visited many houses built entirely with materials from the forest, designed in traditional manner with subtle differences that marked one group from another. In village after village people talked of the fruits, herbs, roots, and medicines they gather from the forest. Even where the forest appeared to be extremely degraded, they explained that in it there were still resources of great importance to them and that they also would travel far behind their villages, into better forests deeper in the hills, to gather what they needed. People also showed us their hunting equipment—the bows and arrows for which the Bhil and Bhilala are famous. We also saw—and listened to—the drums that are used for tribal ceremonies. We witnessed shamanic ceremonies at which tribal deities were propitiated. And at many occasions people took pains to explain the meaning to their culture of objects and ceremonies. They also told us about ways in which resources were shared, and how groups collaborated, on the basis of kinship, to plant, harvest, and build houses.[16]

In all this people sought to show us that they had their own ways of looking at and living in the world. They wished to explain their tribal identities. Often they referred to the Goddess Narmada to explain that their links with the river valley were timeless. In these ways we saw and heard something of the tribal life that is integral to the villages of the Satpura and Vindhya mountains of the Sardar Sarovar submergence zone.

We also saw signs of Hindu influence, or of symbols and practices that Hindu and tribal life have in common. Some of the innumerable small shrines that are to be seen at the edges of every tribal village contain a mixture of tribal and Hindu effigies. In particular, we noticed effigies of Shiva. In fact, the people did not repudiate Hinduism; rather, they affirmed their separateness. Often this was linked to people's apprehension about resettlement. Again and again we were told: "Our gods cannot be moved from this place, so it is difficult also for us."

The history and customs of tribal peoples affected by Sardar Sarovar Projects has direct relevance to resettlement and rehabilitation policies with re-

---

[16] Dr. Nandini Rao of the Tata Institute, in a submission to us on the Bhils, points to the extent to which tribal societies are more egalitarian than caste or peasant groups. Dr. Rao's submission is based, in considerable measure, on her firsthand experience of isolated tribal villages in the submergence area of Maharashtra, where she noted that, "This (largely) egalitarian ideology in tribal society permeates all interactions, so that problems of indebtedness and crime . . . appear only in situations where the society has been influenced greatly by inegalitarian values" ("The Bhils," p 3).

spect to the issue of "encroachers." These are the people who, as a result of successive political and economic pressures over a long colonial history, find themselves to be illegal users of what they have believed to be their own lands. This history takes us back to the original economic system practised by the *adivasi* of the forests.

We were told that originally many of the Bhils and Bhilalas dwelt in the plains and were pushed into the hills, first by successive Aryan invasions and then by stronger agricultural castes. In the forests and hills, these tribal groups depended on hunting, gathering, and shifting agriculture. This agricultural method, known as slash and burn, meant that tribal groups cleared a small area of forest and cultivated it for a few years, after which they moved to another patch. In effect, this was a long-term form of rotation, suited to conditions where soil fertility deteriorates quickly under intensive use. Fields were used for three to four years and then, when crop yields declined, they were left to regenerate as forest. Meshed with the arable component was the use of other resources of the forest and river: animals, fish, and plants.

In the nineteenth century, the British administration sought to put an end to shifting agriculture; they saw slash and burn as destructive of the forests and inconsistent with orderly administration. The British government of India made shifting cultivation illegal, "reserved" the forest, and established sources of revenue there. At the same time increase in population gradually led people to adopt a more intensive form of agriculture, and the two forces resulted in a heavy reliance on domestic animals, especially goats,[17] and permanent fields becoming the norm, although shifting agriculture was never entirely abandoned. In so far as these permanent fields were regularized within the British administration, they constituted "revenue lands," and the owners paid an annual tax. In so far as the tribals were using or creating anew fields that were not recognized, they became "encroachers." In this way a large section of tribal economic life became illegal. Periodically, successive administrations recognized encroachers and increased the extent of revenue land. The scale of the problem, however, is reflected in the fact that in the Narmada valley many entire villages are identified as "forest villages," that is, as lying outside the revenue system altogether. Thus arose the hostile (though also symbiotic) relationship between the tribal cultivators and the Forest Department guards, who levied fines and bribes. Encroachers paid (and pay) what is asked of them in order to be able to harvest their lands.

---

[17] Goats are able to range freely in forests and survive even the worst drought conditions. They provide the economic equivalent of a savings account in a market economy. If a crop fails, goats can be killed and eaten, or taken to market and sold.

This gave rise to a further set of complications. Isolated as tribal people were from administrative centers, and reluctant to pay any revenue on their land, disparities developed between interests in land registered in the Land Record Office and what existed in tribal reality. When sons inherited under tribal conventions their share of the land, this was usually not recorded in the Land Record Office. Land being farmed by several households continued to be registered in a single name, even in the name of a landholder who had died. The devices by which administrations sought to regularize ownership and use of forest land resulted, paradoxically, in extremely unreliable records.[18] Moreover, many villages of the Narmada submergence area could only be reached by arduous journeys on foot. Revenue collectors and other administrative officials were not eager to make routine visits to such places. Indeed, the Bhils became famous in the nineteenth century for their fierce resistance to external administrations and had their own tribal kingdoms.[19] At a meeting in Bombay in November 1991, officials of the Revenue and Forests Department, Government of Maharashtra, told us that when it came to the remoter regions of the Satpuras, lying at the northernmost edge of Maharashtra, revenue collectors and others were loath to make the arduous journeys to communities where they were unsure of receiving a welcome and unlikely to collect much in the way of revenue or taxes due.

This discussion of tribals does not raise merely academic questions. In Chapter 3 we touched on some aspects of World Bank policy for projects that affect tribal populations. Given the distinctive cultural heritages of these people, the isolation within which they were preserved, and their long history of resistance to external administration, the condition of the tribals of the Narmada valley raises the kinds of concerns expressed in Bank policy statements.[20] Indeed, the existence of special policies for tribal people and the doubt thrown on the status of those of the Narmada valley leads us to examine the Bank's statements in greater detail. Its 1982 Operational Manual Statement observes that in the absence of special measures designed for their protection, "tribal people are more likely to be harmed than helped by development projects." It goes on to say:

[18] Amita Baviskar described this for Madhya Pradesh villages in a submission to the review, "Land Ownership," pp 1-2.

[19] In a report on this Nandini Rao notes that several Bhil tribal kingdoms took advantage of isolation to maintain their own cultural and economic practices ("The Bhils," Tata Institute of Social Sciences, 1992, pp 13-20.)

[20] The April 1987 mission pointed out that tribal villages have a critical dependence on forest resources, and recommended that land for grazing and "social forestry" be sizable components of land allotted at resettlement sites. This recommendation did not find its way into the mission's Aide-Memoire or subsequent policy considerations.

As a general policy, the Bank will not assist development projects that knowingly encroach on traditional territories being used or occupied by tribal people, unless adequate safeguards are provided.... The projects should be designed so as to prevent or mitigate such effects. The Bank will assist projects *only* when satisfied that the Borrower or relevant government agency supports and can implement measures that will effectively safeguard the integrity and well-being of the tribal people.[21] [emphasis in original]

The 1982 Operational Manual Statement seeks to define "tribal," therefore, as a basis for special policy measures by which they are to be protected. It is instructive to apply the Operational Manual's clauses to the people of the Sardar Sarovar Projects area.

WORLD BANK DEFINITION (1982):	APPLICATION TO SARDAR SAROVAR PROJECTS:
2. The term "tribal people" refers here to ethnic groups typically with stable, low-energy, sustained-yield economic systems, as exemplified by hunter-gatherers, shifting or semi-permanent farmers, herders, or fishermen. They exhibit in varying degrees many of the following characteristics:	Virtually all of the tribal peoples of the submergence zone operate low-energy, sustainable yield economies. They told us in many places that they avoid purchase of fertilizers, and rely on cow dung to provide soil nutrients. Until relatively recently, the people of the Satpuras were hunter-gatherer / shifting agriculturists, which includes all Maharashtra, all but 5 Gujarat, and 45 Madhya Pradesh submergence villages. All these villages depend to some extent on forest produce for subsistence and supplementary income; many are heavily reliant on fishing.
(a) geographically isolated or semi-isolated;	Approximately 95 villages are isolated or semi-isolated, to the extent that markets and other mainstream or urban facilities are at least 10 kilo-

---

[21] Operational Manual Statement, No. 2.34, February 1982, p 1.

meters away; approximately 40 villages are about one day's travel from such facilities.

(b) unacculturated or only partially acculturated into the societal norms of the dominant society;

It is evident from the details given in this chapter, from anthropological findings given to this review in the form of submissions, and from details available in monitoring and evaluation studies conducted in the submergence area after 1987 that a large proportion of those to be affected by Sardar Sarovar are only partially acculturated into Hindu social, religious, and economic norms.

(c) nonmonetized, or only partially monetized; production largely for subsistence, and independent of the national economic system;

Subsistence in the more isolated villages (i.e., at least 95) constitutes a major part of economic life. Researchers in the villages of Maharashtra and Madhya Pradesh have given us estimates of 50-60% of nutrients coming from non-agricultural subsistence, and have pointed to the dominance of subsistence over market crops in agricultural production.

(d) ethnically distinct from the national society;

The evidence of this chapter and other sources (see item (b) above) show that there is a clear ethnic distinction between the tribals and others in the society, though this is subject to various interpretations. Also, at the interface between tribal groups and non-tribals there is a considerable "porosity" between various groups.

(e) nonliterate and without a written language;

Illiteracy is between 75% and 95%; the cultures do not have a tradition of written language.

(f) linguistically distinct from the wider society;

There are two tribal languages in the submergence zone, though some people understand (and some can speak) the official language of the state where they live or go to market.

(g) identifying closely with one particular territory;

Virtually all identify very closely with their ancestral lands. Some of the Ratthwa of Gujarat are recent immigrants, but they constitute a very small proportion of total tribal population. We were told that Bhilala groups moved into the area many generations ago, and that the region as a whole has witnessed a flow of tribal population from the plains into the fastnesses of the hills as a result of political shifts and up-heavals. The Nayaks and perhaps some other Bhil subgroups are said by some anthropologists to be the original *adivasi* of the Narmada valley as it flows through the Satpuras, but these are matters of conjecture. The people themselves (except for the Ratthwas) regard the lands they now use (including the adjacent forest lands) as their territories. Their creation stories, in which their world is made by the Goddess Narmada, express this relationship to place.

(h) having an economic lifestyle largely dependent on the specific natural environment;

Use of the forest and river reveal an economy that is linked very closely with the environment. A forceful ex-pression of this is the house style, in which all major components—teak for pillars and beams, bamboo for walls, baked mud tiles for roofing, a variety of plants for ropes and stor-age baskets—are harvested in the immediate neighborhood. Virtually all the houses in the remoter villages, and a majority of those in the Nimad, are built of these materials.

(i) possessing indigenous leadership, but little or no national representation, and few, if any, political rights as individuals or collectively, partly because they do not participate in the political process; and

Leadership in the villages is complex. There appear to be indigenous leaders whose authority is rooted in tribal tradition, and also police Patels whose authority comes from the British administrative arrangements. At the same time, there have in recent years been intense efforts to bring tribal groups into the electoral process, especially at the local government level. Also, implementation of Sardar Sarovar Projects has inevitably resulted in significant shifts in leadership, in part proceeding from divisions of opinion about whether, when, or where to go in response to pressure from outside resettlement agencies and non-government organizations.

(j) having loose tenure over their traditional lands, which for the most part is not accepted by the dominant society nor accommodated by its courts; and having weak enforcement capabilities against encroachers, even when tribal areas have been delineated.

The transition from shifting to settled agriculture has been accompanied by administrative efforts to create revenue landholders in most of the tribal villages. In virtually all, however, there is a mixture of regularized and non-regularized land use. The non-regularized, including encroached fields and extensive use of government forest lands, has created many conflicts between the people and authorities—notably Forest Department officials. The traditional system of tenure, which appears to have the informal and pragmatic characteristics typical of shift-

ing agriculturalists and hunter-
gatherers, is not acknowledged by
government officers or institutions.
Outsiders' encroachment on tribal
lands and resources, therefore, have
for the most part gone unchallenged.
For example, the removal of timber
by contractors and the pressure on
tribal "encroachers" to pay fines or
abandon their plots are not matters
that tribal people in the region (or
elsewhere in India) can challenge in
the courts. Their systems of use and
ownership have no standing in the
dominant society.

The Bank's 1982 Operational Manual Statement observes that as a consequence of these tribal characteristics the people tend to live outside "national
or local services," and refers, in particular, to health, education, and communications. In the Sardar Sarovar submergence zone, this applies to all the remoter tribal villages. Only in the Nimad in Madhya Pradesh are villages well
serviced; only there are there schools and medical facilities that can be reached
with the help of regular bus services on relatively good roads. Similarly developed services are also available in most of the command area, and hence to the
tribal villages along the first sections of the canal. In the Shoolpaneshwar
Wildlife Sanctuary, however, the degree of isolation increases as one goes
deeper into the forest. Even here, however, forest roads provide reasonable
communications, though bus services are extremely limited.

Lack of project appraisal means that we have limited data on the economic
and social systems of the tribal villages. However, on the basis of the monitoring and evaluation reports prepared since 1987 by the Centre for Social Studies, Surat, Tata Institute of Social Sciences, Bombay, and Doctor Hari Singh
Gour University, Sagar, it is possible to see the distinctive characteristics of at
least some of the villages. They indicate (as has already been noted) that many
people's economic life depends heavily on forest and river resources. This finding is reinforced by a submission on tribal villages of Madhya Pradesh.[22] This
submission provides many details of tribal spiritual and economic life, and de-

---

[22] Chitraroopa Pallit and Perveez Mody, "On The Tribal Path, A study of the S.S.P. affected villages of Kakrana, Jhandana and Anjanwada, Madhya Pradesh," submission to the Independent
Review, 1992, pp 32-6.

scribes an integration of culture and economy that is typical of tribal society. A government-commissioned study of fishing[23] is of limited use in its description of tribal villages. Access was severely restricted by opponents of the dam, and the study focused heavily on full-time fishing families rather than the subsistence fishing characteristic of tribal communities. Nonetheless, it found some 6,000 "active fishing families" in the submergence area and downstream of the dam (p v). Most important of all, perhaps, evidence presented to our review and our own visits to tribal villages indicate that a large proportion of people there are holders of non-revenue land—that is, they are said to be landless according to the terms of the Tribunal award and state policies that adopt the award's approach to compensation. Along with the large proportion of major sons, many of whom are in effect separate families with shared or encroached lands of their own, this may mean that between 60 and 80 per cent of tribal oustees are at risk from any policy that offers adequate land on resettlement only to revenue landowners.

Our opinion is that the evidence demonstrates the tribal status of a large proportion of people to be affected by Sardar Sarovar Projects. There has, since before the beginning of these Projects, been an acute shortage of sociological and anthropological expertise. Consultant anthropologists have gone on missions, but their roles have been circumscribed and have lacked continuity. The amount of time available to a social scientist in the course of a mission is extremely limited. The information that is needed and lacking requires fieldwork, and appraisal requires continuity of field workers. Much of this is made clear in the Bank's 1988 exhaustive treatment of forced resettlement.[24] A continuing result of lack of basic information about the peoples of the submergence area has contributed to uncertainty within the Bank about the tribal issue. And it has allowed those who have wished to minimize the issue to assert, on the narrow basis of the findings of the 1987 mission, that the tribal population of the submergence area is limited to a very small number of extremely isolated villages.

From the point of view of the people themselves, the intent of the Indian Constitution, basic anthropological findings, and the criteria embedded in World Bank policy directives for tribals and indigenous peoples in Bank-aided projects, a substantial proportion of those likely to be affected by Sardar

---

[23] Central Inland Capture Fisheries Research Institute, Barackpore, *Sociological Survey of the Fishing Families of the Narmada River*, Indore, 1991. The report also gives the number of active fishermen and women as 33,000.

[24] See Michael Cernea, *Involuntary Resettlement in Development Projects: Policy Guidelines in World Bank Financed Projects*, World Bank Technical Paper No. 80, 1988. This document is an extremely useful summary of policies, and indicates the kind of social science field procedures that would be appropriate to implementation of these policies.

Sarovar Projects are tribal people and entitled to the benefit of special measures that will defend and secure their distinctive interests. The Bank's failure to build this into the credit and loan agreements represents a failure to comply with the 1982 Operational Manual Statement.

The number of tribal people living in the Sardar Sarovar submergence area, along the path of the canal, and on land to be used for basin development or catchment treatment is uncertain. Bank policy is clear that detailed research must be done to establish the scale of impacts and nature of societies to be affected before a loan is approved that will result in compulsory resettlement. This was not done as part of the 1969 to 1979 Tribunal proceedings, nor was it carried out as part of project appraisal between 1980 and 1985. Since then, monitoring and evaluation agencies have devoted some attention to the particular circumstances of the tribal people of villages in the submergence area. But no policies have been devised by the Governments of Gujarat, Maharashtra, or Madhya Pradesh that pay attention to the particular needs and concerns of Sardar Sarovar tribals. The whole problem raised by locating highly integrated, isolated groups—be they tribals or semi-tribals—has never been given the attention it requires.

Disregard for the people who come within the Bank's definition of tribals is inconsistent with Bank policies. These policies, formulated in 1982 and restated in 1991, are emphatic in their concerns, and seek to avoid definitions of what it means to be tribal that are stereotyped or narrowly applicable to the aboriginal populations of the Americas. Thus there is use of "semi-tribal" and emphasis on isolation, subsistence, and low-energy economic systems. Concern for such groups is an aspect of the world's increased awareness of how isolated cultures have all too often paid an appalling price for development. The mechanisms by which they become separated from their lands and stripped of their own cultural integrity are all too well known.

The Bank's principles with respect to tribal peoples arose from a concern for human rights. Failure to design or implement policies that put these principles into effect places these rights at risk. It is disturbing to find, therefore, that in March 1992 the Bank's India Country Department wrote to the Ministry of Water Resources, Government of India, asking for: ". . . clarification on how tribals, who constitute about half of the Maharashtra oustees and about 24 villages of Madhya Pradesh, will be treated under these R&R policies." The letter goes on to ask: "Would tribal people be fairly judged as landed by the policies, processes and appeal mechanisms. . . ."[25]

Although Bank attention to tribals' interests is to be welcomed, the March

---

[25] Letter of March 11, 1992, from Heinz Vergin, Director, Indian Country Department, to Mr. M. A. Chitale, Secretary of Irrigation, Ministry of Water Resources.

1992 letter reveals persisting confusion. The issue of tribals cannot thus be narrowed to "half" of the Maharashtra oustees and 24 of the villages in Madhya Pradesh. To do so is to continue to misrepresent reality in the villages, and thereby to confound the Bank's own policies and principles. Yet none of the state policies we discuss in the following chapters were designed with tribal villages in mind. In the course of the discussion of Maharashtra and Madhya Pradesh we raise aspects of tribal culture that create especially acute problems for implementation. But it must be made clear at this point, in a general way, that what has been termed the "original sin" of the implementation of Sardar Sarovar—namely, the failure to appraise and provide basic data—is revealed with a special poignancy when it comes to the region's tribal people. Continuing confusion about who they are, and persistent denials that they represent a distinctive part of the cultures of the submergence area, raises a large question mark over the very possibility of their being successfully resettled and rehabilitated.

Looking towards houses of Gadher, which has a total population of over 600 families and is the largest submergence village in Gujarat.

Chapter 6
GUJARAT

INTRODUCTION

GUJARAT is at the center of the Sardar Sarovar Projects. The dam site is within Gujarat; the drinking water and irrigation benefits are directed towards Gujarat's drought-prone areas. The Tribunal's 1979 award directed that Gujarat should provide resettlement and rehabilitation for those in Maharashtra and Madhya Pradesh who were to be displaced by the reservoir and who chose to leave their home states. Thus it is in Gujarat that we find the impacts of construction, at both the dam site and along the irrigation canals, and where we find most of the resettlement sites. It is to Gujarat that we must look in order to judge whether rehabilitation could become a reality for something like 20,000 displaced families.

The total number of families who might eventually relocate in Gujarat depends on implementation of policies in the other states. As we shall see (in Chapters 7 and 8), considerable pressure has been brought to bear on many villagers in both Maharashtra and Madhya Pradesh to move to relocation sites in Gujarat. Also, a very large proportion of those who are being relocated in Gujarat come from tribal villages. The population of the Gujarat submergence area is approximately 95 to 98 per cent tribal, composed of Tadvi, Bhil, and Ratthwa. The distribution of these tribal groups largely follows the course of the river: the Tadvi villages are those closest to the dam site; the Bhil villages lie farther upstream in the remotest part of the Gujarat submergence area; while the Ratthwa are concentrated in villages nearest the Madhya Pradesh border.[1]

---

[1] For some details of the population distribution and some interesting observations on Bhil culture and economy, see Vidyut Joshi, *Submerging Villages: Problems and Prospects*, Ajanta Publications, 1987.

Although construction on the dam did not begin in earnest until 1987, it was in the 1960s that work in Gujarat on project infrastructure began to affect a significant number of families (most of whom were Tadvis). Others were displaced by the first stages of construction of the headworks of the canal system in the early 1980s. This was at a time when Gujarat's policy for resettlement and rehabilitation was limited, and was based on cash compensation to landed oustees who were left to buy replacement land. Considerable hardship ensued, and intense protests were registered by both Gujarat non-government organizations and Bank missions.

In 1987-88 Gujarat developed a policy for its Sardar Sarovar oustees that has since been welcomed as among the most progressive packages of measures ever devised for securing the long-term rehabilitation of people displaced by large-scale development projects. Many told us in the course of our review that the Gujarat policies should become Indian, if not worldwide, norms by which resettlement policies should be guided.

The post-1988 Gujarat policy refuses to make distinctions between landed and landless and offers the benefits to major sons that we judge to have been the intent of the Tribunal's award. By comparison with what has been done in all too many other development projects, in India and elsewhere, Gujarat may be providing a basis for rehabilitation that represents a real advance.[2] Moreover, the implementation of the policy has been assisted by the energetic and committed work of non-government organizations, notably Arch Vahini and Anand Niketan Ashram, based in the Narmada valley with long-term involvement with Gujarat submergence villages.

In this chapter we look at the evolution of Gujarat policy, at the circumstances of the communities affected by construction and displacement prior to formulation of the policy, at resettlement sites for Gujarati oustees, and at the nature of implementation, especially since 1989. Implementation of the projects in Gujarat takes place in particular contexts, some of which complicate or restrict our assessment.

First, the policy adopted by Gujarat follows closely the central measures laid down by the Tribunal award of 1979. These were designed to protect Maharashtra and Madhya Pradesh oustees, and to guarantee for them a resettlement package in Gujarat. But as we saw in our discussion of project appraisal (Chapter 4), the measures prescribed by the Tribunal were not based

---

[2] In fact, it should not be forgotten that other projects in Gujarat—notably the Medium Irrigation Projects—have given rise to serious misgivings, and even alarm, in Bank officials who have observed them. The terms of the policy for Sardar Sarovar are deemed not to apply to these other projects, and resettlement in their cases has caused, and continues to cause, considerable hardship.

on a careful scrutiny of oustees' existing conditions or their resettlement needs. Also, the award defined "oustee" in such a way as to restrict application of its measures to families threatened by "submergence." This allowed Gujarat to avoid analogous responsibility for those affected, even displaced, but not "submerged."

Second, Gujarat policy was changed by successive government resolutions. Implementation therefore had to keep adjusting to meet differing circumstances. Families who had not been eligible at first were subsequently included. Members of families who relocated under the earlier compensation arrangements suddenly were entitled to land in their own right. Retrospective application of the policy was often required. Where this was done for families or communities that had already begun the relocation process, a multitude of difficulties inevitably ensued.

Third, resettlement and rehabilitation is a protracted process. It begins with displacement, and is followed by relocation and resettlement. Gujarat has demonstrated considerable success at implementing these first steps for a large proportion of its oustees. Rehabilitation is another matter. Social scientists who have specialized in resettlement and rehabilitation take the view that its success cannot be judged for many years, possibly not until the next generation. The Bank's overarching policy requirement, that those relocated are entitled to achieve a standard of living at least as good as the one they left behind, means that before rehabilitation can be assessed, sufficient time must elapse to allow oustees to readjust and for long-term social and economic forces to act. In the case of families resettling on land in new environments these long-term factors may be decisive. The most serious threat to achievement of resettlement and rehabilitation policies may well lie in entanglement in debt cycles, and the resultant loss of land to money-lenders or local landowners. In the case of tribal groups, long-term wellbeing may depend on people's ability to retain, or adjust to loss of, social and economic customs on which their personal and material strength have always depended.

In the case of the relocation sites in Gujarat, relocation is recent, resettlement is beginning, but rehabilitation is for the most part a set of promises about the future.

Fourth, the impacts of a development project start on the day that the people to be affected hear about it. Their anxieties then begin. From that moment investment in local resources is likely to decrease. In the case of subsistence or isolated communities this may not be an important factor. But an equivalent reluctance to invest in project-affected communities and their infrastructure typically afflicts government, and starts at an even earlier date. Once a region is said to be targeted for submergence, road building, development of schools, and even provision of community pumps all become lethargic.

If a project is on the drawing board for a long period, this can produce a pervasive slowing down. In the case of Gujarat, where the Sardar Sarovar Projects have had an important place in regional planning for some thirty years, officials claim that normal investment continued until 1988. Since then, they agree, investment in amenities and services has been minimal. However, many of the Gujarat submergence villages, including the Bhil villages of the interior, lack roads, medical facilities, and functioning schools. This may be the result of a generation of administrative neglect, or it may be a regional norm. In either case, the standard of services is depressed. Achievement of their equal in a resettlement site may come as a welcome surprise to oustees, but this cannot be said to represent fulfilment of the spirit of either the Bank's or the state's resettlement and rehabilitation policies. To provide only the limited amenities that were available in submergence villages because of government neglect is not rehabilitation.

These four considerations arise in the following discussion of Gujarat. We emphasize them at the outset in order to make clear that our assessment, in the case of Gujarat, takes us into a particularly complex set of circumstances.

POLICY

Work on Sardar Sarovar began in 1961. Construction of infrastructure at Kevadia and near the dam site displaced people living in Gujarat, at the six villages adjacent to Kevadia Colony. This was 18 years before the first major policy statement on resettlement, that of the Tribunal's 1979 award. Between the award and the 1985 credit and loan agreements with the Bank, intensive work was carried out on the dykes for the head of the irrigation system. This produced major impacts on five Gujarat villages.[3] Between 1985 and 1987, displacement at the dyke villages increased. After 1987, construction on the Sardar Sarovar Projects intensified, with environmental clearance being granted for the dam and work beginning on the main canal. By 1992, 4,300 families from the submergence area were in varying stages of relocation and resettlement, while a considerable number of families had been affected by work on the irrigation system.

Gujarat has never enacted legislation that lays out policy for treatment of people affected by its development projects. Nor did the Tribunal's 1979 award stipulate measures applicable to Gujarati oustees; it set out measures for people in Maharashtra and Madhya Pradesh, particularly those who were likely to be affected by a Gujarat project.

[3] Two villages, Limdi and Navagam, were affected both by construction at Kevadia and by the rock-filled dykes.

Gujarat's own policy for its oustees has been created by a series of government resolutions. There is no one document that sets out a comprehensive policy position. In 1979, a Gujarat Government Resolution defined "oustee" and facilities to which oustees would be entitled if displaced by "major and medium irrigation projects."[4] This resolution defined oustees as people "residing in submergence area" and earning a living there one year prior to notification under Section 4 of the *Land Acquisition Act*.

This resolution echoes the Tribunal's award. Its definition of a family includes the words: "Every major married son shall be considered as a separate family." It offers a minimum of two hectares to any affected family losing 25 per cent or more of their land. Fifty per cent of the compensation for land acquired is to be retained as a downpayment for replacement land, the balance repayable as a 20-year interest-free note. Similarly, following the Tribunal's formula, civic amenities are allotted in relation to the number of families at a resettlement site.[5]

On August 25, 1981, the Chief Ministers of Gujarat and Madhya Pradesh co-signed a Memorandum of Understanding which stated:

> In view of large number of persons who will be displaced by the reservoir that will be gathered behind Sardar Sarovar dam and hardship that will be caused to the displaced persons in spite of the arrangements that may be made for their rehabilitation in the command area of Sardar Sarovar in terms of the decision of the Tribunal, both the states . . . agree to explore the possibility of reducing the distress of the displaced people as much as possible.

This accord indicates that neither Gujarat nor Madhya Pradesh took the view that the Tribunal's award had established measures adequate to deal with anticipated hardship. They recognized that there was a burden on them to find policies that really meet the needs of oustees. In the coming years Gujarat's policy was enlarged.

In 1984, a Government Resolution established a land purchase committee "to arrange for private land at reasonable prices for the oustees of SSP who are

---

[4] GR No. MISC/RES/1078/Amenities/PART-III/K-5, June 11, 1979.

[5] The policy thresholds for numbers of families required for the provision of civic amenities are: primary school—100, community hall—500, dispensary—500, seed store—500, children's park—500, well with trough—50, pond—500, tree platform—50, religious place of worship—100, approach roads and link roads—3 km per *abadi* (dwelling) site, electrical distribution lines and street lights—2 km per 100, water supply and sanitary arrangements and site levelling—no thresholds.

not interested [in] the allotted land" (Government Resolution No. REHAB-Narmada-7082-48-K-5). The 1984 Narmada Control Authority report, which outlines plans for resettlement and rehabilitation, contained 15 pages on Gujarat, but was no advance on existing Gujarat policy. On November 1, 1985, the Government of Gujarat (GR No. RHB-1085-D) endorsed the main objectives for resettlement and rehabilitation embedded in the 1985 credit and loan agreements with the World Bank. It adopted, for example, the overarching policy formula: oustees are to be enabled to "improve or at least regain the standard of living they were enjoying prior to their displacement"; they have a right to be relocated as village units or families according to their preferences; "the plan for Resettlement and Rehabilitation of the Oustees shall ensure adequate participation by the oustees"; and it was established that landed oustees shall be allotted no less than two hectares of "irrigable" land, whereas the landless shall be "entitled to stable means of livelihood."

Meanwhile, criticism of Gujarat's policy and the way government resolutions were being implemented on the ground began to build. Arch Vahini, the newly formed Gujarat non-government organization led by Dr. Anil Patel, wrote to the Bank in 1983 protesting vehemently on behalf of families being displaced by the early stages of project construction. Arch Vahini referred to the "*ad hoc* and non-imaginative policies of rehabilitation adopted by the Government of Gujarat." It complained that the "poor and illiterate tribals" were "expected to buy their own land," and had to wait for all basic amenities. They characterized the 1979 Government Resolution as "empty ritual." Arch Vahini also lobbied Professor Thayer Scudder, who carried out the first Bank appraisal of resettlement and rehabilitation for Sardar Sarovar oustees.[6] Between 1983 and 1985, Professor Scudder expressed many reservations about Gujarat's intentions. He told our review that he doubted, at that time, that Gujarat would implement a policy in a way that would secure the Bank's overarching objective.

With each passing year during which no remedial action was taken, alarm at the effects of displacement within Gujarat continued to grow. The Bank's 1986 supervision mission identified "serious inadequacies" in the Narmada Control Authority's 1984 plan for Gujarat, referring to the treatment of the landless and noting that existing provisions for dealing with this problem were unworkable. It also noted the poor conditions at resettlement sites and warned that the cumulative effect of these difficulties for oustees was likely to be "great hardship." The 1987 missions (April and November/December) continued to uncover fundamental problems, and doubts began to arise in the Bank about the "consistency with legal agreements" of Gujarat's policy. It noted as "seri-

---

[6] See Chapter 4 above for details of Professor Scudder's role at this time.

ous and flagrant" Gujarat's refusal to accept and honor the "covenanted agreement" that oustee families should receive not less than two hectares of land.[7] Attention was also being directed to the suitability of the policy for the region's tribal peoples (see Chapter 5).

Pressure on the Government of Gujarat to improve its policy benefits continued to mount and culminated in the November/December 1987 World Bank mission, which seems to have helped bring about a spate of new government resolutions. By the end of December 1987, Gujarat government resolutions had accorded full benefits, i.e. two hectares of land, to all the landless, giving as its rationale the fact that "ninety per cent of them are tribals; whose main occupation has been agriculture and collection of forest products" (GR No. REH-7087-(76)/D). Then on May 30, 1988, a further government resolution (GR No. REH-7088-57-D) extended the whole benefit package, including the minimum of two hectares of irrigable land, to "major sons of the landed, landless and encroacher oustee family." This was followed with a guarantee of irrigation by well or tube well if no other irrigation system is possible, and in the event that this cannot be provided "the displaced family would be allotted a minimum of 4 hectares of land instead of 2 hectares. . . ."

Many people spoke to us about the effect of these government resolutions. They appeared to meet all the main criticisms of implementation in Gujarat, and they have been held up as a model of correct resettlement and rehabilitation for the rest of the world to follow.[8] Some of the Projects' critics were astounded, and changed their position on the dam. This created the opportunity for Arch Vahini and Anand Niketan Ashram to become part of the implementation process.

Others remained skeptical about the eventual outcome. An investigation into tribal people during the Bank's April 1987 review mission had concluded that "there should be ample provision for: (i) Adequate grazing land near the resettlement site. (ii) Adequate area for social forestry. . . ." The new resolutions did not guarantee grazing lands, and they assumed that people could move from forest to plains without risk of cultural and economic losses. The Bank, as we shall see, continued to seek assurances from Gujarat that the overarching principle of maintaining standards of living really could be achieved.

Since 1988 Gujarat policy has not changed in any major respect. Its implementation, however, has evolved considerably. In 1989, given the paucity of

---

[7] The mission report stated, in fact, that Gujarat government data showed that "while arrangements have been concluded with more than 900 families, less than 35 ha have been found acceptable by oustees." The role of Bank missions is discussed below.

[8] The 1988 expanded policy does not apply to other Gujarat projects. This means that the 1987-88 improvements to policy do not address Gujarat's overall record of treatment of oustees.

suitable government-owned land, the purchase of private lands for resettlement sites became the norm. This was followed, in 1990-92, by refinement of
the overall site selection and resettlement processes. We consider these in the
final section of this chapter. In the other sections we look at how displacement
and resettlement have occurred in both submergence villages and relocation
sites.

The division between displacement and relocation, on the one hand, and
resettlement and rehabilitation, on the other, is to some extent artificial. As relocation gets under way, oustees who agree to move begin by dividing their
time between old and new villages, seeking to harvest crops in both. This is
their right: land acquisition is not legally complete until their houses have
been moved, which is required only a minimum of six months prior to scheduled submergence. Some families have maintained a double existence for up to
five years.[9] Impact occurs first in the existing villages, after which come the
consequences of resettlement and the process of rehabilitation at relocation
sites. The recognition that displacement precedes relocation directs attention
to the loss and hardship by which relocation tends to be accompanied. This is
the traumatic dimension to the process that Bank policy aims to minimize.

Our consideration of Gujarat's implementation of resettlement and rehabilitation policy took us to many villages and sites, and we spoke with people
from many places we were not able to visit. We do not have space to describe
all these places nor all the submissions that were made. We give details here in
order to illustrate the main facets of displacement and resettlement, and to
consider places that were said to be representative of both the most and least
successful features of the process. Prior to 1988 virtually all resettlement took
place under circumstances that were likely to militate against success: the policies simply did not provide an essential benefit—land—to a large proportion of
oustees. Both policy and its implementation now having changed their charac-
ters, the prospects for success have improved. But there have been many
delays.[10] This means that we were able to look only at displacement and resettlement; but not at rehabilitation. The implementation of appropriate measures under suitable conditions is too recent for rehabilitation to have had a
chance to occur. The real test is yet to come.

Gujarat policy, based as it is on the Tribunal's award, provides measures
only for oustees from "submergence" villages. The impacts of the canal, the

---

[9] The Centre for Social Studies, Surat, Report No. 13 states that 18 per cent of five villages
surveyed took three to five years to resettle permanently (1991, p 31). This had not, however, been
an option for people of the six villages at Kevadia or, in many cases, those from the rock-filled
dyke villages.

[10] According to the Tribunal's 1979 award, most of the resettlement process was to have been in
place by 1983.

expansion of the Shoolpaneshwar Sanctuary, and secondary effects of relocation are all part of the Sardar Sarovar Projects' consequences for Gujaratis. Gujarat's policies, however, have not thus far been extended to potential oustees who are not resident in submergence villages. The lands of others, mainly those in the path of the canal, have either been acquired under the *Land Acquisition Act, 1894*, or, in the case of those downstream, their circumstances have not yet become part of any socioeconomic assessments. These are issues to which we return in Chapters 8 and 12. Here we look at the villages and relocation sites only of the Sardar Sarovar infrastructure and submergence areas.

THE SIX VILLAGES AT KEVADIA

In 1961 work on Sardar Sarovar dam began with the preparation of extensive infrastructure at and around Kevadia. Work on roads, guest houses, office blocks, and accommodation for engineers and their staff, as well as development of the dam site itself, entailed the acquisition of land in and around six villages. As well as the village of Kevadia itself, these were Kothie, Gora, Vaghadiya, Limdi (which included also Barphalia), and Navagam (which included Malva).

We were told that the villages lost about 70 per cent of their revenue land. Overall, more than half the total holdings of the villages was acquired. These were all agricultural villages, with predominantly tribal populations, for the most part Tadvi. They were market-oriented economies, with a number of landless laborers as well as landholders.[11] We were told that 165 revenue landowners and 120 landless families were displaced.

According to data gathered by Arch Vahini in nearby Gujarat villages in the 1980s, and on the basis of detailed breakdowns we have for communities affected by the first 60 kilometers of the canal, we estimate that for each revenue landholder there would be between two and five families dependent on that land. The average for the canal is approximately three at the present time. According to Arch Vahini's 1982-83 data, the average for 16 of the submergence tribal villages is 3.4. If we assume that numbers of revenue landholders and landless correspond to numbers of heads of households, we estimate the total number of families affected at about 950. This compares to the figure reached by Father Joseph, of the Rajpipla Social Services Society, who told us that application of the policy criteria of the Gujarat relocation and rehabilita-

---

[11] According to Vidyut Joshi (1987), up to 17 per cent were landless, though his data have been criticized by Arch Vahini for overstating landlessness. Professor Joshi is here taking the landless only to include those who do not have agricultural plots. Encroachers are therefore not included.

tion program would yield a total of approximately 800 "project-affected persons"[12] from the six villages.

We have not received data that indicate the number of houses that were lost to construction in these six villages. Villagers told us that houses that have not been physically taken up were nonetheless legally acquired.

It has been almost impossible to establish how much compensation the villagers have received for their losses. At the time that the Government of Gujarat acquired the land and houses of the six villages, some compensation was paid. Many villagers told us that they had been given between Rs. 90 and Rs. 250 per acre. Some said that this represented an assessment of the value of the crops that were destroyed during construction; some believed it had been the value attached to the land according to the *Land Acquisition Act, 1894*.

Still others told us that they had, at the time and subsequently, been promised various compensation packages, including secure employment at the Sardar Sarovar site, patches of alternative land, and social benefits at their villages. At several different meetings with villagers, we were told that a senior official of the Nigam, the Government of Gujarat's agency responsible for the Projects, personally guaranteed a full compensation package. Some said that two or three years ago they were promised compensation that included two acres for every householder who had lost agricultural land.

Resentment has built up among many of the people of these villages about the low level of compensation. Some spoke of insecurity they felt living in houses that had been acquired but not yet taken from them. Several said to us that they were ready to make sacrifices in the interests of the people of Gujarat as a whole, but resented the fact that promises that had been made to them had not been kept. They felt cheated.

They also told us that employment opportunities that were supposed to be available for them as a result of the Sardar Sarovar construction being within easy reach of their villages had not really materialized. Government officials insist that this is not so, and both they and Arch Vahini told us that many of the villagers had been employed since the time of their displacement. Bank officials were unable to give us any firm figures for the number or duration of such jobs, nor were any provided by Gujarat government sources. Figures submitted to us by critics of the Projects, however, suggest that employment opportunities for the villagers have been limited.

Moreover, there are radically different accounts of what people are in fact paid. Gujarat officials insist that all laborers receive at least the minimum

---

[12] "Project-affected person" is a term widely used to mean an oustee family.

daily wage.[13] Of the villagers who had secured jobs, many told us that they were paid by contractors, on a casual daily rate, at far less than the minimum daily rate—according to some accounts, as little as Rs. 10 per day.

When the Arch Vahini organization began to work at Kevadia, they came to the conclusion that all the villagers impacted by Sardar Sarovar infrastructure should be regarded as oustees under the Gujarat policy, and should therefore be eligible for a minimum of two hectares of irrigable land for each family, landed or landless, and including major sons. However, by 1988 Father Joseph of the Rajpipla Social Services Society had placed a worker in the villages, and Arch Vahini decided at this point to subordinate its work to theirs. Since then, tensions between non-government organizations that have taken opposing positions on the Sardar Sarovar issue have somewhat confused the picture.

In 1989, the Sardar Sarovar dam site and its adjacent area were placed under Section 144 of the Indian *Official Secrets Act.* This meant that no more than five people could gather together for political meetings. Villagers nevertheless took part in demonstrations as part of the campaign that began in 1988 to secure oustee status. According to Mr. Girish Patel, a lawyer who has represented villagers in court, approximately 200 people have been charged under the Act.

The villagers have continued to press for oustee status. However, senior officials in Gujarat told us that retrospective application of their 1988 policy would create a potentially unmanageable precedent: people affected by other projects all over the state might thus be able to seek similar benefits. Moreover, a precedent of this kind would open up 30 years of history, and create the opportunity for thousands of families affected by projects too long ago for a reconsideration of their circumstances to be practicable.[14] The Kevadia villagers' demand for oustee or project-affected person status has been persistently rejected.

In 1990-91 the Government of Gujarat and the Nigam made a new offer to people in the six villages who had lost revenue land to the development of Sardar Sarovar infrastructure. This offer was Rs. 7,000 per acre up to a maximum of five acres.[15] The offer also provided land for a house site. Landless and major

---

[13] We were told by Nigam engineers that 8,500 people work on the dam, 2,100 as laborers at minimum wages of Rs. 36 and Rs. 25 per day for skilled and unskilled respectively. A further 10,000 work on the canal. All labor is organized by contractors.

[14] Since the benefits offered by the 1987-88 policy are not available to oustees of other projects in Gujarat, the problems of precedence seem to be overstated.

[15] Land in the area of the six villages costs between Rs. 15,000 and Rs. 25,000 per acre. This raises a question about the appropriateness of a compensation offer pitched at Rs. 7,000 per acre. Is this based on retrospective valuation? Or is it, perhaps, adjusted to take account of other benefits that may have been, or are planned to be, available to the villagers?

sons were not included in the offer. Accounts differ as to how villagers have re-
acted to this new proposal. According to John Clark, recently of OXFAM, some
50 per cent of former revenue landholders in the six villages have indicated
their willingness to accept. According to representatives of four of the villages,
a much smaller proportion has accepted. This difference of opinion may be a
consequence of rival interpretations of the total number of persons who are entitled to the compensation package. OXFAM's informants may be measuring acceptance against the total of 165 revenue landholders; it seems that the villagers are basing their estimate on the 800 families their representatives have
identified as qualifying for oustee status under the terms of the Gujarat policy.

A compensation proposal that excludes the landless and major sons is inadequate: it means that many people lose a stake in the land—the resource that is
most important to them. They are therefore unlikely to maintain or regain the
standard of living enjoyed before construction began. Government of Gujarat
officials, on the other hand, told us that application of the Gujarat policy to the
Kevadia oustees would not be appropriate. They pointed out that it is over 30
years since these lands were taken, and said that the present generation has
therefore not grown up practicing agriculture. Rather, they say, a compensation package that is a mixture of money and employment opportunities, along
with a suitable contribution towards loss of or replacement of housing would
meet their needs.[16]

When we put this to villagers, however, they insisted that they would prefer
the package carried in the Gujarat policy. They told us that agricultural land
could offer them long-term security as nothing else could. They also told us
that many families have continued in some measure to depend on the land.
Not every family lost all of its land; every household that possibly can has continued to maintain animals, grazing them along the river bank and on available government common land. They added that in any case they should be
treated in the same way as other oustees. As one villager put it: "The others
will be submerged by the waters of Sardar Sarovar; we have been submerged
by bricks and concrete."

The degree of frustration felt by the villagers is cogently expressed in this
statement made to us by a woman of Kothie:

They set up a camp in 1962 and said Nehru is coming, we need

---

[16] This kind of compensation package may not be consistent with the provision of the 1985
Development Credit Agreement (CN 1552 IN) that "In no case shall cash payments be made in
substitution for actual rehabilitation" (Schedule 3, §7). Although the Agreed Minutes of
negotiation allow cash payments for oustees who explicitly wish it (§14), in this case it is the
government, rather than the oustees, who are pressing for monetary compensation.

your land for a helicopter pad. They said they would return the
land when Nehru went. There was a crop in the fields, it was
during winter when they started to send up notices. But we refused the notices. Then they said the police would come. So then
we still stayed and they took bulldozers and drove over our crop.
They gave us Rs. 70 or Rs. 80 for the crop.

We'll give you land, they said, and a house plot and jobs, but
they never did. So far, after 30 years, none of these promises
have been fulfilled. So we had to organize ourselves. . . .

The plot that our two houses are on belongs to us, just that, and
a kitchen garden. Many of the other displaced people squat on
government land. Have some tea; my story will last my whole
life time. . . .

We tried to talk to the chief minister, but we did not get to see
him. The police would not let us. So we told the police that they
were squatting on our land and so was the chief minister. We
tried to force our way in and we were beaten. It was for taking
on the police. When we get a chance to fight back we are happy.

The issue of the six villages of Kevadia has been caught up in the polariza-
tion of arguments about Sardar Sarovar. The fact is, however, villagers lost
lands and other resources because of construction of the dam infrastructure.
They fall within the unambiguous language of the 1985 credit and loan agreements' definition of oustees displaced from their "usual habitat due to the carrying out of the Project." The first principle of that agreement, which guides
all policy vis-à-vis Sardar Sarovar, states that oustees should be enabled to improve or regain their former standard of living.

Since 1988, local organizations have spoken for the Kevadia oustees, they
themselves have protested, and World Bank missions have reported that there
is a continuing problem.[17] Both non-government organizations and World
Bank representatives have strongly criticized Gujarat's failure to deal fairly
with the six villages. To refer to problems of precedent (which can be solved by
government action), or to employment opportunities (which we believe cannot, under the circumstances, be a replacement for land), or the fact that

[17] See mission reports of 1988 and December 1989. Also note that in the 1990 mission report the
compensation package for "the Kevadia oustees" is mentioned as evidence of progress on
relocation and rehabilitation in Gujarat.

people have now changed and no longer know how to farm (which is to disregard what they themselves say) looks like evasion of the issue.

In 1985 the Bank's Staff Appraisal Report said "some households were relocated in the mid 1960s under policies less satisfactory than present ones, and their position would be reassessed and appropriate rehabilitation conditions applied so that all oustees are subject to a uniform policy" (Annex 1, p 45). At that time Gujarat had ignored the plight of the six villages for over 20 years. Seven more years have now elapsed.

Retroactive application of the Gujarat policy—granting of oustee status, effecting of a "uniform policy"—appears to be an obvious solution.[18] The procedure may be complicated by virtue of some of those affected having received monetary compensation, either under the *Land Acquisition Act* or as *ex gratia* payments at the time or subsequently. But under the terms of the policy, all oustees from whom land is acquired receive 50 per cent of their compensation as cash. It should not be too difficult to modify the formula to take account of earlier compensation. Affected families should be allowed to choose between whatever compensation they have already received and the new offer of land and an interest-free loan. In this way, a longstanding injustice could in some measure be resolved. For those whose families have now scattered, and for the years of distress that have already passed, there is no adequate compensation. But this adds to the argument for a quick and generous solution to the problem.

THE ROCK-FILLED DYKE VILLAGES

Between 1962, the date by which land and houses at the six villages at Kevadia had been acquired for Sardar Sarovar infrastructure, and 1979, when the Tribunal's award was handed down, development of Sardar Sarovar did not entail further acquisition of land. By 1981, however, when construction of both the dam and the head of the irrigation system got under way, more land was needed from surrounding villages. They were: Panchmuli, Khalvani, Navagam, Limdi, and Zer. For the most part, lands of these five communities were to be submerged by the holding tanks for the main canal. These tanks were to be bounded by immense rock dykes, and the impacted communities have since been known as the "rock-filled dyke villages."

The scale of the displacement for the dyke villages can be gauged by look-

---

[18] It has recently transpired (1991 92) that some of the families of the six Kevadia villages qualify for oustee status by virtue of having land that was taken for the rock-filled dykes. Their number is not known, but is said to be small. This is another example of the confusion that stems from inadequate data.

ing at the number of families who were relocated from those communities between 1983 and 1991. Numbers have been provided for us by Arch Vahini and
Nigam officials.[19] These are given in Table 6.1.

Table 6.1 Total number of relocated families

VILLAGE	ARCH VAHINI	NIGAM
Panchmuli	361	366
Khalvani	79	110
Navagam	145	145
Limdi	212	272
Zer	36	36
TOTAL	833	929

Since the land of these villagers was first acquired in 1981, they were compensated only according to the 1979 Gujarat policy, with a heavy reliance on
the *Land Acquisition Act*.[20] Oustees from the rock-filled dyke villages told us that
their lands were valued at between Rs. 2,500 and Rs. 3,000 per acre, whereas
the price of equivalent land in the same districts was more than Rs. 4,000 per
acre. We have found that the *Land Acquisition Act* process invariably undreval-
ues land. Its assessments are based on records of land sales, in which prices are
typically understated in order to avoid taxes.

For the rock-filled dyke villagers, undervaluation of their land resulted in
two sorts of hardship. First, the amount of replacement land people were able
to purchase was virtually never as great as the amount lost. Second, in order to
secure an economically viable plot of land, people used the compensation paid
for house removal to purchase land. Many families were left without the
means of re-establishing adequate housing for themselves. Moreover, major
sons and "landless" families received no compensation—there was no policy
that granted them any such entitlement. In general, the displacement of these
villagers was a rough and ready process, and those who recall it do so with bitterness. Many say that they continue to endure resultant hardship.

In August 1983, Dr. Anil Patel and Ambrish Mehta of Arch Vahini wrote a
letter to William G. Rodger, Divisional Chief in the Irrigation Division of the
Asia Projects Department of theWorld Bank. They drew attention to the poor
treatment of the rock-filled dyke villagers by the Government of Gujarat. They
said:

[19] In 1984 the Narmada Control Authority reported that 601 ha of private land and 266 houses
were to be submerged. An additional 491 ha of government and forest land were transferred to the
Irrigation Department for the Projects. See *Sardar Sarovar Project: Land Acquisition and Rehabilitation
of Oustees*, April 1984, p 43.
[20] We discuss the *Land Acquisition Act, 1894* in the context of the canal. See Chapter 9 below.

The oustees have been shown the lands which are so poor in quality and so far away from their traditional place . . . that their economic-wellbeing—bad as it is—would even worsen further and that their whole social and cultural life would get totally disrupted. . . . The experience of five villages which are affected by Rock Filled Dykes illustrates this point very clearly.

Relocation took place on a family by family basis. Ties between villages were disrupted, and the network of relationships within villages was broken up. In Panchmuli and Khalvani, these problems became severe. Moreover, since only "landed oustees" qualified for two hectares of agricultural land, major sons, families without land, and encroachers were threatened with dispossession.[21] Figures provided by Patel and Mehta at the time indicate that for every landed oustee, approximately three families who were dependent on the same lands were excluded from benefits.

The first Bank resettlement and rehabilitation review mission, in September 1985, was very critical of Gujarat's policies and their implementation. These judgments were directly informed by what was happening to the five rock-filled dyke villages. Oustees from the dyke villages could be seen camping in extreme poverty at the edge of what remained of their lands. In general, much of the Bank's dismay about the displacement caused by implementation of the Projects, despite the requirements laid down by the Tribunal and the Bank, was caused by consideration of the fate of the rock-filled dyke villages.

In a September 1987 memo, an official of the Bank's India Country Department reported on the need for a meeting to discuss "protracted noneffectiveness" or "apparent noncompliance with legal covenants" which stemmed "in part or largely, from resettlement problems." He went on to describe aspects of the "current situation," and spoke of "inadequate policies" and failure on the part of Gujarat to provide "the necessary minimum of 5 acres [2 hectares]." The problems described here are in large part those of the rock-filled dyke villages. This memo also referred to the difficulties villagers faced in acquiring enough land to secure a reasonable standard of living. The official noted: "Apparently the average amount purchased thus far is 0.8 ha. The concern here is that 0.8 ha [2 acres] cannot provide a family with a modest livelihood."

Some benefits accrued to the rock-filled dyke villagers as a result of the Government of Gujarat resolutions of 1985 to 1988. For example, the 1987-88 resolutions that granted two hectares to major sons, encroachers, and the landless meant that far more families from the dyke villages qualified for the

---

[21] The Gujarat 1979 Government Resolution also excludes co-sharers from "landed" status.

resettlement package. However, more difficulties have arisen in the course of
applying retroactively the newer policies to families who had already relocated
in places where it was not easy to find additional agricultural land nearby.

Paradoxically, the effects of dispersal of families and villages, which had occurred as a result of the original family by family relocation process,[22] were
magnified as a result of trying to implement what would appear to be beneficial compensation. The allocation of two hectares to major sons could not always be accommodated in the site to which they had moved with their extended families. Consequently, some families were split. People from Panchmuli told us of a case where a family came to be divided between six different relocation sites. Under the circumstances, oustees were reluctant to take
advantage of their benefits. Although exercise of free choice came to play a
much stronger part in the relocation process after 1989, by this time the new
circumstances of the oustees of the dyke villages had, in some fundamental respects, been irreversibly cast.

This degree of dispersal, or scatter, of the families of the dyke villages is revealed by data provided to us by the Nigam and Arch Vahini (Table 6.2). Although their figures differ by as much as 100 per cent,[23] even the lower numbers
quoted by Arch Vahini demonstrate that in the new sites social, cultural, and
economic ties of the kind that shaped life in the original villages cannot be
maintained.

Table 6.2 Number of relocation sites

VILLAGES	ARCH VAHINI	NIGAM	
	SITES	SITES	TALUKAS*
Panchmuli	15	23	3
Khalvani	6	12	5
Navagam	12	19	6
Limdi	18	21	9
Zer	7	8	4
TOTAL	58	83	27

(*administrative districts)

Arch Vahini say that they have identified clusters of communities, thanks
to which the potentially deleterious effects of scatter are ameliorated: by exer-
cising their own choices, oustees have effectively established groups of commu-

[22] In their 1983 letter, Patel and Mehta say that the rock-filled dyke villagers had already been
relocated in 15 different sites.
[23] This may be the result of Nigam's data counting as separate sites each small additional
agricultural site, even if it is immediately adjacent to a larger site.

nities that can provide some of the benefits of the kind that they may otherwise have lost. Arch Vahini's tabulation of clusters shows that Panchmuli relocation sites are divided among seven different clusters, Khalvani among four, Limdi among six, Navagam among six, and Zer among five. These figures suggest that even if clusters do provide the integrative functions that help ensure that people are as well off, socially and economically, as they were in their original villages, the scatter of families among clusters is also considerable.

The people of these five villages themselves told us about the difficulties that relocation had caused them. At Gadkoi, for example, a resettlement site near Kevadia Colony and close to the first stretch of the main canal, we spoke to people who had relocated from Panchmuli 12 years ago.[24] They told us that they had received a total of 25 acres of land. They had bought this out of their compensation money at Rs. 5,200 per acre—though, they said, their compensation was between Rs. 2,500 and Rs. 4,200 per acre. Of the 14 families who first came here, nine have still not been given land. When we asked about what had happened to those who had not received land, they told us that they had collectively used house compensation money to buy an additional 10 acres, increasing the total land to 35 acres. They claimed that there were 20 families in the community who ought to be recognized as oustees, but that all of them were depending on the 35 acres they had put together from their compensation money.[25]

When they first came to Gadkoi, the villagers were told that a small hill would be levelled for house sites "as soon as you come." They therefore brought their housing materials to the hill. They told us, however, that the bulldozers never arrived, so they moved the housing materials to their agricultural land and built houses there. Subsequently they were told that bulldozing the hill was too expensive, and that a level patch of land behind the hill would be for their houses. Plots were demarcated, but before construction of houses could begin, a plantation was put there as part of the Sardar Sarovar afforestation program.

They also told us that out of their 35 acres between 5 and 10 are irrigated. In Panchmuli, they said, a larger proportion of their original land had been irrigated, with the help of a pump and the use of a rivulet. A well had been dug at the new site, but their old pump is not powerful enough for its depth. This has limited irrigation at Gadkoi.

---

[24] This meeting at Gadkoi occurred by chance we were visiting the canal, and happened to walk along a path that took us by the Gadkoi resettlement site. A number of people were sitting outside, so we suggested that we hold an impromptu meeting.

[25] Nigam 1991 data give 10 as the total number of oustee families at Gadkoi. One of these families is recorded as coming from Limdi; the people we spoke to who came from Panchmuli probably did not include the Limdi family in their description of what had happened.

We asked the people we met at Gadkoi how they had come to choose this particular site. They said that when they had been told they must leave Panchmuli, they had looked far and wide for an alternative place. But they wanted to stay close to other families of their marriage circles, and when this land at Gadkoi was offered to them, they had decided to buy it. Then, when the Gujarat policy was expanded, and more of them qualified for land, families broke up. There is still a need, they said, for getting together—for work, marriage, and death ceremonies—but often distances and cost of transport make this impossible. The fact that their site is small, therefore, makes realization of the policy very difficult.[26]

We asked them what features of life at Gadkoi were better than those of Panchmuli. The people we spoke with insisted that there were few if any advantages to be found in Gadkoi. The water here had presented them with no problems, as far as drinking was concerned. But in Panchmuli, they said, the river was close to their village site. Also, they told us that they had a school to the fourth standard in Panchmuli, but no doctor. Here there is a school, and also no doctor. Since Panchmuli was not an isolated community, the benefits of being close to Kevadia did not seem to the people with whom we met to represent an important asset.

On the other hand, when we asked about economic change, they pointed to the problems they experience with fodder and water for animals. The family with whom we discussed this in some detail told us that they had had approximately 200 buffalo, 200 goats, 10 pairs of bullocks, and 90 cows and calves between the five brothers who lived and worked in adjacent plots. Here, they have 8 pairs of bullocks, but only 7 or 8 buffaloes, approximately 25 goats, and 22 cows and calves. They say this is a result of lack of grazing, but it is aggravated by their needing to cross a pond in order reach the grazing they do have, which tires the animals. The economic consequences of this change in numbers of animals, they said, lie mostly in the loss of earnings from ghee. In Panchmuli this extended family remembered selling some 15 kilograms of ghee per week. They said that prices had risen, over the last 30 years, from Rs. 12 to Rs. 60 per kilogram. The reduction of their herds has meant that they no longer produce ghee at all, and, because of the grazing problem, often do not manage to get enough milk for their own consumption.

So, we asked them, how do you assess the success of the policy? Are you as well off as you were before? Do you believe that, with a bit more time, you could be as well off? One elderly man said that he believed that they were about the same as they had been in the old place. There were no real difficulties with cash, and if there was any urgent problem, they could go to Kevadia

[26] We subsequently learned that some people had finally selected land at a site 15 km away.

Colony and a rehabilitation officer would come to Gadkoi to help them deal with whatever had arisen.

The other people at the meeting, however, insisted that their life could not improve, if only because they did not have the agricultural plots that they needed, that their grazing land was too restricted, and that the forest was too far away to allow them to harvest its produce and get adequate supplies of fire-wood. Several people insisted that the rehabilitation process seemed to apply to the small matters that arose. These were solved promptly, they said. But the real difficulties—housing, and most of all, land for those who still had not received their two hectares—never seemed to get dealt with. They said: "Lots of people come and write things down, but nothing important ever happens."

Many of the problems that people at Gadkoi spoke to us about appear to reoccur in other relocation sites to which rock-filled dyke oustees have resettled. The monitoring and evaluation reports prepared by the Centre for Social Studies, Surat, make reference to difficulties that have sprung from the application of the *Land Acquisition Act* to the rock-filled dyke villages (see, for example, Reports 8, 11, and 12). Submissions from rock-filled dyke villagers in 15 different relocation sites also refer to the failure of the resettlement process to secure two hectares of land for all oustees, and the widespread tendency for those with insufficient land to spend compensation money given to them for housing on the purchase of land. Also, in many places the disparity between the amounts paid in compensation and actual costs of alternative land at the time seems to be considerable.

We were also told that at the rock-filled dyke villages, houses were not acquired, but people nonetheless had to relocate. In Zer and Navagam, in particular, this has apparently presented considerable difficulties to oustees. And in all the sites about which we heard oustees emphasized the problems that had come from the separation of households and families.

The allotment of land to rock-filled dyke oustees increased substantially after 1989. The figures in Table 6.3 show the scale of increase, but also reveal how protracted and incomplete resettlement and rehabilitation have been for the dyke villages, at least until 1991. Ten years after the villages were impacted by Sardar Sarovar construction, and six years after the loan agreement, nearly 50 per cent of those recognized as oustees had still not been allotted agricultural land. It is not surprising that implementation has been fraught with difficulty.

Yet these are the first five villages to have benefitted from the resettlement and rehabilitation policies set out by the 1985 credit and loan agreement and, subsequently, the Gujarat government resolutions expanding provisions to Sardar Sarovar oustees. There can be no doubt but that retrospective application of the expanded Gujarat policy compounded difficulties.

Table 6.3 Number of agricultural plots allotted at different dates

VILLAGE	AGRICULTURAL PLOTS ALLOTTED UP TO			RECOGNIZED OUSTEES
	Mar 1989	Feb 1990	Feb 1991	Mar 1991
Panchmuli	68	183	219	366
Khalvani	24	37	42	110
Navagam	20	24	37	145
Limdi	55	89	144	272
Zer	10	26	24	36
TOTAL	177	359	466	929

(Sources: Centre for Social Studies, Surat; Monitoring and Evaluation Report Nos 10 & 12; Nigam monthly resettlement reports.)

Some of these difficulties are the result of there never having been a comprehensive socioeconomic impact assessment. This illustrates the crucial importance of making adequate studies, plans, and policies for resettlement prior to the onset of construction. In this case, the real social and economic needs of the rock-filled dyke villages only began to emerge as a result of displacement. Policies that evolve in response to emergencies, rather than from an understanding of conditions prior to any actual impacts, are bound to be beset by problems.

THE FOURTEEN SUBMERGENCE VILLAGES

The Sardar Sarovar reservoir will submerge all or part of 14 Gujarat villages. Five of these—Mokhadi, Surpan, Vadgam, Katkhadi, and Gadher—are within 20 kilometers of the dam site. Two of them, Vadgam and Gadher, are very large, recorded in 1985[27] as having 251 and 376 houses respectively. Both these extensive communities are scheduled for total submergence. The other nine submergence villages of Gujarat are remote, and are often referred to as "interior"—that is, situated in the hilly regions farthest upstream of the dam site. These are Makadkhada, Dhumna, Chharbara, Antras, Ferkada, Kadada, Turkheda, Hanfeshwar, and Pandheria. All except Pandheria are on the north bank of the Narmada.

The differing cultural, social, and economic characteristics of these villages are very marked. The breakdown of tribal groupings is shown in Table 6.4.

[27] Professor Vidyut Joshi, *Submerging Villages: Problems and Prospects*, 1987.

Table 6.4 Tribal Composition of Gujarat submergence villages

VILLAGE	TADVI	BHIL	RATTHWA	OTHER
	%	%	%	%
Vadgam	95.0	0.5	0	4.5
Surpan	65.0	32.0	0	3.0
Mokhadi	82.0	18.0	0	0
Katkhadi	93.0	6.0	0	1.0
Gadher	70.0	27.0	0	3.0
Makadkhada	2.5	95.0	0	2.5
Dhumna	0	100.0	0	0
Chharbara	0	100.0	0	0
Antras	0	97.0	0	3.0
Kadada	0	55.0	41.0	4.0
Ferkada	0	37.0	32.5	30.5*
Turkheda	0	23.5	55.0	21.5*
Hanfeshwar	0	67.0	29.0	4.0
Pandheria	0	97.0	0	3.0

*These are virtually all Nayak, a small Bhil group that may well be part of the region's original *adivasi* population.
(Source: Joshi, 1987, pp 44-5.)

The villages are arranged according to their distance from the dam site, with Vadgam nearest to it. The figures show the dramatic difference in tribal composition between the villages near the dam site and, starting with Makadkhada, those stretching away to the Madhya Pradesh border. The Tadvi have, in general, developed far more extensive market and social relations with adjacent Gujarat towns than have the Bhil and Ratthwa of the remoter villages. The Bhil populations of the villages beyond Gadher have been far more isolated than their Tadvi counterparts. This is reflected in every aspect of their social, cultural, and economic lives. On the other hand, the Ratthwa divide into two groups, those who have been in the area for several generations, and those who are relative newcomers from the Gujarat plain—some came as recently as the 1960s—and who maintain contacts outside the region.

Since submergence has not yet begun in these 14 villages, people have, strictly speaking, not been displaced. But many have been wholly or partially relocated. The Nigam report that by February 1992 approximately 75 per cent of families identified as project affected and entitled to resettlement and rehabilitation had been allotted land and house plots at resettlement sites.[28] This

[28] Arch Vahini data are similar, showing that 3,152 families in Gujarat have been allotted land, out of a total of 4,222 who are eligible. In fact, Nigam tables show the total number of "accepted families" as 4,500. Discrepancies of this kind probably result from the constant reconsideration of

process does not, from a legal point of view, prevent villagers from maintaining homes and farms at both the relocation site and their submergence village, although this is difficult if the new site is a long way from the village. However, even people for whom the journey is a full day or more told us that they were succeeding in growing crops in both places, and had divided their time or their families accordingly. To this extent the resettlement process is incomplete. Administrative displacement may be said to have begun, and in some cases to have been achieved (represented by the moving of the family house from the original village to the new site), but relocation forced by submergence is yet to come for all but the rock-filled dyke villages.

After the 1987 and 1988 amendments to Gujarat's policy for Sardar Sarovar oustees, the resettlement process changed noticeably. As we shall see, from 1989 the sheer rate of relocation accelerated; there was considerable administrative success. Once the decision was made to buy the sites for relocation settlements from private landowners, and a land purchase committee had been set up to acquire the lands and make arrangements for the villagers to move, the process has gone ahead rapidly. But what might be termed the era of successful administration is recent, and, according to at least one Nigam official, began in 1990-91.

One consequence of Gujarat's administrative effectiveness in the resettlement process among the oustees of the 14 villages is new influx of data. Nigam officials gave us, for example, a December 1991 tabulation of the process so far. The table allows us to see at a glance what proportion of people in each village have identified land where they want to settle, where it has been measured, where documentation has been completed, where plots have been allotted for housing or agricultural land, and where *ex gratia* payments have been made. For the 75 per cent of families who have completed settlement formalities, they are classified according to their status as landowner, co-sharer, major son, landless, or encroacher.

This tabulation provides a measure of the work that is being done in these villages by all levels of the resettlement and rehabilitation administration, supported by Arch Vahini and Anand Niketan Ashram. In addition, the data make it possible to assess the significance of the current Gujarat policy to these villagers. We can calculate what percentage of the total resettled population is made up of landless, encroachers, and major sons to discover what proportion stand to benefit now that land is being allotted to these groups (see Table 6.5).

families seeking to be recognized as projected affected in the legal sense, and thus qualifying for the compensation package. Families eligible under the Tapu Land Policy Amendment, for example, as well as major sons who have had difficulty convincing officials as to their age, are always matters for officials to reconsider.

Table 6.5 Landowning and non-landowning families as per cent of total resettled

VILLAGE	LANDOWNERS, CO-SHARERS	LANDLESS, ENCROACHERS	MAJOR SONS
	%	%	%
ROCK-FILLED DYKE VILLAGES			
Panchmuli	55	3	42
Khalvani	71	2	27
Navagam	62	1	37
Limdi	47	1	52
Zer	67	0	33
DAM SITE VILLAGES			
Mokhadi	54	6	40
Surpan	34	6	60
Vadgam	53	7	40
Katkhadi	27	12	61
Gadher	34	13	53
INTERIOR VILLAGES			
Makadkhada	26	40	34
Dhumna	39	47	14
Chharbara	10	53	37
Antras	16	46	38
Ferkada	16	52	32
Kadada	19	48	33
Turkheda	12	57	31
Hanfeshwar	18	42	40
Pandheria	33	25	42

The advantage of these numbers lies in the fact that they depend on data accumulated by the administration in the course of the land selection and allotment process. This means they are not subject to the vagaries of land records or informant hesitancy.

The pattern is striking. An average of 64 per cent of families being relocated would not qualify under a policy that allots land only to landowners and co-sharers. In assessing the results shown in Table 6.5, we should bear in mind that of the large proportion designated as non-landowning, almost all would have been using land in their original villages that they considered to be their own. The increase in landless and encroachers as we move into the interior—that is, down the table—shows the extent to which all remote tribal villages have land use and ownership arrangements that are simply not revealed by land office records, and demonstrates the problems inherent in relying on official records rather than detailed on-the-ground surveys of socioeconomic patterns. There is a great irony here: the isolated villages, where virtually all families use similar amounts of land and share resources, are made to appear to be socially and economically divided between landed and landless. Communities where resources—in the form of agricultural plots, forest lands, and river—are relied on in a way that has led to relative economic equality are treated as if there were profound inequalities. Policy implementation that followed this position could well be responsible for grave injustices.

Data derived from the resettlement process also came from Arch Vahini. By combining this with Nigam data we reveal the pattern of resettlement shown in Table 6.6.

Table 6.6 Distribution of relocated families from Gujarat submergence villages

VILLAGE	OUSTEES "SETTLED"[1]	TOTAL R & R SITES[1]	SITES OF MORE THAN 4 FAMILIES[1]	NO. OF TALUKAS[1]	NO. OF CLUSTERS[2]
Mokhadi	233	9	6	3	5
Surpan	65	5	3	3	3
Vadgam	453	34	17	7	7
Katkhadi	71	8	3	4	5
Gadher	609	31	18	5	5
Makadkhada	160	7	5	4	3
Dhumna	28	5	2	1	1
Chharbara	19	3	2	2	2
Antras	112	6	3	1	1
Ferkada	173	10	7	4	3
Kadada	248	6	4	2	2
Turkheda	162	13	11	3	3
Hanfeshwar	344	23	17	4	5
Pandheria	48	2	2	1	1

[1]Based on Nigam data.
[2]Based on Arch Vahini data.
(NB: Nigam data list all sites, even if they constitute agricultural add-ons to existing plots. The number of sites with more than four families may give the best impression of actual dispersal of families.)

This table shows the degree to which the oustees of the 14 Gujarat submergence villages have been dispersed among numerous resettlement sites. In our discussion of the rock-filled dyke villages we referred to Arch Vahini's concept of clustering. They point out that the resettlement sites form distinct geographical groups. This is the cumulative effect, they say, of many individual choices. Their argument depends on the freedom of these choices, but Arch

Vahini workers, with great experience of the process, have told us that since 1990 families really do select the land that they wish to move to. In fact, we traveled with the land selection committee when villagers were trying to find land, and in the cases we observed the men (and there were only men) clearly felt free to choose or reject the alternatives offered to them.

What is worrying is that the choice they are free to make is between one parcel of land and another. This focuses their attention on agricultural potential. We may ask whether, under these conditions, oustees are able to take account of their social and cultural preferences in forming an opinion of where to move. In their March 1991 annual progress report, the monitoring and evaluation team of the Centre for Social Studies, Surat, discussed the reasons oustee households from four villages gave for selecting land at a particular place.[29] Two-thirds responded that economic factors were the sole criterion for their choice of land. Just under one-quarter said that both economic and social factors had affected their choice.

What are the implications of the dominance that economic considerations have in these responses? First and foremost, displaced families are anxious to have land that will secure a livelihood for them. This gives rise to a set of related questions: are they being forced, in effect, to sacrifice social and cultural needs as a result of an overriding economic apprehension, or, indeed, through a wish to maximize an economic opportunity? The trauma of relocation centers on non-economic factors. Oustees told us many times and in many different ways that loss of both social and natural environment was very frightening and hard for them. For these losses there may be no commensurate recompense, but this does not diminish their significance to the oustees. For the most part these factors appear to be left out of all relocation and rehabilitation calculations. Given that compensation is centered on plots of land, landlessness is oustees' dominant fear, and their choices take place in an extremely narrow range. The monitoring and evaluation work done in Gujarat tends not to seek to penetrate the cultural dimensions of relocation.

A principal issue here is that of dispersal or, as it is termed, the "scatter effect." Each community is being relocated to a number of different sites. Only two have all their relocation sites within one of the clusters Arch Vahini have identified. Among the villages of the interior Bhil region—where, arguably, integration is more of a critical socioeconomic factor than elsewhere—this scatter is less extreme. Arch Vahini cluster theory is reassuring, but the number of sites in relation to the total number of population being resettled is nonetheless alarming. On the basis of data available for the dam site villages, scatter appears to be very broad. Crude as they may be, these numbers represent the

---

[29] Report No. 12, pp 30 1.

framework within which measures to realize the policies of Gujarat settlement and rehabilitation have to be assessed.

Many officials and non-government organization workers told us that resettlement and rehabilitation constitutes an opportunity for the people of the Gujarat submergence villages to escape from poverty and isolation. They showed us places where forests had been felled to make fields on steep slopes, and where rain had subsequently eroded the topsoil. They spoke of population pressure in this environment that causes what they see as severe poverty. They described the lack of medical services, noting that to reach a doctor or hospital villagers often must walk for many hours carrying their sick on stretchers across rough, exhausting terrain. They explained that the monsoon makes isolation extreme, and yet this is the time when sickness is most common. They told us about the inadequacy of schools in all but a few submergence villages. They said that even where there are school buildings, teachers usually fail to turn up. They contrasted this with the irrigation, electricity, schools, hospitals, roads, bus services, and all the other amenities that they say will be found at relocation sites of the command area.

Gujarat is a state with a strong entrepreneurial tradition and a high standard of literacy. Not surprisingly, therefore, Gujarati officials and non-government organizations are particularly forceful in characterizing tribal villages as suffering from deprivation. The Tadvi communities near to the dam site, with their comparatively developed market-oriented agriculture, are said to share this view of the socioeconomic opportunities available in the resettlement and rehabilitation compensation package. According to this argument, for them, to stay in isolated and poorly served villages amounts to a comparative disadvantage they themselves experience and seek to escape. On the other hand, for the Bhil and Nayak communities in the hinterland, this same argument asserts that once such people recognize the economic and social possibilities now being offered to them they can only benefit thereby. This line of reasoning amounts to saying that the Tadvi believe that resettlement and rehabilitation is in their interest; and the Bhil may not see it, but it is nonetheless objectively true.

Arch Vahini argue this position with considerable energy. They are persuaded that resettlement and rehabilitation is a development opportunity and, if implemented with commitment and sensitivity, will achieve real economic and social gain for virtually all Gujarat oustees.

We spoke with oustees, in their submergence villages, at relocation sites and at meetings in Kevadia and Baroda where they sought to explain to us their points of view. A number of Tadvi leaders, who are in the early stages of relocation, and who either have got or anticipate getting irrigated land, told us about the economic progress they expect to make as a result of resettling. They talked about increased agricultural production and access to markets. Some of them talked about the benefits of better schooling and medical facilities. Tadvi women mentioned that they would not have to carry water long distances from the river to their houses. And some of the Ratthwa were equally optimistic.

On the other hand, many we spoke to—both Tadvi and Bhil—did not find it easy to believe in the rehabilitation process. They are not convinced that they are going to be better off. They told us about their herds of goats that graze in the forest. Even in years of severe drought their goats survive. They showed us their houses—big enough for large families and many animals—built of teak and bamboo from the forest and roofed with homemade tiles. They told us that they never have to worry about firewood. They showed us their fishing nets and basket traps, and told us about the fish they catch in the Narmada. They said that their land is poor, but with all the resources from the forest and river they knew they would be all right. They said they would like more schools and doctors, but they talked about their ancestors who had lived in these villages and their gods who created and named the river and forests around them. They explained their marriage customs and how important it is that there are relatives nearby to turn to for help.

They contrasted all this with the lack of essentials at relocation sites: little grazing or firewood, tin sheds that are hot in summer and cold in winter, members of families far away in strange places, dependence on officials whom they say they can never fully trust, dependence on neighboring villagers whom they do not know, dependence on landowners and money lenders whom they fear will somehow take their land away from them. Even people who say they are prepared to move, and can see that there could be advantages, told us that if they had a choice, they would stay in their isolated villages. As people said at meetings at Makadkhada, they do not want to leave their gods behind.

The things people spoke of touched on every aspect of their lives. Sometimes they were puzzling, and often they were given to us by people who clearly were struggling to find a way of expressing that which all human beings find most difficult to express, namely their sense of place and society. Social scientists have often pointed out that the distinction between culture and economy is often overstated. Sense of community is an aspect of a society's cultural heritage; it can also be a major factor in economic wellbeing.

In isolated, subsistence-oriented communities that prevail in the Gujarat submergence area, links between culture and economy are particularly strong. This is one reason why World Bank guidelines pay such careful attention to enforced relocation in the case of indigenous peoples. The importance of community is acknowledged in the high priority that is given by the 1985 credit and loan agreements to oustees' right to be relocated as village units if they so choose. The economic-cum-cultural losses that can result from the decision, be it by the authorities or the oustees themselves, to move in small units are not easy to forecast. Nor are they the kinds of loss it is easy to see or to measure. The policy itself, with a central emphasis on two hectares of land, the conception of development that prevails in the institutions that design and implement policies, and the social scientific difficulties that arise when it comes to measuring non-economic variables—all these factors converge to limit the entire issue to narrow economic concerns.

In Gujarat, where the resettlement process is far more advanced than in the other states, and where one can visit oustees in many different situations, it is possible to look at some of the risks inherent in this narrowing of the issue. Oustees spoke to us often about promises that had been made, and, in their opinion, often not fully kept. This concern with government promises expresses their newly increased vulnerability to a whole range of outside agencies. Many of these families are moving from isolation and self-reliance to some degree of integration into a wider society and immense dependence on public institutions and services to protect them against possible disastrous consequences of this move. The long-term outcome will indeed depend on both the keeping of promises and the relevance of the provisions in the resettlement and rehabilitation package.

PACHISGAON, MALU, KRISHNAPURA, AND AMROLI

Critics of the resettlement and rehabilitation process in Gujarat selected these four villages for us to visit as representative of some of the more serious problems to which resettlement and rehabilitation has given rise. As predicted, in each of these places we saw real difficulties.

In Pachisgaon, when we first arrived (without any formalities, and having given no warning that we were coming), the family we met on entering the village told us they had been there for one year, and explained they were "paying a price" for something that was "good for other people." This, they said, was something "we must accept." This family and all others we spoke to in the community said many times that from most points of view their circumstances in Pachisgaon were far worse than they had been in Kadada, the Gujarat submergence village from which they had come.

The people of Pachisgaon mentioned specific problems: fuel, water, and fodder appeared to present difficulties for everyone there. Several men also spoke about anomalies in the allotment of land. Three brothers told us that they had received land, but that their father had not been included on the list of oustees. They also said they had written many letters of complaint. We were taken to see the land that families had been given, some of which, they said, turned out not to be the plot they had originally selected. They had the impression that a switch had been made between their finding the site and the time the land was given to them. They suspected that landlords had managed to trick the Land Purchase Committee into paying high prices for bad land.

Several people told us that they could not put up their houses because of infestations of white ants, which would eat into the timbers—they were afraid of losing their teak and bamboo house-building materials. They also told us they had suffered greatly from waterlogged ground, and that, in general, living at the new site did not provide them with the economic and nutritional resources that they had had before.

They spoke at some length about the promises that had been made to them to encourage them to move: pukka houses,[30] one job per family, free electric light, and irrigation. They said they had received none of these. There was no point during the visit, which lasted several hours, at which anyone who spoke to us expressed the belief that, in the long term, relocation would secure for them a standard of living commensurate with that they had enjoyed in Kadada. For them, relocation entailed sacrifice.

We heard similar stories from people at Malu. A number of families had received land that was not cultivable. Some of the landowners from whom plots had been purchased had not yet been paid by the Land Purchase Committee. As a result, the original landowners succeeded in taking a proportion of the crop in lieu of the purchase price. People also complained about swarms of rats in their fields and around their houses, and spoke at length about the waterlogging of the land in the previous monsoon.

Most disturbing to the Malu families were the burglaries in theirs and a neighboring relocation site that apparently had been carried out by gangs from the distant hills. In one case, tin sheds had been systematically rifled. May oustees had returned to their home village of Makadkhada. When we asked whether or not people had complained, they said they felt apprehensive about complaining—they feared they would lose the little they had if they made any difficulties. Nonetheless, we were shown copies of letters of complaint dispatched to the authorities, and were told about a long history of attempts to get things that had gone wrong put to rights.

It is possible that those with whom we spoke at Malu, and those who showed us their fields, were not truly representative. Arch Vahini workers told us that things had gone badly wrong for a number of families, though others seemed to be relatively satisfied, and once or twice Malu was even mentioned as a site where relocation and resettlement has had some success. On the basis

---

[30] "Pukka" is used to refer to structures built with concrete, stone, or bricks. Thus both houses and roads are said to be pukka, as opposed to *katcha*, made of earth, mud, or wood, etc.

of what we saw and heard at Malu, there seemed to be no evidence to suggest that life in the relocation site was providing, or promised to provide, a level of wellbeing equal to that of the submergence villages from which the oustees had come.

But the two relocation sites we visited where problems seemed most severe were Krishnapura and Amroli. At Krishnapura, people were living in five lines of tin sheds, and had been there for three years. We heard a litany of difficulties. In the monsoon, waterlogging was extreme; they told us that the interior of their houses became so damp that firewood would not burn, and inside cattle sheds the animals sank into the mud and their fodder rotted. They told us that they had had a school in their old village, but there was no school here. They said they had many problems with their land, both in its allotment and quality. Some family heads, they said, had still not been given plots, while many major sons were still not recognized. They insisted that their landholdings in the original village were larger, if only because there they could encroach on government land as and when they needed.

Having heard this array of complaints and disappointments, we asked them why they had agreed to come here. An elderly man told us: "This dam is going to be built. We'll be submerged. So we had to go." Others interrupted him and added to his answer saying: "We didn't want to move." They told us that they had been influenced by promises the government had made. They said they had been told that every house would have electricity, and that there would be grazing land as before. They were also told, they said, that they would get housing plots with plinth foundations. And that here would be a school, temple, dispensary, and meeting hall.

In discussing these promises, we asked them if they understood how long it would be before the services to the community could be in place. They said that they were told, when they were considering whether or not to move, that work on services and buildings would begin as soon as they relocated. Yet, they said, after three years there was still no sign of work beginning. One man said: "Only God knows how long it will be. We don't know when the problems will be solved. People like you come and ask questions, and we answer them. The government comes and asks questions, and we answer them. But nothing is done."

We asked them about jobs and employment possibilities. They said there were very few. We asked them if there was social contact between the oustees and the host villages. We were told that they could not eat in one another's houses because of caste proscriptions. Their families had been broken up. Some were here, some were there. They said they had lost their animals—especially their goats and cattle. The women said they had nowhere to bathe and no privacy to perform their ablutions.

The case of Amroli was, if anything, even more disturbing. The people had come from Gadher, one of the largest of the 14 submergence villages in Gujarat. They had been in Amroli for three years, but numbered only 19 families. Their experience had been so discouraging, they said, that they had now urged others not to follow them. They complained about the water facility: the pump that had been provided did not work and the well was saline; they said not even their animals could drink there. As a result, they fetch water from a river one kilometer away. They said they had asked many times to have this fundamental problem dealt with, but nothing had happened.

They said that of 19 families who had been given land at Amroli, 12 have land that is adequate while 7 have land that is not cultivable. For all of them, they said, their plots at Gadher had been of better quality. One of the women said, with the obvious endorsement of the others: "This place is not good. Many in our family are sick. The water is not good and is far away. This place is like a crematorium. Our children suffer from vomiting, diarrhoea, and dehydration." As the women spoke, some of the men interrupted them, asserting that the land they had been shown was not the land they were given. A woman said that because of the absence of trees, they had to spend much of their time finding cow dung and small bits of wood to burn in their stoves. The small area for grazing meant that cows did not eat enough to produce an adequate supply of milk. Most of their animals they had had to leave at Gadher, because they could not possibly graze them here. They were especially unhappy about losing their goats, which they said represented their savings and their way of dealing with important rites of passage and crises. One woman said: "Without grazing, without goats, how can we survive?" Apparently they were being forced to sell most of their animals. They spoke of their difficulties with cash flow, and told us that some of them had gone to labor at the dam.

We asked them why they had moved here. They said they had no alternative. Their village was going to be submerged, and they were told they had no choice. They were promised that everything would be good here. They were told about the benefits to their major sons, and were persuaded that there would be good water and grazing. They had also been promised pukka houses. They knew that this land would never get water from the canal, because it is high. But they were told they would have a well for each two-hectare plot. They said they had been promised a subsistence allowance for one year. It was to come in three instalments, of which they had received only the first two. They said they were now told they would get the third instalment when they moved their houses from the old village to the new site. But they had not been given house sites, they said, nor had they been given a school, a dispensary, or free electricity. They said they had asked repeatedly to have these things put in place, but nothing happened.[31] They told us that only seven families remained here, because many had gone back to Gadher. They pointed to locked houses. And they said that they were now thinking that perhaps it would be better if they all moved back as a group.

We asked them if there was anything at all that they could identify as being better here than at the village from which they had come. The women shook their heads and smiled, saying: "Nothing." One of the men said: "There is no good drinking water. How can we say anything is good here?"

It is important to emphasize that at this meeting—as in our other visits to relocation sites—we sought to make sure that people told us what had gone well for them, as well as to identify difficulties. Visitors can easily become an opportunity for the airing of problems, and therefore can cause bias towards negative statements. Our overwhelming impression, however, was that the people at these sites were genuinely experiencing hardships of many kinds. In the cases of Krishnapura and Amroli, it would be impossible to avoid the conclusion that the quality of life—as the villagers themselves see it—including their economic circumstances, has deteriorated continuously over the three years they have been there.

In February 1992, three months after our first visit, we returned to Pachisgaon. In the intervening time, the community had grown. Many families had brought their house materials, though none so far had erected them. House plots were being cleared, and there seemed to be more women and children at the site. We held a short meeting, making a point of talking to some of the people we had met previously. We discussed the changes that had taken place. They told us that the difficulties they had told us about had not been corrected. The father of the three brothers still had not been recognized as an oustee. Others had been told that the land they had received was the land they would have to accept, and their complaints about quality and size seemed to have got them nowhere. They told us that they had sold off animals in order to buy building materials for pukka houses. There appeared to be no process of rehabilitation to help these people through their difficulties. Their mistrust of officials and their anxiety about their circumstances did not seem to have abated.

It is important to note that those who resettle are promised irrigable land, but the sites we are discussing here had not yet received this benefit. In fact,

---

[31] It is possible that the policy's stipulation of minimum number of families per school, dispensary, and other amenities has created confused expectations. However, Gujarat officials also have said publicly that amenities will be provided on an as-need basis. It is more likely that oustees' expectations derive from statements by officials than the specific terms of the policies.

for a large proportion of the relocation sites in Gujarat, irrigation is dependent on the canal network, which, even on the most optimistic schedules, will not deliver water for irrigation until 1995, and possibly not until 1998. It is probable that the advent of irrigation will improve the situation considerably, though in the meantime these families seem likely to continue to be beset by uncertainties. Moreover, in the absence of a strong economy and their familiar bulwark of family assistance, the uncertain or delayed provision of wells, house sites, schooling, and other community infrastructure have special significance.[32]

In our visits to both submergence villages and relocation sites, many people told us that resettlement was certain to be hard for them. Some said they did not like to think about the river and the forests of the place they had come from. Others said, difficult as it was, they had not given up hope that in a few years they would have made the appropriate adjustments. In Pachisgaon, Malu, Krishnapura, and Amroli—as also in other relocation sites—the consensus among those who spoke with us was that their life in their original villages was superior from many points of view. Although they did not express it in so many words, their remarks added up to a simple conclusion: their cultural wellbeing depended on the world they were leaving behind. This cultural loss raises doubts about the possibility of achieving the long-term policy objective—that people's standard of living should be at least as good as it was before. Problems of water, fuel, grazing, privacy, and caste proscriptions—issues to which people in relocation sites referred again and again—suggest some of the links between the cultural and economic settings.

At the level of the individual family trying to make the best of resettlement in an environment with which it is not familiar, and seeking to cope with the shock of cultural losses, resettlement requires piecemeal and continually demanding implementation. The arrangement for plowing that is not made, the repair of a water pump that has broken, the readjustment of plot size where a mistake has been made about its measurements, the securing of land for a major son who has not yet qualified as an oustee, the payment of an instalment of relocation allowance, the need to smooth over conflict with host villages. There is recurring need to deal with oustees' apprehension about petty crime, the need for toilet facilities, anxiety about size of the local rat or white ant population, a dispute within the relocated community over grazing, anxiety about the stoniness of a plot, indignation that the road is part of land allotment, delay in provision of electric light. The lists are very long.

These problems—all of which we heard about at one or other of the reloca-

---

[32] Doubts about the environmental impacts of irrigation are also of great relevance here. See the discussion of the command area in Chapter 14 below.

tion sites we visited—raise two concerns of great importance. First, there is an enormous problem for an administration that has to deal with a plethora of individual crises spread across an ever-widening number of communities. Second, the people of these communities are not accustomed to anything but extreme self-reliance—for the most part they come from isolated villages where there are virtually no social services, and such as do exist have never been particularly responsive to their demands. Yet now their everyday wellbeing and long-term prospects for adequate subsistence depend on administrators or non-government organization workers.

A woman at Amroli said to us: "They made promises. That is why we have moved here. If they don't keep their promises, we have nothing." And at Malu an elderly man said: "We came here like a groom comes to his wedding. He has many hopes. And then there is a marriage."

THE BEST CASES

Workers from Arch Vahini took us to visit relocation sites in the cluster near Dabhoi, where oustees are working irrigated land. As we have seen, Arch Vahini workers take the view that, with the benefit of irrigation and the allotment of two hectares of land per family, resettlement and rehabilitation constitute a real development opportunity. They also told us that although prospects for adequate rehabilitation were not secured until the 1988 Gujarat policy changes, the implementation process had improved immensely since 1990. By looking at conditions in relocation sites established in the past 18 months, in an area where irrigation is already available in the command areas of other rivers, they helped us to see the beneficial results that proper implementation of the current Gujarat policy would achieve in the long term.

The land base for the whole Dabhoi cluster is approximately 1,620 hectares. This is enough to provide agricultural plots for 600 to 700 oustee families (land is also needed for house plots, roads, public buildings, etc.). One recently added area comprises enough land for 100 families, available to the people from three Gujarat villages. At these villages, we visited the land and held meetings with groups of men and women.

At Kukad, Ramatia Koyla Ratthwa took us to see his rice harvest. Ten day-laborers were working in the fields, at Rs. 15 per day. He had brought them from Nawchitli, a village outside the submergence area, in the Gujarat plains. Ramatia Koyla was extremely proud of his agricultural success at the relocation site, and told us that he expected to make over Rs. 25,000 from that harvest alone. He also expressed considerable satisfaction in the provision of services in the new place, and noted that the people there had built the tin sheds for themselves, instead of using contractors, and had therefore been able to design them to meet their needs. In particular, they had included lofts for storage and plinths to protect the sheds against waterlogging. Also, they had sited their sheds on actual house plots, rather than in the barrack-like rows typical of almost all resettlement sites.

After seeing the land, and being told of the harvests that were being achieved, we held a meeting to which some 25 men and 20 women came. Most of these people were originally from Hanfeshwar, the Gujarat village closest to the Madhya Pradesh border. They spoke of the relative benefits of the relocation site, mentioning the fact that they had been encroachers before whereas now they had their own land, and pointing out that here they could already raise two crops a year and anticipated being able to increase to three. They spoke of having to walk 10 kilometers from Hanfeshwar to the nearest market town. They told us that some of the families from their village had gone to a resettlement site at Panasoli, so they were not far away. They insisted that they had chosen where they wanted to go for themselves. Some of the women spoke of how well adjusted the children were, and when one woman asserted that "even our children are happy," others indicated their strong agreement. The women also talked about how hard it had been to get enough green vegetables in their submergence village, because they could not carry enough water to irrigate the plots. They also spoke of the hardships they had endured in bringing even enough water for drinking: "We had to stop on the way for rests."

They said they were confident that the government was going to honor the promises that had been made. They said they fought for what they had now got, their irrigated land and their house sites. They said that electric poles were already in place, and they were sure that light would come to their houses. They pointed out that road construction had started, to provide access to the site. They said, "The government is slow. Things will take time." In general, the group exuded a quiet confidence.

They also told us about problems they were facing. They spoke of the difficulty of getting fuel wood and the absence of trees. But they were sure that they could plant trees, and these would grow well.[33] And they insisted that grazing was not a problem here. They said in Hanfeshwar that they had had to keep their goats as the only insurance available to them against drought. They said the goats were their survival mechanism, and with irrigation they do not need that insurance, and in any case they will be able to provide fodder themselves from their plots. They also mentioned difficulties about allotments of land. Families whom they believed to qualify as oustees had still not been al-

---

[33] Stalks from irrigated crops, notably cotton, can also provide fuel. Some people told us that they anticipated an easing of the fuel problem from this source; others expressed skepticism, saying that cotton stalks burn too quickly.

lotted agricultural plots. And some said that promises of tractors had been made to help with plowing; they claimed that a senior official of the Nigam had guaranteed that they would get their land plowed at the start and that it would be paid for by the Nigam. But this had not been done. Even here, they complained only about the breaking of the promise, saying that if there had never been a promise they would have managed without help. They also spoke about conflicts with nomadic herders who were now settled in Dabhoi and who had a tradition of grazing this land. There had been considerable tension, culminating in a court case against the grazers. They also said, however, that the local Patels had warned them to be careful, and had helped them in other ways. The dominant mood of this group was optimistic. They talked enthusiastically about being able to grow rice and wheat. They said that for the first time in their lives they felt no need to be anxious about the failure of the monsoon.

Virtually everyone at Kukad is Ratthwa, most of whom had only migrated to Hanfeshwar in the 1960s. Ramatia Koyla had moved to the Narmada valley in 1967, having been born at Nawchitli, hence his ability to find workers there for his rice harvest. He told us that he had worked as an agricultural laborer on irrigated lands. He knew perfectly well how to manage planting, harvesting, and maintenance of an irrigated system. In general, Arch Vahini told us that the Ratthwa of Hanfeshwar were especially enterprising, and were eager to seize the opportunity offered to them by the resettlement and rehabilitation policy of re-entering the mainstream of Gujarat agricultural life.

Evidently the conditions at Kukad and the history of those who relocated there were complementary. This appeared to be a real development opportunity—a model, perhaps, of how resettlement and rehabilitation policy can achieve its fundamental objectives.

The second Dabhoi cluster community we visited, Karanet, is even newer than Kukad. There were 10 houses, although some 50 families had been allotted land there, while over 85 were expected to move there eventually. We held a meeting with some 30 men. Unlike the Ratthwa from Hanfeshwar, these Vasava from Makadkhada were shy. Hesitantly they told us that it had been very difficult to move. "We left our native land. To leave that is very painful and difficult." But they went on to say that the land here was far better than at Makadkhada and they believed their prospects to be good. One man said that it had been extremely difficult to leave "the land of my forefathers," but that he had had to go. There was no option, he said, because of the dam. On the other hand, this same man went on to say how many difficulties there had been in his original village. He spoke of how little help they ever got from government officials, and how hard it was to get the sick to a doctor. He said it took a whole day for him to walk to shops, one day would then be spent shopping, and a third day would then be taken up to walk back. Here, he said, there was the government to help them and good shops available in Dabhoi town.

An elderly man also expressed gratitude to the government for having warned them that they would have to move, and having provided them with a plan that got them their land. "If we hadn't been told, the water would have risen, and we would have had to run helter and skelter and we would have lost our animals. This is a saving grace. And the land here is good."

The men here had very little to say about the agricultural possibilities. This was their first year and they had not harvested a crop, but they were optimistic. On the other hand, several of them spoke about their concern for their sons. Those who hadn't qualified as major sons, but who were in their teens, would soon be needing land. What would happen to them?[34] They also said herders had been grazing cattle on their land, and they had to maintain all-night watches to protect their crops. They needed to go back to Makadkhada because many of their wives are still there and also some crops. To get there they took a bus that left at six in the morning and they would reach their village by the afternoon. They also spoke of the lack of firewood and grazing. But there was confidence: they would plant trees, and they would get fodder from their crops.

At the end of the meeting, the men said that they needed a school badly and they needed motors for the pumps on their wells. The owners had taken these away. The Nigam had promised replacements, but nothing so far had been done. And again they returned to their worries about minor sons. The people of Karanet were manifestly less sure of their prospects than those at Kukad. Yet their mood was optimistic.

Harivalabh Parikh of Anand Niketan Ashram also took us to three other relocation sites where implementation seemed to be proceeding with relative success. These were Untkoi, with 20 families from Hanfeshwar living on 40 hectares, Bakha, where eventually 36 families from Turkheda and Ferkada will be relocated, and Vadala, where eventually there will be 33 families from two hamlets of Hanfeshwar.

At Untkoi, which is a new site, people were not yet able to judge the agricultural potential, but seemed optimistic. They said they had been promised irrigation, and expected that they would be given one well per unit. Apart

---

[34] Although land for new families is also a problem in many submergence villages, encroachment and a wide range of forest and river resources combine to create a relatively elastic economic base. The relocation site is a precisely measured plot of arable land. Its rigid boundaries cause apprehension about the future. Fear of loss of land as a result of debt adds to this concern about the fate of the next generation.

from some apprehensions about waterlogging (four hectares of the 40 hectares available to them tended to be waterlogged), they told us that they expected life would be better for them here than in Hanfeshwar. Similarly, at Bakha, where some people had moved their houses already, there was optimism, though here again it depended on the promise of irrigation. People said that once the land was irrigated, they were sure they would be economically more secure than they had been at Hanfeshwar, where trouble with the Forestry De-partment, they told us, had made their economic lives very difficult. They said they had been promised additional grazing land at Bakha. When we asked if, in general, they felt worse or better off than they had in their original villages, they said—with some giggling amusement and apparent reluctance—that things would improve. They missed the forest, and said life had been hard and, in some ways continued to be hard, but they expressed determination to make everything work out.

At Vadala, people said that when they had first moved, their land had been afflicted by waterlogging. They had found the tin sheds unbearably hot in summer and cold in winter. This may have been particularly trying for them because Vadala is far away from Hanfeshwar, and they therefore had to spend more time in their sheds than would otherwise have been the case. But people here were enthusiastic about the productivity of their land. They told us that they had got between Rs. 10,000 and Rs. 30,000 for their cotton crops, while also producing large supplies of rice, millet, maize, and chickpeas for domestic consumption. Some of the farmers estimated that their outlay on fertilizers was approximately Rs. 4,000 per family, but the returns on this investment justi-fied it. Nor did the people we spoke to at Vadala have any complaints to make about schooling and other services. They said they missed the forest, and needed far more fodder for the animals that they would like to bring there. But the mood was optimistic.

At Bakha we visited families who have already brought their houses to the relocation site. Some of these are large and beautifully constructed. As a result, the site did not present the usual grim spectacle of rows of tin sheds. Here we had a conversation with oustees about housing. They told us that they wanted brick houses rather than their traditional teak and bamboo homes.[35] When we asked them about their reasons for preferring pukka houses, the people ex-

---

[35] By coincidence, there was an engineer from the Nigam visiting Bakha when we were there. He told us that the teak used in the construction of a house of the kind we were visiting has a replacement value of approximately Rs. 600 per cubic foot. We asked him to estimate how much teak there was in the house where we were at that moment. After spending a considerable time examining the building, he calculated the total at 80 cubic feet, representing a value of Rs. 48,000. He emphasized to us that this did not include an estimate for the many, but slender, rafters and other wood the house was built from.

plained that the homes they now have are better built and are, in many ways, more comfortable than would be the case with the kind of pukka house they envisaged. But they pointed out that every monsoon their traditional houses need repairs. This requires finding bamboo and other materials, none of which are within easy distance of the relocation site. As a result, repairs could only be done through purchase of materials. Therefore, they said, they could not expect to be able to manage the economics of living in the traditional-style homes.

At another meeting in the same village, women talked about the river and the forest. They said that they followed their men in adopting the view that now they must think about land, and not the river. Apparently, in Hanfeshwar they had suffered much insecurity as a result of their dealings with the Forestry Department—a large proportion of the land there is encroached. They said that people had been forced out of their lands, and complained that women had been assaulted by forestry officers. They also told us that in 1983 the government had issued 5,000 eviction notices, resulting in a great deal of protest and confrontation. Escape from harassment seemed to be the dominant factor in their belief that life at Bakha would be more secure for them.

The women also told us that at Bakha the absence of the forest made their work more arduous. They had to walk a long way to find enough wood for their fires, and suffered from a lack of privacy. We asked them if this meant, in a day-to-day way, that their life seemed to be worse for them here than it had been in Hanfeshwar. Their answer came after a great deal of hesitating. They said they believe that, eventually, it would improve. "Now it is hard for us," they said. "This is only the third year we are here."

These three sites—Untkoi, Vadala, and Bakha—are among the 30 or so whose oustees are visited regularly by workers from the Anand Niketan Ashram organization. They take the view that Sardar Sarovar is "bad medicine that Gujarat must take if it is to cure its drought ills." And their workers told me that they were determined that all the rehabilitation measures of the policy must be implemented, and believed that this is already yielding real benefits in the communities with which they deal.

These visits to resettlement sites chosen by Arch Vahini and the Anand Niketan Ashram as indicative of resettlement and rehabilitation's prospects of success lead to no clear conclusion. Irrigation holds out the prospect of new cash crops. And the provision of irrigable land has been an integral component of all the policies from the Tribunal's 1979 award onwards. Policy planners in India and at the World Bank have maintained that irrigated land represents a necessary condition for the achievement of policies. However, it has not been seen as a sufficient condition, and much of oustees' optimism arises not from present benefits, but from the belief that promises that have been made will be kept. In addition, the kinds of concerns that arose in the relocation sites of Dabhoi and elsewhere leave questions about those aspects of policy which do and do not address issues of culture and community.

In the end, successful rehabilitation must depend—as World Bank operational manuals and supporting documents make clear—on a package of benefits and an implementation process that recognizes a wide range of needs.

MONITORING AND EVALUATION

The 1985 credit and loan agreements required monitoring and evaluation of progress in resettlement and rehabilitation so that the Bank would be able to judge whether the provisions of the agreements were being carried out. Despite some difficulties—including a good deal of mutual suspicion between government and academics—a monitoring and evaluation agency was in place in all three states by 1987.[36] In Gujarat, the Centre for Social Studies, Surat, was already doing research in the submergence villages. In 1985 the Centre contracted with the Government of Gujarat to continue this work as the monitoring and evaluation required by the Bank. The result was a series of reports looking at a number of aspects of resettlement at selected relocation sites.

Monitoring and evaluation was never intended to be a substitute for assessment of the impacts of the Projects, nor a way of accumulating information on which policy could be formulated. This information was required well before 1985, the year of the credit and loan agreements. The work done at the Surat Centre for Social Studies between 1982 and 1985 included a survey of Gujarat submergence villages. But this work had not been designed to be the kind of impact assessment that was needed for the Projects, did not influence policy,[37] and appears not to have been drawn upon as part of the Bank's 1983-84 postappraisal process.

Between 1985 and 1987, the Surat Centre's monitoring and evaluation continued, but the Gujarat government's response to its findings was less than sympathetic. Reports focused on the fact that oustees were not receiving the two hectares of land to which they were entitled, while Gujarat officials countered that oustees were rejecting land that was being offered to them. The Bank's April 1987 mission report included a comment to the effect that Gujarat was not responsive to the Surat reports' findings, and mentioned the researchers' "fear of censorship" that "has led to [the] resignation of the social

---

[36] See Chapters 7 and 8 for discussion of the work of agencies in Maharashtra and Madhya Pradesh.

[37] Report No. 5 notes that the monitoring and evaluation team was unable to obtain access to crucial documents, and therefore "suggesting effective policies is not possible."

scientist in charge of the project and most [of the] enumerators." The Bank's objective at this time was to ensure that monitoring and evaluation continued, and that it be independent. The 1987 mission, though expressing apprehension about possible tensions between the Surat team and the government of Gujarat, did conclude that the work had "survived" this difficult period.[38]

Senior staff at the Surat Centre for Social Studies, however, told us that tension did not end in 1987. They also explained that some of their difficulties sprang from doubts about the criteria embedded in policy for judging the nature of the Projects' impacts. They felt deeply uneasy about the concept of "standard of living," fearing that it was interpreted by the Bank to exclude important social and cultural factors.

Nonetheless, the Surat Centre's reports set out recommendations that, at least after 1988, received attention from Gujarat resettlement officers. A review of the recommendations made and the Nigam response to these recommendations is revealing.[39]

We have already mentioned that the Center reported problems surrounding allotment of land are raised in Reports 6, 8, and 10. The streamlining of the documentation process is urged (10).

The need for amenities and anxieties about the long-term prospects for getting them are discussed (Reports 6 and 7. In general, it is noted that rehabilitation needs to be seen broadly rather than as a "target oriented physical replacement exercise," and that the population of relocation sites is unlikely to reach the numbers at which they qualify for the amenities set out in the policies (7). The reports suggest that all promises of facilities be bound by a "time clause" (7). The need to provide water tanks and wells is also emphasized, along with the importance of their being repaired promptly (10).

Problems related to scarcity of fuel and fodder recur (Reports 8, 10, and 12). One report states: "There is the problem of grass and fodder everywhere" (10). Another says that fodder "is going to be the major issue for these oustees" (12). They warn about conflicts between oustees and host villagers over available grazing near relocation sites, and recommend that grazing be provided to all oustees (8).

Problems facing women also give rise to recommendations for better implementation (6, 10, and 12). The suggestion is made that women should play a part in site selection, and that they should be given a chance to stay for a while

---

[38] This is set out in the mission's draft Aide-Memoire, April 1987, Annex 1.

[39] It is to be recalled that the research for monitoring and evaluation was not shaped by problems or priorities that had been identified by prior assessments. Thus, for example, there are no reports that focus on how loss of forest is to be compensated; nor is there a report that centers on the needs and concerns of women, and how these can be mitigated. We make use of the monitoring and evaluation studies, but do not wish to imply that they should deal with issues that they were never expected to address.

in prospective host villages in order to get to know what the difficulties at a particular site might be and begin the process of integration with the host community. There is also a set of recommendations with regard to "women specific development programmes" (12).

Medical needs are addressed (8 and 10), and the importance of dispensaries and regular visits by doctors is emphasized.

Generally, the reports conclude that cultural and social aspects receive too little attention in the resettlement process. They recommend that resettlement policy needs to take account of "dislocation and adjustment" rather than suppose that provision of land will be a "sufficient safeguard" (6). It is also pointed out that Bhils have an "organic link with nature" and must be resettled in forest land. "Special attention should be given to the Bhils at the time of their resettlement" (10).

Another problem the reports raise is the failure adequately to keep oustees informed. "Oustees are ignorant of many facts concerning the Narmada Project. . . . They are ignorant about matters like land acquisition and resettlement which affect them directly. They do not know . . . what right to exercise" (6). The reports also express frustration that the monitoring and evaluation teams themselves cannot get crucial documents, including ones that are essential if their suggestions concerning policy are to have any place in what is being decided and done by government and Bank officials.

The recommendations made in the monitoring and evaluation reports are addressed, on a point by point basis, by Nigam officials. The responses are set out alongside the recommendations. These reveal what might be termed bureaucratic caution. Repeatedly a recommendation is marked as "noted." Most items, including deficient health care and women's problems, are considered to be dealt with by existing services. The shortage of fuel and fodder is said to be something that will be resolved in the coming year or two by new "schemes" or by the fact that "almost all the host villages have grazing lands" (10 and 12). It is evident that officials do not feel able to tackle the source of fundamental problems. They point out that they are restricted by existing agreements, and lack the resources with which to address problems spread across an ever growing number of sites—by 1991 the number of housing and agricultural sites had reached more than 130. The written response to the Surat team's recommendations echoes what officials told us at length: they have had great difficulties in dealing with the day-to-day problems that inevitably arise in the course of relocating and resettling thousands of people, while the basis (in terms of policy and information) for addressing the broader and deeper issues is very narrow.[40]

---

[40] It is disturbing to find that when Surat recommendations speak of oustees having problems

This does not mean that monitoring and evaluation reports have only negative findings, or that institutional limitations cause all their recommendations to go unheeded. Some suggestions are welcomed; small steps to improve conditions are taken. Among the helpful responses are the Nigam's resettlement and rehabilitation officials' statement of intention to appoint a team of experts to study the special problems faced by Bhils, and a decision to appoint two female social workers to help with women's difficulties. Sometimes Nigam officials asked their monitoring and evaluation agency to look at a particular problem at a particular site. But Nigam officials told us that their immediate administrative needs tended not to be met by the work of the monitoring and evaluation team, while leaders of the team told us that many issues they raise tend not to be dealt with by the Nigam. There is a mismatch between implementation that is unable or reluctant to question policy and research that repeatedly encounters and suggests the need for policy changes.

In 1991 the Centre for Social Studies followed up its earlier study of October to March 1988 (6), which looked at the degree to which oustees in five relocation sites had integrated with host communities, with special emphasis on "socio-religious aspects" of this process. The five sites were Ambavadi, Chhindiapura, Khadagada, Tentalav, and Parveta.[41] Although the focus of the research was relations between oustees and hosts, the findings of the 1991 report (13) also contained oustees' judgments of some of their social and economic circumstances.

The report concluded that "participation in the existing village organization is almost negligible." It explained further: "The host villages and oustees of the villages under study are not antagonistic with each other, though there exists subtle tension between the two in some spheres of life." Other indicators also suggested a low level of social and cultural adjustment: visits to markets and celebration of religious festivals had declined in all the relocation sites. All the questionnaire results indicated that, apart from Chhindiapura, where oustees and host villagers are related by kinship ties and knew each other prior to relocation, there is tentativeness and distance rather than either antagonism or collaboration. This is an important finding, since these oustees are Tadvis who have relocated within relatively short distances of their original communities. It suggests tribal links are not sufficient for the integration of oustees with host populations, and that effective socializing only occurs within marriage

moving their "houses," the Nigam response talks of "huts." This usage of "hut" (and even "enhutment" to refer to a hamlet or village) illustrates the stereotyped way in which tribal life tends to be seen. The people's houses, in reality, are large, permanent, and carefully (sometimes magnificently) built, making use of teak and bamboo for beams, rafters, and walls, with locally made tiles for the roofs. By rural Indian standards, many of them are of high quality.

[41] The implications of these and the 1991 findings for Parveta are discussed in Chapter 7.

circles (extending approximately 20 kilometers from the home village). The low levels of integration recorded at these sites do not bode well for integration of oustees from Bhil or Bhilala villages much further away.

The 1991 report emphasized again (as did Reports 6, 7, and 10) the distress caused by the terms of the policy that tie the provision of civic amenities to the number of families residing at a relocation site. It identified this as a serious problem, and pointed out that thresholds for provision of these amenities were designed by the Narmada Water Disputes Tribunal, at a time when officials generally believed that relocation would be by large social units. As we have seen, in reality villages have been dispersed into small relocation units. Nigam data from 1991 disclosed that out of the 131 relocation sites in Gujarat only six contain more than 100 families and none as many as 500. That some of these small sites may be located in clusters does not secure the amenities under the terms of the policy. Despite promises by the Government that services and institutions will be provided on an "as needed" basis, we saw little evidence of this happening. There are probably far more communities without civic amenities than anyone originally anticipated.

The 1991 Surat report concluded that, on the whole, a majority of the oustees in the villages they studied "are happy with their economic condition and standard of living" (p 57). This conclusion suggests that Gujarat has provided adequate agricultural plots to some oustees.

On October 20, 1991, we met with 30 or 40 oustees who came to see us in Baroda as part of a series of presentations to our review by non-government organizations who support Sardar Sarovar. Twenty-seven of these oustees, all of whom were spending at least part of their time in relocation sites, made brief statements about their circumstances.

Although we extended this meeting throughout the morning of the following day, it was difficult to pursue any of the matters raised to any real depth. Each person who spoke listed the benefits he had received as a result of resettlement. Many described the fertility of their land, saying it was adequate, although others were worried that yields were low and the soil difficult to cultivate. Some said that they had received the facilities they had expected, and many identified the particular items they had been given—notably bullocks, bullock carts, plows, house sites, carts, and some hand pumps. At the same time, virtually every person who spoke identified the absence of grazing, fodder, and firewood as persistent serious deficiencies. They mentioned the numerous products they used to gather from the forest and could no longer get.

This kind of meeting away from people's own territory, at which many of those who spoke obviously felt uneasy, is not productive of understanding the ways in which resettlement has affected people. But we did hear a wide spectrum of opinions given by people from many different sites, and a middle-aged man who now lives at Kandewar and is originally from Pandheria, a Tadvi community in Gujarat, made a statement that encapsulated what seemed to be the general mood.

> It is true it is very difficult to leave the place where we have lived for decades. We have to leave the jungle, the leaves, and all those things. We have to settle in places close to highways. We will become happy. . . . At present we remember all things. We think we will move back. But in time, we will settle.

The findings of the Surat Centre's monitoring and evaluation reports and the statements made to us by oustees show similar pictures. The administrators are restricted by policies that reflect particular interpretations of people's needs. As a result, the problems of grazing, firewood, and privacy recur, even in sites where oustees are benefiting from irrigation and achieving agricultural success. These are not issues of minor or passing significance. They go to a wide range of social and cultural factors that may, in the end, bear as heavily on the long-term outcome of resettlement as the quality of people's land.

The reports confirm the extent to which implementation depends on a provision of amenities that have been promised, but are in doubt either because site populations are too small for them to qualify, or because existing government services are inadequate.

The reports also reveal the administrative problems that are in considerable measure a result of the scatter of relocation sites. Each site has daily problems, some of them, such as water and quality of agricultural plots, are of acute importance. The resettlement staff of the Nigam have been fully occupied finding and distributing plots; attention to other matters has inevitably suffered as a result. It is important to reiterate in this regard that resettlement policy did not envisage a scatter of small sites, and was able to anticipate, therefore, economies of administrative scale. The reality on the ground, reflected in the monitoring and evaluation reports, especially as relocation proceeded after 1989, has placed a burden on the Nigam which has proved hard to sustain. The implications for oustees at relocation sites are far reaching.

BANK MISSIONS

Since 1986 the Bank has sent review missions at six-month intervals to supervise the Projects. Each mission includes a resettlement and rehabilitation component. The Back-To-Office Memoranda, Aide-Memoires, and Mission Reports are an important source of information about progress on implementation of many aspects of resettlement in Gujarat.

Virtually all resettlement sites are in Gujarat, and therefore implementation of resettlement policy, especially between 1985 and 1990, fell to the Gujarat administration. With regard to resettlement, therefore, Bank missions tended to center on Gujarat.

In fact, there was only one supervisory mission in 1986, the second having been postponed at Gujarat's request. Its report is intensely critical of both policy framework and actual conditions at existing resettlement sites. The full report also pointed to the unsuitability of existing resettlement and rehabilitation personnel. It observed that if these inadequacies were not removed soon, the principles and objectives of the 1980 Operational Manual Statement would be difficult to meet. Officers who were on this mission reported that the Government of Gujarat (and governments of the other states) viewed resettlement "not as an important issue, but as an impediment to construction of the dam."

We have already referred to the 1987 mission reports.[42] The central finding of the April mission was that Gujarat had gone back on the agreement to provide each oustee with two hectares of land. A post-mission letter (July 1, 1987) to the Government of Gujarat set a ten month deadline by which time this "serious" failure of compliance was to be addressed; in somewhat guarded terms this letter warned Gujarat that the Bank might have to reconsider the loan. The November 1987 mission, although it focused on monitoring and evaluation, returned to the problem of non compliance on the provision of two hectares of land for oustees. It was on the last day of this mission that Gujarat issued the Government Resolution that affirmed the two hectare minimum entitlement.

The April 1988 mission found that oustees and the organizations representing them were "incensed" over Gujarat's reluctance to implement the policy as required, including its "backtracking" on the two-hectare minimum when it came to major sons of landed oustees.

As we have seen, Gujarat broadened its policies in 1988. At the same time, opposition to the dam intensified. All subsequent missions have been conducted in a charged atmosphere that limited their access to villages in Maharashtra and Madhya Pradesh. In Gujarat, however, opposition was diminished by the broadened policy and (as we shall see below) the decision on the part of the Arch Vahini organization to co-operate with government.

Nonetheless, in 1989, a result of Bank disquiet about lack of progress in resettlement and rehabilitation in all three states, Professor Thayer Scudder was called back to participate in the review, together with Mr. Michael Baxter (who was in charge of the Bank's Agriculture Unit in Delhi from July 1987 to

---

[42] See also Chapter 5; the issue of tribals was a focus of the April 1987 mission.

February 1992) and Mr. Abdul Salam (who was a consultant on Sardar Sarovar in 1986 and was the Delhi office specialist on resettlement from March 1987 to March 1991). The formal mission report of May 1989 observed, when it came to the question of Gujarat, that there was "overall improvement" in its relocation and rehabilitation. It said that all major issues were resolved, and that once remaining deficiencies were corrected, it anticipated that Gujarat would achieve its resettlement and rehabilitation objectives.

The Bank therefore appeared to conclude that a corner had been turned. Professor Scudder himself, however, had not taken this view. He felt strongly enough about what he had observed that, in a separate report to the Bank, dated May 29, 1989, he argued that the chances of successful resettlement and rehabilitation had receded, despite improved policies. He also judged that the only way the Bank could redeem the situation was by suspending disbursement until all major issues were fully and finally resolved.

Scudder's 1989 report was leaked to the press, and created much controversy. It is still being debated in the Narmada valley today. Whatever the rights and wrongs of Scudder's conclusions, there is a remarkable disparity between his findings—as the resettlement and rehabilitation expert with most experience of Sardar Sarovar—and the Bank's formal mission report of May 1989. In the mission report, Professor Scudder's conclusions were not merely qualified, they were, when it came to Gujarat, of which he had been particularly critical, more or less repudiated.

But the position taken by the Bank in May 1989 represents the beginning of the a new and continuing approach to the Sardar Sarovar Projects. The India Country Department urged that the Bank use the forthcoming closing date for the loan extension (June 1989) as a lever to pressurize and test the Indian government's readiness to take significant measures that would render resettlement and rehabilitation more successful. This was the beginning of what is now referred to as the incremental strategy. The Bank sought to press for action on identifiable and remediable problems, and to stay away from an approach, exemplified by earlier mission reports, that sought to focus attention on the source of much that was going awry. It appears that the 1989 review mission marked the beginning of a phase of intensive supervision of Sardar Sarovar by the Bank. But if the earlier phase of supervision was marked by legal and bureaucratic adherence to covenants and conditions, this new phase represents a determined effort to achieve changes in policy and improvements in implementation on a piecemeal basis.[43]

After 1990, Bank missions' criticisms of policy and implementation focus

---

[43] Bank officials told us that the May 1989 decision to change strategies was taken because the previous approach had failed to deal with problems in all three states. We shall see, however, that

increasingly on Maharashtra and Madhya Pradesh. The achievements of Gujarat are repeatedly highlighted, to show that resettlement and rehabilitation are continuing to improve, and, perhaps, to hold up an example before the other states. This does not mean that concerns about what was happening in Gujarat had disappeared. But the strategy depended on the working assumption that all was fundamentally well.

THE ROLE OF NON-GOVERNMENT ORGANIZATIONS

In 1988, the umbrella organization, Narmada Bachao Andolan, decided to oppose the Sardar Sarovar Projects, and sought to mobilize the affected populations of Maharashtra and Madhya Pradesh. Opposition to the Projects also attracted the attention of national and international non-government organizations. Articles and monographs were published on the environmental and social costs of the Projects.[44] On the other hand, Arch Vahini, the Gujarat non-government organization that had been active in submergence villages and relocation sites since the early 1980s, regarded the 1988 Gujarat policy as the basis for support for the government. By 1989 there was active cooperation between the Nigam and Vahini workers, who threw themselves into this task, becoming active in every step of the implementation process. Their contribution was augmented by their personal knowledge of many of the Gujarat submergence villages.

After 1989, the rate and effectiveness of relocation in Gujarat increased. Most important of all, the Nigam set up a land purchase committee which was able to acquire private land and distribute it to oustees. Although this initiated the scatter effect that we have already discussed, it made it possible to put in place an institutional process. Identification of land, its purchase and selection by oustees, and many other aspects of the relocation process were greatly assisted by the collaboration between non-government organizations and Nigam officials. In particular, the resettlement process came to rely heavily upon the work of Arch Vahini and another non-government organization, the Anand Niketan Ashram.

Anand Niketan Ashram, whose central figure is Mr. Harivalabh Parikh,

the new, incremental strategy has not secured the results that may have been hope for (see Chapters 7 and 8).
[44] See Ashish Kothari and Shekhar Singh, *The Narmada Valley Project, A Critique*, Delhi: Kalpavriksh, 1988; Baba Amte, *Cry, The Beloved Narmada*, Chandrapur, Maharashtra: Maharogi Sewa Samiti, 1989; Vijay Paranjpye, "High Dams on the Narmada," *Studies in Ecology and Sustainable Development*, No. 3, New Delhi: Indian National Trust for Art and Cultural Heritage, 1990; Pravin Sheth, *Sardar Sarovar Project: Dynamics of Development*, Ahmedabad, Gujarat: Vikas Bharati, 1991.

has used its longstanding connections with villages closest to the Ashram—notably Hanfeshwar and Turkheda, but is well known throughout the Gujarat tribal belt—to encourage acceptance of government policy and to begin the process of land selection, and then to follow up oustees at new sites. The Ashram has also provided material services to oustees: it has contracts with Nigam to supply Gobar gas units (which are made at the Ashram), and has developed a house style for oustees at relocation sites that makes use of earth bricks, also made at the Ashram. By 1992, Anand Niketan was active at some 30 sites—a little under half of those in Gujarat with residential plots. Moreover, Ashram workers are constantly updating oustee lists, seeking to ensure that those they believe to qualify for the benefit package do indeed become officially eligible.

If an oustee family identifies land of its choice, the purchase must be effected and arrangements made for temporary accommodation there. Arch Vahini became integral to this part of the process, working constantly with oustees, potential land sellers, and the Nigam administration to ensure that this is done quickly, accurately, and without corruption; and that ownership documents reach the oustees. Given the rapidly accumulating irregularities in this process up to 1991, Arch Vahini managed to avert potential disaster through their influence over this part of implementation. Like Anand Niketan, it also has been active in design of housing sites and accommodation.

Once oustee families are beginning to relocate, they are entitled to cash support and other benefits. Arch Vahini and Anand Niketan contribute in a vital way to this simply by being the organizations to which oustees go if they have problems. The Nigam is stretched beyond its limits when it comes to meeting the needs of those who have chosen to move.

The contributions made by these non-government organizations could continue. Indeed, in a crucial sense they ought to continue, for rehabilitation, as opposed to resettlement, reaches far into the future. Moreover, this joint government-non-government system is straining under the weight of approximately 4,000 mainly Gurjarati oustee families who have begun to relocate. Without Arch Vahini and Anand Niketan, the process to date would have been little short of disastrous. And a real danger continues: it is one thing to persuade people to move, and to provide them with a house and some land at a resettlement site; it is another thing to ensure their long-term rehabilitation. When we raised this potential for future difficulties with government officials, they assured us that there would be intensive non-government organizational effort to make sure that the policy was a long-term success.

We have referred at length to the work of the non-government organizations because it illustrates the peculiar nature of resettlement and rehabilitation. They are not amenable to the same degree of control that can be applied to technological implementation. Nor can ordinary, bureaucratic structures easily be adapted to the case-by-case, family-by-family, detailed, on-the-ground activity that is needed.

In India there is a strong tradition of participation of non-government organizations in public life. In Gujarat, the birthplace of Mahatma Gandhi, this is especially so. The contributions made by Arch Vahini and the Anand Niketan Ashram draw on the Indian tradition of community and spiritual leadership. Also, in the absence of state welfare, non-government organizations in India have worked at many levels of society, from social services to local economic development. The role of the non-government organizations in the case of Gujarat has been played out against this distinctively Indian background. To recognize this is to help us to see the immense importance of non-government organizations to the implementation of measures designed to mitigate the impacts of the Projects.

But there is a limit to what non-government organizations can achieve. They may be effective at the level of community mobilization and policy design; they may have the ability and experience to shape policies in a way that no one else could; and they may be able to help the process of implementation. But their resources do not allow them to achieve all this for thousands of families spread across several hundred villages. They may be able to gather detailed data for 19 villages; they cannot do this for all the communities or for all aspects of the project, from submergence to the canal to the Shoolpaneshwar Wildlife Sanctuary to the problem of malaria. Nor should they be expected even to attempt so vast an undertaking.

From both the government and the non-government organization point of view, there is a degree of reliance of the one upon the other that can only compromise the best contributions of both. Governments can benefit from criticism and scrutiny by well-informed and independent non-government organizations, and should not be able to relinquish responsibilities to them; non-government organizations that become overburdened with government activities or too deeply integrated into government systems of activity are less likely to achieve their most important task. Neither side should become too dependent on the other.

As well as the help provided by non-government organizations, changes of personnel within the Nigam itself established a much improved administrative atmosphere and process. Land purchase, which we were told had been afflicted by a degree of malpractice, benefitted from new appointments. Mr. Vinod Babbar assumed central responsibility for implementation of resettlement and rehabilitation in 1990; his commitment to achievement of the main policy objectives is recognized on all sides. Mr. Babbar himself told us that his task is daunting, but he takes the view that since 1991 real progress has at last begun to be made.

The pace of relocation in Gujarat has accelerated since 1990. The total number of relocation sites assigned to oustee families at the end of 1989 was 35; by the end of 1991 it had reached 143. Officials told us that the rate of resettlement had been quickened because of directives from the highest levels of the Gujarat Government and pressure from the World Bank. With submergence in both Gujarat and Maharashtra scheduled to begin in 1992-93, the pace of resettlement is also dictated by legal obligations: the Tribunal's 1979 award established that resettlement of a village had to be completed a minimum of six months before its first inundation. These pressures have contributed to speedy, but not necessarily adequate implementation—despite the tireless efforts of non-government organizations. Moreover, resettlement under pressure is liable to spawn a plethora of difficulties on the ground. These difficulties can relate to provision of resources and amenities that are fundamental to oustees' material, social, and medical wellbeing. Given the degree of reliance placed on non-government organizations, who cannot be expected to act in lieu of government, this is a reason for real concern.

SOME CONCLUSIONS

Resettlement and rehabilitation depend on a large number of specific provisions and administrative measures, many of which require administrative skill and integrity. Actual relocation—the moving of houses, possessions, animals, etc.—is a matter of demanding logistics. For people to be able to live at new sites, basic services have to be in place—water and temporary housing being the most important. In the longer term, a range of amenities is important—medical facilities, schooling, bus services, electricity, public buildings (including a *panchayat* or meeting house and temples). All these depend on institutional commitment to making sure oustees get that to which they are entitled, and the essentials for maintenance of their standard of living. All this depends on administrative capacity, flexibility, and continuity.

In the early stages of resettlement, as we shall see in the case of Parveta (see Chapter 7) and as we saw in the case of the rock-filled dyke villages, provision of basic resources and facilities left much to be desired. Not even allocation of the basic two hectares of land was achieved. This was prior to the adoption by Gujarat of its broader policy: at that time, encroachers, landless, and major sons received no land.

After 1988, when Gujarat completed extension of its resettlement policy, the provision of land continued to be beset by difficulties. The burden falling on administrators trying to implement the policy inevitably proved to be onerous. Officials in Gujarat told us that from 1988 to 1990 problems of land acquisition, land allotment, and staff morale within the resettlement division of the

Nigam all combined to create a multitude of difficulties at every stage of the re-settlement process and at virtually all resettlement sites. Discussions with oustees at many of these sites, as has already been suggested in this chapter, revealed the accumulated consequences of these implementation difficulties.

Doubts about Gujarat's readiness and ability to implement an appropriate resettlement policy were expressed, in 1989, by Professor Scudder. Officers at the Bank have told us that his misgivings were considerably reinforced by the limited success of Gujarat's resettlement of oustees from other projects, nota-bly the Medium and Major Irrigation schemes, which between them displaced in excess of 100,000 people, many of them tribals.

Senior officials at the Nigam told us that implementation was indeed com-pounded by many acute difficulties, but that the situation was radically im-proved in 1990-91. This, they said, has been secured by the work of non-government organizations and better staffing in the resettlement and rehabili-tation department of the Nigam. Even with these advances, however, the Nigam resettlement administration is having to cope with an immense load of work—sites are scattered and oustees' needs are many.

Some of the problems derive from the original lack of research and impact assessment. The policies—though extended by Gujarat to include all oustees, and therefore avoiding the major flaws that come from attempts to provide two hectares only to those who have revenue lands—had never been designed with the particular social, economic and cultural needs of the oustees in mind. Hence the hardships caused to oustees by loss of lands for gathering housing materials and other forest produce, firewood, and grazing their animals, along with loss of river resources.

There are social and cultural factors that could well determine the long-term outcome of a resettlement and rehabilitation program. A society's wellbe-ing cannot be reduced to yields per hectare. Indeed, agricultural production is itself dependent on a whole set of social and cultural factors. When people at even the most successful relocation sites raise questions about grazing and pri-vacy, or wonder what will happen when their population grows, or foresee the impossibility of maintaining their traditional houses in new surroundings, they are implicitly, if not explicitly, raising issues of great importance. These are is-sues that might have been raised fully at the early stages of appraisal and plan-ning, if only on the basis of an appreciation of the people having the particular needs and vulnerabilities that arise from their being tribal.[45] They are impor-tant, moreover, because they will in the long run bear directly on people's ma-terial prosperity. But the problems of tribal economic and cultural realities were not built into resettlement policies. Implementation of appropriate miti-gative measures has therefore tended to be an after the fact attempt to deal with problems on a case-by-case basis.

A particular failure of implementation concerns consultation with women. This is not helped by cultural norms (though, according to many anthropologists, women in Bhil society enjoy a higher status than is the case in the wider, Hindu society), and is hindered by language differences. Virtually none of the women in the remoter villages speak official state languages. This was a problem that we encountered in the course of our work in relocation sites and submergence villages. How, under these circumstances, are the concerns and needs of women met? Are there staff who have been trained in tribal languages? Does consultation draw on accumulated understanding and experience of the people's cultures?

Gujarat has indicated that it is prepared to provide resettlement and rehabilitation to all the oustees from Maharashtra and Madhya Pradesh who wish to take advantage of Gujarat's policy measures. This could mean the resettlement and rehabilitation of an additional 15,000 oustee families. There is little basis for concluding that Gujarat would be able to achieve such a task. Moreover, some of the problems of resettlement increase in direct relation to the distance between relocation site and original village. To resettle oustees from Maharashtra and Madhya Pradesh, other than those from the few villages on the border with Gujarat, raises this problem in acute form.

This brings us again to the core problem. Resettlement and rehabilitation have been effected *pari passu*. The best efforts of Gujarat since 1990 have shown that it is possible to get people to move: with the help of committed non-government organizations and hard-working, sensitive officials, there is real efficiency to the process. But the Bank must ask itself how an accelerated process of this kind, supported by neither fundamental planning nor an appropriate time frame, can be said to be consistent with its 1980, 1982, and 1991 operational directives. When the Bank drafted its policy guidelines in the early 1980s, it did not envisage the kind of process that has taken place in Gujarat.

No one can deny that Gujarat has achieved successes in implementation of its policies, and it is properly acclaimed for having extended its policy as per the 1987 and 1988 government resolutions. The provision of irrigated land to the more entrepreneurially minded or market-oriented oustee families could secure a long-term economic basis for their lives. This group seems to us, however, to constitute a minority of the total oustee population in Gujarat. When it comes to the prospects of others affected by the Projects, in the submergence area itself as well as along the canal, serious doubts must arise. Given the history of the process, and the circumstances within which this process continues to take place, the relocation of submergence oustees can no doubt be achieved.

[45] For a discussion of the degree to which this aspect of the problem was minimized or overlooked, see Chapter 5.

As to their rehabilitation, especially with reference to the Bank's 1980 Operational Manual Statement, the 1982 and 1991 policy guidelines vis-à-vis tribal peoples, and the overarching policy principle of the 1985 credit and loan agreements, serious misgivings must remain.

The interior of a house in Manibeli, a village in the Maharashtra submergence zone. The posts and beams are teak. The floor is built up by regular spreading of a mixture of cow dung and mud. Walls are made of woven bamboo. The villagers make their own roof tiles.

Chapter 7
MAHARASHTRA

INTRODUCTION

THE submergence area of Maharashtra lies in the Satpura mountains. Manibeli is the submergence village closest to the dam site, and is immediately adjacent to the Gujarat border. But even its lands are relatively inaccessible; behind the village, forest lands reach up into the hills.

All of the villages in these hills are tribal. Their economies depend on a wide range of resources, including forest and river products, and extensive grazing. Much of the forest land is harvested and grazed on a communal basis, while many agricultural plots are encroached. As is typical of tribal communities in the Narmada valley, the disparity between government administration of land and the people's way of owning and using resources is profound.

The Tribunal's 1979 award did not take these social and economic factors into account when it made its provisions for Maharashtra oustees. The Bank never appraised the kind of information about the tribal people of Maharashtra that could have constituted a basis for policies that would be most likely to mitigate the impacts and compensate for losses caused by the Sardar Sarovar Projects.

Lack of adequate appraisal and failure to take account of people's tribal characteristics have combined to cause a number of fundamental resettlement problems. At the same time, pressure has been, and continues to be, exerted on Maharashtra oustees to take advantage of the relatively more generous terms of Gujarat's resettlement policy. The findings of previous chapters (notably 4, 5, and 6) thus establish the themes for much of what follows here. As we shall see, these include the possibility that a large proportion of Maharashtra oustees—perhaps as many as 80 per cent—are faced with some degree of dispossession as a result of implementation of existing resettlement policies.

POLICY

The most comprehensive statement of policy for Sardar Sarovar by the Government of Maharashtra was published in its 1991 *Master Plan.*[1] General policy objectives were set out, and follow very closely the 1985 credit and loan agreements. Thus:

> The Resettlement Policy of Sardar Sarovar Project PAPS[2] in Maharashtra attempts to substantially improve their living conditions while causing minimum disturbance to their social and ethnic conditions. . . . PAPS must:
>
> (i)   Improve or at least regain the standard of living they were enjoying prior to their displacement.
>
> (ii)   Be relocated as village units, village sections or families in accordance with the PAPS preference, as far as possible.
>
> (iii)   Be fully integrated in the community in which they are resettled.
>
> (iv)   Be provided with the appropriate compensation and adequate social and physical rehabilitation infrastructure including the community services and the other facilities which are normally available under the various development schemes. (p 4)

The specific provisions designed to achieve these policy objectives were set out in Government of Maharashtra resolutions dated June 29, 1989, and February 26, 1992.[3] The latter resolution tried to clarify entitlement to benefits and made minor changes in them. Under the updated 1992 policy, benefits are allocated according to whether oustees are classified as "landed" or "landless."

"Landed" oustees include those who own land "in occupancy rights" and encroachers who encroached prior to March 31, 1978, and whose encroachments were regularized. As in the 1989 Government Resolution, these "landed" oustees are to be allotted a minimum of two hectares of land, as are all joint holders.[4]

It is in regard to "landless" oustees that the 1989 and 1992 Government Resolutions mainly differ; we discuss the probable repercussions of these changes below. Under the 1992 Government Resolution, "landless" oustees

---

[1] *Sardar Sarovar Project: Master Plan for Resettlement & Rehabilitation of Project Affected Persons of Maharashtra State*, Dhule: Office of the Additional Collector, 1991.

[2] "PAP" or "Project-affected person" is a term widely used to mean an oustee family.

[3] Resolution No. RPA-3188/CR-130/88/ R-5, 29 June 1989, and Resolution No. SSP-3192/R&R/ CR-40/R-5, 26 February 1992.

[4] The land will either already be irrigated or the oustee will receive irrigation facilities as a grant-in-aid. A joint holder is someone who shares revenue land with the title holder. In many tribal

include major sons and major unmarried daughters of "landed" oustees (except those recorded as "joint holders"), encroachers who encroached after March 31, 1978 and encroachers whose encroachments were not regularized, landless agricultural laborers, village artisans, and persons engaged in non-agricultural trades and callings. All these will be allotted on a "first come-first served" basis a maximum of one acre of irrigable land *if* it is available near the relocation site and *if* the "landless" oustee moves with other oustees to the re-location site. For those "landless" oustees unable to obtain land under this system, a grant-in-aid is offered "to ensure that they acquire stable means of livelihood so as to improve or at least regain the standard of living that they had prior to their displacement."[5] Major sons of the "landless" still have no status as either "landed" or "landless" and hence do not qualify for any land.

In accordance with the terms of the Narmada Water Disputes Tribunal award all oustees are given the right to choose to relocate in Gujarat or Maharashtra, and receive house plots and resettlement grants. The 1992 resolution established a committee to handle disputes arising under the resolution and made all oustees eligible for an interest-free house-building loan.[6] The 1991 *Master Plan* also outlines an elaborate package of developmental programs (see pp iii, 61, & 145-51). On the basis of these measures, the Maharashtra *Plan* expresses its confidence that: "The resettlement policy in Maharashtra... amply ensures the raising of standards of living of all categories of PAPS..." (p 5).

The 1989 Maharashtra policy was the object of much criticism. The most serious attacks were directed towards definitions of landed and landless and provisions for the landless. It was in response to pressure on these points from the World Bank and non-government organizations that the Government of Maharashtra formulated the 1992 resolution. Under the 1989 Government Resolution major sons were not included as landed or landless oustees and did not qualify for land. Since major sons of landed oustees now have legal status as landless oustees, they may apply, along with all other landless oustees, to receive, on a "first come—first served" basis, one acre of irrigable land.

The available evidence strongly suggests that a majority of the population of the submergence villages will be adversely affected by this policy. The socio-economic realities of the Maharashtra submergence villages mean that the distinction between landed and landless is virtually meaningless. The *Master Plan* concedes that people termed landless have encroached land, making them

families there can be as many as 10 individuals holding revenue land on a shared, co-owning basis.

[5] Resolution No. SSP-3192/R&R/CR-40/R-5, §(9)(b).

[6] It seems reasonable to suppose that, given the discrimination against "landless" oustees under the Maharashtra policy, that group is likely to be more in need of a house-building loan than are the "landed." However, the "landed" are eligible for Rs. 8,000, the "landless" only for Rs. 4,000.

landless only for official purposes (p 10). It records that its oustees are "tribals relying basically on rainfed traditional agriculture ... with hardly any marketable surplus. ... A major portion of lands have been encroached after 1978 thus disqualifying the PAPs from being termed 'Landed PAPS'" (p i).

The artificiality of the distinction between landed and landless is well illustrated by the monitoring and evaluation studies carried out in Maharashtra by the Tata Institute of Social Sciences in Bombay. The studies show that even in the less remote communities of Akkalkuwa there is, in reality, almost no such thing as landlessness. Those who do not hold revenue land are cultivating encroached plots of similar size and making the same use of grazing and other forest resources as those who do have revenue land.[7]

All of the villages of Akrani District are said to be without revenue lands. Major sons of these villagers have no status even as landless oustees and are not entitled to land. That major sons constitute a significant sector of the population is indicated by data collected during implementation in similar villages in Gujarat, where major sons make up between 30 and 50 per cent of oustees.[8]

Whatever the realities of landlessness are on the ground, one acre, even of irrigated land, is widely regarded as a non-viable agricultural holding, and would leave the majority of those defined as landless worse off than they were before displacement, especially if they no longer had access to river and forest products. Furthermore, the number of landless oustees who receive one acre will depend on the land available at relocation sites. There is no policy commitment on the part of the Government of Maharashtra to acquire sites in the future that are large enough to accommodate both landed and landless oustees, even at the level of one-acre plots.

Maharashtra sets great store by its offer of training and employment opportunities for the landless. For those few who are truly landless these may assist rehabilitation. For the vast majority who are only landless under law, but are in fact farmers with both family plots and forest resources, these "opportunities" represent a fall in economic status—from farmer to laborer. The 1984 Narmada Control Authority report on land acquisition and resettlement acknowledged this as a real economic loss, stating that, "For tribals, there is no rehabilitation more effective than providing land as the source of livelihood" (p 66). This same conclusion is expressed in the writings of many who have been engaged with resettlement and rehabilitation of tribal and other isolated

---

[7] Data for Sindori, Bamni, and Manibeli show that holdings of "landed" and encroachers are of the same size. See Tata Report No. 4, June 1989, pp 130-1. See also discussion of Manibeli below.
[8] See Chapter 5 above and Nigam data from their R-1 forms showing performance in resettlement on a monthly basis, December 1991. See also the Maharashtra *Master Plan*, p 123.

agriculturalists or gatherers. It is also noted by several Bank officials.[9] Our considered view is that the existing Maharashtra policy is in fundamental conflict with the 1985 Bank agreements. While adopting the overarching objective from the legal agreement with the Bank, the specific provisions of the policy are not capable of securing that objective.

Some of the consequences of resettlement without measures that take the particular circumstances of tribal and isolated oustees into account caused Gujarat to amend and broaden its policy in 1987 and 1988. The present Gujarat policy evolved by a process of testing specific benefits against the objective of improving or regaining standards of living. If Gujarat extended its policy provisions in order to overcome the probability that under the original provisions many, if not most, oustees would be unable to regain their previous standard of living, then the same objections must be levelled against Maharashtra's policy. By giving equal entitlements to land to revenue landholders, encroachers, and all major sons, Gujarat went a considerable distance towards establishing a basis for compliance with the overarching principle of the 1985 credit and loan agreements. A policy that offers less than Gujarat, while applying to a population with comparable socioeconomic characteristics, is vulnerable to the charge of non-compliance. If Gujarat was right to extend its policy provisions, then Maharashtra is wrong not to have followed suit.

This is not only a matter of logic. Maharashtra oustees are threatened with resettlement conditions that do not meet their needs. However, they do have an alternative. If they elect to resettle in Gujarat, they receive the benefits of its policies. In that case, all encroachers, landless, and major sons would be treated as landed and be allotted two hectares of irrigable land in Gujarat. This discrepancy in the policies of the two states compromises the right of choice between Gujarat and Maharashtra accorded to oustees by the Tribunal's award, the 1985 credit and loan agreements, and Maharashtra's own policy. It is true that the bare right of choice remains, but if the discrepancy in land allocations between the two states makes the difference between an economically viable and non-viable agricultural holding, then the choice is hollow.

Interstate discrepancies in major elements of policy also jeopardize the principle of the 1985 credit and loan agreements that "Oustees shall . . . be relocated as village units, village sections or families in accordance with Oustees' preference" (Schedule 3, 1(ii)). When economic survival of some members of a family or village is in question, unless all move to Gujarat, there is little prospect of fulfilling oustees' preferences as to the size of group that re-

---

[9] These include William Partridge and Michael Baxter, both of whom have immense experience in India.

locates together. Here is a built-in mechanism for fragmenting villages and even families. In this way the Maharashtra policy spawns a cluster of difficulties.

Maharashtra officials told us that it would be very difficult to make any major changes in their policy. They took the view that its provisions were consistent with, and to some extent even improved upon, the Narmada Water Disputes Tribunal's award. They interpreted the statement in the award that "Every major son will be treated as a separate family" (1(3)(ii)) as applying only to the provision of grants and amenities, not to the allotment of land.[10] They also pointed out that they must pay attention to the creation of precedents that could hamper other development projects. One senior official reminded us that his department would be dealing with 200,000 relocating families that year (1991); he compared this with the total of 2,500 families he anticipated would be displaced by Sardar Sarovar. He said that in this regard—as in several others—the administration in Maharashtra was caught in what he referred to as "cross-fire": if they refused to change their policy, the Narmada Bachao Andolan and other critics would insist that people in the Sardar Sarovar submergence zone were badly treated, but if the policy were improved for them, the government would soon be attacked for mistreating families being displaced by other projects.

Maharashtra's justification for its policy rests on the terms of the Tribunal's award and the 1985 credit and loan agreements. We have already pointed out that these were themselves policy principles and measures that arose from a limited set of concerns and an inadequate database. The Tribunal anticipated the resettlement of less than 500 Maharashtra families, and was not in a position to take account of the socioeconomic and cultural information that policy measures require. As a result, important dimensions of the issue are left unaddressed by the Maharashtra policy. It ignores the extent to which special provisions are necessitated by virtue of all the Maharashtra villages being tribal, and some of them being in extremely remote regions. It also overlooks the fact that economic and cultural needs in these villages are met by substantial use of forest resources. And it neglects the possibility that there may be people who will be impacted by the Projects who are not, according to the criteria set out by the Tribunal's award and the 1985 agreements, given any form of compensation.[11] These are lacunae in the policy.

In the Preamble to the 1992 Resolution, the Government of Maharashtra

[10] It is our view that this is a misinterpretation of the award. See Chapter 3 above.

[11] For example, families losing less than 25 per cent of their agricultural land but who are dependent on the submergence area, herders who make seasonal use of submergence land, and merchants who may lose markets.

states that it "has deemed it necessary to amplify and amend" the policy thus far in place "with a view to ensuring speedier and harmonious implementation of the process of resettlement and rehabilitation of the oustees of the Project." This highlights the fact that a major constraint on implementation of resettlement and rehabilitation in Maharashtra lies in the tardiness of the adoption of a policy and development of the *Master Plan*.[12] Senior officials of the Maharashtra Department of Revenue and Forests told us that in order to begin implementing the policy all land ownership records would have to be brought up-to-date. Lands and houses in the first village, Manibeli, may be submerged in 1992. In January of 1992 notices were served on five other villages on the grounds that, in the event of a one-in-one-hundred-year monsoon, they too could experience some submergence. To correct land records requires an immense effort on the ground, by officials who are often reluctant to travel to remote forest villages. Senior officials in Bombay told us: "Two or three years elapsed, and we did not manage to do the necessary surveys." By 1988-89, when they were finally in a position to begin surveying, they could no longer gain access to villages because of intense opposition to relocation. The basic records required for resettlement and compensation do not exist.[13]

World Bank missions suggest that these delays were in part a result of, and at the same time encouraged by, the hope that the majority of Maharashtra oustees would choose to relocate to Gujarat, where they would receive the benefits of irrigation in the command area and the advantages of the Gujarat policy. The deficiency in land records was noticed by the Bank in April/May 1988, the first time a World Bank resettlement and rehabilitation review mission visited Maharashtra. The mission noted "the necessity of updating the oustee survey and land records." Lack of records was not the only problem. Maharashtra still had no resettlement and rehabilitation policy—its 1976 *Resettlement of Displaced Persons Act* did not apply to interstate projects like Sardar Sarovar—and implementation was restricted to encouraging its own oustees to move to Gujarat. The situation in Maharashtra reported by the April/May 1989 review mission resulted in the Bank imposing as a condition for extension of credit for the loan beyond June 1989 that Maharashtra policies

---

[12] The extent of the delays occurring in Maharashtra are indicated, in part, by the requirements of the Tribunal's award. Within 18 months of publication of the award, Maharashtra was required to have told Gujarat the number of families willing to relocate there from Maharashtra (*Final Order and Decision of the Narmada Water Disputes Tribunal*, IV(2)(i) & (iii)). The Tribunal also established the timescale for serving various notices under the *Land Acquisition Act, 1894*. In effect, the Tribunal required that this process be completed by 1983.

[13] The 1991 *Master Plan* states that the Tata Institute has "a separate Computer File on each family containing all relevant information" (p 14). This is puzzling since the Tata Institute team told us they had not done any work in the 24 villages of Akrani.

should meet the requirements of the Tribunal's award and "legal aspects of the Projects." Maharashtra quickly passed the June 1989 government resolution setting out the provisions discussed above.

In response to Bank pressure, the Maharashtra Government created a deputy collector in the Dhule District, with special responsibility for resettlement and rehabilitation. The appointee, Mr. Maninder Gill, has shown immense energy in his dealings with the oustees of the Sardar Sarovar region. Maharashtra has thereby been able to make progress in what are undoubtedly difficult circumstances. It was Mr. Gill, for example, who prepared the *Master Plan*, an impressively detailed account of measures that the government says are being and will be taken to compensate and mitigate the Sardar Sarovar impacts on the 33 Maharashtra villages. He has also managed to negotiate with villagers from Akrani who are amenable to possible relocation in Maharashtra. But the deficiencies embedded in the policy make Mr. Gill's task extremely difficult. In the course of this chapter, as we look at the 33 submergence villages, at what has taken place at Manibeli and Parveta, and consider the circumstances at Taloda, we shall see some of the obstacles that stand in the way of Maharashtra's policy achieving "the raising of standards of living of all categories of PAPs."

AKRANI AND AKKALKUWA

Thirty-three villages in Maharashtra lie in the submergence area, all of them in the remote and hilly land of the Satpura mountains. Sixteen are on the south bank of the Narmada, opposite the Gujarat submergence villages, and 17 on the south bank of the river opposite the first submergence villages of Madhya Pradesh. The villages fall in two different administrative districts, or *talukas*: 24 lie in Akrani, and 9 in Akkalkuwa. The population of these districts is almost entirely tribal, made up of various Bhil groups including Tadvi, Vasava, and Paura.

Since 1987, the Tata Institute of Social Sciences, Bombay, has been doing monitoring and evaluation work under contract to the Government of Maharashtra, in accordance with the World Bank requirement that each state constantly provide information to help assess relocation and rehabilitation processes.[14] The reports of the Tata Institute provide insights into aspects of village social, economic, and cultural life in the nine villages of Akkalkuwa. In particular, their studies of Sinduri and Bamni (completed in 1989), Taloda (1991 and 1992), and Manibeli (completed in 1992) proved extremely valu-

---

[14] Maharashtra is required to perform monitoring and evaluation under the Maharashtra Project Agreement, §2.10.

able to us.[15] However, when Tata Institute fieldworkers were ready to extend their research into Akrani, opposition there to the dam made data gathering impossible.

This means that for about three-quarters of the submergence villages in Maharashtra monitoring and evaluation case studies do not exist. The non-government organization active in the area after 1985, the Narmada Dhangrast Samiti based at Dhule, began detailed house-to-house administration of a questionnaire. But in 1988 this organization joined the Narmada Bachao Andolan, which decided, in August of the same year, to oppose the dam. The Maharashtra non-government organizations took the view that house-to-house data gathering was inappropriate. Having no detailed surveys of its own, the Maharashtra *Master Plan* for resettlement and rehabilitation of oustees has been assembled with the benefit of very limited information.

Also, displacement in Maharashtra thus far has been on a far smaller scale than in Gujarat. There is no equivalent of the Kevadia or the rock-filled dyke villages. Nor has the kind of intensive resettlement effort made in the 14 submergence villages of Gujarat taken place in any communities of Maharashtra—despite the fact that 16 of them share a submergence schedule with the 14 of Gujarat. This means that Maharashtra has not generated statistics as part of a relocation process. There is no equivalent of Gujarat's monthly resettlement up-dates, in which those relocating are classified according to whether they are "landed," "landless," "major son," etc.[16]

Conscious of the fact that for Akrani there are virtually no field data, we decided to visit villages there to assess to what extent they resemble or differ from the case studies of Akkalkuwa carried out by the Tata Institute. The Akrani villages are divisible into two cultural regions. In the center, contiguous with Akkalkuwa villages, the population is predominantly Vasava. The eight villages that lie nearer the Madhya Pradesh border are mainly Paura. The Paura are closely linked to the Ratthwa of Gujarat, and we were told by some experts that they constitute the same people under a different name.

We visited several villages in Akrani. We held a large meeting at Bhusha,

---

[15] The strength of the Tata Institute reports comes from their reliance on intensive field work. Data for the village studies were gathered during four field trips spread across 18 months (see Report No. 4, p 1). The work is guided by social scientists with high academic standards and extensive background anthropological knowledge.

[16] The problem of data in Maharashtra is revealed in the extraordinary disparity between the Tribunal's 1979 estimate of 456 oustee families, on the one hand, and 2,464 given in the Maharashtra 1991 *Master Plan*, on the other hand. The latter is still no more than an approximation; some officials told us that they expect this number to increase to 3,500. Tata Institute researchers, in 1992, estimated the number as 2,784. Critics of the project have insisted that it would reach as much as 5,000. The Narmada Water Disputes Tribunal Award required that complete oustee lists be finalized within 18 months, i.e., by 1981. They are not yet done.

attended by more than 200 villagers, including representatives from other Akrani communities. We also went to Varvali, a Paura village farther downstream. At Bhusha and Varvali, both of which are scheduled for virtually total
submergence, we spoke with many people who told us that they are now in favor of resettling. They showed us their fields, and said that deforestation followed by soil erosion was drastically reducing the productivity of much of their
land. They also described the difficulty of getting sick patients to the nearest
doctor at Dhadgaon some 25 kilometers away.

Some of those who spoke to us at Bhusha told us that they had been prominent activists in the campaign against Sardar Sarovar, but had now come to
the conclusion that the resettlement and rehabilitation process might offer
them an opportunity to secure a better agricultural base. People told us that
they all work some land, and every family appeared to be dependent on agriculture, though they explained that they supplement this with fish from the
river and forest products. When we tried to talk to them about these supple-
ments, however, people said with some passion that they wanted to talk about
land; their lives, they insisted, depend on their agricultural plots. They evidently feared that resettlement might entail landlessness. All the oustees we
spoke to expressed anxiety about Maharashtra's policies, saying they were not
prepared to accept resettlement except on the terms of Gujarat's policy,
though they were intent on staying in Maharashtra.[17] Even among those who
have distanced themselves from the opposition movement, and have become
ready to resettle, the indignation was palpable.

Leaders from Bhusha and adjacent Akrani villages also told us about the
problem of *tapu* lands, those lands that will be surrounded by water but not
submerged. As we travelled through the steep and rugged hills that make Akrani such an inaccessible district, they pointed at valleys where flooding by
Sardar Sarovar will isolate groups of people on headlands and at the foot of
steep hills, causing some hamlets to be almost completely cut off. They showed
us Savardigar, where they said 100 families will be marooned; Bhamana, with
105 families; then Udadia, with 110 families. They also talked to us about
Tinasmal, where a whole village of 60 households will, in their opinion, become a non-viable community.

As we travelled through this terrain, and listened to the kinds of difficulties

---

[17] The Maharashtra *Master Plan* is confusing in the data it gives for Akrani. For Bhusha, Annexure
II gives 131 landholders, no encroachers, and 29 major sons. The number of landholders in all villages of Akrani totals 855. Whereas Annexure XVIII lists no landholders in Akrani district and
855 encroachers. This seeming contradiction may be explained as one of the many consequences
of the basic lack of information at planning stages. Maharashtra officials told us that originally the
government had not realized that the whole of Akrani is "government forest," and hence the
oustees must be encroachers. This provides the basis for oustees' anxieties on this score.

that Akrani leaders anticipate, we could see how a sense of injustice might easily arise. Everywhere the land is steep and fractured, with virtually no roads, and footpaths that depend on stream crossings and access along the lower parts of the valleys. To survey such a place would be an immensely difficult task. Yet to proceed with implementation, or even the design, of policy without detailed and accurate surveys is to invite a plethora of real problems. Officials working from topographical sheets and desktop data are unable to gauge the nature and extent of impacts. The resulting anomalies go to the very foundation of people's social and economic lives. The people of Bhusha, anxious as they are to cooperate with Nigam officials and non-government organization workers who support resettlement and rehabilitation, were bewildered about the apparent unfairness of the process. At every meeting we had with them, they restated their view that a policy that did not recognize everyone as landed, and did not acknowledge the rights of those marooned on *tapu* lands to be given full oustee status, was unacceptable to them.

We also visited villages of Akrani where the people maintain an adamant opposition to Sardar Sarovar, many insisting that they would never relocate. We spoke to people at Bilgaon, Sawarya, Kherdi, Mal, and Junmana. At Kherdi and Mal there was great uncertainty about the extent to which the villages might be affected by submergence. The people of Mal, for example, said that they had originally been told that ten landholders there would be affected, and showed us where the survey had identified fields that would be flooded. They pointed out to us that other fields, at lower elevations, were said to be above the Sardar Sarovar reservoir. They also said, however, that subsequent information had reached them according to which none of the Mal landholders would be affected by the dam. In Kherdi people took us to fields which they had heard were to be submerged, and showed us others, farther down the hills, which were supposedly not to be submerged. In fact, Kherdi, like Mal, is a village high in the Satpura hills, and according to 1988 government data has only one hamlet which will be partially affected, with a total of 12 potential oustees.

People in these Akrani villages asked us what really was going to happen. They said that no officials had ever described to them the possible impacts of the dam. They also expressed anxieties about possible afforestation. All their villages are said to be "forest villages"; all of the families living in them are considered to be encroachers. They feared that the planting of trees in the catchment area of the dam might result in their losing land. In three of the villages, we asked people if they had ever been to the Dhadgaon forestry office, 30 kilometers away, to look at plans. They told us this was something they could not imagine doing.

After leaving the higher villages of Kherdi and Mal, we walked down to

Junmana, a village of 60 households close to the banks of the Narmada. Here we also met with oustees from Shelda, the next Akrani village downstream. People told us about their economic system, describing how they live on a mixture of subsistence farming and gathering, supplemented by the sale of fish and forest produce at Dhadgaon market. They were sure that their lives were far more secure here than they would be at any relocation site, whether in Gujarat or at Taloda, the site in Maharashtra that had been shown to some of them by the government.

We suggested that their fields were suffering the consequences of deforestation and erosion, as the people at Bhusha had reported, and that therefore life in the submergence zone must be unacceptably hard. They would not agree. They pointed out that the supply of fodder, fuel, and fish meant that in any case it was not a question of replacing agricultural plots. They gave us the prices they get for fish, identifying four different species. They explained that they fish all year round, stopping only during the monsoon, when they need to spend all their time preparing their land, or when harvesting. They agreed that their population had increased, some of the elders saying they thought it had trebled in their lifetime. Yet they insisted they were still able to live well on the same resources as had always been available to them. Men and women alike spoke of the mixture of social and economic "freedoms" that they enjoyed. They said, quite simply, they could not imagine leaving their forest and their river.

They agreed that medical and educational facilities were very poor. But this was something they hoped could be corrected in the places they now lived. A woman from Shelda said: "Suddenly the government is so concerned about us, about our health and about our schools. Since they are so concerned, they can make sure we get a doctor and a teacher here."

The villagers' insistence that their economy is strong was endorsed by what we could see for ourselves. At Junmana we saw buffaloes, animals that are kept for milk and which require relatively high quality grazing. The houses were large and well maintained. In their storage lofts were baskets full of grain, and bundles of forest produce. The people looked healthy.

These signs of material wellbeing, reinforced by many indications of cultural strength, were evident in all the Akrani communities we visited, including Bhusha. Indeed, the leader at Bhusha who made a special point of taking us to see some of his land that is suffering from deforestation and erosion, had the largest and best equipped house we saw in any of the tribal villages we visited throughout the Sardar Sarovar submergence zone.[18] In these important re-

---

[18] Our largest meeting in Akrani took place in this house. Without crowding, at least 250 people sat on the floor.

spects, our visit to Akrani is consistent with the descriptions we find in the Tata Institute reports on Sinduri and Bamni, Akkalkuwa villages for which detailed data are available. There appeared to be extensive reliance on forest and river produce, strong cultural ties with the land and an overarching sense of distinct cultural identity.

We noticed during our visits to Akrani villages that Paura leaders were articulate and outspoken, and that their households showed many signs of strong Hindu influence—the most striking, perhaps, is the way in which Paura women observed Hindu conventions.[19] This may explain why some leading families are inclined to look to resettlement and rehabilitation as a way of building on social and economic changes that are already taking place.

The Bhil villagers of the least accessible parts of Akkalkuwa and Akrani, set in the central region of the submergence area of Maharashtra, are being strongly encouraged to consider relocating to Gujarat. Both Nigam officials and the Anand Niketan Ashram have been arranging for truck and bus loads of oustees from these remote villages to visit Gujarat sites. They also arrange for oustees to see the dam site—to persuade them that the project is inevitable and that they must reconcile themselves to being displaced. These tours are a consequence of the policy gap between Maharashtra and Gujarat[20]—the lack of benefits available to oustees under Maharashtra policy is the source of Gujarat's attraction for Maharashtra oustees who might otherwise far prefer to remain in their home state.

These pressures arising from policy differences effectively nullify choice, and in so far as choice is part of the implementation of policy defined in principle by the Tribunal's 1979 award and 1985 credit and loan agreements, can only be said to offend the spirit of the agreements: the oustees' right to choose between Maharashtra and Gujarat for resettlement is compromised.

This recurring problem of policy is inseparable from the associated lack of information. The Tribunal established measures to protect families potentially to be submerged by the Sardar Sarovar reservoir. We have seen that the Tribunal underestimated the total number involved, but it did at least alert others to a potential problem. The Tribunal did not go into the cultural characteristics of the submergence communities, but census returns establish that the villages of the Satpuras are to all intents and purposes 100 per cent tribal. By use of census returns and topographical maps, the basic information about the dam can generate some sense of the scale of the impacts on these tribal com-

---

[19] At Bhusha, the Akrani village where Paura leadership is especially strong, we were told that it was not appropriate for us to ask questions about the women's opinions.
[20] The struggle between the Nigam and Narmada Bachao Andolan to influence the people also contributes to this pressure on people in Maharashtra.

munities. Neither original nor field research was required for the Bank to establish a first measure of the problem; it would have been easy enough to recognize that several thousand tribal people were at risk of being forced to relocate.

Bank policy at the time, 1980 to 1985, directed that careful attention be paid to the impacts of involuntary relocation, especially on tribal populations. Yet no special studies of Maharashtra villages were required by the Bank. The 1983 and 1984 missions conducted by Professor Scudder did not include visits to Maharashtra villages. The Tata Institute work, begun in 1987, gives an indication of the dimensions of the problem. By that time, however, everyone—including Tata research directors—inevitably had to attempt to fit research to the terms of the existing policies, as established by legally binding agreements. We saw for ourselves that in Akrani the implications of policy discrepancies are even more striking than in the case of Akkalkuwa. The entire resettlement and rehabilitation exercise in Maharashtra suggests an *ex post facto* rationalization.

Opposition to Sardar Sarovar has been particularly intense in Maharashtra. Medha Patkar, who in 1988 became the central figure in the Narmada Bachao Andolan, first chose Dhule as a base, and then Akkalkuwa villages. Resistance by villagers to surveyors and other government officials, as well as to Tata Institute field workers, has limited what could be achieved. But this limitation arose only after 1988. Bank policies and principles set out in 1980 and 1982 provided an opportunity to, and indeed, imposed an obligation on the Bank to ensure that appropriate studies were done, especially in the tribal villages of the remoter regions.

On the basis of what we were able to see in the course of our review, and with the help of the Tata Institute reports, a central conclusion is inescapable: the implementation process in Maharashtra fails to comply with both the spirit and the letter of many of the most important of the Bank's own principles.

MANIBELI AND PARVETA

Implementation of resettlement in Maharashtra began in the mid-1980s by moving some oustees from the Akkalkuwa village of Manibeli to a relocation site in Gujarat, near the village of Parveta. As we shall see, the rationale behind the move was to a large degree based on the belief that cultural and economic ties between the people of Manibeli and their neighbors in adjacent regions of Gujarat would facilitate the process. As we shall also see, however, in the early phases of relocation the people were not given a choice between

Gujarat and Maharashtra for relocation, while policy discrepancies subsequently continued to minimize the reality of any such choice.

Manibeli is made up of four hamlets, each of which is composed of a set of related households who trace a common ancestral lineage. According to the oral histories of the lineages, ancestors of the households of two of the hamlets came to Manibeli six generations ago. In fact, migration to Manibeli has been from two different directions—from other parts of Akkalkuwa, the administrative district in which Manibeli is one of nine submergence villages, and from across the river in Gujarat. Akkalkuwa immigrants have for the most part been Vasava, whereas Gujarat immigrants are Tadvi.[21] Each of the two tribal groups acknowledge the other as having a right to clear and cultivate land, which, over the years, has also been extended to men who, unable to pay bride price, have come to live with their wives' families.[22] The Tadvi and Vasava did not permit other groups to farm in Manibeli. Cattle-grazers and temple priests were invited to settle in the village, but "never had the sanction to clear land." Cattle-grazers, although they were invited to take care of the community's animals, "remained landless in the past five generations."[23]

Although the Vasava and Tadvi have shared the village and adjacent resources for several generations, they nonetheless are strictly endogamous: marriage between the two groups is forbidden. Also, Tadvi will take neither food nor drink from Vasava. This concern, often referred to as "*beti* and *roti*," women and bread, is integral to community life in all submergence villages. It has many implications for community functions. Tadvi, for example, have responsibility for preparing food for feasts at which both Vasava and Tadvi are expected to attend. It also has many implications for resettlement and rehabilitation. The two groups have marriage links that lead in different directions, and the "*beti* and *roti*" proscriptions invite the possibility that resettlement for the two sub-communities might follow the apparent divide.

The history of Manibeli also provides understanding of land use and the place of encroachment in the community's economy. Before 1917, Manibeli was part of an estate recognized by the British and known as the *Kathi*. In

---

[21] For these and other details of the evolution of Manibeli community see: Tata Institute of Social Sciences, *Resettlement and Rehabilitation of Manibeli People in Parveta: A Process Report*, Monitoring and Evaluation of Resettlement and Rehabilitation of Sardar Sarovar Project Displaced in Maharashtra, Report No. 16, February 1992, p 3ff.

[22] All the Bhil communities of the submergence area are strongly patrilineal and patrilocal. This means that a woman leaves her father's home on marriage and takes up residence in the home or the hamlet of her husband. This is the basis for concern about marriage circles which is a theme running through monitoring and evaluation reports.

[23] Tata Institute Report No. 16, p 7.

Kathi villages, there were two types of cultivators.[24] One of these was granted permanent occupancy rights and was recorded as a landowner in village records. These were the *kathedars*, and they paid taxes to the estate. The second category of cultivators held land by virtue of an 11-month contract between themselves and *Kathi* chieftains. They paid an annual rent and were entitled to use as much land as could be tilled with two bullocks.[25] These contracts were not recorded, but were negotiated verbally. Both Tadvis and Vasava cultivated their lands under this double system of tenure. Distinctions between revenue land and encroached land did not arise; and everyone had a right to cultivate the forest as their needs dictated.

In 1975 Maharashtra introduced the *Private Forest Acquisition Act*. Through this Act they took possession of the forest lands of the *Kathi* estates, and proceeded to "regularize" land ownership and land use. Under the terms of this Act, all people who had been cultivating lands prior to 1975 were entitled to ownership rights. All land not registered under the Act by 1978, and any land taken into cultivation after that date, would be deemed "encroached." However, the Tata Institute report states that this was "not properly implemented in a large number of cases" (p 7). This was the beginning of an increasing divide between administrative perceptions of ownership on the one hand, and the people's practices on the other. The Tata report notes: "As far as the people were concerned, they owned all the lands they cultivated. But according to the government, the people [held and used] two categories of lands, own[ed] and encroached" (p 7).

Despite the distinction between *kathedars* and contract land owners, the actual area under cultivation differs little between the two. Each Manibeli household cultivates between two and three hectares. Other rights and resources—forest land, grazing, and access to the river—are held in common. In these important respects Manibeli exhibits the characteristics typical of tribal villages of the submergence area. Different Bhil groups share a village, while maintaining a strong sense of cultural distinctions. Within their joint communities resources are distributed and used in ways that establish a broad equality in standards of living.

The Government of Maharashtra is aware of the land use patterns of the people of the submergence villages. Its 1991 *Master Plan* refers to some of the distinctive characteristics of these people. It recognizes that the population is mainly tribal and lives "on rainfed traditional agriculture." And it observes, as we have seen, that "A major portion of lands have been encroached after 1978" (p i). It seems to recognize that these people are bound to be economi-

---

[24] See Tata Institute Report, No. 16, p 6.
[25] The rent was known as *aut*, or "pair of bullocks."

cally worse off under a policy that offers only the possibility of one acre of land in an area with no opportunity for future encroachment to supply the needs of subsequent generations (pp 11 and 15).

The *Master Plan* goes on to say also: "Education standards are dismal and health facilities appalling. Every year there are a number of deaths due to water contamination" (p i). Villagers from Manibeli told us that their educational facilities were limited. We saw for ourselves that communications to the village are difficult, and we were told that they are much worse during the monsoon. On the other hand, Manibeli people told us that they do not have to worry about getting enough food and other things they consider essential, and that they do not feel that their health has been any worse than that of people in other places they have visited. When we asked monitoring and evaluation agency field workers about medical problems in Manibeli and other Maharashtra submergence villages, they told us that the evidence available to them suggested strongly that water-borne diseases constituted a far more serious problem outside the submergence area, in villages higher in the Satpura hills, than in those adjacent to the Narmada. They said that people of the submergence villages tended to be comparatively healthy.

Descriptions of Manibeli are often colored by rival points of view. Those who oppose Sardar Sarovar seek to show the strengths of submergence communities like Manibeli; those who support the Projects emphasize the weaknesses of the villages' social and economic conditions. Such social scientific data as we were able to find, however, and the judgments of the Manibeli oustees who discussed their lives with us, create the impression that Manibeli has been a successful community in the past. The difficulties of isolated village life are real enough, but the urgency that has surrounded resettlement has created a widespread tendency for those who implement the Projects to exaggerate hardships.

Extensive clear cutting of forests in the Manibeli area, after 1975, seems to have been the first indication to people there that Sardar Sarovar was to be developed. In 1980, village leaders were summoned to meetings at which officials told them about the probable submergence of the village. Apparently people were not asked to discuss the implications of this, and there were "no consultations."[26] Between January and July 1981, the first notices under Section 4 of the *Land Acquisition Act* were served in Manibeli, and the first compensation for lands acquired was paid in 1984—though most compensation awards were processed in 1987 and 1988.[27]

---

[26] See Tata Institute Report No. 16, p 12.

[27] Compensation was paid in a single instalment. According to the terms of the policy, 50 per cent was set against the cost to the government of the land allotted to the oustees. Apparently the

Manibeli villagers say that they were bewildered by what they were told about resettlement and were unhappy about the compensation being offered to them. In 1984, amid tension and confusion, the first relocation of Manibeli oustees took place. The problem of major sons and encroachers, along with indignation about the compensation package even for those who were eligible, gave rise to many questions. In their summary of this period of Manibeli history, the Tata monitoring and evaluation researchers note that: "The lower level government personnel had no idea about [what answers to make to] the questions to which people wanted answers. The senior officials were not around to give them the answers" (p 14).

In the first phase of resettlement and rehabilitation (1980 to 1985), the assumption was that Maharashtra oustees would more or less automatically relocate to Gujarat. Although the 1979 award stipulates a right for oustees to choose between Gujarat and their home state, there was no attempt to establish relocation sites in Maharashtra itself at that time.

As early as 1980, degraded forest land near the Gujarat village of Parveta was identified as a possible location for resettlement and rehabilitation of Manibeli oustees. This was an extensive area, allowing the possibility for resettlement of a substantial proportion of Manibeli families, with the possibility of whole hamlets relocating together. Since Parveta is situated in southeast Gujarat, some 35 kilometers from the Narmada, it was thought that relocation there would be within the Tadvi culture area, and therefore facilitate good relations with host villages.

Parveta therefore came to be seen as a site with many possibilities for successful resettlement and rehabilitation, at least for the Manibeli Tadvi. From the start, however, Vasava families of Manibeli were not enthusiastic about Parveta. They had few links with the Gujarat side of theriver. Also, a large proportion of Vasava were encroachers, and did not qualify for an allotment of land in Gujarat at that time.[28]

Of all the Gujarat relocation sites, Parveta is the most studied. This is in part the result of its having been established early. Social scientists with World Bank missions visited the site from 1983 onwards, and researchers from both the Centre for Social Studies, Surat, and the Tata Institute have conducted research among Parveta oustees since 1987. Parveta has also been a focus for

---

people did not realize that this was the case, and it "came to them as a rude shock, when they eventually learned that the GOM [Government of Maharashtra] had transferred this money through its Treasury Office to the GOG [Government of Gujarat] in lieu of the land allotted... according to the NWDT [Narmada Water Disputes Tribunal] provision" (Tata Institute Report No. 16, p 13).

[28] After 1988 the revised Gujarat policy meant that they did qualify, but only for land at a site in Gujarat.

much non-government organizational activity, and has become a place to which visitors are often taken to be shown the various aspects of the rehabilitation process. The Government of Gujarat arranged for our review team to visit Parveta during the first stage of our work in India.

When the first few Manibeli oustees came to Parveta in 1984, land was allotted on a first-come first-served basis. This measure was adopted to encourage oustees to move rapidly, despite the fact that facilities at Parveta for oustee families consisted of temporary shacks, limited water supplies, and no cultivable land. This is now said to have "invoked a feeling of bitterness and relative deprivation among many at Parveta, as well as in Manibeli, and continues today."[29]

The first years at Parveta appear to have been beset by great difficulties. Pumps for drinking water were not kept working and development of infrastructure was slow. People were faced with converting unworked government forest land into fields. Removing stumps and rocks absorbed their energies and resources. The subsistence allowance of Rs. 15 per day for 25 days of each month for their first year at Parveta was insufficient to meet the costs of purchasing food and clearing land. Sixty Manibeli oustees qualified for Parveta land in 1984; by 1990 42 had been given land, but only 18 had managed to start cultivation. A further ten attempted to clear their land, but never succeeded in removing the stumps and rocks. Fourteen had judged the land too intractable to be worth even trying to convert it into arable fields.

Relocation from Manibeli took place in stages. First, a small number of individuals moved to Parveta and began to establish an agricultural base and accommodation. Subsequently, families moved their houses to Parveta and women and children moved out of Manibeli. Where they were able, even oustee families who had moved their houses left one or two family members in Manibeli in order to continue to cultivate their fields there. The relocation process, from first attempts to clear land to moving of houses and household goods, took approximately five years. Those who relocated in 1984 completed the full process by 1989. A second group of oustees began to clear land at Parveta in 1985. Most of these moved their houses by 1990, though a small number continue to spend much of their time at Manibeli. Subsequent groups, who moved in 1986 and 1987, have not all completed the relocation process. In January 1992, there were still 70 houses at Manibeli.[30]

After 1988, when opposition to Sardar Sarovar began to increase in intensity and Manibeli became one of the main centers of activity, relocation of

[29] For a discussion of this process, and some of its consequences, see Tata Institute Report No. 16, pp 16-17.

[30] Nigam estimates put this number at 80 (submission to the Independent Review, April 29, 1992).

oustees to Parveta achieved symbolic importance. Activists urged villagers in the submergence area to oppose the dam, and encouraged them not to relocate. On the other side, Nigam officials and some Gujarat non-government organizations urged them to resettle. Each oustee who accepted land at Parveta was seen to represent a political achievement for the Nigam; oustees who refused land or returned to Manibeli were said to represent the effectiveness of the anti-dam campaign. Inevitably charges of bribery and intimidation flourished in this symbolic tug of war. Oustees' individual preferences and needs could all too easily be obscured by the political storm in which the entire resettlement and rehabilitation program had become engulfed. This storm reached a climax in March 1992, when 38 houses belonging to families who had relocated to Parveta were removed from Manibeli. This was done by a large group of Gujarati oustees (estimated by some to be as many as 400), who—accompanied by government officials, workers from several Gujarat non-government organizations, supporters of the Sardar Sarovar Projects, and protected by several hundred police—after being confronted by Narmada Bachao Andolan activists, moved into Manibeli, and carried out dismantling and removal of house materials.

But resettlement problems at Parveta predate the rise of the anti-dam movement. In 1988, the Tata Institute reported unusually high mortality rates among Manibeli oustees, especially children, for the first years of relocation. Eleven out of 17 deaths were of children less than 4 years old. Their 1992 report, in a reconsideration of the 1988 events, tentatively attributed the deaths to a number of causes:

> Low birth weight and the consequential nutritional deficiency related illnesses and measles seem to have resulted in most of the infant deaths. Life in a very different environment, and poor water quality might have contributed to the deaths. Caloric and protein intake of the Parveta people was relatively low. (p 52)

The Tata Institute 1988 report created a stir. Several Nigam officials referred to its findings with great skepticism when they discussed Parveta with us. The researchers themselves told us that they did not claim to understand all the dimensions of the morbidity rates they noticed, and in any case had great difficulty in putting together benchmark data for the years preceding relocation. But they point to the *ad hoc* character of implementation during the first years at Parveta, and their account of the land and water problems by which the oustees were, in the early stages, bedeviled, is clear enough.

In a memorandum of May 29, 1989, to Michael Baxter, Professor Thayer Scudder wrote of "a very serious deterioration" in relocation and rehabilitation, both vis-à-vis policy and implementation, between 1984 and 1989. He described conditions at Parveta, observing that economic pressures on oustees—in large measure as a result of the intractability of the forest land they were allotted—have caused them to take money from their house compensation in order to deal with the land problem. He noted:

> One result of this is that quality of housing is below that in their village of origin. In this case people who were willing to move early, and hence should be "congratulated," will end up the most indebted. Obviously if they had known the price of government land at the time, they would have opted for purchasing private land.[31]

The evidence strongly suggests, therefore, that the resettlement and rehabilitation policy was not, at least until 1989, implemented in a way to minimize hardship and suffering. The question arises: has the new policy and its implementation, from 1989 to the present, redeemed this set of failures?

We have seen evidence that workers with non-government organizations and Nigam officials have sought to ease difficulties. The Tata Institute 1992 report[32] noted the central role that both government and non-government agencies continue to play at Parveta. Basic services now function well and are keenly appreciated, especially the school. The provision of Gobar gas plants has eased the problem of firewood for a number of families. Income from wage labor, at the dam site and from sugar cane harvesting, has buttressed the agricultural economy. The Tata Institute report also noted that: "Most of the men and women found the productivity potential and actual crop yield of Parveta land, as being superior to the land in Manibeli" (p 38).

But fundamental problems, in both social and economic aspects of life at Parveta, continue. In 1991, 80 per cent of Parveta families borrowed money (between Rs. 1,500 and Rs. 3,000) to buy agricultural inputs and "to meet the shortfall in consumption" (p 47). As a result of people being settled in the Parveta area from other project-affected villages, shortage of grazing land in the area had become acute.[33] The problem has been alleviated in the short term by a reduction in animal herds and conservation of crop stalks for use as fodder. Some have said that this may not have been at too great a cost to the people,

---

[31] Professor Scudder also recalls in this memorandum that in 1985, according to the Government of Gujarat "water supplies were in fact polluted and dysentery present" (p 3, I(2)).

[32] Tata Institute Report No. 16.

[33] 1991 Nigam schedules for relocation show 102 families relocating to Parveta from Gujarat villages, of which 92 are from Gadher and 10 from Vadgam.

though it is an element in the shift towards cash-oriented agricultural economics, which is in turn allied to the debt issue. The consequences of this set of
changes will take some time to reveal themselves.

In conformity with the requirements of the 1985 credit and loan agreements, the monitoring and evaluation team at Surat has been collecting data,
through the use of standard questionnaires, on resettlement and rehabilitation
at relocation sites. Their 1991 report is a survey of five long-term resettlement
sites and includes Parveta.[34] We have reservations about the representativeness
of their findings, since the Parveta results are based on a sample of only 23 respondents out of a total population of approximately 100 families. However, it
can at least give us an indication of the types of problems residents are facing.

All respondents rated Parveta worse than their original village for drinking
water, cremation ground facilities, possibilities for keeping livestock, and opportunities for casual labor. Although forest labor and milk cooperative societies have been set up, only one person among those surveyed had become a
member. Other services that were rated worse by the majority of respondents
included medical and transport facilities. Education facilities were generally
rated higher at Parveta than at villages of origin. The Surat questionnaire also
asked about relations between Parveta oustees and host villagers. They found
that about half of those asked "are yet to develop social relations." The report
observed that the host village is two kilometers away, and that, "The social
groups are also dissimilar. They were quite unknown to each other" (p 47, see
also p 45). This is remarkable given the widespread belief that for the Tadvi of
both Manibeli and Gujarat dam-site villages relocation to Parveta has the immense advantage of being within existing cultural, economic, and marriage
circles.[35] Nonetheless, it is striking that the report's authors, in comparing Parveta with the other four resettlement sites in the survey, conclude that "the
oustees of Parveta are least happy among them all and have many complaints" (p 57).

The 1992 Tata report, based on a large number of interviews and having
given credit for recent improvements, concludes:

> Parveta is a classic example of how a resettlement should not be
> done. . . . People were shifted first and the basic infrastructure
> created later. . . . Land was being cleared for over three years
> which made proper cultivation in the initial years very difficult.

---

[34] *Monitoring & Evaluation of Resettlement And Rehabilitation Programme for Sardar Sarovar (Narmada)
Project*, Report No. 13, April-September 1991.
[35] The survey results indicate that there are probably problems with soil fertility and religious ob-
servance, but the data are too scanty to be conclusive.

At least 15 per cent of the households received lands that were not good for cultivation. Seven years after shifting, these households could cultivate only parts of their land. Those persons who were landless or had their lands under "tapu" condition in Manibeli, were given land five years after they shifted to Parveta, and that too in Lunadra [3 kilometers from Parveta] and Siyadra [10 kilometers from Parveta]. The major sons are being given lands in Lunadra and Siyadra.... The prolonged social and economic disorganization that was created by the ad-hoc resettlement process has had a telling effect on the morbidity and mortality condition of the people. Seven years after the first batch of people left Manibeli, nearly 50 per cent of the households still continue to remain in the village itself. (p 81)

We also received, from Parveta, a submission that expresses women's experience. It is in the form of a letter to our review, and includes (in translation) the following:

The government wanted our land to build Sardar Sarovar Dam and some of our men agreed to move to Parveta village in Gujarat. Since then, we have known only grief and the strain of trying to build our lives in an alien place.

This village, Parveta, is different from Manibeli. Earlier, we lived by the river, and the forest was close by. Our children would take cattle to graze and make them drink from the river. We could go to the forest and get wood. We could catch fish in the river. We got so much else from the forest—bamboo with which to build, fiber to make rope with, food to eat, all kinds of herbs, and animals to hunt. Now all that is gone and we are poor. Here we do not have the forest. Where do we go to get wood, fodder, or fiber? Instead of wood, we have to burn jowar stems. We were used to plenty. Now we have to work all day to gather what was earlier easy to come by....

We now have to pump water for all our cattle and goats. And the pump itself—how can it replace our wide, freely flowing river where we could bathe and wash and drink?...

The soil in Parveta is different from Manibeli. The land here calls for water, fertilizer, and pesticides which we haven't used before. We need money for this, but since we do not have titles to the land, it is hard to get loans.... If we manage to buy all that the land demands, we have to spend much more time in the fields than before, weeding and spraying pesticides several times. . . . Forty households moved from Manibeli to Parveta. In our first year here, we watched 38 of our children die. . . . Now we live far away and, though Parveta is by the road, we cannot go home, because it means spending money for the bus. So only men travel; we cannot. We have to stay in Parveta where our presence is resented by the people who live here from before. We lived in the mountains. Parveta is on the plain and flat so you see everything around. In Manibeli we could defecate when we wanted to; the hills would hide us. This is one of the many freedoms we have left behind. Here we have to wait until dark or rise before dawn.

We have to live here now in this land where we and our children go hungry, even though we get no rest from work. The promise of new wealth lured our men, but we now wish we had stayed behind in Manibeli, among the people and on the land we call our own.

When we visited Parveta ourselves, in October 1991, our hosts there, notably the president of the Gujarat Chamber of Commerce and workers from non-government organizations helping to provide services at the site, told us that all was well. They said that the people at Parveta were all very happy. In subsequent discussions with a Nigam official with extensive experience of Parveta, we were told that it was a relocation site "with no problems." Later in the course of our review a government social worker at Parveta insisted that the community was "free from difficulties."

During our visit to Parveta, the review team divided. While three of us were taken on a tour of various facilities, one member, finding himself surrounded by villagers, asked a number of informal questions about economic conditions there. Several of the older men spoke of their dissatisfaction with the land and many expressed their concern about increasing indebtedness. There was, evidently, a willingness to speak of problems, but this occurred only in an informal setting.

It is perfectly understandable that officials who feel accountable to outside agencies should seek to emphasize their success, and minimize appearance of failure or non-compliance. Yet available evidence on Parveta is overwhelmingly negative. Supporters of the Sardar Sarovar Projects, including Arch Vahini workers and members of other pro-dam non-government organizations, subsequently told us that Parveta was known to be suffering from fundamental problems, which in substantial measure they attributed to the initial choice of land and a policy change in midstream. They also emphasized that implementation at Parveta had presented a succession of difficulties, giving rise to the confusion and improvisation that the Tata Institute report detailed.

Neither the circumstances of resettlement nor the process of rehabilitation at Parveta thus far indicate that people there have achieved a standard of living equal to that which they left behind in their submergence villages. Moreover, in so far as the policy states that this should occur promptly, it is important to point out that the disturbing consequences of the policy and its implementation are noted and emphasized in the Tata Institute 1991 and 1992 monitoring and evaluation reports, seven years after the first Manibeli oustees began to relocate.

Genealogical and household data for three of the four hamlets of Manibeli show that in each there are individuals who qualify for land under the Gujarat policy but have not yet been allotted or have rejected land at Parveta. They total 36, and are for the most part Vasava.[36] Some of those who continue to refuse to accept the resettlement and rehabilitation package that has been offered to them have houses that are threatened by submergence in the 1992 monsoon.[37]

Critics of Sardar Sarovar continue to say that immense pressure is being put on Manibeli oustees to continue the relocation process at Parveta. The Maharashtra Government accepts, meanwhile, that some of those who are directly at risk from the first phase of submergence will not relocate this year. Mr. Gill, the Deputy Collector with special responsibility for resettlement and rehabilitation of Maharashtra oustees, has said that he will provide temporary accommodation on high ground above Manibeli and a flood warning system. Those who remain will thus be offered some degree of government protection. Yet the evidence available to us on conditions at Parveta, and the special difficulties the Vasava of Manibeli anticipate as concomitants of relocation there, do not provide encouragement to remaining Manibeli oustees to have faith in rehabilitation at Parveta.

Forced relocation cannot be achieved without human costs. The objectives of a resettlement and rehabilitation policy center first and foremost on the attempt to minimize these costs. The case of Manibeli and Parveta reveals the problems that arise from a policy that has not been developed with careful attention to the needs of the affected populations. Implementation has been unable to overcome policy deficiencies. Yet we find that, in the interests of

---

[36] Based on genealogical tables for the Patilpada, Vavipada, and Sarpanchpada, updated in January 1992. The numbers include those who, in 1991, returned land allotted to them at Parveta.

[37] In a letter to the Bank, Mr M. A. Chitale, Secretary to the Government of India, Ministry of Water Resources, noted that there will be "no permanent submergence of agricultural lands or houses in Manibeli during 1992. The temporary submergence in Maharashtra may extend only to six villages even if a flood of 1 in 100 year frequency impinges during the monsoon period of 1992" (Letter of February 25, 1992, p 1).

pressing forward with the Projects, the conclusions reached by Professor Scudder, the Centre for Social Studies at Surat, and the Tata Institute, in 1989, 1991, and 1992 respectively, have been obscured by protestations of optimism, while Gujarat has repeatedly been commended by the Bank for its progress in resettlement and rehabilitation. Implementation that disregards uncomfortable conclusions is hardly consistent with the tenets of World Bank policy. Worse still is the escalating probability that the first Maharashtra oustees to resettle will suffer a long-term reduction in wellbeing.

TALODA FOREST

Maharashtra oustees who relocated to Parveta were offered no alternative site in Maharashtra itself. The 1984 Narmada Control Authority land acquisition report noted that: "At present there is no such land [i.e., irrigable] available which can be offered to the oustees" (p 31). This represents a failure to comply with policy requirements laid down by both the Tribunal award in 1979 and the credit and loan agreements in 1985. Cultural links between Maharashtra Tadvi and Gujarat may help explain, or even justify, this deficiency. But all except two of Maharashtra's submergence villages are inhabited by Vasava, Nayak, and Paura, most of whom have marital and economic ties in Maharashtra. The principles by which resettlement and rehabilitation are supposed to be guided required that sites for them be found in Maharashtra itself.

Between 1985 and 1988, critics of resettlement and rehabilitation in Maharashtra concentrated on the need to locate suitable sites within Maharashtra. A non-government organization working in the villages, Narmada Dhangrast Samiti, repeatedly insisted that successful resettlement and rehabilitation depended upon provision of forest land. A growing understanding of market links and marriage circles of the Akkalkuwa villages, especially with the findings of the first monitoring and evaluation reports of the Tata Institute, invited the conclusion that relocation should be to areas contiguous with the Satpura hills.

Bank missions went to Maharashtra in October and December 1988, by which time opposition to Sardar Sarovar had reached intense proportions in Maharashtra. This opposition was centered in the Akkalkuwa and Akrani submergence communities. In 1989, the formal mission report described inaction on the part of Maharashtra vis-à-vis both policy and "a clear strategy" for resettlement. The mission attributed this to activists' success in persuading oustees not to cooperate with the government. The 1989 mission concluded, however, that the situation in Maharashtra was "not unredeemable."

The hope was that the situation would be redeemed by lands being released for resettlement in the Taloda area, a forested region at the southern edge of the Satpura hills. In order to show the difference Taloda would make to implementation of resettlement and rehabilitation in Maharashtra, the November/December 1990 mission reported that 150 Maharashtra oustees had indicated their readiness to accept land there. Six months later, the April/May 1991 Bank mission estimated the number of willing oustees as 36. Nonetheless, the Bank maintained its pressure on Maharashtra and the Government of India to make the necessary forest available for relocation sites at Taloda.

Release of such forest requires clearance by the Ministry of Environment and Forests of the Government of India and cabinet-level approval. In 1990, the Cabinet made the necessary exemption and 2,700 hectares became available for Sardar Sarovar oustees. A proviso was attached to this release requiring that other lands in Maharashtra must be afforested by way of compensation. The terms of the release insisted, moreover, that this afforestation must come first. Then Taloda could be cut. The Maharashtra Government, however, decided to fell 16 hectares of Taloda forest in order to establish a first Taloda resettlement site. This was done in defiance of the clearance requirements set out by the Ministry of Environment and Forests. Senior Maharashtra officials told us that they were determined to establish credibility for their resettlement and rehabilitation program, and therefore felt they had no choice but to press ahead.

Supporters of Sardar Sarovar welcomed the release of Taloda Forest land as a major breakthrough for implementation in Maharashtra. However, critics of the Projects—including some who had previously insisted that forest was the only acceptable basis for resettlement—denounced the release of forest land, deeming it to be environmentally unacceptable. Nor did work at the Taloda site overcome opposition in the villages. The November/December 1990 Bank mission reported very strong hostility in Maharashtra; the April/May 1991 mission was told not to go to Maharashtra at all.

The dispute over Taloda came to center on three questions. Was the forest area released large enough? Was it already occupied by encroachers and herders of the Taloda host villages? Were the cultural links between the oustees for whom it was intended and the people already in the region likely to facilitate the integration of the oustee resettlement population? Maharashtra and Nigam officials told us that the answer to all the three questions was reassuring, saying that the area could accommodate a sizable proportion of oustees' land requirements, that the forest was encroached only to a very limited extent, and that cultural ties between oustee and host communities would greatly help the resettlement and rehabilitation process.

In 1991, the Tata Institute monitoring and evaluation team completed a report on the Taloda Forest.[38] This report looked at the suitability of the region for the resettlement of Vasava oustees, and the compatibility of the cultures of host and oustee populations. The report goes some distance towards answering the hotly disputed questions about Taloda. It notes that "the host and oustees belong to the same tribal group i.e., the Bhils." And it observes that many of their customs and rituals are "very similar" (p 54). On the other hand, it concludes that agricultural practices and dietary habits of the two communities differ sharply, and warns that "the quantity and quality of food items could diminish seriously . . . if care is not taken to ensure proper R and R [resettlement and rehabilitation]" (p 54). They also note that the "overall nutrition status of the oustees" was better than that of the hosts. But in a concluding section, the report states that "resettlement and rehabilitation could be a smooth process if undertaken with sincerity, care and devotion" (p 58).

These optimistic conclusions are to some extent offset by the report's prediction that resettlement would "put tremendous pressure on the forest resources." There is also a caution that availability of grazing is a potential source of conflict (p 29). The authors note: "People who are living in unauthorized villages and cultivating encroached land in Taloda are being displaced from the land. The process of their eviction is currently under way." The report also warns about waterlogging during the monsoon, and observes that "the quality of the soil is uncertain." The authors say: "It is evident that under these circumstances, the new settlers will almost certainly have to face a host of problems, most of them unpredictable, in the initial years."[39]

During the course of our review we made two visits to Taloda. We saw the first stages of site preparation, and met with a small number of oustees who were spending time there, some of whom had accepted land. During our second visit to Taloda, we met with a group of oustees who were staying at temporary accommodation on the site, most of whom did not qualify as "landed," and had not been allotted any agricultural land.[40] These people had come to Taloda in the hope of finding wage labor opportunities.

The situation at Taloda seemed to be severely compromised by the policy

---

[38] *Resettlement in the Taloda Forest Area, A Study of the Area and its Inhabitants*, Report No. 14, May 1991.

[39] See pp 23-9 and p 56. See p 63 for a map showing locations of 10 villages in or adjacent to Taloda Forest and the basis for an estimate of 3,800 people who are already grazing animals there. See pp 31-2 for concerns about prospective indebtedness and inescapable cultural loss.

[40] At the time we visited (before February 1992) only "landless agricultural laborers" were entitled to 1 acre and then only if they moved with other (presumably) "landed" oustees. The June 29, 1989, Government Resolution does not say anything about post-1978 encroachments, therefore it could be that the people we met did not qualify for any allotment of land. On the other hand, the *Master Plan* states that "though there is no agriculture land provision, the post 1978 encroachers would be treated as landless and hence entitled to 1 acre of irrigated agricultural land" (p 15). This is confusing on paper and may well be a source of confusion to oustees.

limitations. Since all of the Akrani submergence communities are identified as "forest villages," none of their oustees qualify for two hectares of land at Taloda.[41] Rather, as "landless," they are eligible to apply for one acre and the various benefits for employment and rehabilitation identified in the 1991 Maharashtra *Master Plan*. Since they reject this policy package, very few Maharashtra oustees stay at Taloda even temporarily. Thus the issue of policy looms large.

In the course of our second visit to Taloda, we met with a number of people at Chhoti Somaval, the host village closest to the resettlement site that is being developed. They told us that they were indeed concerned about recognition of their encroached lands, but said that they were not unduly alarmed by the prospect of a resettlement site being established in an adjacent village.[42] These findings appear to contradict the conclusion arrived at by the Tata Institute research team. However, their work is more extensive, and took them to all 10 of the villages directly at risk as a result of use of Taloda Forest for resettlement sites. Moreover, in visiting remoter villages, the Tata Institute team met with families who are far more dependent on encroached lands and forest produce than is the case with Chhoti Somaval, which is an accessible community.

The issue of implementation is addressed in a second Tata Institute report on Taloda Forest land.[43] This study is based on additional field work, and is a reassessment of the prospects for resettlement and rehabilitation at Taloda sites by the authors of the 1991 report. They consider the three contentious issues—the size of the available land, the nature of its prior occupation, and the cultural links between oustee and host communities.

The second Tata report points out that the number of families to be resettled in Taloda is still not known. Tata's own work in Akrani has been curtailed as a result of the non-cooperation of the opponents of the dam. They say that if the terms of the Gujarat policy were to be available in Maharashtra, they estimate the number of families entitled to two-hectares plots of land at 2,784. Of these, they say that 400 Tadvi families can be expected to settle in Gujarat. The remaining 2,384 families could elect to resettle in Maharashtra. This would create a need for 4,768 hectares (pp 18-19). On the assumption that something like 2,700 hectares of forest is available for agriculture at Taloda, this creates a potential shortfall in agricultural land of approximately 2,000

---

[41] Despite contradictions in the *Master Plan* on the status of Akrani oustees, government officials to whom we spoke confirmed that none of these oustees qualify as "landed."

[42] Ironically, people at Chhoti Somaval expressed as their first and foremost concern the regularizing of 47 one-acre encroached plots. They said this had been promised to them in 1957.

[43] Parasuraman, Rao, and Kumar, *Issues on the Resettlement of Displaced People in the Taloda Forest Land*, February 1992.

hectares. Further land would also be needed for house plots and community facilities.

In fact, this amount of land would not be required if Maharashtra does not alter its resettlement and rehabilitation policy to match Gujarat's. But even if only some of the oustee families receive land, the other families would still be entitled to house plots in the forest. The Tata report calculates that this could mean as many as 13,000 people will be seeking to make use of resources there, be it agricultural, grazing, or forest products and firewood (p 20). Some of the people we spoke with at Chhoti Somaval expressed concern about losing their forest, saying "there is no other grazing land." They also spoke of the loss of the flowers and fruit of the *mahua* tree, from which they make valuable liquor and oil.

This raises the question of prior occupation. The second (1992) Tata report estimates that the 10 villages now in the Taloda Forest area depend upon 800 hectares of the Forest for grazing and firewood.[44] They say that this underestimates the pressure on the land being allotted to oustees, for it does not take into account villages on the periphery of the Forest, which also make use of its resources (p 70). They state, both in their 1991 report and in submissions to our review, that large numbers of encroachers have already been displaced to make way for resettlement needs. The 1992 Tata report says that encroachers there "have been threatened, abused, their cattle and firewood seized by the authorities; they have been prevented from digging wells...." (p 18).

This leads us to the issue of cultural links between host villages and potential oustee immigrants. The 1992 report notes that, "The host population is completely set against the proposed rehabilitation" (p 17). It gives as the main reason for this the problems of pressure on the Taloda Forest resources and the fate of host encroachers. But it also takes issue with the view (endorsed by their own 1991 findings) that resettlement and rehabilitation in Taloda will be facilitated by virtue of the close cultural links between the Bhil populations of the two regions. In fact, in a 1992 discussion of the Bhils of the region, Dr. Rao argues that the links between the Vasava of the submergence area and the Bhil sub-groups of Taloda are ambiguous.[45] The 1992 report observes that "smooth interaction between the displaced and hosts cannot be guaranteed." It refers to tensions that already exist between encroacher and revenue villages in the

---

[44] The 1991 Report includes a map showing six villages within the Taloda Forest boundary and four at its periphery. The total population for the six villages within the boundary is given as 1,832; and for the four at the periphery, 2,411 (p 63).

[45] Dr. Nandini Rao, "The Bhils," 1992. Her conclusion to this paper is to the effect that resettlement of the Akrani and Akkalkuwa Vasava is likely to fracture their "traditional patterns of land ownership...and rights over the forest" and will therefore "result in indebtedness, bonded labor and finally migration to the urban areas" (p 26).

Taloda area as an indication of the kind of difficulty that can arise. It also notes that Taloda groups reflect a strong Hindu influence, exemplified by a refusal "to acknowledge that they eat meat," whereas the Vasava of the submergence area readily acknowledge that meat is part of their diet (p 4). The danger for the Bhil who relocate is that they will, once they find themselves in a more Hindu setting, be accorded low status in the hierarchal caste-type arrangements.[46]

Some of the concerns raised by the Tata Institute 1992 report are being addressed by Nigam officials. In February 1992, an additional 1,000 acres of agricultural land was identified for resettlement close to Taloda in Gujarat. This has been earmarked for Maharashtra oustees. Also, Nigam and Anand Niketan Ashram workers have been collaborating in an attempt to get more Akkalkuwa families to select land at Gujarat sites. Most important of all, perhaps, a new people's organization centered in the farthest villages of Akrani has declared its readiness to relocate. These people told us that they were eager to get land in Taloda Forest. Yet they insisted that the first and essential condition for their resettling at Taloda consisted in their being offered the same benefits as contained in the Gujarat policy.

This brings us back to the overriding difficulty. If the Maharashtra policy is fundamentally unacceptable, in that its measures are such as to leave many oustees worse off than they were, then no implementation package or process that aims to put it into effect will achieve adequate rehabilitation. This concern overshadows the problems at Taloda itself, but there is strong evidence to suggest that these may in any event be severe.

SOME CONCLUSIONS

Maharashtra committed itself, in its 1989 policy for Sardar Sarovar oustees and its 1991 *Master Plan*, to the overarching principle of resettlement and rehabilitation policy. Oustees must be at least as well off after relocating as they were in their original villages.

But the effect of Maharashtra's resettlement policy is that a large proportion of its oustees are deemed to be landless. In the case of Akrani, all the villages are said to be "forest" villages, and to have no revenue lands. In the case of Akkalkuwa, families who have been cultivating land for many years—

---

[46] On p 22 of their 1992 report, the authors also direct attention towards the environmental impacts of resettlement at Taloda; these all flow from the intense pressure that would result on all forest resources, including those that accompany encroachment by families displaced from the forest—thus spreading environmental impacts and forest clearance beyond the perimeter of the Taloda site itself.

perhaps for generations—but who do not have revenue land are also deemed to be encroachers. Encroachers are landless according to the policy, and qualify for a maximum of one acre of land. For them resettlement means a drastic reduction in their resources.

No one in Maharashtra is entitled to compensation for loss of forest resources. These are government lands, and cannot be part of that which is compensated under the policy. Yet every family in the Maharashtra submergence area is heavily dependent on the forest. Every household has animals that graze, including substantial herds of goats. All families gather firewood for cooking. Most families gather fruits and vegetables, roots and medicinal herbs for daily use. Many people gather leaves and fruits that they can sell in nearby markets. All these things come from the forest.

The Narmada River plays an important part in people's daily lives, economically as well as spiritually. Many families depend heavily on fish for food. All oustees who relocate to sites far from the river—and this, at the moment, means all Maharashtra oustees—lose access to this resource.

According to monitoring and evaluation research in Maharashtra villages, the yield from the forest and river represents up to 60 per cent of daily nutrition. This immensely important component of the people's economy is under-reported in virtually all assessments of oustees' wellbeing, and is not considered in determining their compensation. This is an indirect result of policy having been formulated in the absence of comprehensive socioeconomic analysis. By the time any research into Maharashtra tribal life was done, the policy was set. For all who are resettled away from the forest and river, or with reduced access to forest, resettlement brings a substantial contraction of resources.

Within the extended family major sons play an important economic role. Many major sons are in reality householders in their own right: because revenue records tend to be chronically out of date and inaccurate, land can be recorded in the name of a father who has long since passed on most of the property to his sons, or may even have died. This means that major sons, who are not recognized as separate families for the purpose of compensation, stand to lose their status as landholders. Under Maharashtra policy major sons of the landed are only entitled to one acre of land on a first-come-first-served basis; major sons of the landless are not entitled to any. For both, their primary means of livelihood is in jeopardy.

The answer that Maharashtra policy makes to these limitations on land available to oustees lies in plans for alternative sources of income. These are set out in great detail in the 1991 *Master Plan*. But for isolated communities with strong links with the land, and whose inhabitants have few if any of the skills that might make it possible to take good advantage of alternative employment options, the reality is a shift from farmer/gatherer to landless laborer. This shift, in the context of rural India in general and tribal society in particular, is experienced as an economic disaster. It is for this reason that the Government of India's guidelines on displaced tribals notes that "for tribals there is no rehabilitation more effective than providing them with land as the source of livelihood. . . . it must be ensured that some land is provided so that the family is not completely uprooted from its traditional occupation;. . . ."[47] Worldwide experience of resettlement has shown that most who experience forced relocation suffer a drop in their standard of living. This is a stark and widespread reality. Provision of a land base has been welcomed as a breakthrough in overcoming this problem; the belief that the Tribunal award of 1979 and the Gujarat expanded policies of 1987-88 were providing land for land caused these measures to be hailed as unprecedented achievements.

Oustees who relocate to Gujarat can avoid some, but not all, of the potential losses. Relocation sites in Gujarat are far from the river, and do not offer forest or adequate grazing; arable plots are the only compensation under any policy for loss of land. Even in Gujarat there is no compensation for loss of non-arable sectors of the economy. Nonetheless, the Gujarat policy is considerably more generous than its Maharashtra counterpart. An Akrani family with two major sons would get less than one-half hectare in Maharashtra; the same family would get six hectares in Gujarat. This restricts the right to choice. It exists as a technical reality: oustees can *choose*. But they must choose between very different packages.

Those who have made the choice in favor of Gujarat, notably by relocating to Parveta, have not had an easy time. Parveta has been, in the words of the Tata Institute assessment, "a model of how resettlement should not be done." Pressure is now mounting—through the efforts of the Anand Niketan Ashram, Nigam officials, and Arch Vahini workers—on villages in Akkalkuwa and Akrani to consider a move to Gujarat. Some are reconsidering their earlier refusals. They told us that the dam is inevitable, and that they must do something to escape from places that are to be flooded. These people do not look upon resettlement as a development opportunity.

Taloda Forest sites have been welcomed as achievement of a resettlement option in forest lands close to the submergence area, and therefore the basis for a new standard of implementation. People in Akrani told us again and again that Taloda may be acceptable, but only if relocation is according to the terms of the Gujarat policy. Maharashtra policy—even with its 1992 amendments—does not come near to offering the same benefits. And even if it did, the fact

---

[47] Cited in the 1984 Narmada Control Authority report *Land Acquisition and Rehabilitation of Oustees*, pp 66-7.

that the Taloda Forest is already serving the needs of many people creates uncertainty about just how well it can accommodate oustees without causing secondary displacement. Reports of people there being forced off forest plots raise serious doubts.

Since 1988, the Maharashtra submergence area has been a center of opposition to Sardar Sarovar. As a result, government officials' access to the communities has been extremely restricted. This has impeded consultation, gathering of information, and surveying. The *Master Plan* was prepared during this difficult period. But the gathering of information and preparation of resettlement plans should have taken place long before 1988, and in fact was required by Bank policy as a precondition for appraisal in 1983-84. In any event, the preparation of a *Master Plan* at a time when consultation with villagers, and even visits to villages, are all but impossible means that there is a real danger that its provisions are not informed by the affected people's points of view or even their needs.

Thus we find that the Maharashtra policy is not consistent with the requirements of Bank policy, and its implementation reveals immense shortcomings. These are grave deficiencies. In our view, they cannot be put right through *ad hoc* improvisation. Officials have sought to design a resettlement and rehabilitation package, and have worked tirelessly on the ground to achieve the best possible results. But their efforts are cramped by the policy by which their efforts are shaped. The conditions in Maharashtra reveal the continuing need for full assessment of the Projects, consultation with affected people, and a reconsideration of their real economic and cultural needs. On that basis a policy could be shaped to meet the Bank's overarching principles and objectives. In the absence of such procedures, the Bank's directives are flouted and its objectives rendered very unlikely of achievement.

A pulse crop growing in the Nimad region of Madhya Pradesh, widely known for its fertile soils and productive agriculture.

INTRODUCTION

THE Sardar Sarovar reservoir potentially affects two different regions of Madhya Pradesh. The plains of the Nimad, at the eastern end of anticipated submergence, are occupied by peasant villages composed of many caste and tribal groups. The hills of the Vindhya range, where the Narmada becomes the border between Madhya Pradesh and Maharashtra, and where Madhya Pradesh and Gujarat meet, have long been the isolated lands of Bhil and Bhilala communities.

This difference in geographical and cultural settings has many implications for resettlement and rehabilitation. These implications have not found their way into either policy or implementation plans, for they were not the subject of any studies prior to either the Tribunal's 1979 award or the 1985 credit and loan agreements. As we found in the case of Maharashtra, the themes of this chapter are largely shaped by an absence of fundamental data. When we come to Madhya Pradesh, we discover that the problems generated by absence of knowledge have been aggravated by a pervasive tendency for project planners not to consult with the people at risk. A host of speculations and uncertainties have arisen amongst villagers about who will be affected, how great the effects will be, and what compensation they are entitled to. Many people expressed to us deep skepticism about the reliability of surveys, and distrusted what they had heard about the extent of backwater effects.

Lack of information about the people of the submergence area has meant that the implications of relocation for tribal groups have received minimal attention. In particular, compensation is seen as an issue that centers on revenue lands, whereas tribal economies of Madhya Pradesh are dependent on forest, river resources, and encroached plots, in addition to revenue land. In the Nimad, many peasant villages have sizable populations of fishing families. Barely any data about the fishing economy of Madhya Pradesh oustee families appear to have been collected, and they appear largely to have been left out of compensation calculations.

Of the three riparian states, Madhya Pradesh is likely to experience the most severe impacts as a result of the Sardar Sarovar Projects. Submergence will displace at least twice as many families as in the other two states combined. Moreover, flooding in the Nimad affects low-lying, fertile lands that are intensively farmed and that already benefit from an elaborate irrigation system. On the other hand, Madhya Pradesh is not a direct beneficiary of Sardar Sarovar irrigation—the Projects' command area is all within Gujarat (with the exception of a small extension into Rajasthan).

Madhya Pradesh's implementation of resettlement and rehabilitation for Sardar Sarovar has been a source of considerable disquiet within the Bank since the earliest missions. This chapter focuses on the sources of this disquiet, and on how plausible or otherwise implementation plans in Madhya Pradesh have now become. Behind this issue lie the broader ones of project appraisal and tribal people's distinctive interests and rights (see Chapters 4 and 5). Although these have already been discussed, parts of the argument are necessarily reiterated here.

POLICY

In 1985 the Madhya Pradesh Government enacted its own, statewide legislation for the resettlement of people displaced by any public utility project (*Madhya Pradesh Project Displaced Persons (Resettlement) Act*). This Act sets out a resettlement process that begins with assessment of the extent of lands to be acquired and a census of persons to be displaced (Section 12), requires assessment of land available for resettlement and stipulates that these lands be in "the benefit [i.e., command] area of other projects in the vicinity" (Sections 3 & 14), and establishes a principle to the effect that all displaced persons "shall be resettled by allotment of irrigated land . . ." (Section 18).

The 1985 Madhya Pradesh resettlement statute has been described, even by the government's critics, as "a highly progressive and egalitarian piece of legislation."[1] By combining the terms of this act with the requirements of the Tribunal's award, Madhya Pradesh effected a policy package for Narmada projects. In 1987 the Government of Madhya Pradesh approved a policy for Narmada Sagar oustees. In 1989 this was revised and extended to Sardar

---

[1] M. N. Nadkarni, submission to the Independent Review, 1991, Part 3, §1.

Sarovar oustees in Madhya Pradesh. This 1989 revised policy, along with sub-sequent amendments, is included as Annexure III of Madhya Pradesh's most recent policy statement, the *Action Plan* of January 1992.[2]

Madhya Pradesh endorses the four main objectives of the 1985 credit and loan agreements and the terms of the Narmada Water Disputes Tribunal's award. The policy detailed in the *Action Plan* spells out the overarching principle: "The aim of the State Government is that all displaced families as defined hereinafter, would, after their relocation and resettlement improve, or at least regain, their previous standard of living within a reasonable time" (A.1.a.)[3] It lists 14 "Broad Principles for Rehabilitation of Displaced Families," with which the specific terms of the policy do not always concur. Its definition of "displaced person" is more restrictive than the Tribunal award's definition of "oustee," in that to qualify an oustee must have cultivated land for at least three years prior to notification under Section 4 of the *Land Acquisition Act*, rather than one year as specified by the Tribunal. The Madhya Pradesh policy defines "landless" as only those who have no land for agriculture, so that encroachers and major sons are not "landless." However, these definitions are misleading since encroachers and major sons are not entitled to the same benefits under the policy as revenue landholders. Only revenue landholders are entitled to land on resettlement.

The policy provides that "displaced families" with legal title to their land (according to government land records) will receive compensation for the land acquired from them and be allotted a minimum of two hectares of land. If it is not irrigated, they will receive assistance with irrigation. If it is deemed unirrigable, they will receive a minimum of four hectares. Compensation for those who are not submerged but whose land or houses become inaccessible by being surrounded by water will be considered on a case-by-case basis.

Encroachers who encroached prior to April 4, 1987, will receive compensation for the land acquired from them and will be allotted a minimum of one hectare and a maximum of two hectares of land, even if more than two hectares was acquired from the encroacher. No mention is made of irrigation nor of the means of establishing the date of encroachment.[4]

Land will not be allotted to major sons, encroachers who encroached after 1987, or the "landless." Special benefits for the "landless" (to which major

---

[2] *Sardar Sarovar Project: Action Plan of Rehabilitation & Resettlement of Oustees of Madhya Pradesh*, January 1992.

[3] The wording of the 1985 credit and loan agreements is "promptly," not "within a reasonable time."

[4] In a letter to the Bank, Mr. Chitale, Secretary to the Minister of Water Resources, says: "The State Governments had formalized the dates [prior to which encroachments had to have been established] to discourage farther encroachments on Government lands" (February 25, 1992).

sons are also entitled) include occupational training and a three-year income supplement grant.

All "displaced families" are entitled to a house plot and in some cases a house grant; free transport to the relocation site for themselves and their goods; a rehabilitation grant of Rs. 6,400 for landless agricultural laborers, Scheduled Tribes, Scheduled Castes, and small and marginal farmers, and Rs. 3,200 for the landed. Civic amenities are to be provided at least to the minimum level stipulated by the Tribunal's award.

The overall effect of this policy is that encroachers and major sons, who are agriculturalists on lands they regard as their own, are threatened with dispossession.

The Madhya Pradesh policy differs only in detail from that of Maharashtra, and several of our misgivings about it are therefore the same. Any policy that distinguishes between "landed" and "encroachers" in the allotment of land is likely to leave encroachers with a reduced standard of living after relocation, and hence is incompatible with the overarching principle by which all displaced families are at least to regain their previous standard of living. From figures given in the *Action Plan* for 161 of the 193 submergence villages it appears that encroachers represent a much smaller proportion of oustees than in Gujarat or Maharashtra. However, in isolated tribal areas, where some 40 Madhya Pradesh submergence villages are situated, encroachment is integral to people's economic lives. Failure to recognize encroachers' rights is therefore a matter of central importance. Even in the villages of the fertile agricultural areas of the Nimad, many people told us they had small plots of encroached land.

The fact that encroachers are entitled to some land if they encroached prior to April 1987 ignores the realities of tribal life. We were told that proof of encroachment could be established by producing receipts for fines paid to forest guards. Without knowing of their future usefulness, it is unlikely that anyone would save such documents. Given that encroachers are for the most part tribals and illiterate, there is even less likelihood of their having kept them for five years.[5]

In general, policy distinctions of the kind made in the Tribunal's award and the Madhya Pradesh provisions rely heavily on the accuracy and appropriateness of revenue records. Yet much evidence presented to us indicated that in Madhya Pradesh, as elsewhere, these records of ownership tend to be

---

[5] In his letter of February 25, 1992, to the Bank, Mr Chitale outlines an appeal process "for resolving disputes regarding the claims for being considered as landed oustees etc." (p 6). But this letter reaffirms the basic classifications of oustees, or displaced persons, used by both Maharashtra and Madhya Pradesh policies.

out of date and provide an inadequate picture of current land ownership. Several years can elapse between change of actual ownership and the recording of such change at the *patvari* (record keeper and revenue assessor) level. Also, recorded transfers tend to pertain to land sales, whereas in the villages themselves, land changes hands between generations or is partitioned among members of extended families. These are transfers that sometimes go unrecorded, often for generations. Moreover, in particularly remote regions (for example, in the hills of Alirajpur *tehsil* of Madhya Pradesh) fields beyond easy travelling distance have simply gone unregistered.

In a discussion of this issue in relation to tribal communities of Madhya Pradesh, Amita Baviskar concludes that: "The classification of land utilization had lacunae that worked against poor people, for much of the land that they cultivated was not recognized as legally theirs."[6] Given the historical and cultural realities of Madhya Pradesh, the terms of its policy for encroachers, major sons, and "landless" oustees are deficient.

Major sons, who are not entitled to any land under the Madhya Pradesh policy, probably comprise about 40 per cent of total oustee families.[7] As in Maharashtra, the discrepancy between Madhya Pradesh and Gujarat in these items of policy is likely to limit the freedom of major sons and encroachers to choose to stay in Madhya Pradesh rather than migrate to Gujarat, and to promote fragmentation of families and villages.

A major difference between Madhya Pradesh and the other two states is that approximately 140 of the 193 submergence villages in Madhya Pradesh are situated in the fertile agricultural belt of the Nimad where a large proportion of the population is made up of agricultural laborers. These are people who, by going to Gujarat, would receive substantially greater benefits than if they remain. But many of them told us they want to stay in Madhya Pradesh; they feel strongly attached both to the lands where they now work and to the social structure that supports them.

Concern about both Madhya Pradesh policy and the nature of its implementation has been raised repeatedly by World Bank missions. The first resettlement and rehabilitation review mission in 1985 reported that Madhya Pradesh officials were saying that all oustees would go to Gujarat. This ap-

---

[6] Amita Baviskar, submission to the Independent Review on land ownership, p 1. This submission also provides details of the ratio between revenue and encroached land for five families in Anjanvada, a Bhilala village in the Alirajpur *tehsil*. In all but one case, encroached land is larger than revenue land by a factor of between 20 and 80 per cent (p 2).

[7] The *Action Plan* gives figures for 161 villages which show major sons as 7,619 out of a total of 16,618 oustee families, i.e. 45.8 per cent. Figures for Gujarat that have come from the implementation process in the 14 submergence villages show a similar ratio of major sons to total oustee population.

peared to compromise the requirement that they should have a choice in the matter. The April/May 1988 review mission observed that Madhya Pradesh, when it came to implementation, appeared to have done nothing.[8] The April/May 1989 review mission was told by the Government of Madhya Pradesh not to go into the submergence region because of opposition there to the project. The formal mission report noted that Madhya Pradesh was unable to make progress with resettlement because of the non-cooperation of its oustees. But it also noted that a central problem in resettlement and rehabilitation included the lack of policy in Madhya Pradesh.

The December 1989 mission reported that Madhya Pradesh's data on oustee numbers and preferences were "impressive." In the light of what we have learned, the mission's finding in this regard is implausible. In May 1990, the review mission was again told not to make Madhya Pradesh field visits because of the increase in opposition to the Projects. This mission also noted that 44 oustees had now accepted land in Gujarat, and observed the beginnings of action on previous World Bank recommendations, notably with regard to preparation of plans. In November/December 1990, the Bank mission team encountered such fierce opposition in Madhya Pradesh that their visit had to be cut short. They reported that very little progress had been made in Madhya Pradesh, and laid down seven conditions for extension of the credit closing date past June 1991. The mission noted the persistence of major problems related to Madhya Pradesh's continued insistence that a majority of its oustees would resettle in Gujarat and to resettlement and rehabilitation policy weaknesses.

The 1991 April/May review mission observed that there was now greater commitment towards resettlement and rehabilitation on the part of the Madhya Pradesh government, and remarked on a positive development, namely that the Government of Madhya Pradesh had begun to recognize that a significant number of oustees was likely to resettle within the state. This mission also noted that the continuing problems in Madhya Pradesh included a failure to finalize the oustee list and the need to harmonize its policy provisions with those of Gujarat. In August 1991, Michael Baxter visited Madhya Pradesh again. His mission report characterized progress in Madhya Pradesh as "disappointing," the situation as "very serious," and the resettlement and rehabilitation organization as virtually dysfunctional.

The November/December 1991 review sought to be optimistic, and noted "signs of progress" including a determination by the Madhya Pradesh government to undertake preparatory work for resettlement and rehabilitation, though sometimes with police protection. It also noted that land purchase

[8] Abdul Salam, submission to the Independent Review, 1992, p 6.

committees had been set up, and had received offers for the sale of approximately 250 hectares of private land. This mission recommended that the policies of Madhya Pradesh should be reviewed and adjusted to ensure that these meet the overall objectives of resettlement and rehabilitation as per Schedule 3 of the credit and loan agreements.

Mr. Baxter and Mr. Salam told us that after 1989 the Bank sought to nudge Madhya Pradesh policy forwards, hoping that by insisting on a limited number of conditions that were "realistic"—that is, stood some chance of being acceptable to Madhya Pradesh—progress on both policy and implementation would eventually be secured.

Mr. Salam characterizes this as the Bank's mechanistic approach to the issue, and has expressed considerable skepticism about its ability to achieve any real success. In a submission to our review, he states that the 1991 mission recommendations could only raise serious doubts about the Bank's strategy. He wrote: ". . . the recommendations are, in their way, an indirect admission of the Bank's failure—the failure of its mechanistic approach to R&R management, an admission that a series of disparate, disjointed actions do not lead anywhere, but only create an illusion of hectic activity and postpone the day of reckoning."[9]

Several Bank officials, on the other hand, have defended the piecemeal approach the Bank had taken. They also took the view that Madhya Pradesh's wish to secure loans for its Narmada Sagar Project would influence the eventual outcome. He believed that a combination of cajoling and warning of suspension of the loan would effect a change in Madhya Pradesh policy of the kind that would result in its oustees receiving benefits, in the short term and the long term, sought for them by the Bank.

In the final stages of our work in India, we held a number of discussions with Madhya Pradesh Government officials, in which we raised the issue of the adequacy of the state's resettlement and rehabilitation policies. They told us that they regarded their policies as more generous than anything anticipated in the Tribunal's 1979 award. They also pointed out, as had the Government of Maharashtra, that whatever measures were established for Sardar Sarovar oustees would have to be provided to other Madhya Pradesh project-

---

[9] These recommendations were that (1) the resettlement and rehabilitation policies of Madhya Pradesh and Maharashtra should be reviewed and adjusted to ensure that they meet the overall objectives of resettlement and rehabilitation; (2) the feasibility of establishing a single multi-state resettlement and rehabilitation agency separate from the construction agency should be considered; (3) the plans being prepared by each state and the Narmada Control Authority should be the basis of progress monitoring, and all plans should be discussed with affected people so that their suggestions could be taken into account; and (4) each state should prepare comprehensive development plans for reservoir rim villages.

affected persons. In particular, they told us their central concern was Narmada Sagar, as it presents a potential oustee problem larger than Sardar Sarovar. They repeatedly told us that given the size of the state and the large number of projects it anticipates, an over-generous settlement in the case of Sardar Sarovar could cause an escalation of costs of other developments that would raise questions about their financial viability. Officials also took the view that policy questions are a matter of state jurisdiction, and should not be the object of World Bank "conditionalities." These are understandable points of view, but there remains the issue of inconsistency between the provisions of Madhya Pradesh policy and the overarching principle of the credit and loan agreements.

The policy and its implementation have legally binding objectives—the resettlement and rehabilitation of oustees must give them (*inter alia*) the choice between Gujarat and Madhya Pradesh, the opportunity to relocate as whole communities or families, and must ensure that they do not suffer a drop in their standard of living. Failure to achieve these objectives because of Madhya Pradesh's insistence on policies that are legally deficient and fly in the face of realities in the submergence villages is a matter of real concern. The Bank has hitherto chosen to believe that eventually these policy problems are amenable to piecemeal adjustment. It is our view that the problems are long standing and, in several regards, fundamental. They undermine the possibility of oustees being resettled in a way that will ensure they do not suffer a loss in standard of living and quality of life. They create a real possibility that the devastating experiences of oustees in other projects, in Madhya Pradesh and elsewhere, will be repeated. This is precisely what the Bank, since 1980, has established as the outcome to be avoided.

The problems of Madhya Pradesh reveal the consequences, for the oustees and others impacted by Sardar Sarovar Projects, of the Bank's failure to follow its own guidelines and appraisal procedures. It seems reasonable to suppose that if the Bank had examined social and cultural realities in the Madhya Pradesh villages, and had assessed the actual social, cultural, and economic impacts, discussions of policy there would have followed a very different course—one which perhaps would have more effectively protected the rights of those who live in the Madhya Pradesh submergence area.

THE 193 VILLAGES

The people of the Nimad are prosperous. The communities of this wide, fertile valley are large, close together, include sizable market towns, are linked by good roads, and are provided with all the educational and medical facilities that would be normal in rural India. Of the 193 villages in Madhya Pradesh said to be affected by Sardar Sarovar submergence, some 140 lie in this area. The populations of these 140 villages are a mixture of caste and tribal groups. For the most part the larger landowners are members of Non-Scheduled Castes, while those who own small plots and live primarily by labor are members of Scheduled Tribes (Bhil and Bhilala) or *harijans* (Scheduled Castes). Implementation of the Sardar Sarovar Projects bears differently on each of these groups.

In a submission to our review, Amita Baviskar offers insight into the people of the Nimad. She says:

> The fertile plains of Nimad were settled in the last century by Kanbi-Patidars from Gujarat. The emergence of the Patidars as the dominant land-owning caste which, with the encouragement of the British, grew cash crops, coincided with the creation of a class of marginal farmers and landless laborers which included Bhils and Bhilalas in its ranks. Living within a system of occupational specialization closely matched by caste divisions, Bhils and Bhilalas have become more and more assimilated into the caste system, so that, in the plains, they are even described as a caste.[10]

The complexity of the caste system in the Nimad region of Madhya Pradesh is revealed in a study done by the Indian anthropologist Jayanta Sarkar, who lists the caste and tribal communities in two villages.[11] In each case the people ranked each social group in hierarchical order, giving 18 castes in one village and 13 in another, two of which were tribal.

In recent years, farmers of the Nimad have installed a plethora of irrigation pumps with a network of pipelines reaching as far as five kilometers from the river. This was made possible by the gradual electrification of the region in the early 1970s. As a result, landholders with two to five hectares can grow three crops a year, including chilies, cotton, papayas, bananas, sugar cane—produce with high market values. When we traveled in the Nimad, people showed us their abundant crops, their herds of milk cows in stalls, their stacks of cotton ready to be taken to market. We saw for ourselves whole sections of villages turned red by a blanket of chilies spread to dry, and we were handed baskets of bananas and tomatoes to take away with us as evidence of the land's fertility. In many villages we talked with farmers who have accumulated large hold-

[10] Amita Baviskar, "The Bhils and Bhilalas of the SSP Submergence Zone," submission to the Independent Review, 1992, p 3.
[11] *Social Mobility in Tribal Madhya Pradesh*, Delhi: B. R. Publishing Corporation, 1986, pp 22-3.

ings. We visited families who told us they farmed 20 to 30 hectares, and employed as many as 30 to 40 permanent farm workers. This region is a part of what might be called mainstream India.

Implementation of the Projects, in these circumstances, carries a particular developmental burden. If people are to be as well off after relocating as they were in their original communities, the level of services and facilities found in the Nimad must be reproduced for both the landowning and laborer groups. It should also be noted, however, that people's lives are not guided—especially in the tribal and Scheduled Caste communities—by an attachment to profit rather than to place. On the contrary, we were told repeatedly, in many of the villages we visited, of the spiritual and social meanings of the river itself. In fact, the Narmada has immense spiritual importance for many Hindus. We were told about riverside rituals that the women conduct at dawn of every new moon. The name of the river—Narmada—literally means "giver of bliss." Born of the body of Lord Shiva, every stone on her bed is said to be a miniature *Shivalinga*, an object worthy of worship. The people who live along the banks often claim the Narmada to be more sacred than the Ganga. They relate a Hindu proverb that says, "as wood is cut with a saw, so at the sight of the holy Narmada do a man's sins fall away." Local legends aver that Ganga herself must dip in the Narmada once a year. According to many, to die on the banks of the Narmada is to be granted a place in heaven.

There are thousands of devotional songs, *bhajans*, in praise of the Narmada in Marathi and Gujarati as well as in Hindi. They are sung in temples throughout the valley. Many of them speak of the mother's power to help her children in times of trouble. One of these songs is sung in full (it is said to have several thousand verses!) in the village of Koteshwar during the monsoon. People from neighboring villages gather for this event.

It is not surprising, therefore, that we had glimpses of the deep anxiety that the thought of moving away from the Narmada causes in the minds of the people of the area. Many identify with the river as a source of religious strength. They also see their communities on its banks as essential to their material security. Again and again the men and women of landless families expressed to us their reliance upon a place in community life. They have secure working relationships with particular landowners. They have small plots—some encroached, others in the river drawdown—or grazing on government lands. They also make extensive use of the fishery. Indeed, in the Nimad we saw and heard more evidence of both subsistence and market fishing than anywhere else in the submergence zone. In one village we counted 27 fishing boats. In several others we were told that many households depend exclusively on fishing. This social placing of landless workers, and reliance on local resources other than revenue lands, means that even in villages where a large proportion of the population is landless, there is profound fear about what will happen to them if they are forced to relocate. People attribute their economic security to a long-established web of human and geographical links within their community.

The prosperous farmers, many of whom are well educated and have connections with members of the professional and political groups of the region, are competent to use the *Land Acquisition Act* process to ensure that compensation for their lost lands is not minimized, although in so far as they work areas of land over and above the state ceilings they are at some economic risk. The Scheduled Tribe and Scheduled Caste families, a large proportion of whom are not literate and whose land is not recorded in government records, are more vulnerable. Their sense of security comes from occupying a particular place in an integrated network of laborer-landowner relationships, which is threatened by resettlement processes.

As the river flows downstream, the plains of Nimad give way to the hills of Alirajpur. Here the river flows through high and fractured land, the hills and forests of the Satpuras and Vindhyas that have long been the tribal lands of the region. In the submergence villages of this part of Madhya Pradesh we met with Bhils and Bhilalas, who live far from markets and whose geographical isolation has played an important part in enabling them to live at the very edge of or beyond the modern state. Periodically, successive administrations have intruded in order to deal with people farming encroached land by recognizing them as revenue landowners. But for all the reasons we noted when speaking of Maharashtra, access was limited by administrative and geographical difficulties. Thus, great disparities developed between what was registered in the Land Record Office and what existed in tribal reality.[12]

Visiting these isolated and strongly traditional villages, we realized something of the complexity and texture of these cultures. In submissions to our review, anthropologists have helped us to understand some of these in greater detail. It is clear that there are many features of these communities that bear directly on the impacts that construction of the Sardar Sarovar dam would be likely to cause. But we must acknowledge that we have only learned enough to appreciate that a great deal more needs to be understood if policy design and implementation are to be successful.

Between 1986 and 1989, World Bank mission reports repeatedly called for baseline data to be compiled for the Madhya Pradesh submergence villages. Failure to collect this information was tantamount, in the opinion of many Bank officials, to a failure of implementation and therefore an aspect of non-

---

[12] Amita Baviskar provided the details for this process in Madhya Pradesh on the basis of her intensive field work in Anjanvada.

compliance with agreements. Notwithstanding state government analyses that suggest numbers are lower than might have been supposed, more families in Madhya Pradesh anticipate displacement and relocation by the Sardar Sarovar reservoir than in the two other states combined.

The scale of the displacement in Madhya Pradesh, alongside the immediate intention to relocate large numbers of oustees by 1993, are measures of the need for comprehensive detailed data. In fact, Madhya Pradesh's 1992 *Action Plan* is based on a household survey, often known as the 64- or 66-point survey because of the number of its columns. Madhya Pradesh officials told us that this had been completed in 165 of the submergence villages, and would soon be ready for all 193.

Many questions were raised in the course of our inquiry about the reliability of this survey. It was carried out in recent years, when opposition to the dam in Madhya Pradesh villages was intense. Opposition included refusal to cooperate with officials, and non-compliance with any information-gathering exercise. Activists in Madhya Pradesh insisted that very few villages had allowed surveys to be done house to house. This is to some extent confirmed by the Madhya Pradesh monitoring and evaluation reports in their frequent references to difficulties of gathering data. They speak of the "non-cooperative and often violent attitude of the people belonging to these badly affected villages,"[13] and state that: "The path of data collection in submerging villages is now not an easy going task. Many times, point blank they refuse to give any information to us."[14] The 1989 and 1990 reports speak of the same problem and describe the devices and even deceptions that monitoring and evaluation field workers have adopted in order to elicit proper information. These tactics, they report, include posing as anti-dam activists themselves, and, generally, finding every possible way of establishing that they are not government officials. These unfortunate circumstances obviously cast some doubt over any claim on the part of government that reliable house-to-house survey work has been completed in the submergence villages.

Researchers familiar with data gathering in Madhya Pradesh and government officials told us that a large amount of information can be gathered by a "desktop" procedure. By this they mean that discussions with local officials and well-informed individuals from selected communities can achieve a more or less adequate completion of questionnaire forms. This may well result in useful approximations, and an initial basis for assessing the scale of the prob-

---

[13] Doctor Hari Singh Gour University, Sagar, *Monitoring and Evaluation*, Bi-Annual Report, September 1991.
[14] Doctor Hari Singh Gour University, Sagar, *Monitoring and Evaluation*, Bi-Annual Report, March 1991.

lem. At the individual level—which is what ultimately counts for the oustee families themselves—"desktop" data gathering cannot be adequate.

In its September 1991 report, the Doctor Hari Singh Gour University monitoring and evaluation team provided a brief critique of the 64-point survey. They note "the area of discrepancy in the description between the government record and our own observation" (pp 265ff). They expressed their findings and concern at a case-by-case level, giving the names of persons who are on the lists but not resident in the villages, or said to be resident but who are no longer alive, etc. They also compare the findings of the 64-point survey with land acquisition notices issued by the collector in a number of villages. Here they find large numbers of discrepancies. For three villages, the person-by-person listing of affected lands recorded by the 64- point survey is at odds with land acquisition and revenue records—the survey omits some oustees entirely and sometimes misrepresents the size of lands by a factor of two or more.

The monitoring and evaluation reports of the Doctor Hari Singh Gour University do not fill the gap left by the tardiness and deficiencies of the Madhya Pradesh Government data. They seek to establish the basis for monitoring resettlement and rehabilitation; they are not designed to underpin an action plan.

It is obvious that in a large area of uneven topography flooding and associated displacement of people will vary considerably throughout the region. The Government of Madhya Pradesh and the monitoring and evaluation team concur on the extent to which each village will be affected. They told us that 79 villages will suffer inundation of more than 10 per cent of their lands.[15] They argue that in the more level lands of the Nimad, farthest from the dam site, it will be mainly house sites, rather than land, that will be submerged. In the heavily tribal areas—Alirajpur, Kukshi, and Badwani—villages are more severely affected.[16] Of the 79 communities that are expected to suffer extensive inundation, 76 are in these three areas. The first 17 villages to be submerged according to the Madhya Pradesh government *Action Plan* schedules are all in Kukshi or Alirajpur, with tribal populations of 42 per cent and 90 per cent respectively.[17] The flooding of the first, Akadia, is anticipated for the monsoon of

---

[15] Details of this estimate are set out in: Doctor Hari Singh Gour University, Sagar, *Monitoring and Evaluation*, Bi-Annual Report, September, 1991. See also our discussion of probable increased backwater effects upstream of the dam as a result of sedimentation (Chapter 12).

[16] This is true even if the exact numbers given by the monitoring and evaluation report are not correct.

[17] According to data prepared by Amita Baviskar for our review, Scheduled Tribes as a percentage of total oustees in the other Madhya Pradesh *tehsils* is as follows: Badwani 60%, Manavar 21%, Thikri 24%, Dharampuri 9%, Kasravad 15%.

1994-95, followed by 16 more in the monsoon of 1995-96.[18]

Because of the unreliability of government statistics, we asked anthropologists and others who know Madhya Pradesh well about landholdings there. Those who have given us submissions state that, as in Gujarat, there is virtually no landlessness in the tribal communities of Alirajpur and Kukshi, whereas in the caste villages of the Khargone and Dhar districts significant percentages (up to 50 per cent) of village populations are laborers on others' farms. Even in these cases, we were told—both by social scientists and villagers themselves—that very few people are absolutely landless: most farm laborer families have either a small private plot, access to public grazing land, or drawdown agriculture on the river bed.

Despite the absence of precise numbers, the vital importance of the policy issue to the people of these villages is clear. Madhya Pradesh officials confirm this. They have estimated that approximately 50 per cent of oustee families will move to Gujarat, but that this 50 per cent will need 23,000 hectares of resettlement land; the 50 per cent staying in Madhya Pradesh are expected to require only 2,000 hectares (*Action Plan*, Part I, Annexure v). When explaining these numbers, senior officials said that their estimates are based on two assumptions: first, families losing houses but not land, or very small proportions of their land, are likely to wish to stay close to home; second, since those who settle in Gujarat will do so under the terms of the Gujarat policy, those losing lands would "naturally" (the word chosen by both the Deputy Chairman and Director of Rehabilitation and Resettlement at the Narmada Valley Development Authority) opt for Gujarat rather than Madhya Pradesh.

In fact, since late 1990 some 400 families have relocated to sites in Gujarat. Families from Bhawati, a village in Badwani *tehsil*, have chosen land at Gutal, and are spending some proportion of their time in tin sheds there.[19] A group of families also moved from Sondul to Morkhala, while people from Jalsindhi and Akadia, villages in the Jhabua district, have moved to Gaulagambi and Suriya. Akadia and Jalsindhi are both villages in the first phase of Madhya Pradesh submergence, but Bhawati and Sondul appear on the submergence schedules for the year 1996-97. Professor Gouraha, head of Doctor Hari Singh

---

[18] The villages in order of submergence, according to a map of all villages in the Sardar Sarovar area given to us by the Nigam, are as follows: (1) Akadia, (2) Sirkhedi, (3) Anjanvada, (4) Jalsindhi, (5) Bara Amba, (6) Dub Khadha, (7) Khundi, (8) Sakarja, (9) Kakarsela, (10) Chikalda, (11) Chameli, (12) Jhandana, (13) Sugat, (14) Bhitada, (15) Roligaon, (16) Kukadia, (17) Temla.

[19] Tin sheds have been used as temporary accommodation at virtually all relocation sites—sometimes for as long as three years. The sheds are unsightly, not suited to the climate, and have been the object of much criticism. However, many oustees need accommodation that can be locked up when they are away, and they anticipate making use of the tin in future as housing for animals. Oustees' opinion about them is divided.

Gour University Monitoring and Evaluation Unit, told us that relocation from Bhawati and Sondul has been a direct result of "landless" persons seeking benefits in Gujarat. Unfortunately, we do not have detailed data for these villages that can confirm or qualify this statement.

It is important to note here that workers of the Anand Niketan Ashram and Nigam officials have sought to speed up resettlement to Gujarat from Madhya Pradesh. Groups of oustees have been bused around Gujarat sites and encouraged to choose land there and then. Monitoring and evaluation reports (see especially March 31, 1991) indicate that oustee families from eight villages have inspected land in Gujarat at at least 15 different sites. Also, by spring 1991, Gujarat had identified at least 30 other villages where private land could be acquired for Madhya Pradesh oustees, with a total of some 1,500 hectares of agricultural land being available. In this way, Madhya Pradesh resettlement takes advantage of the Gujarat process, in particular the energy and thoroughness of that state's Land Purchase Committee. At that time (1990-91) no equivalent provisions were being offered in Madhya Pradesh; both the policy and the implementation of the first stage thus constituted a direct pressure on large numbers of families to move to Gujarat.

We discussed this issue with officials at every level of the Madhya Pradesh government that has responsibility for resettlement. We were told repeatedly of the problems they have encountered with resistance at the village level, and they assured us that they had time on their side: the resistance was beginning to decline, they said, and submergence was still a minimum of two years away. They continue to reassure: the surveys will be completed; those who do and do not wish to move to Gujarat will have a chance to make their preferences known; alternative sites will be identified for both land and house sites.

We visited many villages in both the Nimad and the tribal areas of Alirajpur and Kukshi. We held small meetings with one or two families in their homes, in villages that could be reached only by walking many hours. We had discussions with groups of women, in both tribal and mixed caste communities. We talked to individuals as we walked along the river. And we were invited to meetings where more than a thousand villagers had gathered to see us. Sometimes as we were travelling, we would find the road blocked by crowds of people, who, having been told that we were coming, wanted to make sure we saw their fields and villages and heard their points of view. Also, we visited several places where Madhya Pradesh resettlement and rehabilitation officials have begun to establish new house sites. And for three of these sites, we visited the submergence villages, from which it is intended that people will relocate.

Virtually everywhere we went in Madhya Pradesh people in or close to the submergence zone gave us to understand that they felt badly treated by the entire resettlement and rehabilitation process. They told us that there had been virtually no consultation. This is borne out by a 1987 report on consultation prepared by the Multiple Action Research Group, which stated:

> Even more pertinent is the total illegality of the whole operation [of notification]. Section 4 of the Land Acquisition Act 1894 (and its successor 1984) requires that the occupier must be given a notice that his land is likely to be required for a public purpose. Only after giving the notice can any work of surveying, soil testing etc. be done on that land. Admittedly the notice does not have to be served individually in Madhya Pradesh. (In Maharashtra it is necessary to do so.) But what sort of a public notice is it, if no one, not even the Patil, has seen it? What sort of democracy is it if the stone markers are implanted with indifference and silence at best and callous secrecy at worst? *No where in the valley did we meet anyone who had actually seen a public notice or had it read out to him.*[20] [emphasis in original]

In villages with close to 100 per cent illiteracy we found that the only information about submergence schedules and land acquisition had come in the form of posters put up in market towns as much as a whole day's walk away, or on cards sent to families through the post. Knowledge about policy, including discrepancies between Gujarat's and Madhya Pradesh's provisions, seemed to have come from non-government organization workers. Since many of these are intent on stopping Sardar Sarovar, information that they share with villagers cannot be said to constitute a positive aspect of implementation.

Officials told us that their access to submergence villages had been very limited since 1988. We have already discussed the implications of this for the database. The implications for consultation are commensurate.

Some of the Doctor Hari Singh Gour University monitoring and evaluation reports take the view that there are many families in the Madhya Pradesh submergence zone, particularly in the more remote tribal villages and among the poorest of landless laborers in the Nimad, who would be happy to take advantage of resettlement and rehabilitation. But the reports also indicate that the terms under which such resettlement could work for them are, in many regards, very different from anything that is being set out in the Madhya Pradesh policy. The early reports, notably a study of Kakarana, indict the process and the provisions of the policy alike. One report calls for construction of

---

[20] Multiple Action Research Group, *Sardar Sarovar Oustees in Madhya Pradesh: What do they know?* (3), Barwani, Madhya Pradesh, 1987, p ii.

Sardar Sarovar to stop until an adequate policy is designed.[21] Another report, which analyzes land use in a tribal village, concludes that pastoralism is at least as important as arable agriculture, and takes the view that on average each family requires 19 hectares of land.[22] A thrust of the early work of the Doctor Hari Singh Gour University monitoring and evaluation program is towards a fundamental reappraisal of Madhya Pradesh policy. Discussions we had with Professor Gouraha confirmed this impression. He emphasized the extent to which oustees had many good reasons to maintain extreme skepticism about both policies and their implementation.

When we visited Madhya Pradesh in October 1991, government officials there told us that their plans were well advanced, and that despite difficulties over access to submergence villages they foresaw no real obstacle to successful resettlement and rehabilitation. When we visited submergence villages in Madhya Pradesh in October and then again in December we saw no sign of progress in any aspect of resettlement and rehabilitation in Madhya Pradesh. On a third visit to villages, in February 1992, some activity was visible. A number of sites were being prepared adjacent to submergence villages to accommodate houses of people losing homes but not land. The ones we were shown were being set up for communities likely to be affected by backwater submergence. Madhya Pradesh officials said that this means that the villagers will be at risk only in high monsoon years after 1997.

In the course of discussions with Madhya Pradesh officials who were responsible for the establishment of these sites, we were told that the hope was that their creation would establish the government's credibility in the minds of oustees, and that villagers would therefore begin to accord more respect to the resettlement and rehabilitation process. In effect, these new sites appeared to be an element in the political struggle in the submergence area.

We visited three of the villages for which these new sites were designed. At Khalburj the people told us that they were happy about the new house site, that they were looking forward to improved services of all kinds, and that officials had discussed this move with them for at least eight months. When we went to Arbarpura, however, we were given the impression that consultation

---

[21] Doctor Hari Singh Gour University, Sagar, *Studies on Resettlement*, Report No. 12, 1988-89, p 48. It states: "No society can afford to go with a development project which envisages to bring prosperity for one section of its people at the cost of destruction and even annihilation of another section with equal population."

[22] Doctor Hari Singh Gour University, Sagar, *Studies on Resettlement*, Report No. 15, 1990-91, p 39. See also p 30. For further details of the importance of animals and grazing, see *Village Studies for Resettlement*, Report No. 4, 1988, pp 55-60, and *Monitoring and Evaluation*, Bi-Annual Report, September 1990, p 58. The Bank's April 1987 review mission reached a similar conclusion for tribal villages in Gujarat.

with the people had been minimal and that there was considerable unease about the site itself. A woman interrupted our meeting there, protesting that no one should be forced to leave the Narmada, the mother from whom they receive the milk of life. When we asked other people whether or not they were satisfied with the new site, their answers were equivocal. There seemed to be difficulties with access during the monsoon, water supply, and accommodation for animals. Most troubling to us, however, was the fact that the villagers had apparently played virtually no part in the design of the new site. They told us that they had never been shown any plans, and when we asked officials if they had brought provisional designs of the new site to the villagers, the officials remarked that since they were illiterate, the people would not have been able to understand them.

At Chichli, where over 100 households are expected to relocate, people were especially insistent that they had played no real part in the choice of resettlement site. Indeed, several people we met with there told us that virtually everyone in the village was opposed to the site. They also told us that there was a hill which would have been far more suitable. It transpired that a Madhya Pradesh official had visited Chichli to obtain approval for the new village, but had met with only a dozen individuals and had gone with only five of them to the site itself. The official herself told us that she had not managed to consult with the women because they do not attend public meetings. We asked her if she had made a point of going to visit them in their houses to talk to them about relocation. She said she had not done so. Yet officials of Madhya Pradesh took the view that they had secured approval of the Chichli people for the site. When we pressed Madhya Pradesh officials on this, they responded by saying it was only a matter of time before they would succeed in persuading the people of Chichli that in fact their new village would be ideal for them.

Nothing we saw in Madhya Pradesh led us to believe that implementation of the resettlement process in the submergence villages was being carried out in the spirit of the various undertakings by which it is supposed to be guided. Activism in the region after 1988 may well have become a severe obstacle. Yet this activism is itself a measure of failure of implementation, in particular a failure of consultation with the oustees themselves.

The Bank missions of April/May and November/December 1991 again criticized Madhya Pradesh. Progress with the database was noted, but the issue of policy was once more identified as a real problem. The second of the two 1991 missions recommended that the policies of both Maharashtra and Madhya Pradesh be reviewed in order "to make sure that they can achieve the overall objectives."[23] The fundamental difficulties in Madhya Pradesh persist.

---

[23] Abdul Salam, submission to the Independent Review, 1992, p 92.

Pressure on oustees to go to Gujarat and failure to provide a real alternative in Madhya Pradesh are part of the continuing problem.

GUTAL, SURIYA, AND GAULAGAMBI

Oustees from Madhya Pradesh have selected land at a number of Gujarat sites.[24] The earliest of these was established at Gutal, 50 kilometers east of Baroda, and the first families visited the site and began to use the tin sheds there in 1990. We went to Gutal in December 1991. Among the more recent Madhya Pradesh resettlement sites in Gujarat are Suriya and Gaulagambi, which we visited in late January 1992.

Nigam officials told us that Gutal exemplified the opportunity that resettlement in Gujarat provided to oustee families of Madhya Pradesh. Thanks to the provisions in the Gujarat resettlement policy for encroacher and landless oustees, they said people who could never otherwise have expected to become landholders and who did not qualify for land under their own state's policy, were being provided with a unique opportunity. One official, speaking of those who had relocated to Gutal, said: "They could hardly believe their good fortune; they were no longer landless." He said oustees' circumstances now were "beyond their wildest dreams."

From the people of Gutal we heard many complaints. Some people told us they had been given to understand that they would, once they had relocated, be provided with large, pukka houses, not unlike the ones belonging to some of the landowners in the neighboring host village. When we asked why they did not bring their own houses from Bhawati, people said, laughing, that their houses in Bhawati were large pukka ones; obviously they could not be moved. They said that between them the 80 different families now at Gutal had owned 44 such houses.

We asked if they were pleased to have got land. The people we met with told us that they had all had land at Bhawati, albeit very small plots. One person explained that he had had one and a half acres that he had received from his father. Most important, they said, that virtually all land at Bhawati was irrigated, and they could get three crops per year there. At Gutal, they said, there was only one crop. Therefore, they went on to say, one and a half acres at Bhawati equalled five acres at Gutal.

In general, they said, their living standards and the quality of their life as a whole had gone down. Surprised to be told this, we sought as complete a clari-

---

[24] Pressure on Madhya Pradesh oustees to accept land in Gujarat means that the number of sites is increasing as we write.

fication as possible. We asked each person at the meeting whether they thought their standard of life was equal here to what it was before. Everyone claimed that now they were worse off, even though they had owned so little land before. Some did say, however, that if they had irrigation and good pukka houses, things might be all right in the end.

The people at Gutal spoke to us at some length about what it had been like to live right on the banks of the river, have forest lands, and be able to fish. Also, they said they had harvested leaves for making cigarettes as well as fruit, fodder, firewood, building materials, medicine, gum, herbs, vegetables—the list was long. As they identified the items, the people conveyed real grief.

They also told us that at Bhawati they had a good school and a government hospital, whereas here they have to go two kilometers to get medical help, in which they appeared to have little confidence. A group of women told us that none of them would give birth at Gutal, but would, if at all possible, have their babies at Bhawati. Similarly, they told us that they try to make sure their marriages take place in the old village. They said: "Our society is not here. We do not know the rituals, or how we'll be treated. Perhaps, later on, if many Bhawati people come, we will have our own society."

The women went on to say that they felt as if they had lost their parents as a result of coming to Gutal. They had never seen Gujarat before. They had not been consulted before coming, and had not made any preliminary visits.

Late on in the meeting at Gutal, Bihar Lal, the community leader, arrived. He said: "We got many promises and had faith. We trusted that they would keep their promises, therefore we did not get anything written down. Now we're not getting the houses or the irrigation—the most important things that were promised to us." He also said: "We are like dead people. What is the point of living like dead people? When you are submerged, you are dead."

Having heard these and similar expressions of intense dissatisfaction, we asked how they would now do things with the benefit of hindsight. They told us they realized they should have made sure that everything was provided for their livelihoods before they moved.

At Suriya and Gaulagambi people were much more optimistic. They told us that they had decided to move to Gujarat from Akadia and Jalsindhi, because they had no choice. The dam was going to flood them out, they said, and though some of their neighbors had decided they would move farther up into the forest when the waters came, they said that they did not believe the land deeper in the hills could support them. Several men said they would have preferred to stay in their villages in Madhya Pradesh, but given they had no choice, now they would make the best of what was available to them.

Several people at Suriya said they had been shown land in four different places, and had finally opted for Suriya because they judged the productivity of the soil to be high. They missed the forests and many other parts of what they called "our own lifestyle," but said that they are able to adjust. They have to manage without fish, they told us; in Akadia, they estimated that they would catch up to five kilograms a day. They also pointed out that they did not have enough grazing land at the new sites and badly needed a cremation ground. People said they were having to sell most of their animals.

But people in these two villages expressed some confidence that the government would keep its promises. They believed that they would eventually get the means to put up their houses here, build new houses if necessary, establish irrigation, get electricity, and achieve agricultural success. They also thought that relations with their neighboring villages would not cause them any difficulties.

We were puzzled by the differences in what we heard between Gutal and the other two sites. It may have been due in part to the fact that Gutal is considerably larger than either Suriya or Gaulagambi, and we spoke to far more people there. Another possible explanation may be that once people have been persuaded to resettle, provision of services to them declines. A number of oustees at several different relocation sites told us that they believed this to be the case. They told us that they suspected they were encouraged to move with promises, but that the objective was to get them to accept land rather than to rehabilitate them. This would mean that the experience of the implementation of the policies gives rise to a growing sense of discontent. People had been at Gutal long enough to begin to think that promises might never be kept. It is also possible that implementation at the site-by-site level has improved recently, and that officials and non-government organization workers are now seeking to ensure that resettlement takes place more smoothly. Non-government organization workers suggested to us that anxiety about implementation of policy in Madhya Pradesh has resulted in an intense and recent effort to make sure that its oustees are provided with as much of what they need as quickly as possible. They said both Gujarat and Madhya Pradesh governments recognized that the credibility of resettlement and rehabilitation, especially in the eyes of the Bank, depended on Madhya Pradesh oustees being willing to move to Gujarat sites. We noticed that tin sheds at sites for Madhya Pradesh resettlement were provided with plinths—that is, concrete flooring—and tiles, and therefore were for the most part superior to anything available to Gujarat oustees. Also, officials told us that some of the best land being acquired by the Gujarat Land Purchase Committee was being set aside for people coming from Madhya Pradesh.

Each of these possible explanations creates uncertainty about the basis for long-term implementation. There can be no doubt but that the resettlement and rehabilitation process depends upon persuading people to move, and at effecting their move with a minimum of confusion. The process is therefore likely to be accompanied by promises of benefits. Given the persistent criticism of policy and implementation, and the extent to which relocation and rehabilitation are driven by construction schedules, this emphasis is inevitable.

So little actual rehabilitation has been done for Madhya Pradesh oustees that their long-term prospects can only be judged on what is embedded in policy and the limited implementation we describe. We are left with a narrow basis on which to assess the likely outcome. We have already seen how few sites are likely to accommodate more than 100 families. Moreover, the scatter effect has negative impacts on the integrity of culture and community. In the end we return to the problems of policy, its appropriateness to the various communities of Madhya Pradesh, and to the low degree of regard that Madhya Pradesh officials have shown for the ultimate social and economic welfare of Madhya Pradesh oustees. Compliance with the broad principles and objectives that the Bank requires depends on both policy and implementation. On neither count is the case of Madhya Pradesh reassuring.

SOME CONCLUSIONS

Resettlement and rehabilitation in Madhya Pradesh has not proceeded very far. This in part is a natural outcome of its location at the upper reaches of the reservoir: submergence is not anticipated until 1997-98 for a sizable proportion of its villages. But given the scale of the impacts in Madhya Pradesh, all possible time should have been used to ensure that suitable measures would be in place, both as to policy and implementation.

In fact, the basis for resettlement and rehabilitation measures and plans for Madhya Pradesh has always been, and continues to be, severely limited. No comprehensive data were gathered prior to the onset of the resistance in the valley which has virtually denied authorities access to many villages. Such information as is on hand, as the result of the government questionnaire, appears to be of little value. Findings are not sufficiently solid to ensure that plans based on them will address problems accurately. In particular, Madhya Pradesh's claim that oustees have chosen where they wish to relocate does not stand up to scrutiny.

Generally, consultation with those likely to be affected by the Sardar Sarovar Projects has been minimal. This was documented by MARG, an independent research institute, in 1987, and has been confirmed by our own meetings with large numbers of Madhya Pradesh oustees. This failure applies to both the tribal villages of the Alirajpur hills and the caste villages of the Nimad. It represents an administrative lacuna and serious non-compliance with the 1985 credit and loan agreements.

In its statement of "broad principles" Madhya Pradesh's resettlement policy affirms that the aim is that all oustees will "after their relocation and resettlement improve, or at least regain their previous standard of living within a reasonable time." It also states that it will ensure "that no hardship is caused to the displaced families in moving out from their present habitat in to a new place and way of living," and that "Special care would be taken of the families of Scheduled Castes, Scheduled Tribes, marginal farmers and small farmers." It also affirms that "Families having legal titles to land and the encroachers would be treated on the same footing." And oustees are given the right to choose to move in social groups of their choice, and to either the Gujarat command area or "near the periphery of the affected areas in accordance with their preferences."

But the actual terms of this policy have consequences at odds with its "broad principles." Provisions for major sons and encroachers are open to the same fundamental objections as can be made in relation to Maharashtra policy. It is to be recalled that tribal villages are the homes of people who depend on a range of resources among which agricultural plots are of great importance. These plots are used and occupied by families who depend upon them and regard them as their own. Yet by virtue of historical and administrative processes, a significant proportion of these plots are deemed to be encroached. In so far as land is encroached, and the families who work it are unable to provide proof of their having held it prior to 1987, they are not recognized as landed. This means that they are not eligible for the one benefit—a viable plot of agricultural land—that we believe is a necessary (though not necessarily sufficient) condition for their successful rehabilitation.

Similarly, major sons—who in other submergence areas are known to constitute something like 40 per cent of oustees—do not, according to the measures of Madhya Pradesh resettlement policy, qualify for land. This creates a real potential for the effective dispossession of many families.

These policy failures are compounded by lack of data. No one has carried out appropriate socioeconomic or anthropological analyses of the Madhya Pradesh submergence villages that have informed, still less shaped, either policy or implementation. Monitoring and evaluation provide some important insights into the economy of a number of villages. But these are limited in their data—they represent case studies, not comprehensive baseline data. Also, they were carried out after the policy had been decided, and therefore are guided by its preoccupations and not by the appropriate social scientific concerns. No one is able to tell us, for example, what are the consequences of the provisions for encroachers and major sons; no one can even identify the scale of the problems these measures could cause. This is because the officials involved are required to defend a policy that exists rather than identify what the people need.

Policy, data, and consultation problems therefore mean that large numbers of Madhya Pradesh oustees cannot expect to regain their standard of living as a result of resettlement and rehabilitation. The prospects of Madhya Pradesh satisfying the overarching and controlling principles of Bank policy and the 1985 credit and loan agreements are remote. Indeed, as things stand, many oustees can expect to experience a substantial loss of economic status; the expectation is that they will go from having land to being landless.

The reply that is made by Madhya Pradesh to these criticisms consists in pointing to the relatively prosperous farmers of the Nimad, saying that they are well able to take advantage of the policy as it stands, and to the measures the state promises will secure employment and other benefits to the "landless." It is also said that the difference in policy between Madhya Pradesh and Gujarat means that oustees who are landless or in danger of becoming so can elect to move to Gujarat, and take advantage of land being offered there under more generous terms.

But these replies raise many difficulties. It may be that prosperous farmers of the Nimad will be able to secure greater benefits than others. Many of them, however, have between two and six hectares of highly productive land. They told us that they do not believe that their resettlement is likely to secure equivalent economic security. Given the record of Madhya Pradesh when it comes to resettlement of persons displaced by its other development projects, the farmers' apprehensions appear to be justified.

Even if the richer and more powerful members of the Nimad community can indeed secure adequate compensation, this does not begin to meet the difficulties we describe. The Bank's special obligation under its own resettlement policy is to the poorer and weaker elements of society. Its policies are designed to ensure that development does not mean that the rich thrive while the poor suffer social and economic losses. Yet the very groups most at risk—the tribal encroachers, small landowners, and landless laborers within highly integrated farm and village life—are the ones who express the most poignant fears, and who are most at risk.

Moreover, any suggestion that policy deficiencies can be remedied by virtue of the benefits available in Gujarat flies in the face of the people's right to choose to be resettled in Gujarat or in their home state "near the periphery of the affected areas." Failure to provide a real option in the form of sufficient areas of irrigable land within Madhya Pradesh—which is a persistent factor in Madhya Pradesh's inadequate planning—is to drain the meaning from right of choice.

Very many of Madhya Pradesh's oustees simply do not believe that implementation of the policies that are in place is likely to secure people's long-term wellbeing. On the contrary, Madhya Pradesh oustees insist that resettlement will bring something considerably different than rehabilitation.

Many of these fears are natural, even inevitable. No one likes to move— even if the prospects are not entirely negative. But all that we learned about policy, planning, and consultation in the case of the Madhya Pradesh submergence area invites the very conclusion that apprehensive oustees repeatedly sought to share with us. All in all, we have little confidence that in Madhya Pradesh, where a substantial majority of Sardar Sarovar oustees live, there will not be a repetition of the tragedy that has afflicted so many other development projects. Much of the scene seems to be set for such an outcome: lack of planning, institutional indifference, policies that discriminate against the weakest and poorest of oustees, and a substitution of paper planning for real, on-the-ground commitment to measures that will work.

The Bank cannot escape some responsibility for this. It has allowed the state's policies to be limited to the measures set out in the Tribunal award, and then accepted Madhya Pradesh's interpretation of the loan agreement to result in policies that fail to protect the poorest and weakest oustees. This has roots in the Bank's inadequate project appraisal, and limited follow-up in the earliest stages of implementation. Moreover, mission after mission reported on the failure of Madhya Pradesh to produce adequate data, the weakness of its resettlement plan, its persistent failure to implement even its own policies, and its insistence on setting out resettlement proposals that are "vague to the point of being wholly unresponsive to Bank policy guidelines."

Despite this litany of complaints, the Bank was persuaded to adopt a piecemeal carrot-and-stick strategy for securing Madhya Pradesh's compliance. The carrot was support for the Narmada Sagar Projects, from which Madhya Pradesh anticipates direct benefits on a large scale, but whose construction is likely to require Bank funding. The stick was the implied threat that the Bank would withdraw from Narmada projects, and therefore from Narmada Sagar. Despite the fact that this tactic secured few improvements, it continued. Moreover, when criticism within the Bank reached a high pitch of intensity, it appears to have been allayed by the Bank's country department. This has made it possible for Madhya Pradesh to avoid implementation targets and requests, or even demands, that progress on one or another of the crucial compliance issues be made.

Reluctance to press with real conviction for compliance by Madhya Pradesh has sent a signal not only to Madhya Pradesh, but perhaps to other states in India where the Bank is funding projects with resettlement components. The signal is to the effect that, in the end, compliance does not matter all that much. There are many officials within the Bank who do not take this view—this much is made clear by the substance and tone of many mission reports. But the outcome of complaints has never been decisive; appeals for more time, another chance to set matters right, a conciliatory tack, acceptance of the Madhya Pradesh interpretation of the Tribunal's award, or faith in its latest statements of intention have prevailed.

Had the Bank stood firmly by its principles in the early stages of the Projects, or made its policy principles inescapable in the first phase of implementation, many of the deficiencies we have noted might have been avoided. As it is, the situation in Madhya Pradesh leads to an inescapable conclusion: there are in place neither the instruments of policy nor the institutions that could ensure that Madhya Pradesh oustees receive that which the Bank holds up as their minimal right—to be relocated in such a manner as to ensure they do not suffer a permanent decline in their standard of living.

Construction of a branch canal, showing machinery specially designed for lining the canal with concrete.

A major purpose of Sardar Sarovar dam is to supply irrigation, domestic, and industrial water to Gujarat and, to a lesser extent, Rajasthan. The system to accomplish this consists of a system of canals, all supplied by a main canal, which is planned to run 458 kilometers across Gujarat from the dam site at Kevadia to the Rajasthan border. A 75,000-kilometer network of branch canals, distributaries, and minor irrigation channels is designed to deliver water to parts of central Gujarat, Saurashtra, Kutchch, and into a small area of southern Rajasthan.

The land required for this undertaking is determined by the width of each level of canal. The right of way required for the main canal at its head is 250 meters, and at its northern end is 100 meters. The average width of the Saurashtra branch canal is 160 meters; the other branches are between 50 meters and 90 meters wide. The distributaries vary from 25 meters to 40 meters in width, and the minors from 15 meters to 25 meters.[1] It is estimated that the main canal will cover 12,123 hectares, the branches 24,500 hectares, and the distributaries 48,500 hectares. The total area required for construction of the canal network, therefore, exceeds 85,000 hectares.[2]

Each level of this system—main, branch, distributary, and minor—entails the acquisition of land. In a submission to our review, the Nigam estimated total land to be acquired at 73,000 hectares, and pointed out that their calculations now show that land acquisition is necessary for a total length of 22,325

---

[1] The irrigation network also anticipates watercourses and field channels that run along field boundaries. Given that these would have very small impacts on landholdings, we do not include them in our calculations.

[2] These figures are stated in an Indian Institute of Management report, and restated in a Ragsdale Associates review of canal-affected peoples, whose findings are set out in a memorandum of December 17, 1991, to the World Bank.

kilometers. Our analysis of the canal concludes that 36,600 hectares of land are needed for the main and branch canals alone.

Work on the canal began in 1987. Construction of the first phase, as far as the Mahi River, is well advanced. Nigam engineers told us that they have scheduled completion of this phase by June 1994. Some 11,500 hectares of private land have already been acquired.[3] We toured the area north of the Mahi River, and saw that construction of the Saurashtra branch canal has begun.

A number of questions inevitably arise. How many villagers will lose land and houses to the canal? How much land will each villager lose? Will those who lose land be rendered entirely landless, or marginal, or will the loss of land be without real significance? Do potential irrigation benefits to affected families offset such losses? What provisions have been made to compensate those who are losing land to the canal network?

The canal network forms a major part of the Sardar Sarovar Projects, and Bank policy on involuntary resettlement includes canals and irrigation systems. We looked to the 1985 credit and loan agreements to find what covenants the Bank had secured from India and Gujarat to ensure that its policy would be carried out. In the agreements for the water delivery project we could not locate a reference to canal-affected families, oustees, or resettlement and rehabilitation. Furthermore, it was not until the December 1989 Bank mission that concern was raised about the impacts of the canal, and not until 1991 that any attempt appears to have been made, by either Sardar Sarovar authorities or the Bank, to assess canal impacts. As in the case of the dam and reservoir, there has been no impact study; there are no comprehensive data about landholding and socioeconomic conditions along the canal corridor. Land for the canal has been acquired under the *Land Acquisition Act, 1894.*

In the course of our work in India we met with many individuals displaced by construction of the canal, and we visited several villages along the route of the canal. At Gadkoi, Songam, and Koliyari people told us about losing their land, wells, and trees to the canal right of way. Some of them had lost all their land; others had lost substantial proportions. Many complained that their lands had been valued far below current real costs of land, and therefore the compensation provided by the *Land Acquisition Act* did not allow them to buy equivalent replacement fields.

Everywhere we went along the canal, we heard disturbing accounts of dislocation and dispossession. People told us about wells and fruit trees that had been destroyed but not compensated. They showed us where their drainage channels had been blocked. They pointed out land that had been divided in

---

[3] 1992 data provided by Nigam indicate: 5,701 hectares for main canal, 4,850 hectares for branches, and 963 hectares for distribution network.

two by the canal, where in order to get to the other side they had to go two kilometers to the nearest bridge and then two kilometers back along the other
side of the canal to their land. We saw villages of landless Nayaks who were
being forced to relocate, but to whom little or no compensation had been paid.
We heard repeatedly about gross undervaluation of houses, and visited villages where people who had to relocate were given no alternative house sites.
These were only glimpses of the problem, however, and we were unable to
measure the extent to which they were representative, or what the real scale of
the difficulties might be. And when we sought the overall picture, we found
that it simply had never been drawn.

As a result of this lacuna, and conscious that our terms of reference required us to make an assessment of people affected by the canal, we attempted
to put together whatever data we could find on canal impacts. We requested
that the report of the Indian Institute of Management, Ahmedabad (commissioned by the Nigam and submitted in draft form in September 1991), be
made available to us. We received it in January 1992. We invited non-government organizations to prepare submissions on the canal. Arch Vahini and
Narmada Bachao Andolan both contributed analyses of their own data. We
obtained a copy of the Ragsdale Associates contribution on the canal to the
December 1991 World Bank review mission. And we invited an economist and
a statistician at the London School of Economics (both of whom are Indians,
and one a Gujarati) to take all these data and to judge what conclusions they
might draw.

The Nigam-commissioned Indian Institute of Management study estimated that 222,786 *khatedars* (registered land-owning farmers) will be affected
by the canal. This number is the highest found in any of the surveys, and is
based on projections from data for 165 villages in the command area to the
3,393 villages of the command area. This projection has been criticized on
methodological grounds. Nigam objections to the Indian Institute of Management report seek to show that its estimate is an immense overstatement of the
problem.[4] Our own assessment of total impact yields the number of affected
khatedars as 140,000. This is based on careful extrapolations of data, and a
computer modelling of the canal's impact on landholders that includes adjustments for changes in critical variables.[5] Even so, the gross number of those impacted does not tell us the amount of land lost by each individual farmer nor
the total land to be lost by all displaced farmers.

[4] Nigam, submission to Independent Review, March 11, 1992, and Nigam "Note on IIM Report,"
press release, n.d. [1991/2].
[5] These include: width of right of way, character of landholdings for different sectors, patterns of
total land ownership, and orientation of fields. Some of these variables have a special relevance to
estimates for percentages of land lost by individual *khatedars*.

Our main concern is, how many *khatedars* will either lose all their land or lose so much of it that their holdings become marginal? This is a difficult calculation, but on the basis of data made available for 4,033 hectares of land for the main canal and 1,822 hectares for the branch canal, there is an adequate sample on which to base a useful estimate.[6] From the data we received on average holdings in each region through which the canal passes, it is possible to gauge the percentage of *khatedars* impacted and the percentage of lands each *khatedar* will lose. In effect, the calculation entails laying a model of different kinds of canal (width, etc.) on a model of different patterns of landholding. Our most conservative analysis shows about 1,100 *khatedars* becoming landless, and of those who are left with some land, approximately 25,000 ending up with less than two hectares. Obviously a significant proportion of those who are left with two hectares or less were already marginal farmers. By adjusting the statistics for this consideration, we get the following results: approximately 1,100 *khatedars* become landless, between 5,000 and 6,000 are left with one hectare or less, and approximately 7,500 with less than two hectares.

The Government of Gujarat has pointed out that a *khatedar*, who is treated as a title holder, may hold the land under more than one survey number. This means that estimates based on survey number data could overestimate the total number of *khatedars* actually impacted. On the other hand, Arch Vahini data and our own discussions with families in the region suggest that in many regions, notably among the poorer landholders, one title holder is equal to three or four families.[7] Since it is probably the case that underreporting of actual dependents on the land outweighs over reporting as a result of title holders having land under more than one survey number, the figures we give here can probably be taken as a conservative estimate of land loss caused by construction of the canal.

This kind of statistical analysis which aims to show the scale of the canal's impact looks exclusively at private revenue land. In fact, a significant proportion of land taken up by the irrigation system is owned by the government. The main and branch canals require some 11,500 hectares of government land. This is also part of the economic system: public land provides grazing, fodder, and fuel wood, as well as possibilities for encroachment. The loss of these parcels of land may or may not be a significant factor in the overall impact of the canal on the people's lives; there is no information on which to base

[6] 4,033 hectares represents 33 per cent of total land taken up by the main canal; 1,822 hectares represents 7.4 per cent of total land for branch canals. These are adequate samples on which to base useful estimates.

[7] One cause of this understatement of actual dependents on land is the Gujarat *Prevention of Fragmentation and Consolidation of Holdings Act*.

an assessment. Officials in Gujarat told us that these kind of losses are trivial when compared to the benefits that would come from irrigation. This is something that must be substantiated. Until it is, a matter of crucial importance to the lives of people along the canal remains the subject of estimates and speculations.

Senior officials at the Nigam and non-government organizations with relevant experience told us that the *Land Acquisition Act* is, at best, a rough and ready instrument. Many of the problems associated with the Act's implementation are raised in the Indian Institute of Management report, which notes "a general tendency" towards undervaluation of land so that those compensated were unable to "buy the land at least to the extent of area foregone."[8] The magnitude of undervaluation is reported to range from 30 to 50 per cent. Also, wells and trees very often have not been included in compensation, despite their immense importance to *khatedars*.

Furthermore, there appear to be inconsistencies in the way in which land has been valued. In many cases, we discovered that a uniform figure had been applied to unirrigated land throughout a village, without attention to special features of particular plots. In other cases land of apparently similar quality had been acquired for widely varying amounts. For example, in Gadkoi, farmers told us that they were paid Rs. 2,200 per acre. Others in the same village got up to Rs. 3,200 per acre. Similarly, Koliyari *khatedars* told us they were paid Rs. 2,800 per acre for irrigated land, while in Kunverpura, one kilometer away, farmers were paid over Rs. 4,500 per acre.[9]

In their submission on the canal, the Nigam, in defence of the *Land Acquisition Act* as an appropriate device for dealing with canal impacts, notes that: "landholders are free to approach Courts of Law for enhancement of compensation. Thus, fair dealing is always assured to the landholders" (p 1). Yet we were told repeatedly that the poorer farmers, and therefore those most vulnerable to the impacts of the canal on their holdings, rarely if ever felt equipped to embark upon litigation. Rather, they simply accepted what was offered to them. In fact, we discovered that the success of the small number of richer farmers who have litigated over inadequate compensation has intensified the sense of injustice among those who have not felt able to use the courts.

In a study of rehabilitation and land acquisition, carried out for the Nigam, consideration is given to how land acquisition is working for canal construction.[10] This report notes that the land acquisition process involves "cumber-

---

[8] Indian Institute of Management Report, Executive Summary.

[9] In striking contrast are the prices paid in the past two years for land acquired close to the canal for resettling oustees. These have ranged from Rs. 12,000 to Rs. 22,000 per acre.

[10] See J. K. Sharma, *Project Implementation Schedule: Rehabilitation, Land Acquisition and Environment*, Gandhinagar: Sardar Sarovar Narmada Nigam Ltd, n.d. [1990?].

some legal and procedural formalities." It observes that "the task of land acquisition is now being carried out at war footings." Additional staff have been
put in place by the Nigam in order to speed up the rate at which *khatedars'* land
is acquired for the canal. A likely result of such intensification of the land acquisition process is to reduce the possibility of careful calculation of suitable
compensation and detailed assessment of trees and other immovables.

We believe that considerable weight must be given to the conclusion at
which the Indian Institute of Management report arrives when it assesses the
present method of determining compensation. The authors of the Indian Institute of Management report state that this is "not at all an appropriate proxy
for the assets and income actually foregone by the *khatedars*." They observe
that this compensation "really leads to impoverishment of the affected
khatedars and does not ensure the standard of living enjoyed by them before acquisition" (p 13).

Many who have looked at the canal have urged that those affected by its
construction be granted oustee status. This would mean that those who lose
more than 25 per cent of their land would be entitled to a minimum of two
hectares of irrigable land elsewhere. The definition of an oustee in the 1985
credit and loan agreements for the dam and powerhouse gives some basis for
such a suggestion, *viz.*: "'Oustee' means any person, whether landed or landless, who . . . has been ordinarily residing, or cultivating land, or carrying on
any trade, occupation or calling or working for gain, in Gujarat, Madhya
Pradesh and Maharashtra, and who would be displaced from his usual habitat
due to the carrying out of the Project; . . ." This definition would appear to
cover the case of canal-affected *khatedars*. Ironically, a parcel of irrigable land
would be more appropriate compensation for the canal-affected people than
for the tribal villagers of the submergence area for whom it was intended. Canal communities are already accustomed to farming in the Gujarat plains, are
not dependent on river and forest resources, and can be expected to adjust well
and quickly to relocation in the vicinity of their existing villages—*if* they are
treated as oustees and given a full resettlement and rehabilitation package of
compensation benefits.

Nigam, as an agency of the Government of Gujarat, continues to resist such
a policy change. In its submission to our review on the subject of the canal, it
acknowledges that there is a problem in the case of those rendered landless by
the main canal, and speaks of "some few hard cases" that may have "to be
considered on merits" (p 4). However, its position is that the *Land Acquisition
Act* works quite adequately, and that, in any case, the canal is an immense
benefit to all Gujarat, including those who are impacted by it. The Nigam has
said: "For such a large irrigation project, which is to benefit the community at
large, the farmers have always been ready for slight sacrifices."

In the absence of a comprehensive study, the scale of the anticipated sacrifice cannot be known for certain. We have gathered enough evidence to conclude that the canal is the cause of considerable "hardship and disruption,"[11] potentially on a very large scale. Bank consultants first raised the question of whether people were likely to be affected by canal construction as early as 1983. Only in 1989, however, did the Bank urge that there be a comprehensive study of the problem. The Indian Institute of Management report does not constitute a detailed consideration of the scale of the impact—its terms of reference caused it to focus on aspects of compensation rather than the socioeconomic dimension of the issue.[12] Nor is the Ragsdale contribution to the December 1991 Bank mission an attempt to fill the research gap. It is no substitute for a case-by-case examination of the problem, both in order to see how to address the grievances of those already affected by the canal, as well as to establish the basis for an appropriate compensation.

Assessment of the impacts of the canal is urgently needed. A full account of how those already impacted have fared is essential. The Bank's guidelines require research of this kind.

The 1980 Bank policy makes clear that canal-affected people who lose their homes or their means of livelihood should be recognized as oustees. This means they are entitled to the benefit of the principle that they promptly at least regain their previous standard of living. It is unacceptable that families who lose substantial portions of their lands, vital assets, house sites, and even whole village sites should find themselves economically debilitated.

Those affected by the canal live in the Gujarat plains, and are farmers or farm laborers. This means that the measures for compensating Sardar Sarovar oustees could well be appropriate. The exclusion of canal-affected oustees from these benefits is a result of a missing clause in the credit and loan agreements. The Bank did not include a covenant in the agreements which would require Gujarat to include those affected by the water delivery network as "oustees," as its 1980 policy required.

Families who have been rendered landless or marginal by the canal and who have been compensated under the *Land Acquisition Act* should be offered the measures available to oustees. This would be a retroactive application of policy, much as was the case with the oustees from the rock-filled dyke villages. Such compensation as they have already received could be set against

---

[11] Operational Manual Statement No. 3.22, 1980.

[12] The terms of reference of the Indian Institute of Management report directed it towards formulae for compensation to canal-affected people, the case for differential compensation, the case for other measures of compensation, and the need for paying compensation in other ways than cash. See Indian Institute of Management Report, Executive Summary, p i.

their compensation as oustees. Those who judge that the measures of the *Land Acquisition Act* have adequately compensated them could refuse oustee status. In this way, hardships caused by canal construction would be compensated. The Bank's policies and guidelines could then be seen to be enforced.

The Bank has already included in the resettlement policy for the Upper Krishna (Phase II) Irrigation Project (1988) the stipulation that families whose lands are acquired for canals and distributaries, and who are left with less than 1.5 hectares of irrigated land, should receive the same compensations as those affected by submergence. It should now use its good offices to ensure that the policy applied to those persons displaced by the Sardar Sarovar irrigation project is clear and consistent with its 1980, 1990, and 1991 Operational Manuals and Directives.

The Sardar Sarovar canal is planned to be the largest in the world. Somehow, those vulnerable to its construction were excluded from the resettlement benefits the Bank's policy deems to be essential. A canal of this magnitude involves more than just engineering and construction. The Bank's policies for people must have, and be seen to have, the priority they deserve.

THE ENVIRONMENT

Looking across the Narmada River from Gujarat to Maharashtra.

Chapter 10
ENVIRONMENT:
CONTEXT AND COMPLIANCE

AN environmental review of the Sardar Sarovar Projects must begin in a broader context. Over the last two decades both the World Bank and India have been active participants in a global movement seeking to integrate environmental considerations into economic development decision making. Since the 1972 United Nations Conference on the Human Environment in Stockholm, the Bank has provided leadership among international aid institutions, and India has played a key role among developing countries to bring forward these considerations.

The Sardar Sarovar Projects have been considered in one form or another since the 1950s. They have been under construction over a decade marked by a rapid evolution of ecological awareness throughout the world. Standards of acceptable environmental impact have changed and continue to evolve. Internationally, this movement has been crystallized by the 1987 report of the United Nations World Commission on Environment and Development (the Brundtland report). The December 1987 United Nations resolution adopting this report called upon all governments to strengthen their environmental and natural resource agencies. It also called upon the governing bodies of multilateral development assistance and financial institutions to commit their organizations more fully to pursuing sustainable development. Prime Minister Rajiv Gandhi of India, pledging his nation's support, spoke of the Brundtland report as "a call to concerted political action." He said "the search for the right answers must go on relentlessly. It is a worldwide endeavour to which India pledges unstinting support."[1]

The terms of reference for our review require us to "conduct an assessment

of the implementation of the ongoing Sardar Sarovar Projects (SSP) . . . as regards: . . . the amelioration of the environmental impact of all aspects of the
projects." We are also asked to include, as appropriate, recommendations for
improvement or implementation. We are directed to take account of the 1985
legal agreements between the Bank and India upon which the loan/credit was
conditioned, as well as the 1979 award of the Narmada Water Disputes Tribunal, the 1987 environmental and forest clearances approvals given by India,
and Union and state laws. We are also directed to make reference to existing
directives and guidelines issued by the Bank and by India, keeping in mind
that many of these were promulgated or amended after 1985.

Our review is directed to all environmental aspects of the dam and canal
projects. Thus, it has been necessary for us to consider their full ecological
reach, extending upstream from the reservoir to include the catchment area in
Maharashtra and Madhya Pradesh, downstream from the dam to the estuary
in the Gulf of Cambay, and northward to the canal's command and water service areas in Gujarat and into Rajasthan.

When the Narmada Water Disputes Tribunal made its award in 1979, it
had the technical experience of several decades of dam building in India and
elsewhere to draw upon. At that time, many important environmental issues
were not well understood or well documented. This is no longer the case. The
international controversy over the Sardar Sarovar Projects has arisen because
of hard lessons learned not only in India but in other countries as well. Within
India, there has been a rich exchange in the literature based on past experience of large dams and irrigation schemes. Some authors, like the former secretary of Water Resources, Ramaswamy Iyer, acknowledge the need for such
schemes while recommending extreme caution because of the heavy financial,
human, social, and environmental costs. Others, like Vijay Paranjpye, have
developed more specific critiques.[2] Many more expressions of expert opinion in
books and articles inform this debate. But it is not a debate exclusively among
professionals. Although it does include engineers, economists, environmentalists, and lawyers, it goes beyond them to include others such as non-government organizations and, of course, the people affected by the Projects, all of
whom have experience and knowledge to share. During the course of this review we benefitted by hearing from them all.

---

[1] The Centre for Our Common Future, "What They Said About 'Our Common Future' (The
Brundtland Report), Selected Statements from World Leaders," undated.
[2] R. Iyer, "Large Dams: the Right Perspective," *Economic and Political Weekly*, September 30, 1989.
Vijay Paranjpye, "High Dams on the Narmada: A holistic analysis of the river valley projects,"
Studies in Ecology and Sustainable Development, No. 3, New Delhi: Indian National Trust for Art and
Cultural Heritage, June 1990.

Our review is not responsible for the assessment of environmental impact of the projects. This has been done, or should have been done, by others. We have, however, had to acquire an independent understanding of the ecological issues and the impact of the Projects in order to make our assessment. We are in a position therefore to review not only the success achieved thus far in addressing the predicted environmental impact and proposed ameliorative measures but also the ability of the Projects' proponents, based on their past performance, to meet any new ecological issues that have arisen or may arise because of unforeseen circumstances. The substantive issues related to environmental impacts cannot be disposed of simply by preparing and filing studies and action plans. Environmental compliance must include a responsive system for the continuous development of ameliorative measures, especially where construction is proceeding while studies are being done. This is all the more important for a megaproject on the scale of Sardar Sarovar.

Our environmental review therefore is in two parts. The first is a measurement of actions taken to date against standards required by Indian procedures and law or by agreements between the Bank, India, and the three states. The second is an assessment of the ecological significance of project activities and the suitability of ameliorative measures, whether anticipated or not by the terms and conditions imposed in the mid-1980s.

We have taken a broad view of impacts. Indeed, we have adopted the Bank's interpretation as set out in its Operational Manual Statement of May 1984, in which environmental concerns are described as "those pertaining to the natural and social conditions surrounding all organisms, particularly mankind, and including future generations. These concerns encompass human ecology and occupational health and safety."[3] Recognizing that some environmental effects may not become identifiable for a long time, the 1984 manual states that the environmental aspects of projects should be considered in a longer time frame (for example 25 to 50 years or more) than may be appropriate for most other aspects of cost-benefit analysis. We have adopted this time horizon.

In 1989, the Bank issued an Operational Directive dealing with environmental assessment. This directive was updated in September 1991 when our review was beginning its work.[4] The Bank's directive noted that the purpose of an environmental assessment is to improve decision making and to ensure that the project options under consideration are environmentally sound and sus-

---

[3] Operational Manual Statement No. 2.36, May 1984.

[4] Operational Directive 4.00, Annex A: Environmental Assessment, October 1989. Operational Directive 4.01: Environmental Assessment, September 1991.

tainable. The directive states that environmental consequences should be recognized early in the project cycle and taken into account in project siting, planning, and design. It goes on to say that environmental assessments should identify ways of improving projects by preventing, minimizing, mitigating, or compensating for adverse impacts. These steps are intended to avoid costly remedial measures after the fact. Like economic, financial, institutional, and engineering analysis, environmental assessment is considered to be part of project preparation and is therefore, in the case of the Sardar Sarovar Projects, India's responsibility as the borrower.

Environmental assessments, properly done, are necessary to understand impacts, to clarify what should be done, and to define more clearly how to do it effectively—they are essential to crafting good decisions. Such assessments are meant to anticipate and prevent costly mistakes. We approached the environmental issues related to the Sardar Sarovar Projects with these considerations in mind.

In the course of our review we visited the dam site. We visited sites upstream from the dam. We visited the Shoolpaneshwar Wildlife Sanctuary. We examined the forest and lands designated for catchment area treatment. We visited the area downstream from the dam to the mouth of the river at the Gulf of Cambay. We talked to people about the fishery and about the quality and quantities of water in the river over the last several years. We visited the canal and various other locations throughout the command area as far as Saurashtra, Kutchch, and the border with Rajasthan. We talked to government officials, academics, representatives of non-government organizations, and other concerned people in Bombay, New Delhi, Indore, Bhopal, Baroda, Ahmedabad, and in the villages throughout the submergence area and downstream of the dam. In the villages we spoke to the people who use the forest and those who depend on the fisheries and the waters of the Narmada River.

We also examined official documents dealing with the environmental issues. These documents are especially important for a venture on the scale of the Sardar Sarovar Projects because they set out what is known about the environmental components, how the various components work together, what might happen with the construction of the Projects, and what could be done, and will be done, to ameliorate the impacts. Our purpose has been to assess the studies themselves and to understand how the impacts that are likely to ensue from the Projects are to be addressed.

Our environmental review has focused on the most important ecological issues. This means that our review deals with the issues of most significance rather than providing a description of all environmental concerns. We therefore focus on adverse impacts and how they might be ameliorated.

THE ENVIRONMENTAL REGULATORY REGIME

The Sardar Sarovar Projects are subject to two evolving regimes of environment-related laws, directives, policies, procedures, and guidelines—those of India and the World Bank.

In India, the integration of environmental factors in economic development was raised in India's Fourth Plan (1969-1974) documents which state "planning for harmonious development . . . is possible only on the basis of a comprehensive appraisal of environmental issues."[5] The same theme was emphasized by representatives of the Government of India at the United Nations Conference on the Human Environment in Stockholm in 1972.

In that year, India established its National Committee on Environmental Planning and Coordination, an advisory body attached to the Department of Science and Technology. Under this committee, chaired by the Prime Minister, special task forces addressed controversial environmental issues. The most well-known of these was the Silent Valley Hydro-Electric Project, in the heart of one of South India's most important rain forests, which was stopped for environmental reasons.

In 1980, a year after the award of the Narmada Water Disputes Tribunal, the Government of India appointed the Tiwari Committee to make recommendations on ways to improve measures for environmental protection. In November of that year, the Department of Environment was set up, with the Prime Minister as the minister responsible. In 1985, it became part of the Ministry of Environment and Forests. The main activities of the ministry include: environmental clearance of selected development projects on the basis of environmental impact assessment and environmental management plans; prevention and control of pollution; conservation; eco-regeneration measures; assistance to non-government organizations; implementing environmental and forestry programs; promotion of environmental and forestry research, extension, education, and training; collection, collation, storage, and dissemination of environmental information; and creation of environmental awareness at the national level.

At the time that the Department of Environment was established, there was growing alarm about the loss of forests nationwide in India. The Indian government passed the *Forest (Conservation) Act, 1980*, placing restrictions on use of forest lands for non-forest purposes. By this statute, all projects for which for-

[5] Cited in Government of India, "Summary of Indian Environmental Legislation and Guidelines," *Training Workshops on Environmental Impact Assessment and Evaluation: Proceedings and Training Manual*, Vol. 1, Part IV, Lucknow, January 1988, p 377.

est land is required need the prior concurrence of the Government of India through what is now the Ministry of Environment and Forests. This statute and the clearances issued under its authority have particular relevance for our review. For example, the Taloda Forest, referred to in Chapter 7, had to be exempted under this Act.

Also in 1980, India's Ministry of Irrigation published a three volume report entitled *Guidelines for Preparation of Detailed Project Report of Irrigation and Multi-purpose Projects*. Among other things, it deals with the displacement of people because of submergence and with environmental aspects which are "assuming greater and greater importance." Detailed checklists of information required in project reports are provided in two of the three volumes. Guidelines for making an environmental analysis are provided in Volume II. These reinforce the environmental approach developed two years earlier by what was then the Department of Science and Technology; they cover site selection, physical aspects, resource linkages, public health, and sociocultural aspects.

India's environmental impact assessment procedures were first established in 1977. By 1985, the date of the Bank's loan for the Sardar Sarovar Projects, the central government required an environmental impact assessment for all major irrigation projects, multi-purpose river valley projects, and hydroelectric power projects. The environmental impact assessment regime in India places the responsibility for preparing the impact assessment on the project sponsors. Four documents must be submitted for ministerial approval: a detailed project report dealing with technical and financial aspects; a questionnaire response on environmental aspects of the proposed works; an environmental impact statement assessing the likely effects on air, water, lands, flora, fauna, etc.; and an environmental management plan that proposes mitigative measures, resettlement and rehabilitation plans, and environmental monitoring programs. To assist the project proponents in this process, the Ministry of Environment and Forests has issued guidelines and questionnaires. *The Guidelines for Environmental Impact Assessment of River Valley Projects* (first prepared in the late 1970s and updated in 1985 and 1989) are relevant to the Narmada projects. Under these guidelines, a request for environmental clearance is handled by the Ministry's Impact Assessment Division, which examines the documents and consults with experts and the project sponsors as needed. A multi-disciplinary Expert Appraisal Committee meets once a month to review projects. Generally, if the submission is complete, a decision will be taken by the Ministry within three months of receipt of the proposal. Supplementary information is requested when documentation is incomplete. This information must be provided within three months or the proposal is rejected. A separate Forest Conservation Division and Advisory Committee deals with requests for conversion of forest lands to non-forest use. These requests are handled in six weeks with one month provided for supplementary information.

In 1986, India passed the *Environmental (Protection) Act*. This is a general law on environmental pollution which empowers the central government to take all necessary measures for protecting the quality of the environment. Under the Act, environment includes "water, air, and land and the interrelationship which exists among and between water, air and land, and human beings, other living creatures, plants, micro-organisms and property" (§2(a)).

India has numerous laws relevant to environmental protection. Those that significantly affect dams, reservoirs, and irrigation systems, such as are inherent in the Sardar Sarovar Projects, include:
• *Indian Fisheries Act, 1897*;
• *Ancient Monuments Preservation Act, 1904*;
• *Indian Forest Act, 1927*;
• *River Boards Act, 1956*;
• *Interstate Water Disputes Act, 1956*;
• *Ancient Monuments and Archaeological Sites and Remains Act, 1958*;
• *Wildlife Protection Act, 1972*;
• *Water (Prevention and Control of Pollution) Act, 1974*;
• *Forest (Conservation) Act, 1980*; and
• *Environmental (Protection) Act, 1986*.

There are also a number of relevant central government policies and guidelines, including:
• *Guidelines for Preparation of Detailed Project Report of Irrigation and Multi-Purpose Projects* (Volumes I, II and III), 1980;
• *Guidelines for Collection of Data to Study Environmental Impact of Water Resource Projects*, Central Board of Irrigation and Power, 1986;
• *Guidelines for Preparation of Status Report of Monitored Projects*, Central Water Commission, undated;
• *National Water Policy*, 1987;
• *National Forest Policy*, 1988; and
• *Guidelines for Environmental Impact Assessment of River Valley Projects*, 1989 (third update).

This is the Indian regime. The World Bank has its own environmental regime.

The development of environmental awareness at the Bank has many parallels with that in India. The World Bank appointed its first environmental advisor in 1970 and in 1971 created a small in-house environmental unit which was given responsibility for reviewing environmental and related health aspects of projects being considered by the Bank. Operational policy memoranda at the time required that every appraisal include consideration at an early stage of the possible effects of any project on the environment of the country and on the health and wellbeing of its people. A determination was also required to be made of the measures which might be necessary to prevent or mitigate adverse impacts arising from a project.

In 1978, the Bank's procedures were amended to highlight the need to adopt broad environmental criteria in carrying out screening processes for projects, and to caution against the selection of projects that might have excessive social or environmental costs. Social, cultural, and environmental impacts of a project were to be part of feasibility studies. Two previous Bank publications summarizing these kinds of considerations were cited, namely: *Environment, Health, and Human Ecologic Considerations in Economic Development Projects* (World Bank, May 1974) and *Environment and Development* (World Bank, June 1975). Loan officers were given special responsibility to make sure that all issues related to socioculturally relevant institutions and the protection of the environment were properly considered. This was the requirement when the Bank mounted a reconnaissance mission in November 1978 to review Narmada development plans and "to determine an appropriate means for Bank involvement."[6]

In 1980, Robert McNamara, then president of the Bank, endorsed the *World Conservation Strategy* prepared by the International Union for the Conservation of Nature. In 1984, a Bank directive defined the scope of environmental concerns, outlined environmental policies, and described the principles behind its environmental guidelines. It also outlined how environmental considerations were to be taken into account in the project cycle, noting in particular that the identification and preparation of environmental considerations should be introduced during the early stages of a project. This 1984 directive was the operational statement in force when the Bank was conducting the appraisals for the Sardar Sarovar Projects.

In 1986, the Bank developed formal policies related to wildlands, biodiversity, and cultural property. Then in 1987, as part of a more general reorganization, the Bank replaced its office of Environmental and Scientific Affairs with a much larger Environment Department. Environmental advisory divisions were also created within each of the Bank's geographic operational regions, including India. From this point on, environmental considerations became more specific. For example, in 1989, the Bank sponsored a seminar in Washington on dam safety and the environment to consolidate experience related to the design and management of dams in order to improve their safety and lessen their environmental impact. A comprehensive technical paper based on the proceedings was published by the Bank.[7] In 1989, the Bank also issued a new Op-

---

[6] Staff Appraisal Report, 1985, p 6.

[7] Guy LeMoigne, Shawki Barghouti, and Hervé Plusquellec, *Dam Safety and the Environment*, World Bank Technical Paper Number 115, 1990.

erational Directive on environmental assessment that included a specific policy governing dams and reservoirs. This set out the broad process of assessment relating to costs and benefits, design alternatives, river basin planning,
involuntary resettlement, environmental recognizance, environmental assessment and appraisal, as well as matters related to consultation with non-
government organizations and other affected groups. The directive was
amended in September 1991; it now describes the purpose and nature of environmental assessments and the types of environmental analysis that are required, various institutional aspects related to environment, the environmental assessment procedures that are to be used, and so on. Annexes to the directive provide checklists and outline the issues and project-specific items that
should be considered when preparing environmental assessments.

Finally, in 1991 the Bank's Environment Department published a three
volume *Environmental Assessment Sourcebook* that dealt with: Policies, Procedures
and Cross-Sectoral Issues (Volume I); Sectoral Guidelines (Volume II); and
Guidelines for Environment Assessment of Energy and Industry Projects
(Volume III). Volumes II and III contain sections that are particularly relevant
to our review, including:
• Volume II, Chapter 8: dams and reservoirs, fisheries, flood protection, natural forest management, plantation development and reforestation, and irrigation and drainage.
• Volume III, Chapter 10: hydroelectric projects.

Throughout the period of project development and construction of the Sardar Sarovar Projects, there was in place an environmental assessment protocol
and methodology based on the Bank's and India's own environmental directives, guidelines, and procedures. Although this regime has become clearer
and stronger over time, it still has drawbacks. These were summarized by the
Bank in its 1991 *India Irrigation Sector Review*[8] in a way that we have found has
particular relevance to the Sardar Sarovar Projects experience. Under the
heading "Approach to Environmental Problems" it states:

> ... several current drawbacks in the system need attention.
> First, the environmental clearance process is frequently used
> simply as a delaying or blocking mechanism against any project
> with potential negative impact. Unfortunately, political pres-
> sures are frequently employed to get round this constraint with
> the result that projects with real environmental problems may
> be approved without the appropriate overview and addressment

[8] The World Bank, *India Irrigation Sector Review*, Vols I and II, Report No. 9518-IN, December 20,
1991.

of environmental issues. A better approach would be an early assessment of environmental impact with a view to incorporating design features to minimize environment damage. Project blockage may still be appropriate if satisfactory solutions cannot be found, but any decision should take into consideration full project costs, benefits and environmental impacts, rather than the single yardstick of environmental impact. Second, even with the environmental assessment process, project implementation often still falls short of addressing the environmental concerns and objectives identified in Environmental Impact Assessments. (Vol. II, p 76)

ENVIRONMENTAL CONDITIONS

Out of this regime of evolving laws, regulations, guidelines, and policies came the environmental conditions for the Sardar Sarovar Projects. We turn to their application.

In 1965, India appointed a committee to develop a master plan for the Narmada Basin. The committee's recommendations were not accepted by the riparian states. This impasse led to the appointment of the Narmada Water Disputes Tribunal in 1969. Its deliberations continued until 1979. The Tribunal considered the Sardar Sarovar Projects and the Narmada Sagar Projects *together* using the best hydrological, engineering, and other evidence available. The Tribunal did so when environmental awareness had not achieved its current profile. In fact, environmental considerations were not part of the Tribunal's mandate. The Bank's 1985 Sardar Sarovar Projects Supplementary Data Volume describes the state of the project at the time:

> When the NWDT [Narmada Water Disputes Tribunal] made its basic award in August 1978, the GOG [Government of Gujarat] had already prepared a fourteen volume feasibility study for the SSP [Sardar Sarovar Projects] and there was a strong desire to start building the project according to these plans. However, the existing plans had basically been prepared in the 1950s and 1960s.... But the plans were largely prepared against a background of riparian conflicts with the objective to justify the greatest possible allocation of water.... Furthermore, the existing plans were based on design concepts that had changed little since the nineteenth century. There was no clear link between the envisaged mode of operation and the design criteria adopted for the canal system. In short, if the project had been built ac-

cording to those plans, it could not have been operated to meet even the most basic of today's irrigation demands, much less to meet the agricultural goals and requirements of the twenty-first century at full project development. (pp 24-5)

In its 1979 award, the Narmada Water Disputes Tribunal made many of the most fundamental environmental decisions affecting the Sardar Sarovar Projects—dam location, regulation of flows, reservoir levels, etc. Although the Tribunal never explicitly acknowledged them as such in its award, these factors are the triggering mechanisms for almost all environmental impacts (something explicitly recognized in the environmental guidelines of the Bank and India). We discuss this when considering hydrology and water management in Chapter 11.

There are points in the Tribunal award that bear on the environmental aspects of our review:
- the utilizable quantum of Narmada waters at the Sardar Sarovar dam site is specified at 28 million acre feet (MAF) on the basis of 75 per cent dependability (§II);
- apportionment is to be 18.25 MAF for Madhya Pradesh, Gujarat 9.00 MAF, Rajasthan 0.50 MAF, and Maharashtra 0.25 (§III) or in that ratio (§IV);
- the apportionment/sharing of waters (§III and §IV) are subject to review after 45 years (§V and §XVI);
- the canal and dam water levels are fixed (§VI and §VII);
- the multi-purpose character of the project, including hydroelectric power, is affirmed (§VIII);
- Madhya Pradesh is to provide regulated releases of water from the Narmada Sagar Projects to the Sardar Sarovar Projects (§IX); and
- terms of the award are subject to change if there is agreement between all the states concerned (§XIV.17).

The Bank's November 1978 reconnaissance mission to review the Narmada basin development plans anticipated the Tribunal's final award. The mission's three recommendations set the stage for project preparation and appraisal: Gujarat established the Narmada Planning Group; consultants were retained for systems studies and general planning; and key foreign experts were retained in 1979 through the United Nations' Development Program and a $10 million special project preparation component of a Bank credit. In August-September 1980 the Bank mounted a special mission "to review GOG's [Government of Gujarat's] existing plans and to propose a timebound program for the planning and preparation of the SSP."[9] The 1985 Supplementary

[9] Staff Appraisal Report, Supplementary Data Volume, Part I, p 25.

Data Volume says that this mission led "to a close cooperation between the Bank and GOG in defining and guiding the planning process" (Part I, p 25). The documents we have reviewed indicate that environmental issues played little part in this process.

Quite apart from the Tribunal, which had been created to resolve an interstate dispute, the Government of India had regularized its mandatory procedure for sanctioning major projects such as Sardar Sarovar. Prior to construction, technical, economic, environmental, and planning priority clearances now had to be obtained for the Sardar Sarovar Projects from the various ministries and from the Planning Commission of India. Of these, the most important for purposes of our review are the environmental and forest use clearances.

In 1983 *both* the Sardar Sarovar and the Narmada Sagar Projects were before the Department of Environment for clearance. The application was supported by a short-term benchmark study sponsored by the Narmada Planning Group and conducted by experts in zoology, botany, ecology, geology, geography, and soil chemistry at the Maharaja Sayajirao (M. S.) University of Baroda. The information provided did not meet the environmental guideline requirements. A 1991 overview of the Sardar Sarovar Projects environmental conservation program by the Nigam refers to this M. S. University of Baroda study stating: "Relevant literature useful in the Indian context was scarce. Naturally, therefore, the inferences were influenced, largely, by individual insights and limited information sources and perceptions of the overall study objectives."[10] Environmental clearance was not granted and a dialogue between the ministry and the state proponents ensued on the nature of the deficiencies in the submission and the additional studies that would be required. These discussions were taking place while the Bank was considering the loan and credit agreements for the Sardar Sarovar Projects.

In 1985, after several years of discussions, the Bank approved the credit and loan agreements for the Sardar Sarovar dam and canal projects. Consideration of the Narmada Sagar Projects was deferred, even though the Tribunal award and the project designs assumed simultaneous construction schedules. A March 14, 1990 Office Memorandum of the Bank explains the current status of the deferred upstream projects:

> The Bank has indicated to GOI [Government of India] and GOMP [Government of Madhya Pradesh] that it will agree to reactivate the Narmada Sagar projects under the following three pre-

---

[10] *Sardar Sarovar Project, Environment Conservation Programme*, Gandhinagar, Gujarat: Sardar Sarovar Narmada Nigam Limited, October 1991, p 4.

conditions: (a) continued progress on implementation of both
SSP projects [dam and canal], particularly the R&R [resettlement
and rehabilitation] and environmental aspects; (b) an Environmental Assessment, satisfactory to the Bank; and (c) a complete
financing plan, including co-financing, would be agreed upon in
principle. (p 1)

The Bank's 1985 credit and loan agreements for the Sardar Sarovar Projects did cover certain environmental issues. The Government of India agreed
to release forest lands reserved by the *Forest (Conservation) Act, 1980* if required,
and to cause the state governments to implement the project. The three state
governments agreed in collaboration to prepare a work plan by December 31,
1985, to deal with the environmental effects, including: training programs
(plans, schedules, and funding); and studies and implementation schedules
covering fish and fisheries, forests and wildlife, and public health. Each state
government agreed to take necessary measures to minimize risks of malaria, filaria, schistosomiasis, and other water-related diseases. The project authorities in Gujarat further agreed to undertake training programs for project staff
in environmental science and related mitigation measures.

The Bank's 1985 Staff Appraisal Report for the Sardar Sarovar Projects included a discussion of environmental issues, guided, we assume, by the Bank's
1984 comprehensive environmental policy. These issues were summarized in
three pages in the two Staff Appraisal Reports (for the dam-related works and
for the canal-related works), and referred to in five pages in the two Supplementary Data Volumes. The treatment was cursory. No mention was made of
India's environmental approval requirements. No mention was made of the
fact that two years earlier the Ministry of Environment and Forests declined to
provide clearance for the project. No mention was made about the discussions
in India on the nature of the information necessary to have the project cleared
by various central agencies.

In 1985 and 1986 discussions came to a head in India regarding the need
for environmental clearance for both the Narmada Sagar Projects and the Sardar Sarovar Projects; there was increasing pressure for approval to be given.
The Bank's prior approval of the Sardar Sarovar Projects, which included environmental considerations, was a factor in these discussions. The project proponents told the Ministry of Environment and Forests that it would take two
or three years to develop the information that was required by the ministry.
Yet it was necessary, they said, to begin construction. Enough time had been
lost and the Bank's loan and credit were in-hand.

In May 1987, the Chief Ministers of Gujarat, Madhya Pradesh, Maharashtra, and Rajasthan met with Prime Minister Rajiv Gandhi to discuss clearance

of the Narmada projects. A briefing note from the Ministry of Environment and Forests summarized the current status of the Projects. The interdependence of the Narmada Sagar and Sardar Sarovar Projects was described and it was suggested that modifications could be made to the Projects to minimize environmental damage. The more advanced state of readiness of the Sardar Sarovar Projects was acknowledged. The environmental implications of some of the engineering aspects, including the hydrological calculations of dependable runoff, were explored. It was noted that even though "the project formulation has been in progress for more than three decades and the active interaction of the Project authorities has been going on for almost three years, the absence and inadequacy of data on some important environmental aspects still persists."[11]

In June 1987, a compromise was reached. A conditional environmental clearance for both the Sardar Sarovar Projects and the Narmada Sagar Projects was granted. The clearance letter from the Ministry of Environment and Forests notes that although "field surveys are not yet complete . . . complete details have been assured to be furnished by 1989."[12] The letter contained a schedule. Eight matters were included: rehabilitation master plan; phased catchment area treatment scheme; compensatory afforestation plan; command area development; survey of flora and fauna; carrying capacity of surrounding area; seismicity; and health aspects. All were to be completed by 1989. In addition, the clearance letter notes that the Narmada Control Authority had been expanded to ensure that the environmental safeguard measures would be planned and implemented in depth and the pace of its implementation would be *pari passu* with the progress of the work on the Projects. The four conditions of the clearance were:

- the Narmada Control Authority would ensure that the environmental measures are planned and implemented *pari passu* with the progress of the work on the project;
- the detailed surveys/studies would be done as scheduled (i.e., by 1989) and submitted for assessment;
- catchment area treatment and rehabilitation programs would be completed ahead of reservoir filling; and
- the Department of Environment would be kept informed of progress.

In September 1987, under the *Forest (Conservation) Act, 1980*, the central gov-

[11] Cited in Claude Alvares and Ramesh Billorey, *Damming the Narmada*, Appendix 3, Penang, Malaysia: Third World Network, 1988, p 115.
[12] Government of India, Ministry of Environment and Forests, Office Memorandum No. 3-87/80-IA, June 24, 1987, p 1.

ernment gave approval for the diversion of over 13,000 hectares of forest land for the Sardar Sarovar Projects.[13] This approval was subject to eleven conditions in all three states, of which the following are especially relevant for our review:[14]

• detailed compensatory afforestation plans would be submitted by September 30, 1987;

• a proposal for non-forest areas for rehabilitation of oustees would be submitted by November 30, 1987;

• compensatory afforestation would be in double the area of degraded forest lands in addition to the afforestation of equivalent non-forest land, and a scheme for this would be submitted by November 30, 1987;

• a catchment area treatment plan will be prepared by November 30, 1987, failing which a central government team would be appointed at a cost to the project; and

• no forest land would be utilized for the rehabilitation of oustees.[15]

Finally, in October 1988, the Planning Commission of the Government of India granted the State of Gujarat approval for the Sardar Sarovar Projects subject to seven conditions that bear on the environment (as well as resettlement and rehabilitation):[16]

• compliance with the 1987 environmental and forestry clearances;

• adequate funding to meet the construction schedule;

• submission of a detailed program for drainage and ground water balance studies beyond the Mahi River;

• adoption of measures to ensure project revenue from water rates to pay for annual operation and maintenance charges;

• setting up an expert group to study siltation in the main canal;

• drawing up a detailed schedule and plans for the micro-level irrigation network system; and

• an implementation schedule for completion of the canal network so that irrigation benefits do, in fact, start accruing from the financial investment.

As a result of all these endeavors, a rigorous and appropriate arrangement agreed to by both state and central governments was in place before the end of 1988 to ensure that, by the target date of 1989, an adequate assessment of the

---

[13] One month later, forestry clearance was also given for the Narmada Sagar Projects.

[14] Government of India, Ministry of Environment and Forests, Memorandum No. 8-372/83-FC, September 8, 1987.

[15] This condition is of particular interest because it differs from the 1985 Bank Agreement with India. It is also conspicuous in its absence from the forest clearance for the Narmada Sagar Projects.

[16] Government of India, Planning Commission, Memorandum No. 2(194)/88-I&CAD, October 5, 1988, pp 1-2.

environmental impact of the Narmada Sagar Projects and the Sardar Sarovar Projects would be made.

COMPLIANCE

In assessing compliance, we examined the documents required by India's environmental clearances, and under the Bank's agreements. We read the Bank's Back-to-Office and Mission reports from the mid-1980s to 1992. We read the minutes of the meetings of the Narmada Control Authority's Environment Sub-Group, and we reviewed documents supplied by the Narmada Control Authority, the Ministry of Water Resources, the Ministry of Environment and Forests, the three state governments, and the Sardar Sarovar Narmada Nigam Limited. We also interviewed Bank officials and Government of India and state officials as well as officers of the Nigam. We talked with non-government organizations, academics, and others who track Sardar Sarovar Projects issues. Numerous submissions made to us, both verbal and written, also dealt with the compliance issues.

We found that there are fundamental compliance problems. These go beyond a failure to address a checklist of environmental requirements. There appears to have been an institutional numbness at the Bank and in India to environmental matters. The tendency seems to have been to justify rather than analyze; to react rather than anticipate. This is disturbing when it is realized that in most cases both the terms and dates for compliance were the result of negotiations and, often, were based on assurances from the project proponents themselves.

In 1985 the Bank and India entered into legal agreements that included terms on studies and deadlines for completion of those studies. In the Bank's January 1992 Status Rating of key performance indicators for the dam and canal projects, the "Environmental Aspects" are checklist rated as having "moderate problems," with "Health/Malaria Control" rated as a "major problem but being adequately addressed." For both projects the overall status is rated as having "moderate problems." Overall compliance with covenants is rated as presenting "no significant problems" for the dam but "moderate problems" for the canal. The more detailed breakdown on the status of the covenants for Gujarat, Maharashtra, and Madhya Pradesh states that "studies continue,training weak." The Status Rating notes that the original completion date for these studies was 1985 (later extended to 1989).[17]

[17] India Sardar Sarovar Dam and Power Project (Cr. 1552-IN/Ln. 2497-IN) and Sardar Sarovar Water Delivery and Drainage Project (Cr. 1553-IN), January 1992 Engineering and Financial Review: Field Report, Annex 3, Part I(a).

Given the background, this report card is generous. Nevertheless, the covering letter for the report says "the mission was pleased with the excellent progress made on the construction of the dam and noted that the Nigam was considering the possibility of advancing the construction by one year to enable power generation and irrigation to start in July 1994 instead of July 1995." It adds that "obstacles remain in the way of meeting this ambitious target." Resettlement and rehabilitation were mentioned as obstacles. Environment was not mentioned except for the need to address "with the utmost attention" recommendations arising from a recent report on malaria and other health-related aspects of the Projects.[18]

Environmental non-compliance on the Sardar Sarovar Projects is a theme recurring in the Bank files. For example, an environmental workplan (including training programs) was required in the credit and loan agreements to be prepared by December 1985. It was not. Indeed, it probably could not be, because the Projects had failed to be cleared by India two years earlier, and the problems related to that clearance continued. In December 1986, a year after the environmental workplan was to have been prepared, the Bank was arranging a visit to India to review compliance, but correspondence with the Government of Gujarat shows that they were "not assured that GOI's [Government of India's] overall environmental clearance will be received prior to the mission" (December 10, 1986). The June 1987 Bank mission report states that, "The long wait for environmental clearance is over." With the Narmada Control Authority assuming more direct responsibility for environmental issues, the mission recommended that the Authority "furnish the Bank without delay, for its use, review, and comment, a related record of all commitments and/or constraints affecting implementation of the projects . . . as well as the timebound schedule for accomplishing such actions." The subsequent Back-to-Office and Mission Reports show:

• September 1988: Bank staff "expressed concerns about the weakness of environmental management and planning at both the state and central levels" (discussions on this topic were to continue).

• October 1988: "The Secretary of DOEF has also expressed concern about the confusion and absence of an integrated approach to resolving potential environmental problems. . . . It is evident that many of the environmental components of the project are in disarray. . . . It is still unclear what the projects are intended to achieve, what the NVDA's [Narmada Valley Development Authority's] and NPG's [Narmada Planning Group's] operations involve, what the environmental and social consequences of the projects might be, and how State and Federal authorities intend to deal with them . . . opportunities are

[18] Letter from the World Bank to C. C. Patel, February 24, 1992, p 2.

being squandered.... Institutional arrangements for effective coordination continue to prove elusory [sic] and there is much inefficient use of resources."

- November 1988: "A comprehensive environmental management framework should be formulated and then institutionalized.... this is essential to ensure the phasing of all required environmental studies and actions with the engineering components of the Project and the effective coordination between the States and the Central Government.... Outstanding studies concerning fish, fisheries, forests and wildlife and public health should be initiated as soon as possible."
- May 1989: "The preparation of a comprehensive environmental framework (stipulated as a 'workplan' in the Project Agreement) and its subsequent institutionalization in the States of Madhya Pradesh, Gujarat and Maharashtra, and the NCA, and DOEF, has yet to be started." (Terms of reference for preparation of an environmental framework were attached.)
- December 1989: "In meetings in Delhi, MOWR [Ministry of Water Resources], NCA, and MOEF endorsed the urgent need for a comprehensive environmental framework (stipulated as a work plan in the Project Agreement) for application at the state (Nigam and NVDA) and Federal (NCA, MOWR and MOEF) levels."
- January 1990: "The preparation of a comprehensive environmental framework... has yet to be initiated." And, "In meetings in Delhi, MOWR, NCA and MOEF endorsed the urgent need for a comprehensive environmental framework (stipulated as a 'workplan' in the Project Agreement) for application at State... and Federal... levels. The mission stated that the continued absence of the framework poses major problems for the DOEF and NCA in coordinating and monitoring implementation of environmental studies and integrating the work of the concerned states.... The Nigam is to review training needs for environmental planning and management."
- February 1990: (Not mentioned).
- June 1991: "Overall progress continues in fulfilling the conditions of legal agreements and clearance stipulation of the MOEF... [the NCA] currently seems to have only marginal impact on the execution of the environmental studies and action plans and beyond occasional meetings, has done little to help integrate the studies and plans with engineering planning and implementation."
- January 1992: "studies continue, training weak."

The Bank, in sanctioning deficient fulfilment of negotiated obligations, has demonstrated its unwillingness to enforce conditions required by its own environmental policies and which it had required in the 1985 credit and loan agreements. What has happened also belies the assurances offered in the Staff Appraisal Reports.

An assessment of compliance of Sardar Sarovar Projects with India's conditional environmental clearances is not as straightforward. There are differences between the documentation available from the Narmada Control Authority and that available from the Ministry of Environment and Forests. Indeed, the Executive Member of the Narmada Control Authority dismisses as irrelevant the summary of compliance and progress produced by the Ministry of Environment and Forests. His view is that only the Narmada Control Authority, as the interstate agency constituted as a result of the Narmada Water Disputes Tribunal, is in a position officially to define progress. In February 1992, however, Ministry officials reconfirmed that their summary should be considered as the official position of the agency that issued the conditional clearance.

The 1987 clearance required "complete details" in eight areas by 1989. The Narmada Control Authority maintains that, despite some slippage, all are on track and will be completed *pari passu* with the project. The Ministry of Environment and Forests is less optimistic. A summary of its position as of December 1991 is as follows:

- Rehabilitation master plan: works being monitored by the Narmada Control Authority's Resettlement & Rehabilitation Sub-Group and by the Supreme Court;
- Catchment area treatment: completion before impoundment not likely (extent to be treated and budgetary allocations yet to be finalized);
- Compensatory afforestation: details on plans for 1,900 hectares of non-forest land in Maharashtra still awaited;
- Command Area Development: action plans not available, time frame not known;
- Flora, fauna, and carrying capacity: action plans likely to be ready after three years' study in 1993;
- Seismicity: studies in Maharashtra and Madhya Pradesh expected to be completed in 1992;
- Health aspects: final plan awaited from the Government of Maharashtra;
- Archaeological studies: plans for relocation of temples/monuments yet to be submitted; and
- Fisheries Development: studies on migratory species, their breeding grounds with protection measures, design of mechanized lifts, etc., still to be initiated.

Project documents in India say that there is a time-bound environmental plan. But what exists in practice is a highly elastic framework justified by the *pari passu* provision of the 1987 environmental clearance. Detailed studies and surveys were required to be carried out and to be made available for assessment by 1989. The Ministry of Environment and Forests' position is that this has not happened, even to December 1991. We have seen nothing that excuses the Sardar Sarovar Projects authorities from complying with the conditions of the clearance. We cannot believe that these conditions can be set at naught by the *ipse dixit* of the Narmada Control Authority.

The *pari passu* requirement was used for the first time on the Sardar Sarovar Projects (but it has been used since in India with Sardar Sarovar cited as the precedent). When we asked officials at the Narmada Control Authority for a practical definition of *pari passu* as it applies to this project generally and in each of the eight areas specified in the conditional clearance, we were told that what it means is that when the dam is completed the environmental work would be completed also; they would, so to speak, cross the finish line together. We think this is unsound; it subverts any acceptable notion of ecological planning. Without the proper timing and sequencing of surveys, assessments, action plans, and the development and implementation of ameliorative measures, decisions on one aspect of the Projects can prejudice the proper resolution on others.

The agenda and minutes of the August 1990 Narmada Control Authority Environment Sub-Group meetings indicate that the Ministry of Environment and Forests' conditional approval "must be deemed to have lapsed" and, based on revised action plans schedules to be provided, "the Project Authorities should seek renewal of environmental and forestry clearance" (p 13). This matter was discussed by the Narmada Control Authority's Review Committee (composed of chief ministers of the states as well as the federal minister responsible) when they met in Bombay on September 18, 1990. The minutes of that meeting show that the Secretary of Water Resources stated that the conditions stipulated by the Ministry of Environment and Forests for preparation of environmental action plans within the time frame had not been met and that the Ministry of Environment and Forests was seeking to have the state governments request an extension of time for meeting the conditions. After some discussion, India's Minister of State for Water Resources, as Chairman, said that the Narmada Control Authority on behalf of all the states would approach the Ministry of Environment and Forests for an extension.

On November 22, 1990, the Secretary of the Ministry of Environment and Forests wrote to the Secretary of Water Resources to remind him that the chief ministers had decided that a request for a formal extension was to be forthcoming. The request was to address three matters:

• the reasons for delay in the formulation of environmental action plans to date and the steps taken to overcome the identified obstacles;

• a realistic revised time frame for the preparation of comprehensive environ-

mental and forestry action plans along with details of the mobilization of inputs for their timely implementation; and
• a revised construction schedule matching the proposed time frame for implementation of the environmental and forestry action plans.

At the 38th meeting of the Narmada Control Authority held early in 1991, the Chairman began with an inquiry about the scope of *pari passu* implementation. He noted that "some of the environmental safeguard measures are ongoing as per schedule and some others (a major part) are not."[19] The minutes show that the Narmada Control Authority had not applied for extension of time for compliance with the conditions of clearance as had been decided at the meeting with the chief ministers held on September 18, 1990. Some members explained that for the most part they were satisfied that with the revised target for completion of Sardar Sarovar Projects (1997/98), *pari passu* implementation was feasible and an extension on that account might not be necessary.

We have reviewed the correspondence between the Secretary of Environment and Forests and the Secretary of Water Resources from November 22, 1990 to February 17, 1992. The three issues that were identified as requiring attention (cited above) have not been addressed. The position of the Ministry of Environment and Forests is that the clearance, even if it is not regarded to have "lapsed," must be "renewed." The Secretary, Ministry of Water Resources states that "it will be neither appropriate nor desirable to draw up an extended programme of construction of the project...," and he offers assurance "that every attempt is being made to ensure implementation of the environmental safeguard measures *pari-passu* with the *completion* of construction of the project" (emphasis added).[20] It is apparent that an impasse had developed.

We inquired about this impasse. Senior officials at the Ministry of Water Resources and at the Narmada Control Authority told us that if the Ministry of Environment and Forests is unhappy with progress of environmental work under the *pari passu* formula, its Secretary, in his position as Chairman of the Authority's Environment Sub-Group, is in a position to make the necessary changes. We find this difficult to accept. It confuses quite separate functions of a senior civil servant. And if this line of reasoning is pursued, it would quite improperly result in placing the responsibility for implementation with the government's environmental regulators rather than with the project proponents.

This bureaucratic tangle would be of a little importance if it were not for

---

[19] Narmada Control Authority, Minutes of Meeting, Item No. XXXVIII-6(417): Review of Activities of the Environment Sub-Group, p 18.
[20] Government of India, Ministry of Water Resources, D.O. No. 5/30/91-PP, August 22, 1991, p 1.

the fact that wrapped up in the controversy are environmental issues of the first importance. The Bank's legal agreement requires that the project be carried out "in conformity with appropriate . . . environmental, sociological and public utilities practices . . . [supported by] the funds, facilities, staff, services and other resources required for the purposes." What does this mean in the context of the failure to meet the date requirements of the conditional clearances on time or at all?

A May 1991 report prepared for the World Bank by Dr. Gita Gopal[21] points out there is as yet no well coordinated strategy to respond to the emerging environmental crises in India. Nearly every environment-related law has major loopholes and inadequacies. The study states that the most important issue with respect to the environmental regulatory framework in India is the failure to integrate environmental clearance into the process of review and approval of projects. It does acknowledge, however, that the central environmental impact assessment process is by far the most systematic and comprehensive of environmental reviews now carried out in India. The study suggests that the measures to be taken should include:

- expansion of the scope of the projects to which environmental impact assessment is applied;
- strengthening of the legal basis for impact assessment (with the report citing the provisional clearance for the Sardar Sarovar Projects as an example of the need);
- enlargement of the assessment content with more vigorous analysis;
- improvement of the monitoring of implementation of the environmental management plan;
- increase of staff resources for carrying out the assessments; and
- extension of the assessment process to cover state and private sector projects.

Many of the same concerns have been raised by experts in India, including those within the Ministry of Environment and Forests. In the Sixth Plan of India (1980-1984) there is an emphasis on sustainable development which includes this statement:

> The environment must not be considered as another sector of national development. It should form a crucial guiding dimension for plans and programs in each sector. . . .
>
> Environmental problems in India can be classified into two broad categories:
> a) Those arising from conditions of poverty and underdevelopment; and

---

[21] Dr. Gita Gopal, *India National Laws and Regulations on Environmental Protection Checklist*, May 1991.

b) Those arising as negative effects of the very process of development.

The first category has to do with the impact on the health and the integrity of our natural resources . . . as a result of poverty and the inadequate availability for a large section of our population of the means to fulfil basic human needs. . . . The second category has to do with the unintended side effects of efforts to achieve rapid economic growth and development. In this latter category would fall the distortions imposed on national resources from poorly planned development projects and programs as well as from lack of attention to long-term concerns by commercial and other vested interests. Thus it is clear that a concern for the environment is essentially a desire to see that national development proceeds along rational, sustainable lines. Environmental conservation is, in fact, the very basis of all development.[22]

Environmental impact studies, to be most effective, must precede construction. Only in that way can the studies lead to efficient, proactive resolution of problems. It becomes increasingly difficult to anticipate and prevent impacts as a project proceeds towards completion. The 1979 award of the Narmada Water Disputes Tribunal did not consider the environment. The *pari passu* condition attached to India's environmental clearance of the Sardar Sarovar Projects was a difficult environmental compromise required to accommodate other agendas. It is now too late to develop and implement many of the mitigative measures that would have been most effective had the impact been understood at the outset. Most of the Bank's 1985 legal requirements for the environment have not been met. Most of the conditions attached to the 1987 environmental clearances by the Government of India have not been met. By any reasonable standard of the Bank or the Government of India this ought to be unacceptable.

The general Sardar Sarovar history of compliance is a history of omissions, unmet deadlines, extensions, and *ex post facto* revisions. In a Bank Office Memorandum of November 19, 1990, a senior official states "if one looks at what the Bank legal agreements state with respect to environmental studies and training, and the MOEF [Ministry of Environment and Forests] clearance requirements, those who are not fully familiar with the background might con-

---

[22] Cited in Dr. S. Maudgal, "Environmental Impact Assessment in India: An Overview," *Training Workshop on Environmental Impact Assessment and Evaluation: Proceedings and Training Manual*, Vol. 1, January 1988, p 114.

clude that there has been gross delinquency." We did examine the background. We find it difficult to escape that conclusion.

What is the significance of this non-compliance? Is it merely a *pro forma* exercise of legal but otherwise no practical significance? Or have substantial environmental issues not been addressed? Are there real economic, ecological and social consequences? Can ameliorative measures still be taken? We address this concerns under three headings: Upstream Environment, Downstream Environment and Command Area Environment. But first, it is necessary to review the overarching issues related to hydrology and water management.

The Narmada in the Nimad region of Madhya Pradesh, where the river is at its widest. The woman is taking the ritual bath carried out at the time of the new moon.

Chapter 11
HYDROLOGY AND
WATER MANAGEMENT

THE impacts of Sardar Sarovar Projects are determined to a great extent by river hydrology and project water management. A large part of the natural flow of the Narmada, the fifth largest river in India, will be diverted, and its regime will be changed drastically. The resulting environmental impacts will be evident upstream and downstream of the dam and throughout the irrigated area in Gujarat and Rajasthan (the command area).

India describes the Sardar Sarovar Projects as "the largest water resources development project in India and possibly the world."[1] The Bank has described Sardar Sarovar as "one of the most ambitious water resource development projects ever attempted."[2] According to the Bank, the 1979 Tribunal award "opened up the possibility of an immense water resource."[3] In so doing it established many of the most basic conditions that trigger impacts. Understanding the main features of the Projects is a necessary prerequisite to our review of the environmental impact assessment and the proposed ameliorative measures. These features include the location, design, and operation of the Sardar Sarovar Projects' dam, reservoir, powerhouse, and canal system. It also includes the interrelationship of Sardar Sarovar with other projects upstream on the Narmada River.

Sardar Sarovar was not conceived as a stand-alone project. It is part of a

---

[1] Shri P. A. Raj, *Facts, Sardar Sarovar Project (Updated)*, Gandhinagar, Gujarat: Sardar Sarovar Narmada Nigam Limited, November 1990, p 1.

[2] The World Bank, Staff Appraisal Report: *India, Narmada River Development—Gujarat*, Supplementary Data Volume, Part I, p 24.

[3] Staff Appraisal Report, Supplementary Data Volume, Part I, p 27.

basin-wide river development scheme. Over the next half century it is anticipated that there will be 30 major, 135 medium, and about 3,000 minor projects
in the Narmada River valley. Although it is one of the first to be built on the
main river, Sardar Sarovar is to be the terminal project on the river system. Its
design and operation, and hence its benefits and impacts, are linked to developments upstream by the hydrology of the river. This is particularly true with
respect to the Narmada Sagar Projects which are planned to be constructed
immediately upstream and consist of one major dam (Narmada Sagar) and
two medium dams (Omkareshwar and Maheshwar). A 1990 Office Memorandum of the Bank summarized the interdependence of the Sardar Sarovar Projects and Narmada Sagar Projects this way:

> Under the Narmada Water Disputes Tribunal (NWDT) award of
> 1979, the NSP dam was to be completed at the same time as, or
> prior to, the SSP dam. Because the NSP dam was required to pro-
> vide controlled water releases to the SSP reservoir, it was neces-
> sary technically to construct the downstream Omkareshwar and
> Maheshwar dams at the same time.... Live water storage in the
> SSP reservoir and economic benefits to SSP were dependent on
> regulated releases from the NSP dam, and the benefits for MP
> [Madhya Pradesh] from NSP were dependent also on power gen-
> eration and irrigation from Omkareshwar and Maheshwar
> (which in turn would also be dependent on controlled releases
> from NSP). Thus, the three dams of the NSC [Narmada Sagar
> Complex] with their power and irrigation components, together
> with the two SSP projects and the related R&R and area develop-
> ment aspects for all four reservoirs and their catchment areas,
> should be viewed as a technically and economically interdepen-
> dent development complex.[4]

The interdependent nature of the Sardar Sarovar Projects and Narmada
Sagar Projects includes environmental aspects, many of which are integral
parts of the technical and economic aspects. If the upstream projects are delayed, modified, or cancelled, many of the impacts as well as the benefits that
are assumed for the Sardar Sarovar Projects will be changed substantially.
    From 1969 to 1979 the Narmada Water Disputes Tribunal considered the
Sardar Sarovar and the Narmada Sagar Projects together. India proceeded on
the same basis in its 1987 environmental clearance. Yet, in 1985, the Bank
chose to proceed as if the environmental issues arising from the Sardar Sarovar

---

[4] Office Memorandum, March 14, 1990, p 2.

Projects were somehow discrete, orphaned ecologically from the family of projects within which they were conceived and will operate.

For most of the last decade in the Narmada valley, the Bank has invited consideration of the Narmada Projects in discrete consecutive technical and financial slices. This was the 1985 approach to Sardar Sarovar and we find that precedent is cited in the March 1990 Bank Office Memorandum which suggests that the Narmada Sagar Complex could also be "packaged into several projects, and probably also timeslices. This could imply six separate, but interdependent projects: three dam and power projects, two irrigation projects and one area development project...."[5] However convenient financially, this illustrates an ecologically unsustainable concept, a remnant from an era that the Bank's and India's policies have otherwise quite deliberately left behind.

Both the Bank and India now recognize that the watershed is the best planning unit for water resource projects. Both recognize the central theme of hydrology and water management in the assessment of impacts as well as benefits. For example, in its 1980 guidelines, the Ministry of Irrigation has as the first item on the detailed report checklist "the Master Plan for the overall development of the river basin."[6] In the foreword to its 1986 *Guidelines for Collection of Data to Study Environmental Impact of Water Resource Projects*, India's Central Board of Irrigation and Power says that: "construction of water resource projects alter to some extent the ecological and environmental regime; influence the morphological characteristics and dynamics of rivers; and bring about changes in water quality."[7] These guidelines say that environmental information should include data on hydrological conditions of the river basin and on the hydraulic regime of rivers. The same theme is reflected in more recent Bank documents. The section on dams and reservoirs in the Bank's 1991 *Environmental Assessment Sourcebook* states:

> Large dam projects cause irrevocable environmental changes over a wide geographic area and thus have the potential for significant impact.... The area of influence of a dam extends from the upper limits of the catchment of the reservoir to as far down as the estuary, coast and off-shore zone. It includes the watershed and the river valley below the dam.... The major environmental factors affecting the function and life span of the dam are

---

[5] Office Memorandum, March 14, 1990, p 2.
[6] *Working Group Report, Guidelines for Preparation of Detailed Project Report of Irrigation and Multipurpose Projects*, Vols I, II, and III, Government of India, 1980, p 23.
[7] *Guidelines for Collection of Data to Study Environmental Impact of Water Resource Projects*, Miscellaneous Report No. 9, New Delhi: Central Board of Irrigation and Power, October 1986, p 5.

those caused by land, water and other resources used in the catchment above the reservoir (e.g. agriculture, settlement, forest clearing) which may result in increased siltation and changes in the water quality in the reservoir and river downstream.[8]

The *Sourcebook* also contains a section on irrigation and drainage projects:

> Large irrigation projects which impound or divert river waters have the potential to cause major environmental disturbances resulting from changes in the hydrology and limnology of river basins. . . . Reducing the river flow changes floodplain land use and ecology, disrupts riverine and estuarine fisheries, and causes salt water intrusion up the river and into the groundwater of adjacent lands. Diversion and loss of water through irrigation reduces the water supply for downstream users, including municipalities, industries and agriculturalists. A reduction in a river's base flow also decreases the dilution of municipal and industrial wastes added downstream, posing pollution and health hazards. The deterioration of water quality below an irrigation project can render the water unfit for other users, harm aquatic species, and, because of high nutrient content, result in aquatic weed growth that clogs waterways and has health, navigation and ecological consequences. (Vol II, p 94)

In the course of our review, we heard engineers and economists in Washington, New Delhi, and Gandhinagar speak of the Narmada River in terms of acre feet of water and cost/benefit ratios. We heard environmentalists in Bombay, Bhopal, and Baroda speak of the river in terms of habitat, species, and biodiversity. We heard villagers in the Narmada valley speak of these things too, but they also spoke of the Narmada as a home, a provider, and a source of spiritual strength. All were speaking of the same river, sometimes about the same issue, each emphasizing a different dimension of the whole. Our review of the Sardar Sarovar environmental impact assessment begins where these perspectives come together; where engineering and ecology overlap—the hydrology of the river and the water management aspects of the Sardar Sarovar Projects.

---

[8] *Environmental Assessment Sourcebook, Volume II, Sectoral Guidelines, Environment Department*, World Bank Technical Paper Number 140, 1991, p 32.

MULTI-OBJECTIVE PLANNING

India's National Water Policy states that "water development projects should as far as possible be planned and developed as multi-purpose projects."[9] The Policy lists the order of priorities in the allocation of water as drinking water, irrigation, hydroelectric power, navigation, industry and other uses. Sardar Sarovar is designed to provide water for each of these uses except navigation.

Establishing these priorities is only the first step in a multi-purpose water management project. The design and operation of a project such as Sardar Sarovar also requires a balancing of four broad, interlinked objectives: national economic development; regional economic development; social welfare (including public health and income distribution); and environmental protection. Our review takes place in this context, focusing on the latter two items.

Arriving at an acceptable balance of objectives for Sardar Sarovar is not a straightforward technical exercise. Multi-purpose planning requires judgments and policies that cover the full spectrum of "costs" and "benefits," whether these can be quantified readily or not. The award of the Narmada Water Disputes Tribunal dealt with some of these considerations, but not all of them. Since the award, disputes have continued to arise, in part, because important environmental considerations were not understood at the time or were inappropriately valued. The resulting imbalance is a destabilizing element at the center of many of the resettlement and rehabilitation and environmental controversies.

PRINCIPAL WATER MANAGEMENT FEATURES

According to present plans, the Sardar Sarovar dam will divert, on average, 9.5 million acre feet (MAF) of the Narmada River water out of the total of 28 MAF that has been allocated. The reservoir behind the dam will create a narrow lake extending from the dam over 200 kilometers upstream and submerging approximately 37,000 hectares of land once it reaches the full reservoir level. Hydroelectric power will be generated at a riverbed powerhouse discharging downstream and into the estuary at the Gulf of Cambay. In later years, flows through the powerhouse will decrease as water is diverted to the irrigation system. Power will also be generated in the canal head powerhouse to provide some of the energy required for pumping in the irrigation system. The canal is designed for a peak requirement of 40,000 cubic feet per second (cfs) to irrigate 1.8 million hectares in the command area in Gujarat and de-

[9] *National Water Policy*, New Delhi: Government of India, Ministry of Water Resources, September 1987, p 6.

liver a peak flow of 2,500 cfs to the Rajasthan border.[10] Plans for the canal show 19 major river crossings, 244 rail and road crossings, and 31 branch canal off-takes and water canal structures along the route. Two valleys in Saurashtra and Kutchch will be crossed with hydroelectric stations on the falling side and pumping stations on the rising side. A 75,000 kilometer long network of canals will distribute water for irrigation. The irrigation supply will be augmented by an extensive ground water pumping scheme involving thousands of public and private sector wells. Water distribution is being planned to provide for industrial uses and domestic consumption for a forecast population of over 40 million people living in 132 urban centers and 8,215 villages.

About 90 per cent of the Narmada's annual runoff occurs during the three or four months of monsoon rains, usually from June through September. At other times the river flow is comparatively small. The annual floods of the Narmada are intense and sudden, reaching their peaks in a few days, so a large volume of storage is critical to the successful operation of projects on the river. To deal with this type of strong seasonal runoff, the series of dams on the Narmada is designed to capture and store the flood flows for later use during the dry seasons. The Sardar Sarovar Projects will be the last in this cascading series of dams and reservoirs.[11]

The size of the total storage needed on the river was considered by the Narmada Water Disputes Tribunal and a proportion was allocated to the Sardar Sarovar Projects. This "live storage" contains the volume of water to be used for irrigation, power, and other water supply purposes, uses that are dependent on regulated releases of additional water from the Narmada Sagar Projects upstream.

The design of the Sardar Sarovar storage is a balance not only with upstream developments, but also with the rate at which the reservoir will be emptied. According to the Tribunal award, the intent is, on average in three years out of four, to divert 9.5 MAF at Sardar Sarovar and 18.5 MAF elsewhere upstream in the river basin. This 9.5 MAF diversion will be done through the Sardar Sarovar main canal which has a capacity of about 2.4 MAF a month (40,000 cfs). The currently proposed Sardar Sarovar Projects live storage of 4.77 MAF could therefore be emptied by the canal in less than two months. In fact, the dam and canal, as presently designed, are theoretically capable of diverting more than 8 MAF during the three and a half month monsoon. A 1982

---

[10] Narmada Development Department, *Planning for Prosperity: Sardar Sarovar Development Plan*, Gandhinagar, India: Sardar Sarovar Narmada Nigam Limited, November 1989, p 152.

[11] There are a number of dams in existence upstream on the river (including its tributaries), but the functioning of Sardar Sarovar is specifically tied by the Tribunal award to the Narmada Sagar Projects.

report on the planning and operation of the main canal prepared for the Bank by Professor Nathan Buras points out that the canal would flow at less than half its capacity two-thirds of the time and the design flow rate would be achieved only 5.6 per cent of the time.[12] He reports that the canal is probably larger than can be economically justified; a view reflected in many documents in the Bank files and by many of the experts we heard from in the course of our review.

The Sardar Sarovar Projects reservoir also provides water for generating electricity. Hydroelectric power is determined by the product of the height of the water column above the turbines ("head") and the discharge of water through the turbines. Decreasing net head and increasing discharge in the same proportion will result in approximately the same power output. For example, if the height of the Sardar Sarovar dam is reduced, the power capability could be maintained by increasing the discharge capability of the powerhouse. The reverse is also true.[13]

There will be "excess" water available for the riverbed powerhouse during the monsoon because the storage at the Sardar Sarovar Projects is small and the upstream diversions and reservoirs are not being built as planned. During the monsoon, the flow will exceed the combined capacity of the powerhouse and canal, so the excess will have to be stored or spilled. After the flood has passed, the live storage at Sardar Sarovar can be used to supply either the powerhouse or the irrigation canal, or both, depending on water use priorities at the time. During the dry season, a portion of this storage also will hold the water to be pumped back at night from the Garudeshwar Weir, located just downstream of the dam, for release during the peak power demand periods the next day.

In the future, as the full irrigation system comes onstream, the riverbed powerhouse turbines will be idle except for short periods of high "excess" flow and for the periods of pumpback/generation to meet peak demands for elec-

---

[12] Professor Buras wrote six reports from May 1981 to July 1982 that deal with the canal or reservoir. Of particular interest is his report of July 1, 1982, "Narmada/Gujarat (Sardar Sarovar) Project—Report on Project Preparation Mission, May 31-June 11, 1983." The rationale for the canal design is provided in a May 24, 1983, letter report to the Bank by H. D. Fraderiksen entitled "Project Criteria and Plan of Operation." The May 1983 report "The Main Canal its Operation," by the Irrigation Department, Government of Gujarat, also explains the sizing of the canal (pp 9, 15), noting that the surplus waters from rivers on the route of the canal (e.g., Mahi and Watrak) could also be a factor.

[13] The energy, as opposed to the power, produced depends primarily on the annual volume of water that can be passed through the powerhouse. This is primarily dependent on adequate storage to regulate the monsoon flood which may rise hundreds of thousands of cubic feet per second in a day or two. Hence the importance of Narmada Sagar, especially in the early years when the electricity benefits add substantially to the net present value of the Projects.

tricity. There will be no net loss of water from the irrigation system because the powerhouse water would be recycled by pumping at night from the Garudeshwar reservoir.

The riverbed power and energy benefits of Sardar Sarovar are only significant before the irrigation system becomes fully operational. Thereafter, the plan is to divert the water into the canal for the higher priority domestic and agricultural use in Gujarat and Rajasthan. Also, because of the relatively small storage at Sardar Sarovar compared to the monsoon floods, the benefits are substantially increased by the releases of water from upstream projects, particularly Narmada Sagar.

The height of the dam, the reservoir drawdown range, and the size of the canal, which are interrelated, are the triggering mechanisms for environmental impact and resettlement and rehabilitation. The height of the dam and operation of the Narmada River systems is not the result of an economic optimization. The proposed Sardar Sarovar full reservoir level of 455 feet is a compromise decreed by the Tribunal. And there was no environmental impact assessment in the deliberations leading to decisions on the location, design, and operation of the dam. One example presented to our review illustrates the nature of the trade-offs made.

The Tribunal's report concluded that irrigation requirements in Gujarat and Rajasthan could have been met with a full reservoir level of 436 feet. The level was increased to 455 feet to provide hydroelectric power benefits (the third priority after drinking water and irrigation), 57 per cent of which are to go to Madhya Pradesh. But there was a cost for this extra 19 feet. It increased the gross area submerged in Madhya Pradesh by about 35 per cent; the cultivable area submerged was increased by about 50 per cent. The population adversely affected by flooding in Madhya Pradesh was increased by over 70 per cent. Yet the power to be generated, averaged over 100 years, will increase by only about 10 per cent. No doubt, at the time of the Tribunal's award, some of these "costs" were considered to be offset by benefits that would arise from the construction of the Narmada Sagar Projects in Madhya Pradesh which were to be built at the same time as the Sardar Sarovar Projects; this assumption can no longer be made. The Bank has told us that under prevailing circumstances in India there are no assurances that these upstream projects will be built as planned.[14] This means that the Sardar Sarovar Projects would not operate as

---

[14] Late in our review, the World Bank advised us that a contract for construction of the Narmada Sagar dam was signed by Madhya Pradesh on May 5, 1992. We have been unable to assess whether this changes the previous concerns related to project financing and scheduling. The status of environmental and resettlement and rehabilitation work is also unclear. The terms of India's 1987 conditional clearance for the Sardar Sarovar Projects also apply to the Narmada Sagar Projects.

planned. As a result, the levels and drawdowns in the reservoir and the flow regime downstream of the dam and in the canal will be different, as will the resulting impacts. No assessments have been done to determine the nature of these differences.

STREAMFLOW AND THE QUANTUM OF WATER

The impacts of the Sardar Sarovar Projects are dictated to a large degree by the maximum level and drawdown of the reservoir behind the dam, the amount of water diverted into the canal system, and the discharge of water downstream through the riverbed powerhouse or over the spillway. These matters were considered by the Tribunal. In the course of the Tribunal's deliberations, an understanding was reached by the parties about the amount and timing of water that would be available in the river. This became embodied in the term "quantum of water." This is an abstract number that can be measured only statistically. But it is important, not for its absolute value, but rather for what it connotes—a series of daily flows that could be stored or used.

The Tribunal used the agreement on the quantum of water as a basis for apportioning project benefits and costs. The flows implied by this agreement continue to be important because they determine the size, interrelationships, and guidelines for operating the system. These, in turn, are what drive many of the impacts and provide the rationale for ameliorative measures. If the actual quantum of water is not in fact about the same as the quantum assumed, the proportional sharing of benefits would remain the same but the Projects (both the Sardar Sarovar Projects and the Narmada Sagar Projects) would need to be adjusted. This should mean significant design changes to the hydraulic structures and command area. It most certainly would mean changes in operation. Either way, the environmental impacts would be quite different, as would the effect on resettlement.

The question of streamflow and the resulting reliable quantum of water that is available in the river at the terminal storage site (Sardar Sarovar Dam) on the Narmada were contentious issues before the Tribunal. The controversy continues today. Then, as now, there are differences of opinion based on the interpretation of basic data. Actual streamflow measurements are available only beginning in 1948-49. During the deliberations of the Tribunal, to obtain a longer series, an expert committee expanded the sample size using rainfall/runoff "hindcasting" techniques to build a synthetic streamflow record from 1891-92 to 1947-48.

We heard a great deal of debate about how much to rely on the measured flow and on the hindcast statistics. More than a decade of measurements are available since the Tribunal award. The new data fuel the debate and give rise to speculation about their meaning when considering impacts. It is not the purpose of our review to resolve these specific matters, important as they are for design and operation. But we are concerned about the broader matters highlighted by this debate.

In 1974, the flow in the river covering the 79 year period to 1969-70 was agreed to by the states in the presence of the Assessor appointed by the Tribunal. In July, the Chief Ministers of Madhya Pradesh, Maharashtra, and Rajasthan and the Advisor to the Governor of Gujarat agreed "that the quantity of water in the Narmada available for 75 per cent of the years may be assessed at 28 million acre feet and that the Tribunal in determining the disputes referred to it do proceed on the basis of that assessment."[15] The Tribunal accepted this agreement. The 28 MAF is calculated using the 75 per cent dependable yield of 27 MAF less the project estimated evaporation losses (4 MAF) plus regeneration (return flow from irrigation and canal leakage) (2 MAF) and carryover storage (3 MAF). The Tribunal subsequently ruled that this quantity of water would be totally allocated among the four states: 18.25 MAF (65.18%) to Madhya Pradesh, 9.00 MAF (32.14%) to Gujarat, 0.25 MAF (0.89%) to Maharashtra, and 0.50 MAF (1.79%) to Rajasthan. Provision was made for years of lower and higher runoff by agreeing to apportion the available water in the ratio of the allocations. Most importantly from an environmental and social perspective, no allocation was made for flow in the river below the dam.

In 1985, the Bank stated:

> It should be noted that the NWDT used the 28 MAF flow figure only as a base for equitable apportionment. The results of this apportionment in terms of percentage shares, however, would be applied to whatever the utilizable flow in a particular year may be.... In other words, whatever the *actual utilizable* flow in a year may be, it should be shared always in the same way. The figure of 28 MAF and the *absolute* volume allocated to each state out of this becomes irrelevant, particularly with the new hydrological data and as reservoir operations studies for the basin and implied assumptions are retuned.[16] [emphasis in original]

Although it is correct to state that the absolute volume does not affect the way in which the benefits are shared, it would be quite incorrect to assume that it is unimportant. In fact, the assumed quantum provides the rationale for basic project design and operation decisions. And the realization of the benefits and

---

[15] *The Report of the Narmada Water Disputes Tribunal with Its Decision*, Vol. I, 1979, p 8.
[16] Staff Appraisal Report, Supplementary Data Volume, Part I, p 95.

impacts, their nature and magnitude, begins with these same decisions.

Project design and operation are based on the best utilization of the total annual runoff. Because 90 per cent or more of this runoff occurs in a few months, and most comes in sudden floods, a substantial volume of storage in the basin is necessary to deliver the multipurpose benefits of the Projects. The Tribunal's decisions were based on the assumption of construction of projects upstream to regulate the extreme fluctuations in water supply and demand. Indeed, Gujarat is required to share 17.6 per cent of the cost of the proposed Narmada Sagar Projects because of the benefits to the Sardar Sarovar Projects from the storage created upstream.

Regardless of the annual runoff and the controversy surrounding it, even in 1985 the Bank noted that Sardar Sarovar itself is not capable of delivering the quantum of water intended:

> With respect to operation of reservoirs, however, the NWDT [Narmada Water Disputes Tribunal] ordered MP [Madhya Pradesh] to make regular releases from its largest reservoir, Narmada Sagar, to the Sardar Sarovar Reservoir, since the latter would not be able to meet the demand for power releases and, to a lesser extent, for irrigation in Gujarat and Rajasthan through its own regulative capacity alone.[17]

The same conclusion is found in the report of the Tribunal:

> Without regulated releases from Narmadasagar, Sardar Sarovar FRL [full reservoir level] +455 will not be able to utilize its allotted share of water as a good deal of the flood flows would spill down to the sea instead of being stored at Narmadasagar for regulated releases. Due to the spillage and lack of carryover capacity there would be a loss of 17.8 percent in irrigation and power benefits at Sardar Sarovar....[18]

We initially examined the streamflow data simply to understand better the ecological meaning of changes to the river after construction of the dam. We found discrepancies in the data used within different agencies responsible for the Projects. Although some of these discrepancies were resolved by the Central Water Commission in the final weeks of our work in India, many discrepancies remain.

[17] Staff Appraisal Report, Supplementary Data Volume, Part I, p 18.
[18] *The Report of the Narmada Water Disputes Tribunal with its Decision*, Vol. II, 1979, p 102, §15.6.4.

All streamflow data are subject to some measurement error. For a river like the Narmada, these errors are highest during the monsoon, a period when about 90 per cent of the flows occur. The Chairman of the Nigam suggested that the error amounts to no more than 5 per cent on an annual basis. Officials at the Narmada Control Authority told us that it might be about 10 per cent. The Central Water Commission's Chief Engineer (Hydrology) indicated that it might be higher. However, as far back as June 1983, the Bank's engineering consultants on reliability of streamflow data, reported that serious problems existed because of discrepancies of 30 per cent in the data between agencies.[19] Although these were reported to have been resolved, we found similar problems with the data.

In 1991, in response to the growing controversy, the issue of quantum of water was reviewed. The report prepared for the Narmada Control Authority by the Central Water Commission states:

> It is the general experience that, stream flow measurement with desirable accuracy, when the river is in high flood, is difficult to achieve due to the constraints of equipment and facilities at site and also due to widespreading of flood waters. Large errors in measurement of this part of annual run-off vitiate the planning of water use projects with storage...it is considered not prudent to rely only on the observed flow series (1948-49 to 1987-88) without exercising internal and external consistency checks.[20]

No internal or external consistency checks have been made and none are presently under way.

This raises fundamental questions for our review. It starts with reliability and the 75 per cent criterion. This criterion means that, on average, one year in four there will be a shortage. It does not say how much the shortage would be. Also, there could be shortages three years in a row (as actually occurred in the 1980s) followed by surpluses for several years. We appreciate that the 75 per cent figure is an Indian standard for irrigation projects of this type. But we note that the criterion for the priority water use (drinking water) is much higher. However, whether for drinking water or for irrigation this criterion is not specific to the Narmada Projects realities and is therefore not helpful in assessing impact. In its 1991 review of India's irrigation sector, the Bank says that a "common deficiency is that potential irrigable area is often based on a

---

[19] Douglas James and David R. Dawdy, "Hydrologic Modelling of the Narmada Basin," June 1983, p 5.
[20] "Assessment of Utilisable Annual Flow Volumes in Narmada Basin," 1991, §2.12.

standard 75 per cent probability level for water availability. This has no necessary relationship with what is optimal for the command (only simulation analysis can determine this) and also often results in overestimation of potentially
irrigable area."[21] For our purposes, reliability would be better determined by
an analysis that included the amounts of the shortage, their probability, and
the significance of the shortages over time. This analysis has not been done.

There is little point for our review to try to resolve the 75 per cent dependable quantum issue. In any event, the "correct" amount can be measured only
statistically and the debate is about numbers most of which could, arguably,
be correct given the probable errors inherent in the streamflow measurements
and related data.

At the end of the day, the situation is this. In 1974 an agreement was negotiated under the authority of the chief ministers and the Tribunal accepted it.
This allowed certain conclusions to be reached by the Tribunal. The agreement may or may not prove to reflect the streamflow over the lifespan of the
Projects. No doubt, if all the dams are built on the river as planned, and are
monitored, it will be possible to determine more accurately the annual runoff.
But in the meantime, it seems prudent to focus not on abstract statistical concepts but on whether the Sardar Sarovar Projects will work as intended with
the anticipated environmental and social impacts.

The quantum of water, understood as a surrogate for the historical time series of flows in the river, involves two coexisting sets of hydrologic data of importance to the Projects and their impacts. First, there is the *agreed upon, negotiated hydrology* which is used in setting rules of operation for the reservoirs for the
purpose of determining the benefits of upstream storage, utilization of carryover storage, and the volumes of water that can be controlled by optimal operations, and in settling other issues that relate to how well the river basin is
being managed. For these purposes the negotiated hydrology need not be accurate as long as it is accepted by all parties as the basis for decisions. Second,
there is the *actual runoff*, as it occurs in the future. This will be dictated by the
rainfall and runoff characteristics of the watershed and controlled according to
the operating rules developed from the negotiated hydrology. Surpluses and
shortages will result from a combination of the actual runoff and how the reservoirs are used to manage it.

UNDERSTANDING IMPACTS

The important issue is the runoff sequence (timing and amount) that can be
controlled reliably by the Sardar Sarovar Projects to deliver the target
amounts of water. The Bank's economic analysis concluded that a 28 per cent

---

[21] *India Irrigation Sector Review*, Vol. I, World Bank, December 20, 1991, p 40.

error in annual runoff would reduce the economic return to zero.[22] However, it is not clear what this really means. The analysis did not include uncertainty in the hydrologic flow sequence. It was assumed that the future runoff would occur in exactly the same way as the estimated historical streamflows. This will not happen.

As the total storage in the basin increases, the runoff sequence may become less important. Under present circumstances, however, water available for use by the Sardar Sarovar Projects is made more uncertain by the lack of upstream storage. The Tribunal ruled that 85 per cent of the water allocated for use in Gujarat and Rajasthan would be provided in the form of regulated releases from reservoirs upstream in Madhya Pradesh.[23] This will not happen; the Narmada Sagar projects are not being built concurrently as had been assumed. The implications of this have not been studied. According to a March 14, 1990, Bank memorandum, it is a sensitive issue that needs to be explored. We agree. The implications are far reaching. For example, principal benefits of the Sardar Sarovar Projects riverbed powerhouse were to have been achieved in the early years, before Gujarat's irrigation system was fully developed. It is obvious that the value of the powerhouse declines if the upstream storage is not developed and the energy benefits are therefore reduced. In 1979 the Tribunal reported that without the regulated releases from Narmada Sagar, the loss of irrigation and power benefits at Sardar Sarovar would be 17 per cent.[24] A January 2, 1992, Bank memorandum assumes that power at the Sardar Sarovar Projects would decrease by 25 per cent and the irrigated area by 30 per cent without the Narmada Sagar Projects.

The assumptions of reservoir storage at both dams and regulated releases from the Narmada Sagar Projects to the Sardar Sarovar Projects are now questionable. This, along with the trends in the data that we have reviewed above, means that the quantum of water that can be controlled for irrigation, power and energy production, and domestic and industrial use probably will be less than anticipated by the Tribunal. This would change the balance of economic, social, and environmental objectives which can realistically be achieved. These objectives are all interconnected. Not only would the environmental and social impacts be different in and of themselves; they would be strongly affected as officials seek a new balance between the realizable economic benefits and the actual project costs.

Where does this leave our review? Based on the hydrology and water man-

---

[22] Staff Appraisal Report, 1985, p 61.

[23] Clause IX of the Tribunal's 1979 award requires Madhya Pradesh to release 8.12 MAF per year (0.677 MAF per month) below Maheshwar out of the total of 9.5 allocated for Gujarat (i.e., 85%).

[24] *The Report of the Narmada Water Disputes Tribunal with its Decision*, Vol. II, 1979, p 102, §15.6.4.

agement information made available to us, we think that the Sardar Sarovar
Projects will not work as intended. Many previous assumptions now appear to
be unfounded, or are questionable. This has direct implications for environmental impact and for resettlement and rehabilitation. For example, the delay
in construction of storage upstream will have an impact on the operation of the
Sardar Sarovar dam, powerhouse, and canal system. There will be more frequent Sardar Sarovar reservoir fluctuations and greater, more erratic discharges to the Gulf of Cambay. The Sardar Sarovar reservoir will often be
drawn down to the lowest level as the carryover storage from one year to the
next is exhausted.[25] All this will mean different impacts upstream in Madhya
Pradesh and Maharashtra as well as downstream in Gujarat. It will also have
far reaching implications in the command area.

Over the dozen years since the Tribunal award, new information, better
data, and revised project plans have emerged. Our discussions with officials
and our review of the Bank files show that there is a widespread awareness of
the need to reevaluate the Projects. There is a particular sense of urgency related to the impact on the Sardar Sarovar design and operation of delays or
changes in upstream developments.

Our review of the hydrology and water management issues leads to the conclusion that their environmental and social implications have not been properly assessed. Whatever the specifics of these issues, a realistic operational
analysis upon which to base an environmental assessment is missing. The reservoir levels and flows through the powerhouse and canal need to be described
showing fluctuations, ranges, time series, etc., so that the environmental consequences can be determined. Although a number of computer models of various aspects of the Narmada projects have been developed, all of them follow
the assumptions of the Tribunal award. What is happening now on the river
and what is likely to happen in the future are different from what was supposed to happen according to those earlier assumptions.

The Bank recognizes the questions raised by the realities of the 1990s as opposed to the planning assumptions of 1979. In a March 14, 1990, Office Memorandum, senior officials state:

> A satisfactory answer to these questions would require the Op-
> erations Research Group (ORG) in Baroda to re-run the original
> water balance models. This would also be necessary if one

---

[25] It has been suggested that the available storage could be increased by lowering the elevation of
the irrigation by-pass tunnel. This would likely exacerbate upstream impacts by increasing the
reservoir drawdown range. Without proper studies, the true costs and benefits of such a change
are unknown.

wanted to reassess whether the proposed group of smaller dams
upstream could partly or fully substitute for the regulating role
of NSP [Narmada Sagar Projects] . . . the question should be
asked in the context of a *realistic rate* of future diversion or use of
water by MP [Madhya Pradesh], as opposed to the NWDT's [Nar-
mada Water Disputes Tribunal's] unrealistic assumed rate of
18.25 million acre feet (maf) within the next 35 years. . . . it is
unlikely that MP will be able to use (the agreement is on *usage*) its
allocated 18.25 maf within the remaining 35 years of the NWDT
award. Indeed, it is probably technically impossible for MP ever
to use this amount of water. . . . Gujarat could use, and presumably will use for its expansive 1.9 million ha irrigation command
area, rather more than its 9 maf allocation. [emphasis in origi-
nal]

A comprehensive evaluation is needed, including a complete systems analysis of the key features and sequence of development of the facilities upstream of
the Sardar Sarovar Projects. The scope of this analysis should not be restricted. It should include a reappraisal of the basic assumptions in sizing and
operating the Sardar Sarovar dam, powerhouse, and canal. Given the large
command area of the project in Gujarat, the possible integration of the water
resources and storage potential of the Mahi and Sabarmati rivers (both of
which are in the Sardar Sarovar command area) could also be explored as part
of a comprehensive, environmentally sustainable water management plan for
Gujarat.

CONCLUDING OBSERVATIONS

It is not the responsibility of our review to evaluate the engineering hydrology
of the Sardar Sarovar Projects, nor is it proper for us to review the Narmada
Water Disputes Tribunal's extensive treatment of the issue as it relates to the
Narmada Sagar Projects and Sardar Sarovar Projects. Early in our review we
set out to establish the nature of environmental and social impacts of the Projects. We found that there were no comprehensive impact assessments to
which we could relate implementation and ameliorative measures. If we had
stopped there, we would have abandoned the very thing that had motivated
the review by the World Bank in the first place—the need to understand the
basis, if any, for the controversy related to the implementation of environmental and resettlement and rehabilitation aspects of Sardar Sarovar. We felt this
would be irresponsible. So we began reviewing the nature of the impacts upstream, downstream, and in the command area. This led us to a more careful

examination of the origin of impacts—i.e., design and operating features of the Sardar Sarovar Projects. Both features are founded on the hydrology of the river. Both are related to developments upstream.

In our review we came across discrepancies in data and differences in analyses that go to the heart of the triggering mechanisms for impacts. In order to assess what quickly became contentious issues, we engaged an independent hydrologist and asked him to test the key matters raised in the submissions we received and the discrepancies that were becoming apparent from our own assessment. The findings, presented in this chapter, are disturbing.

The work we have done raises important questions about many of the assumptions used to date. At the very least, no impact assessment is possible, and the effectiveness and efficiency of ameliorative measures remain speculative, because there is no appropriate understanding of the hydrology of Sardar Sarovar with or without Narmada Sagar.

Our work on hydrology was designed to better understand impacts. These are described in the following chapters. It was not our purpose, nor was it within our Terms of Reference, to do a complete systems analysis. But in the course of this work we have found that there is compelling evidence that the Sardar Sarovar Projects will not operate as planned. It is not that the results from the work done in the 1970s and 1980s are wrong. We only know that with more data that is now available, it is possible to reach conclusions that will lead to quite different impacts than have been assumed to date.

The Tribunal indicated in 1979 that without Narmada Sagar a 35-foot higher dam at Sardar Sarovar would compensate for the loss of irrigation and power benefits.[26] In a fax to the Bank on May 5, 1992, the Nigam suggested that storage could be created in the command area. Either of these changes would alter in the most fundamental way the nature of the Projects. This, in turn, would change the environmental and social costs, to an extent and in a manner which have not been assessed.

Officials at the Nigam and several others in India have said that the Narmada Sagar Projects will be built. Indeed, the Chief Minister of Madhya Pradesh told us just that in quite emphatic terms. On May 5, 1992, the state signed a contract for construction with Jaiprakash Associates. Work, we are told, is likely to begin soon. But the prospect of the construction of Narmada Sagar does not obviate our concerns about the performance and impacts of Sardar Sarovar. Our recent assessment of hydrology data indicates that if Madhya Pradesh does, in fact, appropriate its allotment of water according to the Tribunal award, the Sardar Sarovar Projects will still not operate as assumed. It is likely that changes in the Projects will be required with all the at-

---

[26] *The Report of the Narmada Water Disputes Tribunal with its Decision*, Vol. II, 1979, p 102, §15.6.5.

tendant impacts. An exhaustive investigation of this is beyond our Terms of Reference. But there is every indication of a problem that needs to be addressed.

Quite apart from the economic, financial, and technical implications, the environmental and social implications are of the first importance.

Draw-down agriculture in the bed of a tributary of the Narmada, in the submergence zone in Maharashtra.

BANK documents provide an indication of the scope and significance of the upstream issues. The 1985 Staff Appraisal Report for the Sardar Sarovar Projects summarized the upstream implications under the heading "Environmental Effects" as follows:

> Characteristically the creation of a large man made lake results in significant environmental changes in the adjacent area. The reservoir would inundate about 37,000 ha. at FRL [Full Reservoir Level] of which 18% is forested, 33% is cultivable land, and nearly 50% is waste or of low utilization potential. Submergence would cause loss of forests and agricultural lands, cultural infrastructure and a limited loss of wildlife habitat. Effects on existing fisheries remain to be assessed. However, creation of a more positive ecocycle on the periphery of the reservoir may be expected in terms of improved soil moisture for nearby forests and other biomass and improved wildlife habitat. Opportunities would be created for improved local river transportation and fresh water fisheries. . . . Measures would be taken through development of implementation programs to ensure the preservation of land and enhancement of the environment. (p 28)

The Bank's 1985 Supplementary Data Volume adds:

> Most of the forest land has been subjected to biotic pressures for many decades and most large wildlife long since overexploited. This statement applies to most of the Sardar Sarovar catchment

area. Wildlife escape corridors and measures leading to strengthened protected areas are being addressed . . . in Madhya Pradesh. It appears that no protected area would be directly violated by the proposed dam. However, the reservoir would damage some wildlife, displace other wildlife, and intensify the biotic pressures on existing reserves by locating resettlement sites nearby. (Part I, p 53)

A Sardar Sarovar "workplan for environmental effects" was required by the Bank's 1985 agreement with India. It was conceived, in part, to address outstanding issues related to upstream impacts on flora and fauna, including fish. To date, there is no workplan, and there is no coordinated approach to impact assessment upstream. We have reviewed therefore the available project data and individual documents. We also travelled throughout the area and consulted experts on forest ecology and sedimentation. We focused our attention on the Sardar Sarovar Projects, but bearing in mind that other projects are planned upstream, especially the Narmada Sagar Projects, that will have environmental impacts in this same area.

Each of the three riparian states has its own study program for flora and fauna. All have experienced delays. Madhya Pradesh has filed interim reports; a final report is expected by March 1993. Action plans are promised for 1994, and "implementation, if any, by 1996 is targeted."[1] In Maharashtra, the terms of reference for a two-year study have been finalized. In Gujarat, a final report was expected in April 1992. Action plans would follow.

The fisheries work has experienced similar delays. Basic information on migratory fish, critical life cycle stages, etc., is described by a Bank consultant as recently as May 1991 as "scarce."[2] A sociological survey of fishing families of the Narmada River was submitted to the Narmada Control Authority in June 1991. The results of a five-year survey on the estuary fisheries will be available sometime after 1993 (see Chapter 13). A three-year pre- and post-impoundment limnological study in Madhya Pradesh is under way. Gujarat has received a report of the first pre-impoundment phase for its work. And fisheries development planned for the reservoir is being pursued with a number of agencies and consultants, some engaged in preparation for the Bank's proposed Narmada Basin Development Project.

---

[1] Ministry of Environment and Forests, Sardar Sarovar Project Status Report, December 1991, p 6.

[2] GOPA Consultants, *India, Narmada River Basin Development Project—Fisheries Component, Final Project Preparation Report*, Annex 6, May 1991, p 1.

The piecemeal approach and early study stages of the work on flora and fauna make it difficult to draw meaningful conclusions. What we have reviewed suggests that if the Sardar Sarovar dam could be considered alone, no significant populations of large mammals or birds are likely to be lost in the upstream area. Because of inadequate information, we can say nothing about other animals and plants and the aquatic ecosystem of the river generally. More information is available on three of the most significant issues: forest issues, catchment area treatment, and sedimentation.

FORESTS

Most of the Sardar Sarovar forest-related issues arise because of inundation of forests by the dam. The Bank's 1985 Supplementary Data Volume summarizes these forest issues in Gujarat, Maharashtra, and Madhya Pradesh as follows:

> The total recorded forest land to be inundated in those states is about 11,600 ha. Of the 6,746 ha. of recorded forest land to be submerged in Gujarat, approximately 4,100 ha. is thought actually to be forested and, within the latter area, the variety of vegetation may vary greatly. An equivalent aggregate (i.e., 4,100 ha.) of compensatory forest would be considered for plantation in tracts to be identified in the vicinity of the reservoir. The forest and other vegetation in the reservoir area would be exploited or otherwise removed before filling. It has been recommended that a narrow 4 m wide strip of trees be left or planted below normal FRL. Since the draw down is protracted, it is thought that a shallow and temporary flooding would not kill the trees in this strip, and would be expected to enhance the reservoir. (Part I, p 53)

The text of the Staff Appraisal Report adds that a work program would be undertaken to assess forest areas and to design and implement measures for protection. India's 1987 environmental clearance of the Projects noted that "complete details" on compensatory afforestation plans would be furnished by 1989. The subsequent clearance under the *Forest (Conservation) Act, 1980* approved diversion of 13,385.45 hectares of forest land of which 4,165.91 is in Gujarat, 2,731.00 hectares is in Madhya Pradesh, and 6,488.54 hectares is in Maharashtra (Maharashtra also needs to compensate for the losses to the Taloda Forest). This forestry clearance was "strictly subject" to eleven conditions, including compensatory afforestation requirements:

Since the project involves violation and also most of the non-forest areas for compensatory afforestation are away from the project area, the State Govts. will raise compensatory afforestation in double the degraded forest lands also in the project impact areas in addition to the afforestation of equivalent non-forest land. A scheme for this will be submitted by 30.11.87.[3]

The program to compensate for lost forest therefore has two parts. Planting on non-forest (i.e., revenue) land, which could be distant from the area affected by the Projects, would be on an equal amount of land to the land lost. If the land to be afforested is already designated as forest land (degraded), twice the area must be treated.

We have reviewed the plans of all three states and the progress in compensatory afforestation documented to the end of 1991. Madhya Pradesh is reported to have achieved approximately 20 per cent of its goals and Gujarat has been reported as accomplishing approximately 35 per cent of its goal. Completion dates for these two states are forecast to be 1994/95 and 1993/94, respectively. Maharashtra, on the other hand, is having difficulty with the planning and execution of its afforestation programs. A scheme was submitted to the Ministry of Environment and Forests but was deemed to require further "clarification." Target dates and physical progress for Maharashtra have not been reported. Issues related to the Taloda Forest also remain unresolved. Nevertheless, the Narmada Control Authority documents show that the "progress reported till the rains of 1991 is 8,425 ha" (i.e. approximately 40 per cent of target in Maharashtra).[4]

There is more to compensatory afforestation, however, than the setting of numerical targets, counting seedlings planted, and documenting hectares covered. When we met with India's Minister of Water Resources, he stated that plantations are not a substitute for a natural forest. The test for implementation of the afforestation program is whether or not there is adequate compensation for the forest lands being lost by submergence. The straightforward 1:1 non-forest land or 2:1 forest land replacement is the real estate component of the compensation. Other factors, from botanical composition to long-term viability, are just as important, if not more so.

Although there are areas that still support a reasonable approximation of the natural flora and fauna (except for large wildlife), much of the Sardar

[3] Government of India, Ministry of Environment and Forests, Memorandum No. 8-372/83-FC, September 8, 1987, p 1.
[4] Narmada Control Authority, Environment Sub-Group, Agenda for the Fourteenth Meeting, Annex XIV(1), February 1992, p 4.

Sarovar submergence area forest is already degraded with lower biodiversity and lower productivity than an undegraded forest. No doubt, some of this has been induced by neglect and over-exploitation pending submergence. But evidence on the ground and in the literature shows that some of the area was already degraded in the last century.[5] Because there is a large area of similar forest in the non-submergence parts of the catchment area, we do not think that the loss of this forest constitutes an important ecological impact *per se*, although there is certainly some cost.

In Gujarat compensatory afforestation is being planted in the arid district of Kutchch. In our opinion this is a questionable decision. By placing the compensatory afforestation in an entirely different ecological zone, one that is marginal for forest development in any case, Gujarat has insured that the forest created will have no resemblance to that submerged.

Gujarat claims to have selected Kutchch because it was the only substantial area available and it is badly in need of reforestation. This, too, is questionable. Productive land has been purchased for resettlement. Presumably it could have been purchased for reforestation as well. A major factor bearing on the compensatory afforestation being carried out in Kutchch is almost certainly that the land there is cheap, being marginal for agriculture and in an area where the countryside has recently been partially depopulated.

Our difficulty with the approach advocated by Gujarat is fundamental. If the practice of replanting marginal forest land in compensation for better lands lost elsewhere continues, productive forest lands will be constantly replaced with less productive ones, mainly because such land is cheap and easily obtained. The amount of forest land may be maintained on paper, but it will be diminished in value. Even if Gujarat's compensatory afforestation program meets the letter of the conditional clearance by the Ministry of Environment and Forests, it offends its spirit and intent. And it does not seem to be what was envisaged for Gujarat in 1985 when the Bank stated that "compensatory forest would be considered for plantation in tracts to be identified in the vicinity of the reservoir."[6]

In Madhya Pradesh, the compensatory afforestation is being done largely by replanting degraded forest land within or close to the Narmada catchment. Maharashtra will be doing the same. This is by far the easiest option because there is a lot of degraded forest in areas adjacent to the Sardar Sarovar Projects. It has been suggested that this practice by the two states will again lead

[5] *Gazetteer of the Bombay Presidency*, Vol. VI, Rewa Kantha, Narukot, Cambay, and Surat States, Government Press, Bombay, 1880. *Ibid.*, Vol. XII, Khandesh, C. E. Luard and R. P. Dube, 1908. *Indore State Gazetteer*, Vol. II, Calcutta: Superintendent of Government Printing.
[6] Staff Appraisal Report, Supplementary Data Volume, Part I, p 53.

to declines in India's forest cover. However, the ecosystem resulting from the rehabilitation of adjacent degraded forests should be a closer approximation to what is lost than the afforestation program in Kutchch. We were impressed with the program being developed in the Jhabua District of Madhya Pradesh where a combination of mixed planting and regeneration of existing coppice has the potential to reproduce a reasonable approximation to the composition of the natural forest of the catchment area. However, the survival of these plantations in the long run is doubtful because of forest management practices, particularly those related to local people as described below.

The true ecological cost of forests submerged by the Sardar Sarovar Projects is not reflected by the compensatory afforestation efforts. However, to put matters in perspective it needs to be said that the amount of compensatory afforestation for Sardar Sarovar is small relative to the amount of afforestation going on in these states under other programs (many with Bank involvement) and the total expenditure is small relative to the cost of the Sardar Sarovar Projects. What is being done is not doing any harm, and some good may accrue. The important issue, however, is the violation of the principle that the quality, not only the amount, of India's natural forest cover should not be allowed to be reduced further.

Taloda Forest

The Taloda Forest is a particularly contentious issue for the Sardar Sarovar Projects (see also Chapter 7). In July 1990, 2,700 hectares of forest land was released for the resettlement of oustees in Maharashtra. The Secretary, Environment and Forests, told us (October 1991) that it was a controversial and difficult decision requiring exemptions under the *Forest (Conservation) Act, 1980*.

The Bank's 1985 legal agreement required India to "take or cause to be taken, all such action as shall be necessary, including, if required, the provision of forest land within the meaning of the Borrower's Forest (Conservation) Act, 1980, for enabling Gujarat, Madhya Pradesh and Maharashtra each to implement, within their respective state boundaries, the Project."[7] India's 1987 approval of the project was "strictly subject" to the condition that "no forest land will be utilized for rehabilitation of oustees."[8] At least some of the

---

[7] Development Credit Agreement (Narmada River Development (Gujarat) Sardar Sarovar Dam and Power Project) between India and the World Bank, May 10, 1985, §3.02.
[8] Government of India, Ministry of Environment and Forests, Memorandum No. 8-372/83-FC, September 8, 1987, p 1.

most basic tensions related to the Taloda issue therefore seem to have been built into agreements from the beginning.

We visited the Taloda Forest on several occasions. Some areas were being cleared for families that will be displaced by submergence in 1993. The land is considered to be of high quality, but the existing forest on the proposed Taloda resettlement area appears to be degraded with a low diversity of vegetation. Parts of the area look well wooded, but most of the trees are a fast-growing species with little value except for fuel wood. Even for that purpose, the trees are less desirable than most alternative species. No significant timber trees remain. Other trees include a lot of *Madhuca indica*, which is used extensively by tribal people.

Although labelled as "degraded," sparse forests are, nonetheless, used in a systematic and productive way by local peoples. Degraded does not mean unused. The surrounding villagers told us of their extensive use of the forest before it was recently "converted" for Sardar Sarovar oustees. A sense of the historical richness of the area is found in working plans prepared by the British in 1931. It is described as "the best timber producing tract in the British Satpuras."[9] The working plans record teak trees in the compartments now being used for resettlement with diameters in excess of 40 inches and heights greater than 75 feet. Such trees are unheard of in the area today.

The decision has been taken by the Governments of Maharashtra and India to use the Taloda Forest for non-forest purposes. If this decision helps to resettle the Sardar Sarovar oustees fairly, the ecological price may be worth paying. However, the high quality of the forest that originally existed in the area means that the lost opportunity in terms of potential forest development has been high. Given the experience with compensatory afforestation elsewhere, it seems unlikely that it will take place on any land in Maharashtra as potentially productive as the Taloda Forest lands. Our concern, therefore, is similar to what we have found in Gujarat—the loss of lands capable of sustaining high quality forests in favor of less productive areas.

CATCHMENT AREA TREATMENT

Catchment area treatment involves interstate cooperation on programs ranging from afforestation, contour bunding, and gully checks, to terracing, fencing, and pasture development. It covers forest and non-forest land, including private, government, and *punchayat* lands. Like afforestation programs, existing conditions in the watershed suggest that the treatment program would be

[9] W. E. Pereira, *Working Plan for the Taloda Reserve*, Bombay: Government Central Press, 1931.

valuable with or without the Sardar Sarovar Projects. The environmental question is what to treat and how. The administrative question is who should bear the cost. The problem is one of definition, identification, and agreement on priorities for the watershed.

The importance of Sardar Sarovar catchment area treatment was recognized in India when the first environmental clearance was being sought from the Ministry of Environment and Forests. In 1984, the Government of India set up an independent committee, headed by Dr. M. L. Dewan, to study measures to minimize soil erosion and sediment transport in the Narmada catchment area (i.e., the area of both the Sardar Sarovar and the Narmada Sagar Projects). The Dewan Committee's 1985 report recommended that the work be done within five years in Gujarat and Maharashtra, and within ten years in Madhya Pradesh. The report emphasized the need to demarcate priority watersheds, to update soil surveys and land use data, to resolve interagency/interstate information discrepancies, to involve non-government organizations, to initiate an integrated soil conservation and watershed management program, to support pilot projects, and to involve tribal peoples and others. The cost for the Projects over ten years was estimated to be Rs. 5,200 million (approximately $200 million).[10]

The Bank's 1985 Staff Appraisal Report and loan agreements with India do not mention catchment area treatment explicitly, although it is reasonable to infer from the wording in the agreements (and certainly from the Bank's files) that this treatment was expected to be included in the environmental work-plan that was to have been submitted in 1985.

India's environmental clearance explicitly required a catchment area treatment scheme to be submitted by 1989, with implementation "*pari passu*" and completion "ahead of reservoir filling."[11] India's forestry clearance required the plan by November 1987. The Planning Commission clearance for the Projects reinforced these conditions. According to the 1987 briefing note to the Prime Minister, three things were required:

• demarcation of critically degraded areas on the basis of aerial photographs, satellite inventory, and ground checks;
• creation of a chain of nurseries of suitable species for biological treatment of the catchment area; and

---

[10] Government of India, Ministry of Agriculture and Rural Development, Department of Agriculture and Cooperation, Soil and Water Conservation Division, *Report of Inter-Departmental Committee on Soil Conservation and Afforestation, Sardar Sarovar and Narmada Sagar Projects, Narmada Catchment*, August 1985, pp 36-45.

[11] Government of India, Ministry of Environment and Forests, Office Memorandum No. 3-87/80-IA, June 24, 1987, p 2.

• preparation of a phased action program for biological and engineering treatment of the degraded catchment area.

The Bank continues to be concerned about the catchment area treatment (something that it hopes to address in the proposed Basin Development Project). In a March 14, 1990, Office Memorandum, two senior officials say:

> If the rules of the central Department of Environment and Forests (DOEF) were followed strictly, reservoir filling could not commence until 100% catchment treatment were completed. This is not only unrealistic, but probably completely uneconomic. At the unit costs being considered, the treatment could cost about US $1 billion. We need to look carefully at the economics of the catchment treatment program. At present, it is evolving as a rather top-down government program. We should focus on something much more participatory, and use experience of our watersheds projects in arriving at something more realistic.

In April 1991, the All India Soil and Land Use Survey submitted a report on prioritization of watersheds. Over 90 per cent of the Sardar Sarovar catchment area is in Madhya Pradesh, with about 7 per cent in Maharashtra, and the remaining portion in the state of Gujarat. Of the total, about 28 per cent is classified for catchment area treatment as "Very High & High" priority. If only the directly draining portions are considered, the "Very High & High" priority areas would be about 6 per cent of the total.[12]

The extent of the area to be treated, and when it is to be completed, are still unresolved. Minutes of the January 1991 meeting of the Narmada Control Authority state:

> The Planning Commission's guidelines cover only corrective action related to direct damage due to the project and the MOWR [Ministry of Water Resources] in its guidelines has relaxed it to treatment of very high and high category of eroding areas in the sub-catchments directly draining into the reservoirs. If the entire catchment is to be treated at project cost, the project will become unviable and this part has to be executed under the National Watershed Development Programme of the Ministry of Agriculture.

[12] Narmada Control Authority, Environment Sub-Group, Agenda for the Fourteenth Meeting, Annex XIV(1), February 1992, pp 1-2.

In a November 1991 letter to the Secretary of Water Resources, the Secretary, Environment and Forests states:

> The catchment area treatment *pari-passu* with construction works has to be taken up as per the conditional approval granted by this Ministry in 1987. The stand being advocated now by the Representative of NCA is that catchment area treatment be limited only to the directly draining areas of the reservoir periphery. This is obviously not acceptable to this Ministry as it negates the basic objective of catchment area treatment and also the very basis of environmental approval granted in 1987. Since the formulation of a comprehensive catchment area treatment plan covering all critically degraded areas in the free draining catchment was not ready with the participating states, we had agreed that treatment work may commence as Phase 1— covering only the directly draining areas. This, however, need not be interpreted as a departure from our earlier stand for treatment of all the critically degraded areas in the free draining catchment which is so essential for optimization of both land and water resources.
>
> I understand that a working group has been constituted by your Ministry under the Chairman, Water Commission to examine the related issues but it could not come to any unanimous conclusion.[13]

In discussions with the Secretary, Environment and Forests in February 1992, it was explained to us that these issues remain unresolved. Only the action plans for directly draining areas have been drawn up by the three states. Maharashtra has still to submit maps and drawings, and has yet to commence the work. Madhya Pradesh and Gujarat have started, work is on schedule (according to their plans), and will be completed by 1996/97 and 1994/95, respectively.

There are several problems with the catchment area treatment program. Obviously the problems of how much to treat, and when, and who will pay, all need to be resolved.[14] But there is an equally important problem that must be

[13] Government of India, Office Memorandum D.O. No. 3-87/80-IA.I, November 25, 1991, p 1.

[14] The guidelines for catchment area treatment have also been the subject of controversy. The agenda for the August 1991 meeting of the Narmada Control Authority Environment Sub-Group notes that the guidelines proposed by the Ministry of Water Resources contain assumptions that "are contrary to the natural principles and processes of hydrology, sediment production and its dispersal, etc." (Annex XII-7, p 52).

addressed—the lack of involvement of local people in the program. Much of the area is degraded. Unless something is done to remove the causes of that degradation, the catchment area treatment program, however acceptable it may be in theory, will almost certainly fail in practice. A program of planting more trees and related works will not help. Because of the pressure on all bio-mass resources produced by the needs of local people, soon after protection is removed (after three years in Gujarat, after five years in Madhya Pradesh) the treated areas will probably revert to their former state (this at the admission of forest officials involved). Moreover, many people displaced by the submergence will remain around the periphery of the reservoir, placing greater pressure on the area. In many parts of the catchment area, people are already cultivating relatively steep slopes. These areas are definitely going to pose a greater soil erosion problem than the degraded forests that are being treated, some of which have reasonably good ground cover, and which develop a much better one in the rainy season when it is especially needed.

In a 1988 article, Arun Ghosh, a member of India's Planning Commission (until 1990), wrote:

> Soil management, water management, the management and proper ordering of "catchment areas" of rains—re-defined as watershed development—are essentially integrated operations wherein the cooperation of the local populace is an essential ingredient for the success of government programmes. Herein lies the essential weakness of the approach of the authorities concerned with the management of water resources.[15]

MAKING THE PROGRAMS WORK

A serious program to stabilize the catchment area and compensate for the loss of forests to submergence and resettlement must include provisions that involve the local people and give them a stake in protecting the lands, waters, and forests of the region. This will mean opening a dialogue with villagers, and establishing the means that will enable them to derive benefits from the cultivation and protection of the forest and other lands.

The importance of this is well known to officials in India as well as at the World Bank. When we met with the Secretary, Environment and Forests in October 1991 he emphasized the need to have popular support and participation in each stage of catchment area treatment. When we spoke with the Chief

[15] Arun Ghosh, "Management of Water Resources," *Economic and Political Weekly*, October 1, 1988, p 2034.

Secretary of the Government of Madhya Pradesh in February 1992, she said "none of the Catchment area treatment or afforestation programs will work unless the people participate."

Our main concern with issues relating to forests and terrestrial ecosystem management in the upstream area, whether compensatory afforestation or catchment area treatment, is related to failures of current forest management practices. This is evident from the enormous amount of forest degradation in the three states involved (although somewhat less in Gujarat).

We have found that there is widespread recognition of the need for a new approach based on a new kind of performance commitment. Many people spoke to us about the need to begin by removing the traditional lack of rapport between forestry officials and local populations. This is not a recent problem and it is not confined to the Narmada. But the anxieties and hostilities created by the Sardar Sarovar Projects make the situation especially difficult.

Under the heading "What is Expected of Systems for a Sustainable Use of Forest Land," the Bank's 1991 forest sector policy paper states:

> Given the experience, especially, of government-sponsored ef-
> forts to utilise forest-lands, it is prudent to be highly skeptical
> about proposals to develop forests. In view of the diminishing
> areas of forest lands, especially tropical moist forests, highly de-
> manding environmental and policy analyses should precede any
> significant new development or utilisation efforts. These analy-
> ses should include assessment of soils, hydrology, the institu-
> tional and incentive framework, and the value of conservation
> for all concerned, particularly indigenous forest dwellers.[16]

New directions for forestry management in India were described to us dur-
ing the course of our review. In the villages people spoke of the need for new ways of doing things. Non-government organizations, academics, and state and federal officials often raised the same issues. We noted with interest the December 1991 order from the Madhya Pradesh Forest Department which would set up village-based forest committees and would result in a local sharing of income arising from reforestation efforts. We found a good description of schemes for involving local populations provided by Aggarwal and Narain in a publication from the Centre for Science and Environment, New Delhi.[17] And

---

[16] *A World Bank Policy Paper: The Forest Sector*, 1991, p 43.

[17] A. Aggarwal and S. Narain, *Towards Green Villages*, New Delhi: Centre for Science and Environment, 1989. See also M. Poffenberger, *Joint Management for Forest Lands: Experiences from South Asia*, New Delhi: Ford Foundation, 1990; M. Poffenberger, K. Bhatia, and B. McGean,

we met with and reviewed the documents of Dr. S. B. Roy, Chairman of the Indian Institute of Biosocial Research and Development, which is a leading agency in the development of cooperative forest management, primarily in West Bengal.

The Narmada Control Authority says that all three states involved in the Sardar Sarovar Projects are proposing some form of joint forest management with local people. However, everything is hypothetical at present. Aggarwal and Narain stress the need for local solutions tailored to the needs of local people and the peculiarities of local societies. It is clear from the studies carried out so far that such schemes cannot be generated in a few years. Sources of funding will have to be identified. But perhaps more importantly, time is required for careful groundwork to develop appropriate institutions, including village committees, women's cooperatives, etc.[18]

It will require a lot of work, goodwill, and time to develop the infrastructure and the trust necessary to implement these forest programs in the Sardar Sarovar area. There is little evidence that anyone has begun a dialogue with the affected peoples. The pace of development of the dam will not allow the necessary time, even if money is made available. We therefore conclude that very little of the catchment area treatment and compensatory afforestation in the three states will be effective unless more time is allowed for their implementation. As discussed in Chapter 16, it is unlikely that the Bank's proposed Basin Development Project will effectively address these issues.

SEDIMENTATION

Sedimentation is not just an upstream issue, although the problems that it presents largely originate there. It is important for three reasons when considering environmental impact and resettlement and rehabilitation measures. First, the useful life of the dam is related to the rate of erosion upstream which, in turn, is addressed by the environmental programs of afforestation and catchment area treatment. Second, the coarse materials carried by the river

---

Forest Management Partnerships: Regenerating India's Forests, New Delhi: Ford Foundation, 1990; K. C. Malhotra and M. Poffenberger, *Forest Regeneration Through Community Protection: The West Bengal Experience*, Calcutta: West Bengal Forest Department, IBRD, Ramakrishna Mission, and Ford Foundation, 1989.

[18] The Bank's 1991 *Forest Sector* policy paper addresses the issue of forest-dwelling populations (tribals), stating: "Involuntary resettlement of forest dwellers is also rarely practical: suitable land is difficult to find, and usually other settlers quickly move into the cleared areas. According to the Bank's policy and operational guidelines, projects should thoroughly explore all alternatives to involuntary resettlement. Alternative approaches should incorporate forest-dwelling people as direct participants and beneficiaries in the design, implementation, and operation of forest projects" (p 48).

will be deposited in the upstream reaches of the reservoir, creating a backwater effect that will submerge more lands than would be anticipated by a simple extension of reservoir levels and floods. And third, the loss of sediment load within the dam will cause changes downstream. We deal with the first two matters in this chapter; the third is dealt with in Chapter 13.

The Sardar Sarovar dam will act as a large sediment trap in the river, causing a buildup in silt behind the dam and a change in the river downstream. Ramchandra Singh Deo, the former Irrigation Minister of the Government of Madhya Pradesh, made a submission to our review that contained a description of the upstream issue as follows:

> A stream or river carries with it silt, sediment and coarse particles in suspension. When its flow is obstructed by the construction of a dam there is a transition in the river from flow to still water conditions. When the river is flowing freely it transports the sediment, but with the dam intervening very little silt load goes down. As it approaches nearer and nearer the still water conditions in the pool, the velocity of the flow gets reduced and the silt gets deposited on route. The coarse particles brought down by the river begin to settle as soon as the river flow begins to be retarded by the back-water effect of the dam. When the dam [reservoir] is not filled the area of deposit will be fairly close to the dam. But as the reservoir starts getting filled the area of deposit moves upwards and becomes closer and closer to the shoreline of the full reservoir. The finer particles can be carried in suspension in slower flows also. Hence after the deposit of coarse particles near the fore-shore the finer particles get deposited closer and closer to the dam. This can well be compared with the process of delta formation when a river joins the sea. The same delta formation takes places when a stream is terminated in a man-made lake. . . . It is clear that the silt deposit takes place all over the bed and is not confined to the dead storage zone alone. The pattern of deposit is conditioned by the size of the sediment particles, their concentration and the dominant water elevation of the reservoir. Eventually every reservoir dies from loss of capacity but depending on the competence of its watershed to arrest silt, we must try to get the maximum service life out of it. Unfortunately, however, the rate of silting in most of our reservoirs is much higher than that estimated in the project.[19]

[19] Ramchandra Singh Deo, "Civilisation in a Hurry," undated, pp 3-4.

The engineering design requires calculations of the volume and pattern of sediment deposit behind the dam. Many factors, including river hydrology and past silt load data, storage capacity, length and shape of reservoir, and future land use in the basin are used to predict the life of the dam and its environmental and socioeconomic effects.

The rate of siltation is intricately related to climate, rainfall, geology, topography, and plant cover. In the Narmada valley, where siltation is already a problem, afforestation and catchment area treatment programs are required to minimize erosion. But these are long-term solutions. The beneficial effects in the river and at the dam would not likely be felt for a decade or more after programs are implemented.

The implications of siltation are well known. In 1982-83, India's Public Accounts Committee cited Ramchandra Singh Deo as follows:

> In India on a rough estimate we are losing a staggering 2 MAF live storage capacity annually in our major and medium dams, corresponding to a loss of 7 lakh [700,000] acres of irrigation potential every year. It costs them about a minimum of Rs. 6,000 to create a potential for irrigating one acre of land. Accordingly, we are losing over Rs. 400 crores [4,000 million] in the form of Capital assets annually.[20]

In 1990, the World Bank published a technical paper on watershed development in Asia.[21] It describes the siltation for eight dams in India showing that the rate of siltation assumed in design is consistently, and often alarmingly, below the rate actually observed after construction. One of the reservoirs cited is the Ukai—a World Bank funded project on the Tapi River in Gujarat just 80 kilometers south of the Sardar Sarovar Projects. The observed rate of siltation was shown to be almost 200 per cent greater than assumed in design, thus reducing the expected life of the reservoir by two-thirds. This is not atypical. The Kadana reservoir on the Mahi River, just north of the Narmada, is also silting up twice as quickly as predicted before construction. There are a great many other examples.[22] The authors of the World Bank technical paper conclude:

---

[20] *Report of the Public Accounts Committee 1982/83*, New Delhi: Lok Sabha Secretariat, p 102.

[21] J. B. Doolette and W. B. Magrath, eds., *Watershed Development in Asia: Strategies and Technologies*, World Bank Technical Paper Number 127, 1990.

[22] In January 1991, the Central Water Commission in New Delhi produced a report entitled "Compendium of Silting of Reservoirs in India." It contains information that also shows that siltation rates are generally higher than assumed in design, although the increase often differs (often higher, sometimes lower) from that documented elsewhere (e.g., the Bank's 1990 Technical

It is clear that sedimentation imposes a high cost in terms of shortened investment life, high maintenance requirements and reduced services . . . comparisons of the design in currently estimated lives of reservoirs in India show that erosion and sedimentation are not only severe and costly, but accelerating. It is now obvious that the original project estimates of expected sedimentation rates were faulty, based on too few reliable data over too short a period. (pp 7-8)

The Bank summarized the environmental impact arising from siltation in its December 1991 *India Irrigation Sector Review* saying: "the strategic need for long term sustainability of irrigation investments dictates that greater attention is paid towards realistic appraisal assessment of siltation rates" (Vol. II, p 74).

The effect of siltation and the remedial measures proposed in the Sardar Sarovar Projects are a subject of controversy. Numerous submissions dealt with the causes. We sought additional information from experts in India and elsewhere. We reviewed the literature and went back to the officials at the Nigam, the Central Water Commission, and the Ministry of Water Resources to review their assessments. Important questions seemed unanswered, so we obtained the raw data on sediment in the river from 1962 to 1987, and we examined its meaning for environmental impacts and resettlement and rehabilitation.

In 1991, Dr. P. R. Rao, Chief Engineer (Hydrology) for India's Central Water Commission, wrote a paper, with his deputy director, C. M. Pandit, which highlights four things important for our review:[23]

• sediment erosion rates vary widely from year to year;

• large quantities are carried with major floods, which complicates evaluation of mean annual deposition rates;

• deposits spread throughout the reservoir, reducing incremental capacity at all elevations; and

• deposits in the upper reaches of the reservoir may result in a significant increase in the water surface elevations upstream, particularly during periods of high water inflow.

The Sardar Sarovar dam has a "dead storage"[24] capacity of 2.95 MAF avail-

---

Paper Number 127). It concludes that part of the controversy stems from the higher sedimentation rates during the first 15 to 20 years of operation.

[23] "Effect of Sedimentation Rate on Reservoir Planning Decisions," *Fourth National Symposium on Hydrology of Minor Water Resources Scheme (Madras, 25-27 October, 1991)*, pp 215-17.

[24] Dead storage is the part of the reservoir below the lowest level of the spillway or penstock (or whatever is designed to take water out). The useable volume of water is in "live storage" which is above the dead storage.

able for the accumulation of silt before it encroaches on the live storage of the reservoir. The Central Water Commission in a submission to our review in February 1992 concluded that the planning for the Sardar Sarovar reservoir meets the prescribed stipulations of the code; i.e., the reservoir life will be greater than 100 years.[25] In 1991 the Chairman of the Sardar Sarovar Narmada Nigam Limited, Dr. C. C. Patel, stated:

> The rate of siltation in Sardar Sarovar will depend upon the construction of 29 reservoirs in the Narmada basin as planned by Madhya Pradesh, especially Narmada Sagar. All the assessments of useful life show that if these upstream reservoirs are built in a reasonable time, the life span of Sardar Sarovar dam will be not less than 233 years. In the worst case of NSP being inordinately delayed for 25 years after the Sardar Sarovar dam is completed, the lifespan of SSP may be reduced to 180 years.[26]

Using data available to us, we were not able to replicate the siltation results claimed by the Projects' proponents.[27] The sediment concentrations used in these calculations are based on grab samples of the suspended sediment. These concentrations were then scaled up to the whole river by using the estimated discharge. Thus, the errors in sediment loads include errors in discharge which are greatest during the monsoon when the sediment assumes the greatest importance. The grab samples themselves are selective, and may or may not be representative of the entire stream. When taken together, these factors lead us to believe that it is not unreasonable to anticipate that the calculations of annual sediment loads may be underestimated by a factor of two. The documented difference between calculated and observed siltation rates for other dams in India tends to support this view. Because there is no comprehensive environmental assessment, we are not in a position to judge the significance, if any, of this underestimation.

But there is a second and much more immediate problem from the environmental and resettlement perspective. The backwater effect of siltation will have startling effects upstream of the reservoir. This will occur whether or not catchment area treatment programs are successfully implemented.

---

[25] Central Water Commission, Hydrology Studies Organisation, "Sedimentation Studies for Sardar Sarovar Reservoir," submission to the Independent Review, February 1992, p 2.

[26] C. C. Patel, *Sardar Sarovar Project—India: What It Is & What It Is Not*, Gujarat: Sardar Sarovar Narmada Nigam Limited, September 1991, p 61.

[27] The basic document on sedimentation, and apparently the one relied on by Dr. Patel in the statement quoted, is: Narmada Project Dam Designs Circle, Vadodara, *Sardar Sarovar (Narmada) Project (FRL 455 ft) Sedimentation Studies and Life of Reservoir*, Government of Gujarat Irrigation Department, June 1982.

The effect of sedimentation on backwater has been overlooked. The 1984 backwater studies provided to us estimated the surface water profile along the river above the reservoir.[28] This effect was calculated to extend over 150 kilometers upstream during severe flood conditions. But the study made no allowance for the effect of the sediment-induced reservoir delta on upstream levels. When we asked about this effect, the Chairman of the Nigam told us that these calculations had not been made.

As Rao and Pandit point out in their 1991 paper on sedimentation, "Deposits of sediment in the upper reaches of the reservoir may result in a significant increase in water surface elevations upstream. This may, in turn, endanger upstream installations and developments particularly during periods of high water inflow" (p 217). This is because at the upstream end of the reservoir the coarser material will drop out to form a delta. The data we have assessed indicates this will start within the 145 kilometer reach above the dam, probably near where the Goi and Uri Wauh rivers join the Narmada. This delta will build and extend downstream into the reservoir at an initial rate likely measured in hundreds of meters per year. This rate will, of course, diminish as the delta progresses toward the deeper and wider areas within the reservoir. The backwater from the delta will extend upstream above the elevation of the reservoir and will be cumulative, significantly increasing the inundated area year after year above the levels that might otherwise be anticipated. At higher flows, the backwater will be higher, and it will extend even farther upstream. The impacts are almost certain to be significant. Lands situated above the present submergence area will be inundated. Forest areas will be affected. People's use of the lands will be affected. The degree of the impact and the suitability of the presently proposed mitigative measures are unknown. Clearly, the physical processes of sedimentation in the reservoir need to be examined more closely to establish the rate of growth of the delta where the river enters the reservoir, and the impact of the backwater conditions that will result.

CONCLUDING OBSERVATIONS

The initial environmental evaluations done in the early 1980s, including the 1983 overview ecological studies by the M. S. University of Baroda, presented enough information for the development of proper assessment studies in the upstream area. The follow-up work has been disappointing. The Bank's 1985 credit and loan agreements and India's 1987 environmental and forestry clearances formalized requirements for comprehensive assessments. Dates for

---

[28] Central Water Commission, *Backwater Levels in the River Narmada at Sardar Sarovar Reservoir*, New Delhi: Government of India, August 1984.

workplans and for results from surveys and studies were established. These were not met. This goes to the heart of the *pari passu* issue.

There is a fundamental difference in the meaning and practical value of *pari passu* between environmental assessment (i.e., what is to be affected, how, what can be done in project design, etc.) and environmental mitigative measures, some of which could be expected to proceed concurrently with construction.[29] The paradox we found is that in many areas, mitigation is actually ahead of the assessment. Surveys and studies which are prerequisites for assessment remain incomplete. At the very least, this frustrates even the most genuine effort to anticipate and reduce environmental damage.

Unlike the Bank's 1985 requirements which were specific to the Sardar Sarovar Projects, in India early considerations about the flora and fauna in the upstream area were based on general concerns of the Sardar Sarovar and the Narmada Sagar Projects taken together. The 1987 briefing note to the Prime Minister by the Ministry of Environment and Forests deals with the flora and fauna for both projects and states the need for "a Master Plan showing not just the present status but also the likely scenarios after the project is implemented."[30] The subsequent environmental clearance by the Government of India, covering both projects, specified that a survey of flora and fauna be conducted by 1989. This was not done. The two projects are now being considered separately by both the Bank and India even though from the Tribunal's 1979 award onward they have been planned and designed to function together. In their position as the downstream project, the Sardar Sarovar Projects are especially dependent on the Narmada Sagar Projects to function properly. It is not clear how the ecological interconnections in the Narmada valley are going to be assessed or who will do it.

All the documents available to us suggest that the upstream impacts of the Sardar Sarovar Projects together with the overlapping downstream impacts of the Narmada Sagar Projects will lead to cumulative effects much greater than would be implied by the simple addition of the two taken separately. Our Terms of Reference limit our review to the Sardar Sarovar Projects but we must emphasize the necessity of addressing the cumulative effects of directly related projects. Defining impacts and formulating ameliorative measures within the limits of the Sardar Sarovar Projects alone is ecologically unsound and can quickly become self-defeating.

---

[29] Mitigative measures also should apply to project design and operation, an aspect that has been largely foreclosed by the *pari passu* approach.

[30] "Note to the Prime Minister from Department of Environment and Forests," reproduced in *Damming the Narmada*, by Claude Alvares and Ramesh Billorey, Appendix 3, Penang, Malaysia: Third World Network, 1988, p 113.

Women bathing, washing clothes, and fetching water at the edge of the Narmada near the Rajpipla bridge, 15 kilometers below the dam.

Chapter 13
DOWNSTREAM
ENVIRONMENT

FROM the Sardar Sarovar dam to the ocean, the Narmada River runs for 180 kilometers through a rich lowland region which represents about 10 per cent of its catchment area. In the course of our environmental review we sought information that described the ecology of this lower reach of the river, the estuary, and near shore region in the Gulf of Cambay. We hoped to find a description of the aquatic ecosystem, including parameters indicating the quality and quantity of water and its seasonal changes, biological species, processes, and resource linkages. We looked forward to finding a systematic treatment of flow regimes and geomorphology. We expected to find systematic documentation of resource use, from drinking water to fisheries. We thought there would be documents establishing the kinds of physical, biological, and socioeconomic changes to be expected as the Sardar Sarovar Projects are brought on stream and more and more of the natural flow is stored, used, or diverted out of the river. We looked for a set of ameliorative measures that would be implemented to mitigate impacts. We thought these measures would be scheduled to begin with the phased development of the Sardar Sarovar Projects. We hoped they would also be related to the cumulative effects of other developments on the Narmada further upstream, in particular the Narmada Sagar Project, and to the expansion of industrial activity in the downstream river basin in Gujarat itself. In all our expectations we have been disappointed.

LACK OF INFORMATION

We found that there had been no environmental impact assessment made of downstream impacts of the Projects, and we found that no comprehensive workplans had been prepared. Although there are a few studies or parts of studies in progress that deal with some of the specific issues, we found very little organized information apart from the preliminary environmental information produced by the M. S. University of Baroda in 1983 after its six-month benchmark study.[1]

Officials at the Narmada Control Authority and at the Nigam assured us that the downstream impact of the Sardar Sarovar Projects would not be serious. Ameliorative measures were described, but these were limited to a general commitment to rehabilitate families engaged in the fishery downstream, if they are adversely affected. The number of such families, the extent of the change in the fishery, etc., are not yet known. We were told that some studies on the fishery were under way, and we were referred to the office of the Central Inland Fisheries Research Institute that had been established in Baroda in 1988.

The lack of an appropriate assessment of impacts for the region downstream of the dam left our review in a difficult position. Our Terms of Reference require us to assess the implementation of measures to ameliorate environmental impacts and to make recommendations for improvement. We therefore sought to establish the general nature and magnitude of the downstream environmental impacts. We set up a series of meetings with officials and researchers associated with the Sardar Sarovar Projects. We conducted a broad survey of the literature in India and elsewhere related to important downstream considerations for a dam of this kind. We engaged an independent expert to provide advice on critical issues.

In January 1992, at our request, the Nigam arranged a meeting of their experts and took us to see the lower reaches of the river. Later we visited other places downstream of the dam. We also gathered information on the Mahi and Tapi rivers (north and south of the Narmada) to learn what the downstream impact of dams built on those rivers has been. We went to the Mahi River to see first hand some of the downstream effects. We went through the reports and other material made available to us by the Narmada Control Authority, the Nigam, and the Ministry of Water Resources to extract relevant downstream information. We went back to the 1983 M. S. University of Baroda publication. We obtained copies of the papers used in its preparation, and these provided more detailed information on many downstream issues. We found other unpublished papers and Ph.D. dissertations in India and North America. We sought oceanographic information relevant to the Narmada estuary in the Gulf of Cambay with the assistance of the library of India's National Institute of Oceanography in Goa and the Woods Hole Oceanographic Institute in Massachusetts. Although we would have preferred a complete

---

[1] Department of Botany, M. S. University of Baroda, *The Sardar Sarovar (Narmada) Project Studies on Ecology and Environment*, Gandhinagar, India: Narmada Planning Group, July 1983.

database in order to make a full investigation of the issues, we believe that the information we obtained was sufficient for us to establish the framework within which we could proceed with our review of the downstream issues. Most of this work should have been done long ago by others.

BASIC REQUIREMENTS

The absence of an assessment of downstream impacts is surprising. In India, the need to examine issues related to siltation and erosion, salinity and water quality, critical life cycles and seasonal distribution of fish, as well as the human use of resources, was presented in the 1980 guidelines of the Ministry of Irrigation, the 1986 Guidelines of the Central Board of Irrigation and Power, and the 1978/1986/1989 (update) Guidelines issued by the Ministry of Environment and Forests. At the Bank, publications and operational statements in the late 1970s and early 1980s contained broad requirements which became more specific with the 1989 Environmental Policy for Dam and Reservoir Projects and the 1991 *Environmental Assessment Sourcebook*. There was certainly no lack of guidance from these and a multitude of other publications that dealt with the effects of dams on downstream riverine and estuarine ecosystems.

The Bank's 1985 Sardar Sarovar Projects Staff Appraisal Report and the Supplementary Data Volume both deal with downstream environmental issues. Both begin with similar statements on downstream effects:

> Below the dam, frequent low-intensity flood damages would be controlled, but potential for changes in the regime of the Narmada streambed would be increased and the upward migration of existing fish species would be halted. Measures would be taken through development of implementation programs to ensure preservation of land and enhancement of the environment.[2]

Further discussion of downstream matters in the Staff Appraisal Report is limited to statements that there would be a fish and fisheries work program with "detailed schedules and budgets for determining the environmental effects of proposed actions to mitigate adverse effects of the dam on the important estuarine species (hilsa, prawn and mullet) . . ." (p 28). This program was to include effects on the migration of fish, changes in quality of water from reduced flows, suitability for spawning, as well as breeding experiments for hilsa and large-headed maashir, and measures to enhance propagation of giant shrimp and mullet. Other studies were promised "as the need develops" (p 28).

[2] Staff Appraisal Report, 1985, p 28.

The 1985 Staff Supplementary Data Volume explains the issues further under the heading "The Estuary and Brackish Reach below the Dam":

> Since the Sardar Sarovar dam might impede migration of fish, this has been addressed by the GOG's [Government of Gujarat's] Fisheries Department. Three main groups are involved: hilsa, prawns, and mullet. The Narmada estuary is the better of the two hilsa-breeding sites in India (the other is the Sundarbans in Bengal). Hilsa is exported and is an economically important foreign exchange earner, as well as being lucrative internally. It has been found to migrate up to 106 km upstream (i.e., not quite as high as the damsite), so that the dam is not expected to impede migration, but this is being checked. In addition to migration, hilsa needs fresh water flushes at the appropriate season. The Fisheries Department and the ID Engineers are studying the timing of fresh-water releases from the dam so that the environment conditions for this fish would be enhanced. Further, reduction in the freshwater flushes to the estuary when the river is more fully regulated in the future would be addressed. Experiments with hilsa breeding are also being undertaken, and the twelve-year-old Ukai Reservoir near Surat has been stocked successfully with this fish, where they are thriving, if not actually breeding. The Sardar Sarovar dam is thought to be too high (129 m) for a fish ladder or similar facility. (Part 1, p 52)

Under the heading "The Reservoir" the document adds:

> The large-headed Maashir (Tortor) fish is one of the world's most important game fishes (it exceeds 10 kg in weight) and is found in the Narmada river. Since the Prime Minister, GOI, recently instructed all ministries to ensure the protection of this threatened species, GOG and GOMP [Government of Madhya Pradesh] Fisheries Department would include it in their study. (pp 52-53)

Downstream issues were to have been addressed in the environmental workplan required by the Bank in 1985 as one of the conditions in its credit/loan agreement with India. They have not been. India's 1987 environmental clearance required, by 1989, the "complete details" from surveys of flora and fauna and carrying capacities. Although the survey work has not been completed, the terms of reference and interim reports for the studies that are under way indicate that downstream impacts are unlikely to be addressed in a comprehensive way. There is, however, a five-year fisheries study under way in the estuary, being conducted by India's Central Inland Capture Fisheries Research Institute. It will provide baseline data, but it is not scheduled for completion until sometime in 1993. Although still helpful, this is about a decade later than necessary for proper planning and design.

The deficiency in environmental assessment and planning for the downstream region is, perhaps, well understood even if the serious consequences are not. Two outlines of work and a report by consultants related to the proposal for a Bank-funded Narmada Basin Development Project include sections that propose studies that cover downstream effects in the Narmada River.[3] This we find surprising, given that these should have been included in the studies related to the dam itself if they were to most usefully address impacts and ameliorative measures.

ASSURANCES IN LIEU OF ASSESSMENTS

At a meeting arranged by the Nigam in Gandhinagar in early January 1992, we were told that the downstream impacts could not be predicted. We had been told the same thing by Bank officials in November 1991 in Washington. The problem was described in terms of uncertainty related to releases from the Sardar Sarovar reservoir, its operation (with or without the Narmada Sagar Project) over the period leading to full development of the irrigation system, and a lack of predictive techniques for a complex river and estuary system of this kind. The Chairman of the Nigam told us that the studies to date on the downstream effects were only conceptual and not very helpful. But he assured us that the flows downstream of the Sardar Sarovar would be sufficient to prevent serious impact.

We were told that long-term problems related to increased riverbed scour, similar to those experienced downstream from the Ukai dam on the Tapi River, would be manageable. The possibility of a negative effect on the fishery was acknowledged. Officials at the Narmada Control Authority conceded that they did not know what this impact would be. But they assured us that ameliorative measures would be implemented to mitigate the impacts. We were told that the loss would be offset several years after construction by developing fishery programs in the reservoir, in ponds in the command area, and in the estuary itself.

[3] M.R.I., Memorandum from Donald L. Graybill to Thomas A. Blinkhorn, April 27, 1990. EcoLogic, Memorandum from Ronald D. Zweig to T. Blinkhorn, September 15, 1991. GOPA Consultants, *India, Narmada River Basin Development Project—Fisheries Component, Final Project Preparation Report*, May 1991.

At all of these meetings and others, the flood control benefits of the dam were emphasized. There is no doubt that flooding has a significant impact in the lower reaches of the Narmada River. But the degree to which this will be mitigated by the construction of the Sardar Sarovar Projects is not clear. The Sardar Sarovar dam alone has a very small storage capacity relative to the monsoon flood volumes, so that even if the reservoir were to be operated specifically for flood control purposes (which is not contemplated at present and could in fact compromise some of the other expected benefits) it would make only a minimal contribution to controlling flood damage. This point was made as early as 1981 in reports by the Bank's hydrology consultants. Of course, construction of the Narmada Sagar Projects with their storage would improve flood control benefits.

In response to our concerns about the impacts of changes in flows and our request for evidence to support assurances that downstream impact would be minimal and manageable, in February 1992 the Nigam provided three papers for our consideration.[4] One deals with the effects on downstream hydrology due to construction of projects in the Narmada valley. The other two review experience with respect to availability and use of water after the construction of dams on the Mahi and Tapi rivers. We understand that these papers were prepared for us under serious time constraints and we know that they are meant more for general guidance than as detailed assessments. Even so, they raise a number of questions. They fail to acknowledge important issues related to downstream impact. They adopt a narrow engineering perspective, not a comprehensive ecological one. They make assertions that seem to be at odds with what we saw and heard during our site visits and with many of the points made in the literature we reviewed. For example, we find it difficult to accept the conclusion that dams on the Mahi and Tapi rivers have been "immensely beneficial to downstream areas without any noticeable adverse effects due to the storages." Moreover, we have serious reservations about the conclusions reached about the Sardar Sarovar and Narmada Sagar Projects: "On the whole it can be emphatically said that construction of the proposed dam on the Narmada will hardly have any detrimental effects downstream. In fact, it will be a boon to them." This same conclusion is carried forward in a May 1992 document produced by the Nigam entitled "An Approach Paper on the Environmental Impact Assessment for the River Reach Downstream of Sardar Sarovar Dam." While this paper does sketch out some of the topics that need to be addressed, the analysis falls far short of what is necessary to understand

---

[4] The three undated papers are: "Downstream Hydrology-Effect Due to Construction of Projects in the Narmada Valley"; "Hydrology with Respect to Flow Availability and Use of Mahi Waters"; and "Flow Availability and Use of Tapi Waters—Tapi Basin."

impacts, in large part simply because the necessary data are not available. The paper says that a complete study program has been prepared and the assessment will be ready by the end of September 1992. It would be extraordinary if a proper assessment could be done in so short a time.

The basis for our concerns about the downstream impacts needs to be explained. To begin, we must to return to issues of streamflow.

ASSUMING FLOW REGIMES

The changes in the daily, seasonal, and annual flows caused by the Sardar Sarovar dam will create impacts downstream that need to be addressed. Experience elsewhere indicates that many of these impacts will appear only after several years. Some may take a decade or more to manifest themselves. As noted in Chapter 10, the Bank's 1984 policy states that the environmental aspects of projects should be considered over a period of 25 to 50 years or more.

We have already described the problems inherent in understanding the existing flow regime. We have also described why the Sardar Sarovar Projects are not likely to perform as planned. Although we know that the downstream flow regime will be changed by the Projects, without a proper study, the size, timing, and variations in flow remain unknown. It is not within our terms of reference to undertake these studies. Nonetheless, they need to be done.[5]

Putting to one side the problems of timing and operational performance at Sardar Sarovar, it is possible to establish some idea of the character and magnitude of the downstream impacts by assuming three stages of diversion and use of Narmada water as envisaged by the Narmada Water Disputes Tribunal.

• Stage 1 would begin about ten years after the start of dam construction (including the Garudeshwar weir). During this stage monsoon floods would flow over the dam's spillway and water would flow through the riverbed powerhouse. During the non-monsoon period (November to June), the minimum river flow would likely be greater than the existing base average low flow. The maximum monsoon flood peak would be reduced in most years.

---

[5] Our Terms of Reference require us to assess the implementation of the Projects with regard to the amelioration of environmental impacts. The downstream environmental impact assessment, which would be built mainly from flow regimes, was to have been done by others. It was not. Without such an assessment, the basis for and effectiveness of any ameliorative measure is speculative. Rather than leave our review on that note, we decided to assemble whatever information we could to establish the basis for concern, if any, in the downstream reaches of the river. The fact that we found ourselves in this position at this late stage of project implementation is deeply disturbing. The matters to be dealt with are not trivial. This is why we have expanded our assessment of downstream issues.

Flood peaking would occur only after the reservoir is full, and it may take place later than at present.

• Stage II would begin when the command area irrigation system and canal powerhouse become fully operational. The riverbed powerhouse would function only during periods of plentiful water supply (monsoons). The dry season flow below the dam is assumed to approach existing discharge conditions.

• Stage III will begin when additional hydraulic control would be applied by operation of other dams upstream, Narmada Sagar in particular. The discharge downstream of Sardar Sarovar would virtually cease during the dry season and reduced overtopping would occur during the monsoon season.

During Stage II and III the discharge below the dam would be augmented by flows derived from ground water and tributaries. (It has been estimated that between six and seven per cent of the flow in the Narmada below the Sardar Sarovar site is derived from the lower watershed.) However, there are plans for impoundments on both major tributaries below the dam (the Orsan and Karjan rivers) so their contribution to the Narmada during Stage III may be negligible. This will likely compound impacts.

The 1979 award of the Narmada Water Disputes Tribunal did not include an allocation of water for the river downstream of the Sardar Sarovar Projects. Gujarat had pleaded before the Tribunal for the release below the dam of 1,000 cusecs throughout the year or 0.7 million acre feet (MAF) annually to meet "incumbent requirements as between (a) navigation, (b) domestic use, (c) irrigation, or (d) arresting salinity progress."[6] This plea for apportionment of water for downstream use was not accepted by the Tribunal; we are told that Gujarat no longer feels such an apportionment will be necessary. The situation is confused by what appear to be contradictory statements in the Bank's 1985 Supplementary Data Volume. First it is said "there are possibilities of picking up water that has passed the Sardar Sarovar Dam . . . which would otherwise be spilled and go waste to the sea" (Part I, p 23). But later it states: "The Fisheries Department and ID [Irrigation Department, Gujarat] engineers are studying the timing of fresh-water releases from the dam so that environment conditions for this fish [hilsa] would be enhanced" (Part I, p 52).

The terms of the Tribunal award include a provision for review in the year 2024 (i.e., 45 years after the award) of provisions dealing with apportionment of the water and the sharing of excesses and shortfalls. This might result in operational changes that would change the hydrologic regime downstream. But other factors, including urban growth and intensified industrial development

---

[6] *The Report of the Narmada Water Disputes Tribunal with Its Decision*, Vol. I, 1979, p 91.

downstream, make it unlikely that there will be any net increase in water available below the dam. It is almost certain that there will be a decrease.

NATURE AND MAGNITUDE OF THE PROBLEM

Our review of downstream environmental issues is complicated by the absence of meaningful assessments. Arriving at any conclusions about the nature and magnitude of what is likely to happen is further frustrated by a lack of basic data for the lower reaches of the river and unanswered questions about the timing and amounts of releases of water upstream. Important parameters related to the river's natural hydrology, the operation of the dam, the riverbed powerhouse and canal, and the existence of the Narmada Sagar Project remain vague. Scenarios have not been developed to better understand the implications of project uncertainties and how impacts might be minimized or resolved under different operating conditions.[7] Nevertheless, the nature and magnitude of some of the impacts that need to be studied and ameliorated can be summarized under four headings: geomorphology, salinity, water quality and biota, and fisheries.

Geomorphology

The impact below the dam along the course of the river and in the Gulf of Cambay is uncertain not because the impacts cannot be determined but rather because no comprehensive studies have been undertaken. Basic data are missing or have only recently begun to be collected. Most of the related analyses have yet to be done. For example, we have been unable to find any study on the hydrology of the lower river and estuary. Nor have there been studies on the interactions among biological and chemical components which influence the patterns and trends associated with erosional and depositional conditions.

We know from existing information that the lower reaches of the present river channel have shifted northwards about six kilometers during recent geological time. Survey records over the past century show that Aliabet Island in the river estuary is expanding on its south side. Studies in the Gulf of Cambay indicate a significant concentration of suspended sediment. Estuarine floccula-

---

[7] Predictions based on various scenarios of rainfall/runoff and operating conditions can be made. We recognize that there are uncertainties. However, if cost/benefit models can be developed and various models for engineering and command area design can be used to help justify and shape a multi-billion dollar project, scenarios can also be utilized to help predict downstream impacts and develop mitigative measures. Some impacts are not inevitable. Properly developed scenarios could have helped establish the design and operating parameters of the dam by anticipating and preventing adverse effects. None of this has been done.

tion and biological capture of suspended sediment appear to provide important mechanisms for the accretion of fine silt in the estuary. During the period
of high discharge, the river also carries significant quantities of sediment into
the Gulf. In general, the configuration of the estuary is a reflection of the inter-
play of the regional structural geology, erosion and sediment transport, and
deposition of muds largely derived from the mobile pool of suspended material
in the Gulf.

Is the impact of the Sardar Sarovar Projects likely to influence seriously the
geomorphology of the lower river and estuary? Although it was never in our
Terms of Reference to do the environmental impact statement, we believe that
the likely impacts that would need to be addressed include the following.

• During Stages I and II there will be changes in the patterns of erosion and deposition and these will probably be more evident in the river than in the estuary. Erosion of the existing river channel will increase and will be more severe in areas nearest to the dam structures.[8] Erosion will affect both the riverbed and its bank. Changes in alignment of the river could affect the stability
of the meander pattern of the river. Initially, these changes will be relatively
limited but they will increase and eventually could cause failures in structures close to the existing river banks.

• During Stage III changes in patterns and trends will accelerate throughout
most of the river and the estuary. With much reduced flow, the river will become a misfit and will occupy less of the existing channel. There will be different effects in different reaches of the river. The increased scour caused by
the change in sediment load in waters entering the river upstream will continue to result in localized erosion, especially in the reach of the river closest
to the dam and weir structures. Monsoon flushing and erosion of the lower
river and estuary probably will not occur at all. With reduced discharge during both the monsoon and non-monsoon seasons, estuarine waters will become more saline. Rates of sedimentation are likely to affect the narrow part
of the river near Bharuch and biological fixation may increase rates of sedimentation in the estuary. The main river channel would remain north of
Aliabet Island and the south channel could close completely. Dominance of
marine rather than river-driven flow in the estuary and changes in suspended

---

[8] As explained in Chapter 12, the dam structures act as a sediment trap. The loss of sediment load
means that below the structures (dam and weir) the river will erode or "scour" the watercourse as
it seeks to reestablish the natural sediment loading, particularly under high flow conditions. This
matter was mentioned briefly in the 1982 report on sedimentation by the Narmada Project Dam
Designs Circle (p 28). While we agree that the erosion effect is unlikely to affect the stability of the
dam or weir, it is quite incorrect to conclude that it will not have adverse effects in the downstream
reaches of the river.

sediment in the inflow waters may also result in coastal realignment along the north shore.

- Changes in the hydraulic behavior of the estuary (and associated shoreline changes) are likely to increase the ponding effects of effluent and contaminant loadings within the lower river and estuary. This means that pollution levels may increase independently of upstream loading because of a less effective water and suspended particulate exchange with the Gulf of Cambay.

Salinity

The freshwater-saltwater mixing in the lower part of the river is influenced by the daily and seasonal flow patterns of the river and by the incoming and outgoing tides. At present, tidally induced fluctuations can be measured upstream as far as Nand, 75 kilometers from the mouth of the Narmada. Changing the natural flow regime of the river would have a number of effects. For example, the habitat for freshwater and low salinity brackish water fish and crustacean species would be changed, as would the type and location of the catch of the fishing communities along the lower part of the river and its estuary. Also, freshwater aquifers along the river and for some distance inland would become more saline; a situation that is paralleled by experience on the Mahi River after dam construction.

A comprehensive study of salinity changes is necessary. Without such a study, one that properly deals with the full range of seasonal and operating flow regimes integrated with the physical, biological, and chemical parameters in the river and estuary, an assessment of impacts is impossible. Ameliorative measures will be limited to compensation after the fact. Two examples illustrate the range of issues to be dealt with as the projects upstream become operational.

- In Stage I, the zone of predominantly fresh water may extend slightly downstream into the estuary below Bharuch, but because the estuary widens considerably there, displacement will be relatively small. In Stage II, the non-monsoon conditions will be similar to those at present. Impacts due to salinity are therefore likely to be localized in nature.
- In Stage III, the salt wedge will move a considerable distance upstream. The tidal effect will be enhanced, allowing larger volumes of sea water upstream with obvious effects on ground water. Communities like Bharuch which depend on ground water for consumptive use may experience considerable impacts. For example, during full moon and new moon days throughout the nine non-monsoon months, there is unlikely to be enough fresh water in the river to impede sea water ingress. By matching the existing data on flows and salinity at Bharuch it is reasonable to conclude that the amount of water that

would need to be released below the dam to offset this effect would be large enough significantly to affect the operation (if not the design) of the reservoirs upstream. And not just at Bharuch. Freshwater aquifers up to Jhanor and perhaps beyond would be recharged with saline water and the water would spread inland. It is also probable that there would be growing shortages of fresh water for expanding populations and industry all along the lower part of the river and estuary.

Water Quality and Biota

A general review of the literature along with project-related studies (e.g., from the 1983 M. S. University of Baroda Sardar Sarovar report to the 1991 *Rapid Environmental Impact Assessment of Gandhar Petro Chemical Complex* done for the Indian Petro Chemical Corporation[9]) provides an overview of many of the more important issues of water quality and biota that need to be investigated and synthesized in an impact assessment: net primary production, phytoplankton diversity, numbers of zooplankton, distribution of benthic groups, water temperatures, dissolved oxygen, pH, nitrate and phosphate variations, concentrations of total dissolved solids, domestic and industrial effluent discharges, freshwater and marine pollution, etc. The importance of this can be illustrated by an example.

During the early years of operation, and because almost all of the particulate matter in the river will be retained by the Sardar Sarovar dam, there will be a noticeable decrease in the quantity of nutrients available in the estuarine water. All levels of production will probably decrease substantially reflecting a loss of organic carbon, nitrogen, and phosphorus associated with this particulate matter. Moreover, since, relative to fresh water, marine waters tend to be deficient in nitrogen, there could be a shift towards nitrogen-fixing forms of blue green algae, with a comparable shift in dependent community structures within the estuarine food web. However, as the rapid pace of urban, industrial, and agricultural development continues around the lower parts of the Narmada River, reductions in nutrient loadings from upstream sources could be offset by inputs from point and non-point sources below the Sardar Sarovar dam. Indeed, agricultural pesticides and domestic and industrial wastes will add substantially to the pollutant load in the river, especially over the next few decades. As later stages of Sardar Sarovar come into effect, the flow of freshwater will decrease and estuarine circulation will be reduced. Retention time for pollutants will increase in the lower river. This will pose the additional prob-

---

[9] National Environmental Engineering Research Institute, *Rapid Environmental Impact Assessment of Gandhar Petrochemicals Complex*, Nehru Marg, Nagpur, August 1991.

lem of rising contaminant levels within whatever biomass then remains. It is likely that the existing nutrient balance will change. During Stages II and III, extremely eutrophic conditions could easily develop, resulting in major changes in the aquatic ecosystem.

The range of research questions necessary for an understanding of the implications of the Sardar Sarovar Projects for water quality and biota in the Narmada River has been clearly identified at least since the 1983 M. S. University of Baroda report. Without proper studies, these changes cannot be properly assessed or effectively mitigated.

Fisheries

The Narmada estuary is larger than all others in Gujarat combined. The information available on hydrobiology and other issues related to the fisheries was described as "scarce" in a 1991 consultant's report to the Bank. What is known was summarized in a paper prepared as part of the 1983 environmental benchmark study by the University of Baroda.[10] The authors explain that more than 50 per cent of Gujarat's total inland catch comes from freshwater and estuarine regions of the river. The hilsa is a fish of "high economic value" which migrates into the river during the monsoon to breed. The Narmada is described as the most important river for hilsa in western India, and construction of dams is known to be related to massive declines in hilsa populations. Prawns also breed in the freshwater regions of the Narmada. The eggs are washed out into brackish waters where they hatch. They return during the juvenile stage. The authors state:

> Even a small amount of reflection on the impact of Navagam [Sardar Sarovar] dam on the fishing regimes of the Narmada river leads one to the conclusion that the Narmada fishing is going to be profoundly affected by the dam. The changes will be different in different parts of the river and they will also vary at different stages of the project. Some of these changes will be beneficial and others will be harmful. The effect of these changes will be felt on inland fishing of the whole state and may even extend to the southern coast of the country. . . .
> The Narmada estuarine and freshwater fishing regimes are

[10] M. S. Duble, S. D. Sabnis, and J. V. Amin, "The Influence of Navagam [Sardar Sarovar] Dam on Fish Yields of the Narmada River in Gujarat," 1983, pp 107-131, MS for Department of Botany, M. S. University of Baroda, *The Sardar Sarovar (Narmada) Project Studies on Ecology and Environment*, July 1983.

important to the state fisheries not only because of their yields but also because they supply much needed seed stock to other freshwater fisheries. Normally when a dam is built across a river; the upstream fishing improves and the downstream fishing deteriorates. The fishing regimes change from riverine to lake modes. In the Narmada river also this is expected to occur.

However, in the first stage, the downstream fishing is not likely to suffer, in fact, it may improve considerably in the freshwater regions of the river; because the river is going to be strongly perennial and larger quantities of water will be available all through out the year.[11] If the flood conditions during monsoon are not adequate, there might be some drop in Hilsa fishing. These losses, however, may not exceed 30%. The prawns will continue to flourish and if adequate steps are taken they may replace Hilsa as the important catch of the river. There have been reports of the second hilsa migration sometime in the month of March. This is likely to increase because there would be larger quantities of water available during that month. When the second stage of the dam becomes operative the river is liable to break up into ponds very early in the post monsoon seasons, because only 1,400 cusec. water will flow in the post-monsoon period. When this occurs, the freshwater yields are going to be adversely effected. On the other hand, Hilsa fishing would also be poor in both the seasons. Hilsa needs large quantities of the freshwater before it starts upward migration. If that water is not available the Hilsa will either change its preference or go to other waters or suffer heavily. The Sardar Sarovar yield at this point will not be able to compensate the loss suffered by downstream fisheries. . . .

In view of the importance of Narmada fishing as source of stocking materials in the inland fisheries programme of the state, it is desirable that consideration will be given to ways and means to overcome the effects of Navagam dam on fishing in the Narmada river. (pp 112-15)

In 1988, India's Central Inland Capture Fisheries Research Institute created the Estuarine Fisheries Research Centre in Baroda to do a five-year study focusing on five matters:

---

[11] We note that this assumes the Narmada Sagar Project is built as planned and, in any event, applies only if Stage I provides all year flow at a higher rate than at present.

- biology of the hilsa and prawn (migration, spawning, growth);
- artificial fertilization of hilsa and development of hatching/rearing techniques;
- qualitative and quantitative assessment of planktonic and benthic communities;
- fisheries statistics, population dynamics of commercially important fish/shrimp, and fishing efforts; and
- assessment of water pollution.

The unpublished data from the work to date were made available to our review. Although incomplete, the studies will yield meaningful results for impact assessment and the development of ameliorative measures. Unfortunately, the work is scheduled to end in 1993, and at present there appears to be only the most rudimentary interaction between this work and the work sponsored by state and project officials.

We reviewed a 1991 fisheries study prepared for the Bank in support the proposed Narmada River Basin Development Project.[12] It contains information on impacts connected with the downstream ecosystem in part of an annex entitled: "Ecological Considerations Related to the Project." It begins by noting that: "The magnitude of possible impacts of ssp of the downstream ecosystem *after* the completion of other main dams of the Narmada cannot be predicted with certainty" (Annex 7, p 1). Although this is correct, it should be added that the reason why reasonable predictions of impact cannot be made is because the necessary studies, upon which assessments can be based, have yet to be done. The GOPA report *assumes* that with only the Sardar Sarovar Projects functioning, there will be *no crucial changes* in the downstream system. The report states clearly how downstream impacts from Sardar Sarovar may affect major species:

> The construction of the dam, however, will change to some degree the actual monthly flow pattern in this [downstream] zone and the seasonal load of sediments. These changes will eventually have a negative impact on some important fish/prawn species who select their spawning or breeding grounds according to both salinity and edaphic features. Both the Hilsa and Giant Freshwater Prawn (Macrobrachium) possess a behaviour finely tuned to the salinity gradient of their habitat. Their juveniles are highly selective with respect to other hydrological parameters such as sedimentalogical texture, alkalinity, pH-values, and

[12] GOPA Consultants, *India, Narmada River Basin Development Project—Fisheries Component, Final Project Preparation Report*, May 1991.

turbidity. It is not completely understood how the latter factors act on the physiological system of these species, but their niche requirement seems to be so finely tuned that they are unable to cope with small-scale alterations of these factors. It is likely that these parameters will undergo some change in the downstream river bed, last but not least because fine sediments would be trapped in the main reservoir and pH-values are likely to drop. Even if it is understood that in the present stage—due to the persisting magnitude of the annual spill over the ssp dam—there is no immediate threat to the ecosystem, it seems justified to consider an artificial replenishment of the estuarine stretch with fish and prawn seed.

The water flow situation will *change in Stage* ii when Narmada Sagar Project is functioning and utilisation of spill water for additional power generation is considered. . . . Thus during most of the season very little water will be available in the downstream zone.

Apart from the change in fluvial pattern and restricted water drainage . . . the salinity ingress will most likely change the ecological balance of this river stretch—replacing the present aquatic community with a new one, more adapted to marine and hypersaline regime. Undoubtedly the breeding ground of Hilsa and Macrobrachium will be affected.

Whenever the monthly amount of freshwater flow in the downstream stretch will decrease, additional problems are likely to arise due to human interference. With a rapid development of new industrial complexes (Ankleshwar, Bharuch) and the intensification of agricultural efforts, waste waters of all kinds and toxic components will inflict their toll on the aquatic system and will obviously affect its biological cycles. (Annex 7, pp 1-2).

In a note attached to a January 24, 1992, letter to our review from the Nigam dealing with downstream fisheries issues, the effect of the dam is described:

Due to changes in the fluvial pattern and restricted water drainage, oceanic intrusion towards the river is expected to take place in the absence of compromising factors. This will cause increase in the salinity regime and other conditions deleterious to the system. The biotic communities spectrum in the lower deltaic region and the migratory routes of Hilsa and Scampi shall be affected and this would result in very poor to negligible output from these prime estuarine fisheries of the State.

Without a comprehensive approach to fisheries throughout the Narmada River basin and adjacent coastal areas, planning of upstream water management in isolation from any consideration of downstream impacts can only lead to confusion and even lost opportunity. Already, future options based on the existing hilsa and prawn fisheries are being compromised. Both species are good indicators of change. Both have particular life cycle sensitivities. The loss of freshwater flow in Stage III may virtually eliminate these species from the estuary. At best, they will be present in greatly reduced numbers. Support of cultured fisheries from these stocks on a sustainable basis is questionable. Other Narmada river fish species like the maashir are thought to be migratory, but it is not known what rehabilitation strategies would be sufficient to support their needs as well. If the Bank's 1985 statement about the importance of this "threatened species" is correct, the situation is all the more disturbing.

CONCLUDING OBSERVATIONS

No assessment of downstream environmental impacts has been made. Even rudimentary information on linkages and interdependencies is unavailable. If data had been collected as contemplated or stipulated by India's guidelines from 1978-80, by the Bank's 1985 credit and loan agreements, and by India's 1987 conditional environmental clearance, a reasonable model could have been developed to assist all parties to predict impacts and develop appropriate ameliorative measures. Proceeding without proper information will almost certainly result in a long series of crises which will have to be dealt with one after the other. This will be both inefficient and ineffective.

Some research has been initiated to identify the life history and environmental requirements of key species in the river, but the necessary understanding of the river ecosystem and its link to marine ecosystems in the Gulf of Cambay will require a great deal more effort and time. It is unrealistic to expect that anything like the present downstream food web could be sustained in the river in the long term. Apart from these broad issues, there will be more site-specific impacts that will have to be addressed. The construction of the Garudeshwar weir below the main Sardar Sarovar dam and the use of this impoundment for temporary water storage will have important effects. Changes in channel configuration could undermine river bank structures. Changes in the downstream fish habitat may have complex social and economic effects on numerous river communities, and relocation of these people would need to be addressed.

Any plan to develop and manage the Sardar Sarovar Projects independent of developments downstream will result in significant environmental and social costs. It seems incongruous to proceed with a multi-billion-dollar river development scheme without thoroughly addressing the downstream consequences especially in an area of major urban, industrial, and agricultural expansion. Assumptions and assurances, however well intentioned, are a poor substitute for in-depth studies and assessments. The magnitude of the projects, and the impacts, justify a rigorous multi-disciplinary impact assessment. This assessment could lead to changes in design and operation of the Sardar Sarovar and other upstream projects so that impacts can be avoided or minimized.

It is not appropriate to propose "band aid" solutions to the cumulative impacts of developments which will reshape lower reaches of the Narmada River. On its own, the Sardar Sarovar dam will have an impact on the downstream environment beginning in Stage I and escalating until Stage III. As this occurs, numerous other developments in the region will also affect the river, compounding the impact. A comprehensive outline of urban, industrial, and agricultural development in the region is essential. Gujarat's Minister of Industry announced in March 1992 that Asia's largest and second largest chemical complexes will be built downstream at Jhagadia and Agra. This gives a sense of the scale of the changes. The impacts on the river of development throughout the region, and the effects of reduced freshwater supply should be assessed in an integrated way. The role of fisheries has to be considered. Priorities need to be set. A great deal of important work must be undertaken if one of India's great natural assets is to be properly managed and developed.

Branch canals are designed to take water across the command area. The irrigation network is planned to use 75,000 kilometers of canals and distributaries.

Chapter 14
COMMAND AREA ENVIRONMENT

OUR review of the command area proved to be as frustrating as it was difficult. We expected the challenge posed by the sheer size of the area—1.8 million hectares—and its agro-climatic variability. But arriving as we did well after canal construction had started and many years after impact assessments were supposed to have been made, we did not expect to find so many deficiencies, inconsistencies, and contradictions in basic information. Here are a few examples.

Although we found a widespread acknowledgement that problems of irrigability, waterlogging, salinity, and drainage are significant, we found no comprehensive assessment of these impacts. We were given assurances that mitigative measures based on complex, interdependent technical, social, and political strategies would be used to address the problems. But these strategies remain speculative and the full dimensions of the problems are not yet known.

Although domestic supply is the Projects' first priority for water allocations, we found no urban or rural water supply plans to review. We were told that the commitment to alleviate drinking water shortages is firm and, in fact, the number of people estimated to benefit has increased by more than 25 per cent over the last year. There is no corresponding increase in the amount of water allocated for domestic purposes. And the list of villages to be served includes more than 200 in Saurashtra and Kutchch that India's census describes as uninhabited.

Although the Bank has disbursed over 94 per cent of the credit for the first part of the water supply and drainage portion of the Projects, we discovered that the Bank's own recent review of the irrigation sector in India identifies many problems found in earlier projects that appear to be replicated in the

Sardar Sarovar Projects. We were told that Sardar Sarovar is different from the earlier ones and were referred to documents supporting the new approach. Yet the problems that have emerged are similar to those that India's Public Accounts Committee and others have been seeking to have addressed for at least a decade.

Although the Bank and India both subscribe to the necessity for a holistic approach to environmental issues, we found that construction of Phase I of the main canal was well advanced, with the dam and reservoir at one end which is unlikely to be able to supply the designed flows (see Chapter 10), and three-quarters of the command area in Gujarat at the other end (Phase II) for which basic assessments are just now being planned. We reviewed several good studies for Phase I of the main canal and a few preliminary studies for Phase II. But these are primarily engineering reports, not environmentally oriented assessments.

CONTEXT

In March 1985 the Bank described Sardar Sarovar as "one of the most ambitious water resource development projects ever attempted" and "probably the largest irrigation project to be implemented as one unit."[1] The precedent is not just related to size. The Bank stated:

> In virtually every respect, the SSP represents a break with past approaches to the planning, design, construction, and operation of irrigation projects in India. To a large extent, this is due to a major effort by the Bank to develop local institutions. However, this effort would not have succeeded without GOG's [Government of Gujarat's] strong commitment and the local availability of highly trained scientists and engineers. Indeed, it was just these factors that made the Bank decide to allocate significant staff and consultant resources to the SSP. It was assumed that this project would represent the best opportunity to achieve the Bank's objective of modernizing the irrigation sector in India. (p 24)

Six years later, in December 1991, with the Sardar Sarovar dam and canal well under construction, the Bank published its *India Irrigation Sector Review*.[2] It provides a comprehensive analysis which, if taken together with the 1985 staff

---

[1] Staff Appraisal Report, Supplementary Data Volume, Part I, p 24.
[2] *India Irrigation Sector Review*, Vols. I and II, World Bank, December 20, 1991.

appraisal documents, provides a set of "bookends" within which to place our review of command area environmental issues.

The Bank's *Irrigation Sector Review* provides a general confirmation for our findings related to the command area. At the same time, it is disturbing because it shows that the problems that we have found in the command area are not unique to Sardar Sarovar. The sources of many of the problems related to environmental issues, as well as to resettlement and rehabilitation issues, are recognized by the Bank to be deep seated. They permeate virtually all irrigation projects in India, and are not likely to be susceptible to immediate solution.

The Bank describes irrigation in India as "at a cross roads." The choice is described as one between the status quo, with modest or diminishing agricultural growth rate, and a concerted reform and renewal to match reality to potential. The executive summary to the *Irrigation Sector Review* puts it this way:

> The findings of this review point to poor sector planning and financial management, on the one hand, and inadequate water management and maintenance, on the other, as the main causes of mediocre performance. Paradoxically, India's major engineering achievements over the past half-century, resulting in massive expansion of surface irrigation, have contributed to the sector's current problems. With the focus centered on construction, the broader management needs of the sector were neglected, and the cumulative costs of this neglect are now apparent. Over the past decade, the situation appears to have worsened: . . . India cannot afford an over-expensed and under-performing sector. Sooner, rather than later, the burden will be financially unsustainable, and infrastructure will be physically unsustainable due to declining construction and maintenance standards. The situation is compounded in some areas by environmental degradation. Above all, agricultural growth will suffer. (p i)

The Bank is calling for improvements in many areas of the irrigation sector in India that go to the heart of matters raised in more project-specific terms by our review. Sector-wide actions suggested by the Bank that are particularly relevant include developing and applying state (i.e., Gujarat) water policies consistent with the 1987 National Water Policy; establishing river basin planning commissions for holistic development; refocusing investment on incomplete works and restricting new construction to a few cases for regional development (Sardar Sarovar is identified as one); expanding the irrigation sector only on the basis of "clear-cut viability, available water and sound technical preparation" (p ii), preparing and implementing national policies on environmental, resettlement and rehabilitation issues, including earlier assessments so that they can influence project design and monitoring; shifting from a narrow engineering focus; and moving in the longer term to command area management that is financially independent and managed by users.

We received many submissions that dealt with the Sardar Sarovar Projects in the context of India's experience with irrigation projects since Independence. We were told that Sardar Sarovar's environmental and resettlement and rehabilitation problems have the same roots as similar problems that emerged in previous irrigation projects. We read the 1983 and 1986/87 Public Accounts Committee Reports that foreshadow many of the problems highlighted in the Bank's 1991 *Irrigation Sector Review*. Clearly, the problems are well understood at the highest levels in India. In 1986 Prime Minister Rajiv Gandhi spoke at a meeting of Chief Ministers, saying:

> The situation today is that since 1951, 246 big surface irrigation projects have been initiated. Only 65 out of these have been completed. 181 are still under construction. This is not a happy state of affairs. . . . Perhaps we can safely say that almost no benefit has come to the people from these projects. For 16 years we have poured money out. The people have got nothing back, no irrigation, no water, no increase in production, no help in their daily life.[3]

This, it is said, is all in the past. The Sardar Sarovar Projects are to be a new departure, particularly with respect to environmental and resettlement and rehabilitation issues. This is the essential thesis of the 1985 Staff Appraisal Report. But it is a thesis that cannot be supported by our review of the command area environmental issues. What we have found indicates that many of the problems highlighted by the Bank's *India Irrigation Sector Review* also apply in some measure to the Sardar Sarovar Projects.

ENVIRONMENTAL CONCERNS

The need to address command area environmental issues is well known in India. In 1973, the Government of India's Expert Committee on Rise of Costs of Irrigation and Multi-purpose Projects recommended that guidelines be laid

---

[3] Cited in *Proceedings of the First Meeting and Some Selected Papers on Land Management*, New Delhi: M. P. State Land Use and Wasteland Development Board, March 1991, p 55.

down for the investigations needed to prepare projects for approval of the Planning Commission. In response, in 1980, the Ministry of Irrigation published *Guidelines For Preparation of Detailed Project Report of Irrigation and Multi-Purpose Projects*.[4] Comprehensive checklists and outlines are provided which include environmental issues. Volume II contains subsections on irrigation planning and command area development. Also included in Volume II are the 1978 guidelines of the Department of Science and Technology's National Committee on Environmental Planning and Coordination (which later became the Ministry of Environment and Forests). Volume III deals exclusively with command area development covering environmentally-related issues such as ground water quality, waterlogging, salinity, and drainage.

Based on the reports of three appraisal missions that visited India between March and September 1983, the Bank, in 1985, approved the credit for the Sardar Sarovar command area water delivery and drainage project. The environmental issues in the command area were dealt with in parts of two documents: the Staff Appraisal Report of February 1985 dealing with the water delivery and drainage aspects of the Sardar Sarovar Projects, and the Supplementary Data Volume of March 1985.

The Bank's 1985 Staff Appraisal Report states that the command area environmental issues would be considered as part of the "workplan" which was to include studies being done by the Narmada Planning Group—the Gujarat agency set up as a result of the 1978 Bank mission recommendations.[5] The Group's listing of 24 priority topics for their work was appended to the report, showing as a first priority the rehabilitation and resettlement plans for oustees within the command area and, as a sixth priority, a "detailed environmental assessment and necessary actions for protective measures for the command area" (pp 82-3). Five other "priorities" related to command area environmental assessment were listed: conjunctive water use (#15), ground water modelling (#17), drainage (#18 and #20), and soil and land use surveys (#21). The Staff Appraisal Report also says that workplan studies were to include when necessary the design and implementation of mitigatory measures. Seven problem areas were identified for investigation: groundwater rise, salt accumulation, proliferation of aquatic weeds in canals, proliferation of water-borne diseases, deterioration of soil and water qualities, potential for afforestation, and "other effects" including those on wildlife.

Under the heading "Water Distribution and Drainage Network," the

[4] *Working Group Report, Guidelines for Preparation of Detailed Project Report of Irrigation and Multi-Purpose Projects*, Vols. I, II, and III, 1980.
[5] Staff Appraisal Report, *Narmada River Development—Gujarat, Water Delivery and Drainage Project*, February 12, 1985, p 18.

Bank's 1985 Supplementary Data Volume noted that "environmental analyses thus far completed have emphasized the main dam and reservoir" (p 55). It says that studies of the command area had to that date generally been limited to the Narmada Planning Group's identification of "specific effects and possible mitigating factors" (p 55). The Group "would be responsible for carrying out detailed environmental analysis of the command area" and the "principal environmental requirements" (p 55) were described as what was summarized in the Group's priority listing (cited above). The Bank report says:

> Highlights of the workplan include studies aimed at developing possible mitigation measures (when required) for effects of potential ground water rise, root zone salt accumulation, growth and aquatic weeds, proliferation of water borne diseases by spread of Narmada water, siltation, increased use of fertilizers and insecticides and need for wildlife enhancements and afforestation. In addition, it is expected that training programs... would be required to fulfil the environmental program's administrative and analytic needs over time with respect to the command area as well as the dam and reservoir. (p 55)

While acknowledging that Sardar Sarovar is "the first of a series of large reservoir projects for irrigation and power which are planned on the Narmada River," and is of "unusual magnitude" with features "without precedent," and that there was "limited experience [in India]...in measuring and controlling adverse environmental impacts of large schemes" (pp 55, 56), the Supplementary Data Volume states:

> ...no basic organizational changes at either state or central governmental levels would be required to implement the environmental work plan; that is all-required studies and implementation programs would be possible within the existing organization framework. (p 55)

We have been unable to determine how the Bank arrived at these environmental assurances. There had been no environmental assessment of the command area, as required by the Bank's 1984 directives. The 1980 guidelines of India's Ministry of Irrigation included environmental requirements that had not been fulfilled. The 1983 M. S. University of Baroda environmental overview study did not cover the command area. Clearance had not been forthcoming from the Ministry of Environment and Forests in 1983 because of inadequate information. (Clearance, albeit conditional, was not granted until 1987.) Yet the Staff Appraisal Report and other Bank documents make no mention of any of this.

The Bank's 1985 Sardar Sarovar Agreement with India contained a provision linked to command area environmental issues. The workplan for environmental effects, which would include the effects in the command area, was to be completed by December 31, 1985 (later deferred to 1989), and this was to be implemented with the necessary training programs. This workplan was not produced and has still not been produced.

In 1987, two years after the Bank's credit and loan approval, when the question of whether to grant an environmental clearance for the Sardar Sarovar and the Narmada Sagar Projects came to a head in India, a briefing note by the Ministry of Environment and Forests for the Prime Minister addressed command area issues:

> Command Area Development is aimed at achieving the following:
> —Prevention of water logging and salinity;
> —Optimization of water utilization; and
> —Maintenance of water quality.
> All these objectives require the development of the command area through levelling, grading and provision of sufficient drainage, both surface and sub surface as well as pollution control measures especially against the fertilizers and pesticides run-off. On-farm development works would be detailed and implemented over a period of 30 years starting from 1990/91. A detailed survey of the command area is, therefore, required on priority to prepare a package of the nature and quantity of development and drainage and on-farm works to fully utilize the irrigation potential. The Action Programme is yet to be detailed.
>
> The Ministry of Water Resources is preparing an evaluation report covering:
> (a) Extent of likely water logging and salinity problems.
> (b) Effectiveness of measures proposed or likely to be proposed to combat these problems as per the action programme to be formulated.[6]

---

[6] Note to the Prime Minister from Department of Environment and Forests. Reproduced as Annex 3 in Claude Alvares and Ramesh Billorey, *Damming the Narmada*, Penang, Malaysia: Third World Network, 1988, p 112.

When it was finally given, India's 1987 environmental clearance for Sardar Sarovar contained the condition that complete details for command area development were to be furnished by 1989. This was not done (see Chapter 10). The subsequent project clearance (October 1988) by the Planning Commission reinforced the requirements of the environmental clearance and added a number of other requirements for the command area. Gujarat was to submit to the Planning Commission a detailed program of studies with milestones of achievements, duly vetted through the Central Water Commission, related to the drainage and ground water balance studies for areas beyond the Mahi River. In addition a special group of experts was to be set up to look at siltation within the canal itself. The state was to draw up a detailed plan related to the micro-level network irrigation system within the command area and to provide assurances that the canal system would be completed in all respects so the irrigation waters would be made available from its outlet to its tail end users. No timeframe was given. These requirements are now being addressed in studies that are under way or are planned.

More than three years after the signing of the 1985 credit agreement, the Bank's environmental reports note that although a water management study proposal had been submitted to the Narmada Planning Group, "it lacks linkages with soil and water conservation requirements and fails to rationalize the allocation of water resources over both the short and long-term. The potential for waterlogging and salinization also deserves more thorough treatment" (Item 5, October 1988). Seven months later, some progress was reported in forging the necessary linkages and rationalizing allocations. The mission was "given assurances that the potential waterlogging and salinization was being given adequate attention along with the risk of water pollution from the application of fertilizers and pesticides" (Item 18, May 1989).

The Narmada Control Authority's status report of the studies and activities regarding the environmental aspects of the Sardar Sarovar Projects, dated December 1991, notes that the master plan for surface and subsurface drainage in the command area has been prepared as far as the Mahi River crossing. The services of six consultants have been engaged to carry out studies beyond the Mahi. Their reports were expected at the end of 1991 but are not yet available. The studies would relate to the ground water, drainage, conjunctive use of surface and ground water, silting aspects of the main canal, planning and design of micro-level canal networks, etc. The Ministry of Environment and Forests' December 1991 summary of command area development progress states that the action plans are not available and the timeframe for their ultimate availability is "not known."

A January 29, 1992, Bank memorandum describes the progress in dealing with the issue of salinization. For the first section of the canal (to the Mahi

River) the studies carried out by the Narmada Planning Group were: soil and contour surveys, groundwater/conjunctive surveys and modelling, drainage plans, and irrigation water allowances. Studies beyond the Mahi expected to be completed in two years are described: detailed soil surveys, mathematical modelling of groundwater systems, and pre-feasibility level drainage studies. The memorandum states that these studies address five specific priorities as listed by the Narmada Planning Group and included in the Bank's 1985 Staff Appraisal Report. They do address these subjects. Where they fail, however, is in bringing together in a coherent way sufficient information to provide an environmental assessment with proposed protective measures, something to which the Narmada Planning Group had given high priority.

When we inquired about the state of the environmental studies for the command area, the Executive Member of the Narmada Planning Group told us that the command area development studies are conducted in three phases: pre-feasibility studies; project execution studies (within two years); and operational planning studies (the micro-level analysis necessary for final project implementation). Phase I of the canal, the section to the Mahi River covered by the current Bank agreements, is now past the pre-feasibility stage. Over 75 per cent of Bank funding for Phase I has been disbursed. The Bank is considering funding Phase II.

CRITICAL COMMAND AREA FEATURES

The main purpose of the Sardar Sarovar Projects is to deliver water to Gujarat and Rajasthan for irrigation and municipal/industrial purposes. The 440 kilometer long canal, described as the largest in the world, will carry about 32 per cent of the "dependable" flow of the Narmada river for use in Gujarat and slightly less than 2 per cent for use in Rajasthan. Because Gujarat is the Projects' sponsor and the principal beneficiary of the Sardar Sarovar Projects, we have focused our attention on the impacts of its irrigation, domestic, and industrial water use plans. The Bank's 1985 Supplementary Data Volume provides a perspective on the development of these plans:

> NWDT [Narmada Water Disputes Tribunal] did not rule on the use that Gujarat should make of the allocated water, and neither did it sanction any particular size or specific geographical location of the irrigation command area. However, the plans for an irrigation command, as submitted by Gujarat to the NWDT (with the objective of justifying the greatest possible need and, therefore, allocation of water), quickly became a political reality. In a sense, once the plan for the command area was made public, it

expressed implicit promises of future irrigation services to particular zones of the state. Furthermore, the mandated extension
of the main canal to the Rajasthan border ... created a strong
argument to include a command area close to the maximum
that could reasonably be served by the canal. (Part I, p 27)

Gujarat's Sardar Sarovar water plan is based on a quantity of 12 MAF of
which 75 per cent is expected to come from the Narmada River (the 9 MAF allocated by the Narmada Water Disputes Tribunal award), 2.5 per cent from rivers along the route of the canal, and 22.5 per cent from ground water in the
command area. Conjunctive use of ground water and surface water is therefore
an essential feature of the plan. This applies to agricultural and non-
agricultural uses.

The non-agricultural demand for water by urban, rural, and industrial users is forecast to be 1.37 MAF of which 35 per cent would be met from "local
sources," 10 per cent from "recharge withdrawals," and 55 per cent from the
canal system. With system losses estimated to be 0.25 MAF, the gross canal contribution for non-agricultural purposes would be 1 MAF.[7]

Agricultural use in Gujarat, estimated to be 11 MAF, is to be met throughout
the command area by withdrawals from the canal and other sources. Groundwater pumping will augment supply and help control waterlogging problems.
Approximately 1.8 million hectares, representing about 20 per cent of the area
of the state, will be irrigated (including 0.35 million hectares already under irrigation) through a 75,000 kilometer automated, state-of-the-art, computerized
canal distribution system. The main parts of this canal system will be lined to
reduce water losses and minimize waterlogging in the surrounding area.

About 75 per cent of the command area is in what is described as mainland
Gujarat, 23 per cent in Saurashtra, and 2 per cent in Kutchch. Irrigation
needs in these areas arise primarily because of the timing or amount of rainfall.
The more abundant precipitation in the Sardar Sarovar command area near
the Narmada River decreases as one proceeds northward along the route of the
canal into areas such as Surendranagar and Kutchch. The annual variation of
rainfall increases in the same direction with the coefficient of variability ranging from 35 per cent in the southeast to more than 60 per cent in the northwest.
About one-third of the total area to be irrigated in Gujarat is in districts with a
normal rainfall of more than 800 mm. This is classified as medium precipitation for agricultural purposes. The Bank's current credit agreement funds the
canal in this area.

---

[7] Narmada Development Department, *Planning for Prosperity: Sardar Sarovar Development Plan*,
Sardar Sarovar Narmada Nigam Limited, November, 1989, p 250.

The objective of irrigation is to increase crop yields. Success depends on soil characteristics, climatic conditions, water management, balanced use of manures and fertilizers, and the control of insects, pests, diseases, and weeds. The current crop yields are well below what it is reasonable to expect even without irrigation.[8] Cotton, rice, and pearl millet are planned to be the main irrigated crops during the *kharif* (wet, June-October) season and wheat during the *rabi* (dry, November-March) season. Although at least five sugar factories are already in various stages of planning or construction in the command area, sugar cane crops are forecast for only about 0.3 per cent of the total irrigated area. (The minister responsible for the Sardar Sarovar Projects in Gujarat has said that it will not exceed 0.5 per cent.) This is an important consideration because the annual water requirement for sugar cane in this area would be high: 2,400 to 3,000 mm per hectare.

If the design and operating assumptions are fully realized, an annual average of about 500 mm of water will be available per hectare over the command area in Gujarat. The irrigation system therefore is described as "extensive" rather than "intensive," meaning that a large area is to be covered by a relatively small amount of water. Canal water will not be supplied to farmers between March and May. Also, a volumetric, rotational supply system would require farmers to use ground water to augment the canal supplies.

This "extensive" irrigation is based on calculations that contain critical, but questionable, assumptions. Two examples illustrate how the water requirements of the system may be underestimated.

First, the adequacy of rainfall for crop growth appears to have been assessed on the basis of average (fortnightly) depth of rain without considering its timing or relating it to crop needs and how much of it runs off without soaking the soil.[9] A more realistic analysis would determine the effectiveness of the rainfall in reducing the irrigation requirements, and this would likely show that additional irrigation water is required to achieve the desired crop yields.

Second, the irrigation water use efficiency (i.e., that portion of the canal head water that is actually utilized by the crop) has been assumed to be 60 per cent—significantly higher than the performance of other systems in India. This is justified on the basis of the design and operating parameters in the system from the canal through to field application. Key features, such as lined canals, computerized control, and new pricing and management regimes are

---

[8] When we interviewed an irrigation consultant who did work for the Bank in the early 1980s, he told us that an extension program to assist and provide training to farmers would increase yields substantially in the area, even without the Sardar Sarovar Projects.

[9] Net irrigation requirements have been determined on the basis of a modified Penman method with a significant departure. Instead of effective rainfall, it appears that the 50 per cent dependable rainfall has been used. This gives lower values for water needs.

said to lead to better water management. But our review indicates that many of the assumptions upon which 60 per cent efficiency is based are questionable.[10] For example, recent Bank Mission reports indicate that India wishes to relax standards related to lining of the distributaries and minors of the Sardar Sarovar canal. (The Bank is objecting.) Some assumptions appear unrealistic. For example, the assumption of operating 290 days per year at two-thirds Full Supply Level means that Gujarat would take more than 60 per cent more water than it is entitled to under the Tribunal award.[11] In the chapter on technical performance in its 1991 *India Irrigation Sector Review*, the Bank addressed these kinds of design issues:

> More realism concerning the availability of water and feasible efficiency of water usage is in order. Concern about ensuring an adequate benefit/cost ratio, exacerbated by political concerns to maximize planned irrigated areas, adds pressures to overextend proposed command areas and use unrealistic design assumptions. Irrigation efficiency in India has often been assumed at 60%, whereas a worldwide sample of irrigation commands indicates 37-40% efficiency in regions of low rainfall (below 1000 mm) under reasonably good management, and in higher rainfall zones, an average of 23%. Most irrigation commands in India probably have an irrigation efficiency of 20-35%. If assumed efficiency is 60% and actual efficiency is 30%, actual water availability will be half the assumption at design. Another common deficiency is that potential irrigable area is often based on a standard 75% probability level for water availability. This has no necessary relationship with what is optimal for the command (only simulation analysis can determine this) and also often results in overestimation of potentially irrigable area. (p 40)

[10] For an explanation of how the 60 per cent figure has been justified by the Government of Gujarat, see Chapter 10 in *Planning for Prosperity* (1989). We note, however, that in 1985 the Bank was developing its calculations on an efficiency of 48 per cent (see, for example, Supplementary Data Volume, Annex 4, p 139). In the June 1985 reports of the Operations Research Group dealing with the mathematical modelling of the groundwater system, scenarios are referred to utilizing a "low" of 42 per cent and a "high" of 58 per cent (see, for example, p 50).

[11] In a letter dated April 28, 1992, Dr. C. C. Patel, Chairman of the Nigam, responded to our inquiry about this assumption. He said that in fact this was just an assumption and, in fact, the operation of the canal "will be entirely governed by the corresponding water demands (converted into flow demands) from village service areas, which will be served from the distributaries . . . the canals would run at discharges much less than those corresponding to two-thirds FSL and the seepage losses will be reduced to that extent giving higher overall efficiency than what is estimated."

Assumptions used in design related to crop requirements and system effi-ciency are probably underestimating the need for agricultural water, even with the "extensive" approach being advocated. In the chapter on hydrology we described why it is unlikely that the Sardar Sarovar dam and reservoir will be able to deliver the 9 MAF of water for Gujarat as planned, even if the water ex-ists in that river in three out of the four years on average (75 per cent probabil-ity). The "extensive" irrigation system is based on this quantum of water and a complex but as yet untested conjunctive use strategy discussed below. As well, the non-agricultural use, and particularly the domestic water use, ap-pears to be underestimated. This leads us to conclude that the system of water supply for both agricultural and non-agricultural uses in Gujarat is based on unrealistic estimates: supply appears to be overestimated and needs underesti-mated. We see this Sardar Sarovar situation as part of a trend that the Bank describes in its 1991 *India Irrigation Sector Review*:

> India's historic irrigation development strategy of spreading water as widely as possible ("protective" or "extensive" irriga-tion) has resulted, in practice, in substantial shortfall, mainly due to design and implementation problems, except in the northwest. Stretching water supplies over larger areas to ad-dress protective or equity concerns cannot be applied indefi-nitely without eventual conflict with efficiency and production objectives. Beyond a certain point, economic viability dimin-ishes as net incremental benefits fail to cover the additional in-vestment costs in distribution networks. Eventually, gross out-put will also fall as water quantities become so overstretched that productive impact is impaired or farmers, frustrated by limited water, take more than their share or break the system. Overly optimistic design assumptions concerning availability of water and feasible irrigation efficiency have also meant that many systems do not have enough water to operate as assumed at the planning stage. (p 15)

IRRIGABILITY

Because the Sardar Sarovar command area has such diverse agro-climatic and socioeconomic features, the Government of Gujarat divided it into thirteen re-gions. In *Planning for Prosperity: Sardar Sarovar Development Plan*, we are told that these thirteen regions are defined by four factors: annual rainfall, irrigability class and drainage characteristics, ground water quantity and quality, and alignment of the canal (p 174). Irrigability class is based on the six-part classification of India's 1970 *Soil Survey Manual.*[12] Classes 1, 2, and 3 describe areas with few, moderate, and severe limitations, respectively, for sustained irrigation. Classes 4, 5, and 6 describe, respectively, lands that are marginal, temporarily not suitable, and not suitable for irrigation.

The objective in regionalization was to choose appropriate crops, to allocate and manage water, and to plan for conjunctive use of canal and ground waters. Ten of the thirteen regions are in the mainland physiographic region of Gujarat consisting of the alluvial plains of the Narmada, Mahi, Sabarmati, and other rivers. Two of the regions (8 and 9) are in peninsular Gujarat or Saurashtra. One (Region 3) is in Kutchch. Based on available data, we were told in *Planning for Prosperity* that "all regions are good for irrigation except some critical areas in Regions 4 and 7 which would require special plans for water use" (p 178).

In our review of the command area reports dating from the early 1980s through to 1992, we were struck by the lack of data on soils, aquifer conditions, ground water quality and drainage conditions, crop yields, and land use. Several good reports have been prepared by consultants working on the first reach of the main canal up to the Mahi River. A considerable effort has gone into modelling. But these models are only as good as the reliability and comprehensiveness of the data. We find that these studies raise almost as many questions as they seek to answer. This is especially troubling given the advanced state of construction of the canal.

In 1988, three years after the Bank's loan and credit agreement, C. C. Patel and Associates, in its final report to the Government of Gujarat on the rescheduling of the Sardar Sarovar Projects implementation program, noted the lapse in pursuing the necessary studies and analyses, stating:

> Bench mark data of all types should be collected immediately for recording pre-project conditions, so that the environmental, socio-economic and other impacts of the project can be assessed precisely and appropriate measures taken to exploit all positive results optimally and to counteract the negative impacts.
>
> The detailed project for the canal system beyond the Mahi has not yet been formulated. In this portion of the project, there are serious soil and water-logging problems for which urgent solutions have to be found through R&D for Bhal area, coastal saline areas, lands with drainage congestion and flood-prone areas in North Gujarat. These problems require very careful research studies and pilot experiments using data collected over several

[12] Cited in *Planning for Prosperity*, 1989, p 177.

seasons specially during the monsoons to delineate the problem precisely in each area, and evolve suitable solutions. The Saurashtra and Kutchch branches need such pilot studies, before their planning can be finalised and designs started. This work, therefore, deserves high priority.[13]

We were given assurances by the Narmada Planning Group, the Narmada Control Authority, the Nigam, and others that the studies they are doing will address these problems. We appreciate the serious intent of these assurances, but we found little basis for confidence. For example, we reviewed the prefeasibility level drainage studies for the command area beyond the Mahi River that examined pilot areas within Regions 5 to 13. These studies, produced two years after the C. C. Patel Associates report, reiterate the seriousness of the problems to be faced yet show little progress toward their solution.

In the absence of a proper environmental assessment and mindful of the paucity of data, we sought to establish the general nature and scope of irrigability problems. We did this by synthesizing available information on rainfall patterns, soil types, ground water availability and quality, drainage characteristics, and cropping patterns in various seasons, then matching these with the general irrigation proposals within the command area.

- Regions 1, 2, and 3, representing almost 24 per cent of the total area to be irrigated have relatively high rainfall and deep black soils. Canal irrigation is likely to result in serious soil degradation, particularly in Region 3, and a decline in agricultural production. Region 2 is already 35 per cent irrigated, mostly from ground water; this source offers additional potential in all three regions.

- Regions 4 and 7 are similar and constitute about 12 per cent of the area to be irrigated. Both have poorly draining, highly saline soils, and have been recognized as problem areas for irrigation. Only a small portion of the area seems irrigable. The proposal is to fill dugouts with canal water to supply farmers who would then lift this water for use. The average rainfall in either area (850 mm and 710 mm respectively) suggests that the dug out tanks could be filled without the canal in many, if not most, circumstances.

- Regions 5 and 6 have relatively high rainfall (800 mm to 880 mm) and alluvial soils. These two regions constitute over 16 per cent of the total area to be irrigated. In Region 6, about one-third of the area has a water table within 5 meters of the surface but in most of the area the ground water is classified as

[13] C. C. Patel and Associates, Engineering Consultancy Services, *Review and Rescheduling of the Implementation Programme, Sardar Sarovar (Narmada) Project, Final Report*, Vol. I, Sardar Sarovar Narmada Nigam Ltd., July 1988, pp xxii-xxiii.

bad for irrigation. The pre-feasibility study of drainage conditions indicates that a considerable quantity of water is lost as runoff, which would lead one to conclude that it could perhaps be utilized. In Region 5, more than one-third of the area is already irrigated by wells; the ground water is of good quality at depths of more than 10 meters. Waterlogging and salinity would likely be a problem in the hot months (March to May) when canal water would not be available.

• Regions 8 and 9 constitute approximately 13 per cent of the area to be irrigated. These two regions are characterized by medium black soil and rainfall in the 600 mm to 700 mm range. Region 8, in the upper part of Saurashtra, faces drought about one year in six. Region 9, bordered on the north by the little Rann of Kutchch, has only been partly surveyed and the area surveyed falls into irrigability class 2, i.e., moderate limitations for sustained use under irrigation. About 19 per cent of the area is irrigated. In both Region 8 and Region 9, provision of canal water is likely to present waterlogging and salinity problems.

• Regions 10 to 13, representing about 35 per cent of the total area to be irrigated, are characterized by low rainfall (generally 500 mm to 640 mm) and alluvial coastal or desert saline soils with low moisture retention capacity. Ground water is highly saline. Much of the region has not been surveyed although this is the area where most of the soils fall into classes 5 and 6 (unsuitable for irrigation). In all four regions the proximity of the Rann and Gulf of Kutchch presents problems for agriculture. The vulnerability to waterlogging and the liability to flooding during the monsoon will likely result in degradation and lower agricultural production. The 2 per cent represented by Region 13, a 3 to 4 kilometer narrow strip 200 kilometers long bordering the Gulf, raises especially difficult issues. The rainfall averages 400 mm and the soils are desert saline. Only about 40 per cent of the area is in irrigability classes 2 and 3.

WATERLOGGING, SALINITY, AND DRAINAGE

In his foreword to the December 1991 booklet *Anti-Water Logging and Anti-Salinity Measures in the Command Area of Sardar Sarovar Project*, D. C. Debnath, the Executive Member of the Narmada Control Authority, describes one of the most serious problems that will have to be addressed in the command area:

> Water logging is mainly due to the accumulation of excess irrigation water in the agricultural lands which affects productivity of the soil and also gives rise to salinity. These problems might aggravate in command areas of major irrigation projects under

conditions of liberal application of water and lack of a proper drainage system particularly in very flat terrain. The likelihood of such a situation was kept in view during the planning of the inter-state Sardar Sarovar Multipurpose Project and anti-water logging and anti-salinity measures are built into the planning, design, implementation and operation of this gigantic project.

Measures described by the Narmada Control Authority and Gujarat to deal with these problems begin with soil surveys and include related water allowances, concurrent installation of drainage works, conjunctive water use, the involvement of farmers' associations, and monitoring programs to minimize water wastage.

We reviewed these plans. Most deal with only the first 25 per cent of the command area (to the Mahi River). We received numerous submissions and presentations on the interrelated issues of waterlogging, salinity, and drainage. These dealt with the context of the problem in India since the nineteenth century and proposed solutions to these problems represented by the new approaches being incorporated into the Sardar Sarovar Projects.

We familiarized ourselves with the recent Tawa project, the first major irrigation development in the Narmada basin. We also learned about two projects in Gujarat adjacent to the Sardar Sarovar: the Ukai on the Tapi River which is just south of the Narmada and is currently the biggest irrigation project functioning in the state; and the Kadana on the Mahi River which is northwest of Sardar Sarovar Regions 1 to 4, and southwest of Regions 5 and 6. In all three projects, we found that damage from waterlogging was significant and had been consistently underestimated in design. In these commands some of the best lands are going out of cultivation as a result. Increases in water table levels are presenting waterlogging and salinity problems over large areas. The increased availability of surface water has reduced ground water pumping, which exacerbates waterlogging and salinity problems. Switching to crops such as sugar cane with high water requirements is adding to the rapid rise in the water table. Ground water quality is often deteriorating. We found that these experiences are reflected in the Bank's 1991 *India Irrigation Sector Review*:

> While in most parts of India, such [waterlogging and salinization] problems on irrigated lands are localized to particular commands and most frequently to localized areas in such commands, a particularly serious problem is developing in parts of *northwest India* (large parts of Punjab and Haryana and parts of Rajasthan and Gujarat) . . . the key to tackling most of the above problems is drainage. [emphasis in original] (Vol II, p 72)

In our review of the Sardar Sarovar command area we were looking for specific evidence that demonstrated how the impacts of waterlogging and salinity would be mitigated. We especially focused on provisions for drainage. We noted that these matters were specifically addressed at least as far back as 1980 in India's Ministry of Irrigation guidelines. The same matters were raised in the Bank's 1985 appraisal reports. A "detailed environmental analysis" was to be part of the comprehensive workplan required by the agreement with India. The effect of rises in ground water levels was specifically identified for study. Similarly, these matters were covered by the conditions India placed on its own 1987 environmental clearance and 1988 Planning Commission clearance. We were disappointed in what we found.

In 1988, three years after the Bank's agreement was signed, its back-to-office reports show that only "assurances" were given that the potential waterlogging and salinization were being addressed (May 1988) and the problem "needs more thorough treatment." One year later we again see that "the potential for waterlogging and salinization is being studied" (May 1989). Another year later we see that a lead drainage consultant would be engaged "to develop the master drainage networks" and to "advise on uniform criteria for this" (June 1990). By 1992, studies of soils, ground water availability, and irrigable area have been completed for the first four regions representing about 25 per cent of the command area. For the rest, a Bank memo (January, 1992) indicates that soil surveys, ground water mathematical modelling and pre-feasibility drainage studies would be completed "in about the next two years."

Detailed studies have been carried out only as far as the Mahi River, i.e., Regions 1 to 4. The *Narmada Mahi Doab Drainage Study*[14] done for the Narmada Planning Group in 1982 says that without adequate drainage more than 50 per cent of Region 2, 60 per cent of Region 3, and about 100 per cent of Region 4 would become waterlogged. Horizontal drainage is considered prohibitively expensive. Vertical drainage (by pumping) depends on water quality and quantity and the availability of natural outlets. Detailed studies have not been done even though installation of vertical drainage is planned. Vertical drainage may be feasible in Region 2 and the eastern part of Region 3, but, based on the information we have reviewed, it is unlikely to be feasible elsewhere in Region 3 and in Region 4. All that we have learned points to the need for further studies to discover whether the master plan will work in practice.

Large parts of the rest of the command will be difficult to drain. Regions 5 and 6 have a flat topography and a relatively high rainfall (800 mm). Irrigation will lead to a rapid rise in the water table and ground water quality will likely deteriorate as it has in the Mahi Right Bank canal area. In Region 7 wa-

---

[14] *Main Report: Narmada Mahi Doab Drainage Study*, Government of Gujarat, Narmada Planning Group, October 1982.

terlogging and salinity have already been identified as a problem and surface irrigation will likely make them worse than Region 4. In Regions 8 and 9, 40 per cent and 53 per cent are already classified as saline, which would restrict pumping by individual farmers on the system. A 1991 satellite data study carried out under the All India Coordinated Project on Use of Saline Water and Salt-Affected Soils shows that large parts of the Sardar Sarovar command area, and particularly areas of Regions 10, 11, and 12, are already severely affected by salinity. Region 10 has large areas subject to flooding. Region 11 is reported to be 56 per cent saline. Region 12 has a larger area to be irrigated than any other, but the Bank's Staff Appraisal Report says that it is a "difficult region" which includes saline/alkaline areas requiring drainage and reclamation. Large areas in the west have not been classified. Of those that have, the Bank notes that considerable parts have been classified in irrigability class 5 and 6 (i.e., not suitable for sustained use under irrigation).

A key element in the prevention of waterlogging and salinization for the Sardar Sarovar command area is the provision of vertical drainage. This depends on conjunctive use of canal water and ground water (discussed below). Its effectiveness is a function of the quantity and quality of the ground water—aspects which have not been studied in sufficient detail to make a reliable assessment. For example, the Bank's 1985 Staff Appraisal Report mentions that poor quality ground water will be discharged into "disposal areas" (p 31). No other information on this is provided nor is any detailed information yet available. The potential seriousness and magnitude of this problem appears to have been underestimated. If it is not dealt with, the impact could be enormous. If it is dealt with, there will be an extensive surface drainage system that itself will have significant impacts, none of which have been investigated.

CONJUNCTIVE USE

The report of the Narmada Water Disputes Tribunal deals with the proposal for conjunctive use of surface (canal) water and ground water. Citing a report of the Irrigation Commission, the Tribunal says:

> Planning for combined use of surface and ground waters calls for greater ingenuity than is needed for their separate use. It has to be admitted that so far no projects have been planned on the basis of such combined use of water. Such combined use as is now practised was not pre-planned but has come into being out of necessity.[15]

---

[15] *The Report of the Narmada Water Disputes Tribunal with Its Decision*, Vol. I, 1979, p 56.

Conjunctive use is one of the most important mitigative measures proposed to counteract waterlogging in the command area. It is particularly dependent on the quality of water, a mixing regime where necessary, and the cost to farmers. It will be difficult to plan and complicated to operate and to monitor over such a large and variable command area. Detailed information is needed—information which is not yet available. Existing data are confusing. For example, we have noted that what are supposed to be actual measurements of static water levels in monitoring wells have often been "converted," sometimes several times. Critical elements like the recharge of ground water aquifers and their use as storage in the conjunctive use plan require much more thorough study.

Difficult political decisions on pricing and priorities will need to be made and properly implemented. The Bank's January 1992 mission report notes that the Government of Gujarat's water charge study, which was to have been submitted by September 1989, is still not available. It also notes that policies on water users' associations, a key factor at the field level, are yet to be finalized. (This was listed as priority item #10 of the Narmada Planning Group study as appended to the Bank's 1985 Staff Appraisal Report.)

The Nigam has told us that the conjunctive use strategy has been fully integrated into the master plan for surface and subsurface drainage in the first four regions, and:

> Development of ground water will be left initially to farmers themselves. With the scheme of water allocations and incentives built in, it is expected that ground water development in the private sector will take place healthily. Where the ground water is saline or area is water-logged needing drainage and not useful for irrigation, vertical drainage by pumping will be attended to by the Govt.[16]

Two issues dominated this review of conjunctive use: water quality and private sector pumping. The ground water management problems related to deteriorating quality may pose unexpected limits on the conjunctive use strategy. A large part of the command area has saline waters. Ground water is to be mixed with canal water but without quality and quantity data and without details on how the mixing will be managed (particularly as the quality and quantity of pump water varies over time) no assessment can be made. As noted in the July 1991 Narmada and Water Resources Department's *Report of the High Level Committee on Augmenting Surface Water Recharge in Over Exploited Aquifers of*

---

[16] Shri P. A. Raj, *Facts, Sardar Sarovar Project (Updated)*, Gandhinagar, Gujarat: Sardar Sarovar Narmada Nigam Ltd., November 1990, p 36.

North Gujarat, pumping changes the quality of ground water, usually increasing salinity in stratified aquifer systems.

The incentive for the farmer to pump is tied to the price of and need for water. The "extensive" irrigation approach increases the incentive simply by supplying less water than the farmer needs. Even if that approach works in practice, how will mixing be monitored and adjusted to ensure that the proper quality is maintained? What about the availability and cost of power—factors which already limit irrigation pumping? Will the promised dedicated power grid be more reliable? If the Bank's 1991 report, *India Uttar Pradesh Groundwater Development Issues,* is any guide, "Power availability, in terms of both quality and quantity, remains a major operational constraint for most electricity-driven tubewell systems" (p 28).

The success of the conjunctive use strategy depends on the successful interaction of a host of variables, from ground water quality and mixing, to water and power pricing and field level farmer education and cooperation. This strategy presents technical, social, political, and financial issues that have hardly been addressed. The strategy is conceptually laudable, but it is highly speculative and, as yet, too uncertain from an operational point of view to rely on as the basis for mitigating impacts of the scale presented by waterlogging and salinity across such an enormous command area.

MUNICIPAL AND INDUSTRIAL WATER SUPPLY

The first priority in allocation of water provided by the Sardar Sarovar Projects is for domestic consumption. Areas of north Gujarat, Saurashtra, Kutchch, and Rajasthan face severe shortages, and the situation is getting worse. Large, expensive relief measures are becoming common. A number of places have unacceptably high fluoride levels in the water that is available. Problems with salinity and nitrate are also common. One of the principal justifications of the Sardar Sarovar Projects is the provision of drinking water to these urban and rural areas.

In May 1983 the Gujarat Water Supply and Sewerage Board issued a report on use of the 0.86 MAF of water to supply 131 urban centers and 4,719 villages, a total population of about 32 million people. (Calculations used for the rural per capita consumption includes requirements for cattle.) Last year this was updated to 135 urban centers and 8,125 villages serving over 40 million people both within and outside the command area. Despite the increased service, the total water allocated remains the same.[17]

---

[17] We were told that this is because Gujarat has adopted a policy of not delivering Narmada water for domestic use to areas of the state that have alternative surface and subsurface water supply sources.

The Narmada water would be available for municipal and industrial uses 11 months of the year from an irrigation system designed on a 75 per cent dependability—considerably less than the standard required for urban water supply. Storage plans are not yet available. Water rates are undecided. We are told that a comprehensive domestic (village) and municipal plan is under preparation. The cost is estimated to be "several thousands crores of rupees."[18] Gujarat's Department of Industries is reviewing the requirements of the sector and how to use the 0.20 MAF designated for industry.

The Sardar Sarovar priority for drinking water as set out in India's 1987 National Water Policy has never been in dispute. Delays in formulating specific plans are therefore difficult to understand. The cursory treatment of the issue in the Sardar Sarovar Projects documents appears to be out of keeping with the stated priority. For example, the issue was raised briefly in 1983 by the Narmada Planning Group in Volume 1 of their report *Water Use Plan and Sizing of System*.[19] The benefits are also raised briefly in the Bank's 1985 Staff Appraisal Report, and a loan/credit agreement item was included requiring Gujarat to establish and maintain municipal, domestic, and industrial water charges to cover full operation, maintenance, and capital costs (p 54). These water charges (along with irrigation charges) were also listed in an appendix to the Staff Appraisal Report as the second study priority for the Narmada Planning Group. In 1988, the report by C. C. Patel and Associates for the Government of Gujarat noted that the "highest priority" had been accorded to the domestic water supply scheme:

> . . . an important point on which action has to be taken by the GWSSB [Gujarat Water Supply and Sewerage Board] of GOG [Government of Gujarat] is with regard to the expeditious preparation of detailed water schemes to convey water from canal delivery points to the distribution areas. An integrated water supply pipeline grid needs to be designed to distribute the Narmada waters to needy areas. In urban centres, the distribution system will have, in most cases, to be remodelled. This will be a stupendous task and a start has to be made now, so as to implement the works within 8 years to enable water supply benefits to accrue as soon as the canal construction is completed.[20]

[18] Narmada Control Authority, *Drinking Water From Sardar Sarovar Project*, Narmada Control Authority, December 1991, §6.0.

[19] Government of Gujarat, *Water Use Plan and Sizing of System*, Sardar Sarovar (Narmada) Development Plan, Vol. 1, Gandhinagar, India: Narmada Planning Group, 1983, Chapter 8.

[20] C. C. Patel and Associates, *Review and Rescheduling of the Implementation Programme*, Sardar Sarovar (Narmada) Project, Vol. I, 1988, p xxviii.

The Bank's June 1989 mission report required that the Nigam:

> ... by June 30, 1989, furnish for the use of the design consultants and simultaneous review by the Bank, GOG's Urban, Municipal and Industrial Water Supply Plan for utilization of SSP [Sardar Sarovar Projects] waters, including the location of towns and cities to be served and their respective take-out locations, as well as estimated quantitative demands and delivery services to be provided. (pp 3-4)

The documents made available to us are insufficient for assessment. General criteria and guidelines have been established. Drinking water quality issues have not been addressed, nor have waste water disposal issues, nor have the energy requirements. More specific plans are to be available in a year. The number of people to be served is growing, as is the number of urban centers and villages. Some discrepancies are apparent. For example, in answer to our inquiry in March 1992, the Chairman of the Nigam acknowledged that the number of villages to be served in Saurashtra and Kutchch "are statistical figures which include 236 uninhabited villages."

CONCLUDING OBSERVATIONS

In January 1992 the Bank's consultant for Phase II of the Sardar Sarovar canal submitted a report outlining the environmental information and study requirements to develop the next 75 per cent of the command area.[21] It gives a good overview of what it is reasonable to expect but which has been largely unavailable to date. The consultant's report describes the continuing need for information on and assessment of soils and surface waters, surface and subsurface drainage, waterlogging, conjunctive use, salinity, ground water and water quality, and related factors. It outlines the need for assessment of agricultural chemical use, the impact of pests, and command area health issues. It deals with the necessity of assessing domestic and industrial water supply needs. Although almost all of these issues flow from the Bank's 1991 environmental impact assessment requirements and guidelines, what is remarkable is the overlap with India's 1980 Ministry of Irrigation *Guidelines for Preparation of Detailed Project Report of Irrigation and Multipurpose Projects*. Assurances were provided in the Bank's 1985 Staff Appraisal Report and commitments were made in the

---

[21] T. P. Whitington, *Narmada River Development, Sardar Sarovar Water Delivery and Drainage System, Second Canals Project, Review of Status of Environmental Preparation*, Bangkok: Seatec International Ltd., January 29, 1992.

1985 credit and loan agreements with India that covered many of the same issues. We can find no adequate explanation why a full and proper environmental impact assessment of the command area has eluded the Bank and India for more than a decade.[22]

Although basic information upon which to make an assessment of the command area is unavailable, there is good reason to be concerned about the likely environmental impacts. They are likely to be severe. Many are related to issues that are basic to the design and operation of the Sardar Sarovar Projects. These are summarized in the Bank's 1991 *India Irrigation Sector Review* under the heading "Sustainability":

> Sustainability also has environmental, financial and institutional dimensions. Environmental deterioration is occurring on a number of commands due to lack of drainage to counteract waterlogging and salinization; other adverse environmental impacts are also occurring. . . . Institutional adaptation is also required to provide functionally specialized divisions focused on design, construction and maintenance, and capabilities in environmental assessment. Additionally, farmers and local communities need to be incorporated into decision-making and management so that their influence is contributory rather than passive (lack of participation in operations and maintenance) or disruptive (illicit taking of water and breakages of structures). (Vol. i, p 40)

Then under the heading "Design," the Bank continued:

> Most design problems stem from inadequate data and unrealistic assumptions about water availability and irrigation efficiency. More complete basic data on hydrology, rainfall, soil characteristics and cropping patterns are needed. . . .
> The above practices substantially explain why many surface irrigation schemes cannot perform as hoped for. Design deficiencies are also partly behind the "gap" noted in some government commentaries between assumed created irrigation poten-

---

[22] An environmental assessment is to be completed before appraisal of the Canal II project. However, much of the design is fixed, dictated by the construction of the first stage to the Mahi River. Construction of the second stage has already begun—we visited the site of the work on the Saurashtra Branch canal. This begs the question of how the findings of an environmental assessment will be incorporated into project planning and design. It suggests that ameliorative measures, once again, will be limited to reactive, after-the-fact mitigation.

tial and actual irrigated area. Many schemes cannot deliver water in the amount as planned, and for these situations the command area targeted for coverage should be reduced to cater to these realities. (Vol. i, p 40)

Under the subheading "Environmental Issues and Trends," the Bank's *Irrigation Sector Review* adds:

> The environmental and resettlement impacts of irrigation are widely debated, but due to political perspectives, and lack of data, discussion has often polarized. A balanced yet more operationally responsive approach to environmental and resettlement needs is required. (Vol. i, p 44)

Some good work has been done on specific topics in the first part of the command area of the Sardar Sarovar Projects. It does not, however, come together to meet the requirements of a good environmental assessment. Without data and without an assessment, mitigative measures, however well intentioned, cannot be relied on to work effectively and efficiently. Our review of the command area has raised more questions than it has answered. But, in the end, what we have learned points to the likelihood that far from being a "break with past approaches to the planning, design, construction and operation of irrigation projects in India,"[23] the Sardar Sarovar Projects are likely to perpetuate many of the features that the Bank has documented as diminishing the performance of the agricultural sector in India in the past.

---

[23] Staff Appraisal Report, Supplementary Data Volume, Part I, p 24.

Migrant workers in front of their living quarters at Sardar Sarovar dam site. Ten thousand workers are employed on construction of the dam. Twelve thousand more are working on the canal.

THE public health risks associated with large-scale hydroelectric and irrigation developments are well known. By the time of the World Bank's appraisal of Sardar Sarovar Projects, the dangers of water-borne diseases were well documented, and epidemic levels of malaria, schistosomiasis, and other water-related diseases had been experienced in a number of Bank-assisted projects. The issue was raised in India as early as 1938; a discussion of "engineer-made malaria" observed:

> improper siting and housing; indiscriminate aggregation of labourers; uncontrolled jungle clearing; excavation such as borrow pits, brickfields and quarry pits; obstruction of natural drainage by road, railway and canal embankments, with culverts too few and too high; impounding of water without regard to leakages, seepages and raised water-table levels; irrigation without drainage.[1]

Under these conditions, the vectors for malaria proliferate, while at the same time new species are added to the region. N. L. Kalra, in his 1992 report to the World Bank, characterized this combination of circumstances as an encounter between the "ignition wire" of construction-related stagnant water and the "gunpowder" of immigrant labor. This creates "an explosion of malaria."[2]

The institutional framework for addressing these health risks was well es-

---

[1] P. F. Russell, "Malaria Due to Defective and Untidy Irrigation. A Preliminary Discussion," *Journal of the Malaria Institute of India*, Vol. 1, December 4, 1938.
[2] N. L. Kalra, "Status Report on Malaria and Other Health-Related Aspects of the [SSP] Projects, and Recommendations Regarding Short-Term and Long-Term Remedial Measures," January 1992, p 8.

tablished in India before the credit and loan agreements for Sardar Sarovar were signed in 1985. India's 1980 Ministry of Irrigation *Guidelines* include public health aspects of projects. These are similar to the "Health Effects" section of the Ministry of Environment and Forests' guidelines, first published in 1978 and updated in 1985 and 1989. The same issues are covered under the "Health" heading of the 1986 guidelines produced by the Central Board of Irrigation and Power.

The first substantial consideration of public health hazards related to Sardar Sarovar was a 1983 study on the project ecology by the M. S. University of Baroda. It dealt with the range of problems arising from the vector-harboring characteristic of aquatic weeds that proliferate in irrigation systems, through to contamination of water by human waste. The health benefits of a reliable water supply were also reported.[3]

The Bank's 1985 Staff Appraisal Report identified malaria, schistosomiasis, and filaria as the three principal diseases that could jeopardize public health as a result of construction of the Sardar Sarovar Projects. Malaria was described as "of a generally low level" over the region, schistosomiasis as "thought to have potential," and filaria as "reported close to the dam site" (p 29). The report said that "a specific action plan" would be required.

In the 1985 project agreements, the Bank required that each state:

> within its State boundaries, take all such measures as shall be considered necessary to minimize the risk of malaria, filaria, schistosomiasis, and other water-related diseases that may result from the implementation of the Project.

In 1985, two studies on schistosomiasis were carried out by India's National Institute on Communicable Diseases. This was followed by an investigation by a team that included the World Bank and which was led by the chief of the schistosomiasis division of the World Health Organization. The conclusion reached by all three studies was that the disease posed no threat in the area of the Projects.

In February 1986 the Narmada Planning Group in Gujarat prepared its *Work Plan for Environmental Effects*. Public health was covered under two headings: the surveillance and control of water-related and communicable diseases, and the surveillance and control of malaria. It did not include schemes for

---

[3] For a more recent discussion of this see Steven A. Esrey and Jean-Pierre Habicht, "Epidemiologic evidence for health benefits from improved water and sanitation in developing countries," *Epidemiologic Review*, Vol. 8, 1986, p 117-28. See also the Bank's Staff Appraisal Report, Supplementary Data Volume, Part I, p 54.

monitoring health in the area of the Projects but stated that "it is already in-cluded in the Seventh Plan of the State Government" (p 4). It then noted that the health statistics are only provided on a statewide basis, not by region, which does not help in proper planning, effective monitoring, or management. An alternative strategy that would help was not provided.

In 1987 India's environmental clearance required, as one of eight studies, "complete details" on health aspects of the Sardar Sarovar Projects. These were to be available by 1989 for assessment by the Department of Environ-ment. The 1988 clearance by India's Planning Commission reaffirmed the conditions attached to the environmental clearance.

A consultant's report prepared for the Bank in 1988 reviewed the public health aspects of Sardar Sarovar.[4] It mentioned that the Narmada Planning Group had made no progress on the actions proposed in its 1986 *Work Plan*, and that the August 1988 Bank mission was unable to get information on these plans. For the three diseases that carry greatest risk—malaria, schistosomiasis, and filaria—the 1988 report explained that they "are being studied because they have the potential to increase as a result of the project" (p 162). It warned that malaria presents a serious threat as a result of a possible proliferation of the anopheline mosquito "in the reservoir, the large draw down strip, and the canals and drains" (p 162). It stated that "preventive measures must be uti-lized to keep the mosquitoes in check" (p 162). The report noted that both schistosomiasis and filaria are not present in any numbers in regions near the reservoir. However, it cautioned that these dangers are not to be underesti-mated, and, citing a 1985 Aide-Memoire of the Bank,[5] stated that the potential for schistosomiasis to develop in the project areas "must be viewed very seri-ously" (p 165). It went on to say that if schistosomiasis were to get a foothold "all of the Gujarat and Madhya Pradesh populations would either have to avoid exposure to the reservoirs and irrigation water for all time, which is practically impossible to accomplish, or most of the people in the areas would be subject to schistosomiasis from childhood onward" (p 166). The 1988 re-port urged that public health plans be prepared to deal with all the disease risks "both during implementation and later during operations" (p 168).

It is to be recalled that in 1988, when these recommendations were being reiterated (they were first made in 1985 and 1987), construction of Sardar Sarovar was already well under way. Infrastructural development at Kevadia was extensive (indeed, had been in progress since 1961), major works had

---

[4] D. W. Levenhagen, "Overview of Environmental Impact, Sardar Sarovar and Narmada Sagar Projects, Narmada River Basin, India," April 1988.

[5] R. Goodland, "M. P. Narmada Hydro and Irrigation Project, Environmental Effects," January 1985.

been started on the rock-filled dykes, and work on the main canal was pro-
gressing. Villages were being affected by creation of pools of stagnant water.
Thousands of workers from all over India were being assembled at the dam
site. Yet measures to deal with the health risks appear to have barely reached
beyond the level of recommendations that studies be done and mitigative measures designed.

The December 1991 status report issued by the Ministry of Environment
and Forests stated that all three states had submitted their initial plans on
health but both Maharashtra and Madhya Pradesh had been asked to revise
their plans. Madhya Pradesh had submitted its revised plan; Maharashtra's
final plan was awaited. The agenda notes for the February 1992 meeting of the
Narmada Control Authority's Environment Sub-Group recorded that:

> the action plan submitted by the State Governments should in-
> clude the present health status of the people living in the sub-
> mergence area. Besides, the plan should not include only what-
> ever normal health infrastructure the State Government was
> anyway to provide but also extra amount for special provisions
> arising from implementation of the project like extra equipment,
> more funds for baseline data build up etc. GOMP [Government of
> Madhya Pradesh], GOG [Government of Gujarat] and GOM
> [Government of Maharashtra] are to report the steps taken to
> include the above in their action plans. (p 8)

The agenda notes went on to report that baseline data on health had twice
been requested but were still awaited from the Government of Gujarat, that
Maharashtra's draft health plan had been forwarded to the Ministry of Environment and Forests, and that its final plan was still awaited.

In February 1992, the Bank forwarded to the Nigam a copy of the field report of the January mission which reviewed the engineering, malaria control,
and financial aspects of the Sardar Sarovar Projects. Attached to the field report was a report on malaria and other health-related aspects of Sardar
Sarovar Projects. The findings of this report by N. L. Kalra were presented in
the executive summary:
- the Projects have been planned, designed, and executed without incorporation of health safeguards;
- the vector control measures have "become blunt because of injudicious use"
  and the killer variety of malaria has shown resistance to chloroquine;
- the project area and villages in its vicinity have a high level of malaria with
  the killer type (*P. falciparum*) exceeding 30 per cent; and
- deaths from malaria have been reported since 1990.

The report states that with the onset of peak construction, the rate of fever increased two and a half times, malaria increased by six times, and incidence of *P. falciparum* also increased by two and a half fold. The occurrence of the disease at the Sardar Sarovar dam and the adjacent villages was nearly double that of the other villages served by the health center in that area. Two deaths due to malaria were recorded in 1990, three in 1991. Kalra said that "there was a total collapse of the vector control measures" (p 7). The indoor vector density was over ten times the level considered to be risky.

The Kalra report addressed the engineering aspects of the Sardar Sarovar Projects and considered the malaria-inducing features. Kalra acknowledged the benefits of controlled releases for irrigation and the benefits of lining the canals, but he highlights some disturbing findings.

- Construction of the rock-filled dykes was carried out in violation of established principles of malarial control. As a result, the dykes have "created tremendous potential" (p 8) for increase in malarial mosquito populations. Kalra notes: "These ponds could be designated as death traps for malaria. . . ." There is also a likelihood that they will lead to a high incidence of Japanese encephalitis in the coming 15 to 20 years. (p 8).
- Construction of the canal has been carried out without regard to increase of malarial risks. Drainage works have been done in such a way as to create stagnant ponds. Borrowing of earth from village tanks has "amounted to taking malaria to the doorsteps of villagers" (p 8).
- The water storage and delivery systems for domestic users at Kevadia Colony have been built in such a way as to "offer ideal breeding sites" for malarial mosquitos in household premises (p 8).

The Kalra report also identifies some of the malarial risks that will arise with future construction at Sardar Sarovar. The periphery of the reservoir will increase humidity to distances of three to five kilometers, which in turn increases the lifespan of mosquitos and facilitates a longer transmission period for malaria (p 7). Also, construction of the Garudeshwar Weir, downstream of the Sardar Sarovar dam site itself, will create sluggish water and swamps "ideal for mosquito breeding" (p 8).

In the Bank's January 1992 mission report (dated February 21, 1992), to which Kalra's findings were appended, the checklist rating of project execution lists "Health/Malaria Control" as "major problems but being adequately addressed." In the Status of Covenants section, the Bank listed as "not yet due" the condition in the agreements requiring the three states to take measures to minimize the risk of water-related diseases. It then noted that "no measures have been planned so far. Nigam/GOG need to examine and prepare a comprehensive scheme to tackle malaria and other water-borne diseases as a priority."

In the Sardar Sarovar Projects there is no indication that India's Ministry of Health has had any input regarding health aspects of the Projects. Indeed, apart from the 1985 studies on schistosomiasis carried out by the National Institute on Communicable Diseases, there appears to have been no involvement of the national or state apparatus that is responsible for managing health care.

Against this background of Bank requirements, consultants' warnings, and now Kalra's findings, the fact that construction at Sardar Sarovar has not included comprehensive preventive measures for malaria and other water-related diseases is alarming.

The absence of preventive measures in Sardar Sarovar Projects becomes even less acceptable if we look at a century of well-known historical examples where large development projects in tropical countries have time and again been directly instrumental in spreading disease. One of the best-documented cases is Egypt's Aswan Dam, completed in 1969, where there was a forty-fold increase in the incidence of schistosomiasis. In India, malaria is now endemic in Punjab, Haryana, and the Raichmur district of Karnataka as a result of river basin development projects. Due to the Upper Krishna Irrigation Project the incidence of malaria in Karnataka soared by a factor of over 250. Serious malaria problems have also afflicted recent irrigation projects in Bihar and Sri Lanka.[6] In 1975, *Man-Made Lakes and Human Health*[7] offered several examples of international case histories to argue the need for early planning of health care in water resource development projects. The World Health Organization's 1974 manual entitled "Manual on Personal and Community Protection Against Malaria"[8] warned of the need for early planning.

> At the earliest stage of a major development project, the Ministry of Health should be involved in the planning in order that health hazards of such a project can be properly assessed. . . . At any rate, when the plan of operations is being drafted, the plan for health protection, particularly the part dealing with protection against malaria, should constitute a special chapter in the overall project.

We cannot explain the discrepancy in the public health aspects of the Sardar Sarovar Projects between what is known and required by both the Bank and India on the one hand, and what is not being done on the other. There has

---

[6] Ruwani Jayewardene, *The Impact of Malaria on New Settlements in the Mahaweli Development Project, Sri Lanka*, Ph.D. Dissertation, University of Connecticut, USA.
[7] N. F. Stanley and M. P. Alpers, eds., *Man-Made Lakes and Human Health*, Academic Press, 1975.
[8] Offset Publication No. 10, 1974.

been a sharp increase in malaria-induced fever and related illness. The situation is at its worst near the Projects. People have died. Yet the Bank's status reports simply say that the preventive measures required by the formal agreement seven years ago are "not yet due." This is entirely at odds with the Bank's own policy requirements.

The Bank and the state governments have failed to address the issue of public health adequately. Early planning is critical. Poor engineering design may be difficult or impossible to correct after construction has begun. Once vectors of disease transmission have been introduced to an area, it is costly to eradicate them, and may prove impossible. The diseases in question can quickly reach epidemic proportions, spreading throughout a region and infecting all sectors of the population. It is already too late in the case of Sardar Sarovar to prevent some of these consequences. Construction is under way; the malarial mosquito vectors are already present. Action is required now to put in place an effective health care program that takes into account the impact on the surrounding local populations, the spread of disease, and the long-term costs of ill health on the region as a whole. Omitting the prevention of disease from the assessment and implementation of projects is a perilous oversight.

Tribal women in Madhya Pradesh head-loading firewood for sale in local markets and towns. To reach markets many women carry wood for 25 kilometers.

Chapter 16

A BASIN-WIDE APPROACH

THE Bank and India both agree that the river basin is the basic unit for resource planning. For example, a river basin is the study area recognized in the Bank's 1986 environmental policy and was highlighted in its 1991 *India Irrigation Sector Review*: "Consideration should be increasingly given to a whole basin or sub basin approach to agricultural development" (Vol. II, p 23). In India, the Ministry of Irrigation's 1980 *Guidelines for Preparation of Detailed Project Report of Irrigation and Multipurpose Projects* lists river basin plans at the top of its checklist of issues to be addressed (p 23). And India's 1987 National Water Policy states:

> Resource planning in the case of water has to be done for a hydrological unit such as a drainage basin as a whole, or a sub basin. All individual development projects and proposals should be formulated by the States, and considered within the framework of such an overall plan for a basin or sub basin, so that the best possible combination of options can be made.[1]

As we noted in Chapter 11, this basin-wide approach was taken from 1969 to 1979 by the Narmada Water Disputes Tribunal in its investigation of projects in the Narmada valley. It was the approach taken by India in 1987 when it gave conditional environmental clearance to the Sardar Sarovar Projects and Narmada Sagar Projects together.

A river is the lifeblood running through an ecosystem. It cannot easily be

---

[1] Ministry of Water Resources, *National Water Policy*, September 1987.

sliced into administrative packages. Before properly dealing with individual parts, the natural relationships between the elements, a sense of the system as a whole, must be established. In 1985, when the Bank approved the Sardar Sarovar Projects, it did so without first examining the environmental and social implications for the Narmada River valley. And this is the approach the Bank appears to suggest again for the Narmada Sagar Projects. As recently as March 14, 1990, a Bank Office Memorandum dealing with these projects proposed ways "to package them into several projects and/or time slices." This is being considered despite the hard lessons of Sardar Sarovar. It is not something that can be addressed by the Bank's proposed "free-standing Basin Development Project." Indeed, as we discuss below, this proposed project suggests that very little has been learned from the experience of Sardar Sarovar over the last decade.

LEARNING FROM EXPERIENCE

In a submission for the record to a Committee of the United States Congress in 1987, a professor at the Yale School of Forestry and a consultant to the United States Agency for International Development commented on the environmental aspects of the Bank's 1985 Staff Appraisal Report for Sardar Sarovar.[2]

> It is my opinion that the impact assessment ought to better reflect the massive, long-term nature of this project (really over 30 dams and reservoirs and 400 minor structures such as canals to be constructed over 20 years). Two activities seem to be required:
> • An analysis of the cumulative effects of complete build-out. The Sardar Sarovar must be assessed contextually as it will interact with all other structures, impacts, translocations, etc.
> • A river basin-wide systems analysis should precede impact evaluation.

In Chapter 10 we described the difficulty the Bank faced in getting the "comprehensive environmental framework (stipulated as a 'workplan' in the

---

[2] The submission by Steve Berwick was appended to the testimony of Bruce Rich, appearing on behalf of the Environmental Defense Fund, National Wildlife Federation, Natural Resource Defense Council, and Environmental Policy Institute, before the House Subcommittee on International Development Institutions and Finance of the Committee on Banking, Finance, and Urban Affairs, April 8, 1987.

Project Agreement)" prepared and institutionalized. A memorandum of understanding between the Bank and India was used in December 1988 to reiterate "the urgency of formulating and implementing an environmental impact program" which included the framework. Earlier that year, the Bank had been instrumental in trying to get support for this program. The Bank's environmental review mission had made recommendations calling "for the immediate establishment of a comprehensive environmental management framework within both projects."[3] The Bank drafted terms of reference for the preparation of this framework. And it sought additional assistance:

> For the longer term a basin-wide environmental master plan needs to be established. Both the Sardar Sarovar and Narmada Sagar Projects are likely to generate numerous development activities throughout the Narmada River Basin. CIDA [Canadian International Development Agency] and USAID [United States Agency for International Development] have expressed interest in co-financing a basin-wide planning exercise and the Bank should urge the GOI [Government of India] to adopt it to help impose rational development on areas subject to ever-increasing population pressures and mounting conflicts. (Memorandum, November 23, 1988)

The Bank had taken the initiative to involve both the Canadian International Development Agency and the United States Agency for International Development. However, the Bank's mission report noted:

> A CIDA mission in Delhi at the time of the mission warned of potential difficulties over a Canadian Federal law requiring an EIA [Environment Impact Assessment] for large-scale projects funded by the Canadian Government—to date, no EIA has been conducted for either project. (October 1988, p 9)

In May 1989, the Bank's mission report stated:

> CIDA informed the mission that it is no longer interested in financing a basin-wide environmental master plan. The project was considered "too contentious and too risky.[4]

---

[3] Office Memorandum, October 12, 1988, p 1.
[4] Supervisory Mission (Environmental Aspects), April 22 to May 3, 1989, p 1.

In July 1988, the United States Agency for International Development had written a memo to the Bank asking about river basin planning:

> The Narmada river basin is one of the last major undeveloped rivers in India. A total of 30 major dams have been planned for the river basin. If each project is appraised as a separate project, how does the Bank intend to assess the environmental impact of the system as a whole?

> Could alternative sites or dam heights result in fewer adverse environmental impacts and have such alternatives been considered? (Memorandum, June 7, 1988)

The Bank files show that India's Ministry of Environment and Forests was also concerned "about the confusion and absence of an integrated approach in resolving potential environmental problems."[5] The Ministry set up an Environment Cell to monitor both the Narmada Sagar and Sardar Sarovar Projects. The Bank's mission report said:

> It was essential to encourage the integrated development of the Narmada Valley Basin as a whole and not just monitor the implementation of the two projects. This concept was endorsed by the Chief Ministers and the State Administrators when the project was discussed and decided by the Prime Minister in April 1987. (p 9)

In its recommendations, the same mission report said:

> For the longer-term a basin-wide environmental master plan needs to be established. The Narmada Sagar and Sardar Sarovar projects are to be accompanied by numerous development activities throughout the Narmada River Basin. Thus, to avoid conflicts over water and other natural resources, environmental data will need to be more fully integrated into the planning and management process and used in conjunction with economic and other criteria in ensuring sound development. As far as possible, future development decisions must be based on land capability and an awareness of the potential adverse envi-

---

[5] Environmental review mission of August 16 to September 7, 1988, p 1.

ronmental and socio-cultural costs and not simply on minimizing development costs.

Broadly speaking, the above approach suggests a number of
critical functions or "outputs" of the development process
which have been traditionally insensitive to environmental concerns and yet hold the greatest promise for successful integration: data collection, collation and analysis; development and
evaluation of plan alternatives; formulation of a preferred strategy and plans of action; and management and monitoring of the
integrated environmental master plan.

If proper integration is achieved, the resulting development
decisions should be more sensitive to the biophysical and socioeconomic dimensions of the areas to be developed and the
neighboring areas. (p 12)

All of the above material indicates that for at least the last four years the
Bank has understood the need, and has been an advocate for a basin-wide approach to the environmental issues of the Narmada. But it is an approach that
is not reflected in the Basin Development Project as it is now being proposed.

PROPOSED BASIN DEVELOPMENT PROJECT

In November 1991, the Bank provided our review with an Aide-Memoire and
a Final Executive Project Summary of a proposed Narmada Basin Development Project. Copies of the draft Staff Appraisal Report and Project Implementation Volume delivered to us in April 1992.[6] This project is relevant to
our Terms of Reference because it seeks to address, at least in part, resettlement and rehabilitation and environmental issues related to the Sardar Sarovar Projects. The draft Staff Appraisal Report says, "The *linkages* between the
project and the Sardar Sarovar Dam Project are substantial" (emphasis in
original, p 3).

This proposed project, entailing a Bank credit of $90 million, has six parts
with budget allocations as follows: catchment area treatment (24%), afforestation (25%), fisheries development in the Sardar Sarovar reservoir (6%), village development (36%), wildlife sanctuaries (5%), and basin-wide environmental management studies (4%). A seventh part, training, is to be included
in the sub-components. The draft Staff Appraisal Report says:

[6] Staff Appraisal Report, *India, Narmada Basin Development Project*, March 23, 1992. Project
Implementation Volume, *India, Narmada Basin Development Project*, March 23, 1992.

This project breaks new ground both as the first basin-focused project undertaken by the Bank and as the first project with a broad focus on environmental sustainability issues covering a number of sub-sectors within the on-going irrigation, power and municipal and industrial water development through the Sardar Sarovar Dam and Power Project... and the Water Delivery and Drainage Project..., it will constitute a comprehensive program to tackle the growth and sustainability needs of the basin. (p 3)

The Report adds that a main objective of the project is:

...to introduce a more participatory development approach, particularly with respect to watershed and forestry development, resettlement and environment and human settlement conflict resolution. (p 4)

However, there are fundamental problems with this proposed project. Most of these have the same roots as those that have already arisen on the Sardar Sarovar Projects. And as with Sardar Sarovar, almost all are well documented in the Bank's files but are not reflected in the Staff Appraisal Report. Some examples illustrate our concerns.

First among these is the origin of the project. From the Bank's files and interviews in Washington and India, we have learned that the Basin Development Project began, in 1989, as a stand-alone resettlement and rehabilitation project. The intention within the Bank was to establish a resettlement-oriented loan in order to ensure a more independent and effective resettlement and rehabilitation process, a measure that has been repeatedly urged by officers within the Bank since 1988. This idea was then expanded to include environmental and basin-wide issues. When the expanded plan was taken to India, however, it met with resistance, notably from the Government of Madhya Pradesh. Objections were raised to its resettlement component.[7] In due course, these objections led the Bank to redefine the project, and the resettlement component was dropped. No resettlement specialist was included in the pre-appraisal or appraisal missions of the project—despite the fact that it was already known to be located in a socially sensitive area and to raise questions about the

---

[7] An official of the Bank's India Country Department reported agreement with Madhya Pradesh, on July 13, 1990, that the resettlement component be dropped. At this point the social scientist who had been working on the resettlement aspects of the plan was instructed to work on fisheries.

possible relocation of a large number of tribal villagers. It was said that the Shoolpaneshwar Wildlife Sanctuary component alone "may require the resettlement of scores of villages, which . . . is disingenuously described as 'voluntary resettlement.'"[8] The project became primarily an environmental plan with strong focus on afforestation and catchment area treatment. The resettlement and rehabilitation component became "village development," with most of the funds provided for infrastructure in areas affected by Sardar Sarovar.

The project is not "basin development" within the common meaning of that phrase. It covers an area that is a small fraction of the Narmada River Basin. It is difficult for us to understand how it can be labelled as "the first project with a broad focus on environmentally sustainable issues," when it avoids addressing the most difficult environmental issue pending in the basin—the Narmada Sagar Projects. When the Basin Project was being developed in early 1990, the Sardar Sarovar environmental mission (January 4, 1990) was reporting on "the urgent need for a comprehensive environmental framework (stipulated as a 'workplan' in the Project Agreement)," overdue since the end of 1985. The continued absence of the framework was described as posing "major problems . . . in coordinating and monitoring the implementation of environmental studies and integrating the work of the concerned states." This has not been resolved. It will not be resolved by the proposed Basin Project. And the January 1990 mission noted that:

> . . . the Bank would need to undertake a regional environmental assessment for Narmada Sagar and that the formulation of the framework is critical to the success of this activity.

The major beneficiary state under the proposed Basin Development Project is Madhya Pradesh, and throughout the Bank's files it is clear that the state sees the project as a bridge to the "reopening with the international community the issue of financing of the Narmada Sagar project" (February 23, 1990). The Chief Minister of Madhya Pradesh "indicated that while the Basin project would be helpful, he personally was more interested in Narmada Sagar" (May 1990). The same Back-to-Office Report says that key officials in Gujarat "were less interested in the Basin project than in accelerating work on the SSP [Sardar Sarovar Projects]." In March 1991 it was noted that earlier missions had not elicited any definite proposals from Maharashtra, and "The Bank did not push Maharashtra participation strongly since it seemed likely that [project] components would be small."[9] At the time of the August to October 1991

---

[8] See Office Memorandum, November 18, 1991.
[9] Aide-Memoire, Appraisal Mission, February-March 1991.

mission and a January 1992 mission, Bank memoranda show that Madhya Pradesh did not want the resettlement and rehabilitation part of the project "unless it covers NSP [Narmada Sagar Projects]."

These rather obvious "linkages" to the Narmada Sagar Projects were also described to us in November 1991 by Bank staff, particularly as they related to building the institutional capacity in India (the Narmada Control Authority) to "open up" Narmada Sagar. This bridging function of the proposed project between Sardar Sarovar and Narmada Sagar is not described in the Staff Appraisal Report despite its being a main consequence of the Basin Project and an openly acknowledged objective of key officials in India. The social and environmental impacts of Narmada Sagar have not been assessed, but they are widely acknowledged to be significant; probably much greater than those of Sardar Sarovar.

The proposed Basin Development Project is founded, to a large extent, on the principle of "participatory development." For example, both the catchment area treatment and the afforestation parts of the project (representing 49 per cent of the expenditure) and some parts of the village development component (36 per cent of the expenditure) depend on successful local participation. The plan has been put forward without any consultation with the villagers who are to contribute, and there is no precedent for village participation in Madhya Pradesh. No demonstration projects have been required to verify the feasibility of the approach. And the hostile attitudes within the administrative system and the villages, generated by their experience of Sardar Sarovar, have been overlooked. The situation has reached such an impasse that neither Bank nor government officials have been able to visit many of the villages of the area for well over a year.

The proposed project seeks to "break new ground" and may do so, in part, because of 18 agreements and assurances related to the environmental and resettlement and rehabilitation components. But the last seven years of flawed and deficient compliance with similar kinds of agreements and assurances for the Sardar Sarovar Projects are not discussed. Is there not some need now of proof of performance? Many of the agencies to be involved are those working with Sardar Sarovar, agencies that the Bank itself has noted have been incapable of coordinating environmental work.

Some of the individual components of the proposed project appear to respond in part to the concerns we have raised in our review. This applies to the catchment area treatment, afforestation, fisheries (particularly in the estuary), and environmental studies including water quality, basin resource inventory, environmental overview, and hydrological modelling. These are important. But basic considerations related to development context, proven processes, workable time frames, and realistic budgets remain vague. We are not questioning the need for the Bank to provide its full support to resolve outstanding human and environmental issues in the Basin. Some of the specific activities proposed are what should have been done a decade ago, and indeed in many cases was required by either the Bank's 1985 Agreement or India's 1987 environmental clearances. The proposed project is simply too open-ended, and too uncertain in its outcome to provide assurance that it will succeed in the areas we have identified as needing serious attention.

The proposed Basin Development Project has not been subjected to a formal environmental impact assessment. How is this justified? Correspondence with the Bank in April 1992 and the draft Staff Appraisal documents indicate that, "The project was considered from the outset an environmental project," which is true only if it is understood that resettlement and rehabilitation are environmental. We are told that "each component was subject to careful scrutiny during preparation," but we have not found documents that provide confidence that the emerging basin development issues have been considered.

This proposed project is the Bank's "first basin-focused project" in India. It is addressing "environmental sustainability issues covering a number of sub-sectors within agriculture." But what is the context? Does it address the most important environmental issues in the basin? How will they interact? How are cumulative effects to be addressed? Would similar investments in other areas yield a greater ecological return? Is the investment in any one area enough (or too much) to achieve the desired goal? What are the ecological risks (only administrative and, to a lesser degree, financial risks are raised in the Staff Appraisal Report)? What are the secondary effects? What are the human, including resettlement, implications of the project? What consultation has taken place with the people who could be affected?

Our point is this. A $90 million investment, simply labelled as environmental, does not mean that it is inherently beneficial or appropriate. Nor does it mean that it will deal with real issues effectively and efficiently. Individual environmentally-oriented projects do not substitute for an environmental impact assessment. Much closer scrutiny is necessary. An example from our review of the Sardar Sarovar Projects and included in the proposed Basin Development Project, the Shoolpaneshwar Wildlife Sanctuary, illustrates the point.

SHOOLPANESHWAR WILDLIFE SANCTUARY

The loss of flora and fauna to submergence by the Sardar Sarovar reservoir has stimulated a search for ways in which to replenish the populations in neighboring areas. One solution that is favored by the Indian states and the Bank is to expand existing wildlife sanctuaries and reserves, of which Shoolpaneshwar is one. This proposition poses fundamental questions in which the environmental and human issues are inextricably entwined.

The Bank's January 1990 supervisory mission report demonstrates the project context for protected area initiatives:

> The Secretary, Environment and Rehabilitation, Nigam, agreed that opportunities should be taken to expand existing sanctuaries and reserves in the command area and Kachchh to compensate for habitat loss (including biodiversity loss) by inundation. This would help offset the limited compensation likely to be derived from forestry plantations e.g. none of the 20 proposed tree species are found in the inundated area. It was also agreed that, where possible, the plantation should be contiguous with the existing sanctuaries and reserves to create a habitat mosaic and accrue further benefits to wildlife. These initiatives are consonant with the Bank's Wildlands policies, particularly regarding the compensation for loss of biological resources.

The core area of what is now called the Shoolpaneshwar Wildlife Sanctuary was created in 1972 under Gujarat's Wildlife Protection Act as the 1,500 hectare Dumkhal Sloth Bear Sanctuary. It straddles an area adjacent to the Sardar Sarovar dam on the south side of the Narmada River. In 1983, as a result of their environmental studies, the M. S. University of Baroda recommended that this Sanctuary be extended to the edge of the proposed Sardar Sarovar reservoir. In 1987 the size of the sanctuary was increased to 44,804 hectares and the name was changed to Shoolpaneshwar. In 1989 it was proposed to extend it to cover a total of 60,765 hectares. The notification declaring this extension has been issued. The biological value of these expansions, the priority with respect to other conservation areas in Gujarat, and the implications for people living within the affected area have become the subject of considerable controversy.

Creation or expansion of a sanctuary has, as its primary objective, the protection of natural habitat. The economic lives of villagers are widely seen, by forestry officials and others, as inimical to this habitat. According to this view, people and nature are pitted against one another. Biodiversity can be achieved and maintained only if human activities are restricted. If this view prevails, then enlargement of the Shoolpaneshwar Wildlife Sanctuary means that the people's rights to use the resources around them will be curtailed.

Views about this Sanctuary are based on fundamental conflicts that need to be resolved. Most of these have little to do with the debate about the dam *per se*. Groups like OXFAM and Arch Vahini, both of which support the Sardar Sarovar Projects, told us that they are critical of plans for the Sanctuary. A great deal of their concern has to do with the attitude of the Forest Department and the likely fate of the people who make the Sanctuary area their home. But the current motivation to expand the Sanctuary is to compensate for the loss of wildlife and wildlife habitat caused by the Sardar Sarovar Projects. One issue, therefore, is the biological value of this area.

We visited the sanctuary area with government and university specialists and with non-government organizations, and we talked to the people in the villages in and around the area. We also solicited expert advice. We concluded that many parts of the Sanctuary have high biological value. It includes some of the best preserved pieces of moist deciduous forest in western India. Floral diversity is high. The Sanctuary has little in the way of large animals apart from a few dozen sloth bears, but it does contain some interesting and unusual birds, including birds of prey. Because there is not much wildlife in the submergence area of the Sardar Sarovar Projects either, the protection offered by the Sanctuary probably constitutes fair compensation for the wildlife habitat lost.

However, it does not follow automatically from this that the Sanctuary should be enlarged or that current activities of the local people should be curtailed. Much of the best preserved vegetation is on inaccessible steep hillsides, not suitable for agriculture and difficult of access even for harvesting of forest produce. In fact, if protection of biodiversity were the only concern, the current boundaries are probably larger than necessary. Expansion is therefore not necessary on biological and environmental grounds.

People and their use of the flora and fauna are also part of the ecosystem. There are many management options. Achieving a lasting and workable balance in the management of this ecosystem can only be achieved through cooperation and commitment to common goals.

The forest that exists today is the product of natural and human activities over hundreds, perhaps thousands of years. At the present time the 60,765 hectares of the proposed expanded Sanctuary contain approximately 90 villages. The population of these villages totals between 30,000 and 40,000, all of whom are tribals and for all of whom the forest is a major component of their economy. Some of the villages in the Sanctuary are known as "forest villages," which means that they come under the jurisdiction of the Forest Department and all the lands used by villagers are, technically speaking, encroachments.[10] In the remaining villages, a significant proportion of land is also encroached. All these villages also depend heavily on the surrounding forest for grazing

[10] Detailed data provided by Arch Vahini for one forest village, Dabka, which is only 2 km from the main road and has had a school since 1970, indicate that 54 households between them cultivate 104 ha of encroached land.

cows, bullocks, buffaloes, and goats. In addition, the forest provides these villages with firewood, building materials for their houses, and a variety of other forest produce. The seasonal calendar of use of forest species prepared by VIKSAT[11] shows year-round dependence on products such as gum karaya, timru leaves, behaba pulp, amla, mahua flowers, and mahua seeds (*doli*). The headloading of fuel for sale in Dediapada and other nearby towns is also an important economic activity. In some villages within the forest, agriculture supplies food for only four to five months of the year. Resident villagers support themselves for the rest of the year on minor forest produce and contract work (mainly as laborers in nearby towns). The people of these villages depend upon the forest, and have done so "since time immemorial."[12]

There are also some 50 to 60 villages which are not within the proposed Sanctuary, but whose inhabitants also make use of the forest. These are villages whose grazing and gathering take them into the forest, as does their daily need for firewood. Some of them also have encroached lands in the proposed Sanctuary area. Since no surveys have been done to establish overall reliance on the forests of the region, there are no figures that illustrate people's vulnerability to any changes in administrative arrangements that the Sanctuary could entail.

When we visited Sanctuary villages, we heard people speak with intense feeling about their recurrent conflicts with forestry officials. They told us that their right to harvest in the forest had already been restricted. They said that they were not supposed to get wood to build their houses. They expressed fear even of gathering firewood. They spoke of altercations with officials, and of having to pay bribes to avoid criminal charges being brought against them.

Tensions between tribal peoples and forestry officials are a commonplace of life in all the communities we visited. According to submissions we received, this hostile relationship between villagers and forest officials is institutionalized, in large part because of the current forest legislation. It is against this background that the Sanctuary proposal must be seen.

Reports on the proposed Sanctuary reveal the problem. The Third Interim Report of the Wildlife Management Study Group set up by the Nigam noted that: "Major management issues arise from human-animal-protected area conflict. Many of these conflicts are for land use and resource use.... To protect them a sufficient 'core area' having their population has to be demarcated, from where human and other biotic pressure will have to be removed" (pp 14-15).

---

[11] See VIKSAT, *Peoples Involvement in Wildlife Management, a Preliminary Report of the Field Study,* September 1991, pp 27-8.
[12] See VIKSAT report, September 1991, p 6.

In a study prepared by the Department of Botany at the M. S. University of Baroda, sponsored by the Nigam, the authors note that:

> Perhaps the most waxing [sic] problem of the Shoolpaneshwar Sanctuary is that of human activity in and around the Sanctuary. Three of the needs of human society in this area are in direct conflict with the interests of the Sanctuary. They are the people's need of land for agriculture, their need for fuel wood for daily consumption and their requirements of grazing areas for their livestock.[13]

The report noted that human population in the area is increasing at an estimated 34 per cent per decade, and along with it cattle populations are also rising. The report observed that: "It is possible that the cattle population may have already crossed the carrying capacity of the area" (p 8, see also p 11). The report suggested an action plan that would be based on "inducing a small but steady movement of humans outside the Sanctuary on a voluntary basis, over a length of time. It is expected that in five years' time the pressures on the Shoolpaneshwar Sanctuary area will be reduced; and in ten years they should be mostly eliminated" (p 8).

The enticement of villagers away from the Sanctuary would be achieved by measures that include offering land from other areas to those who live in the core area of the Sanctuary, supplying free fuel and grain in exchange for people giving up cattle, payment of a monthly sum in exchange for cattle and land, training young people for jobs "with industry and other out of area positions," and hiring forest guards from families of the area on the condition that they will neither raise cattle nor practice agriculture. In discussion of the right bank Sardar Sarovar catchment area, the authors suggested that nothing be planted that could be "useful to cattle or to humans for local use in the area" (p 12). The point of view expressed and the plans proposed by these reports can only reinforce the villagers' fears. The figures set out by the wildlife management studies quoted here are a reason for worry. Some new initiatives are no doubt needed if the area is to be preserved. But whatever measures are adopted must be built with and for people who live there. This would entail a break with the past.

The proposed expansion of the Sanctuary came under consideration when

---

[13] J. B. Bhatt, *Eco-environmental and Wildlife Management Studies on the Sardar Sarovar Submergence Area in Gujarat*, Interim Report—II, 1990-91. See also, Sanat A. Chavan *et al.*, *Third Interim Report*, Wildlife Management Study Group, Sardar Sarovar Nigam Limited, August-September 1991, p 15.

the Basin Development Project was reviewed by a Bank mission in 1991. The Final Executive Project Summary[14] observed that "The forestry component calls for a participatory approach to forest management" (p 3), but also referred to Ministry of Environment and Forest guidelines "which call for full forest cover, indigenous species and no timber harvesting" (p 3). The contradiction between these two objectives was pointed out. The Executive Summary went on to focus on the conflicts to which the Shoolpaneshwar Sanctuary has given rise. In discussing the pros and cons of the whole Basin Development Project as a suitable program for Bank funding, the Summary warned that it carries "some risk for the Bank because of the visibility due to its links to the SSP [Sardar Sarovar] projects." The recommendation was that the Bank should stay with the Sanctuary idea, maintaining it as an element in the Basin Development plan, "provided we ensure that any necessary re-adjustment of people within the Sanctuary for wildlife corridors/core areas etc. is minimal and entirely voluntary" (p 4).

Later that year the World Bank made plain that its commitment to the Sanctuary proposal (or any part of the Narmada Basin Development Program) was conditional on there being no involuntary displacement. In a memo of November 13, 1991 the position is set out: "The Bank has also made it clear that it will not finance the component [Shoolpaneshwar Sanctuary] if any compulsory resettlement is involved." While observing that the Forest Department did not envisage "any compulsory movement of people out of the Sanctuary area," the same memorandum reported that Arch Vahini had been critical of the Forest Department role in the area, and acknowledged that "there is probably considerable truth in some of the allegations."[15]

In reality, the villagers who find themselves within the existing Shoolpaneshwar Sanctuary already feel under direct pressure. They told us that fines for encroachment had increased from Rs. 50 to Rs. 500 per year. We saw people hide from forest officials for fear that the wood they were gathering would be taken from them. At meetings with us people said that there had been no consultation. Plans to date, including the Bank's proposal, have not been developed in collaboration with those who are most directly at risk.

Arch Vahini, in submissions to us on the subject of the Shoolpaneshwar Sanctuary, strongly opposed its enlargement unless and until the tribal peoples living there were given rights to forest resources and a real role in forest

---

[14] India—Narmada Basin Development Project, Final Executive Project Summary, July 30, 1991.

[15] Arch Vahini report that harassment of villagers by forest staff has increased since the sanctuary was extended. This confirms that implementation of the sanctuary will limit current practices of forest use. The M. S. University team and the VIKSAT report also come to the same conclusions. Application of sanctuary regulations without compensation for local people can only lead to further antagonism between the government and the tribal people.

management. They say that degradation and over-harvesting of forest is, in part, a result of the people having no rights to their lands. So long as they are treated as poachers and encroachers or, at best, given limited wage labor opportunities by the Forest Department, they can have little interest in the forest as a long-term resource whose future they must defend.

The Bank's Staff Appraisal Report of March 23, 1992, makes it clear that no management plan exists yet for Shoolpaneshwar. It says that "a condition of disbursement" would be that the management plan would be cleared by the Bank. It also says that "assurances would be sought at negotiations that no involuntary resettlement would be carried out" (p 12). The Project Implementation Volume of March 23, 1992 notes that management options cannot be assessed without a clear statement of objects, which are lacking. It goes on to say that a final management plan is "likely" to include 20 items from a land use plan and improved conservation practices, to forest product marketing and pricing policies, and to costs and benefit sharing (Annex 5, Appendix, pp 2-3). This leaves much in abeyance, including the components that strike at the vulnerability of the tribal people of the area. Given the experience with Sardar Sarovar, to which the proposed funding is directly linked, a basic requirement must be a plan that assures the Bank that its policies can and will be met, that the conditions attached to any agreement can be monitored and enforced, and that the Project has some reasonable assurance of success.

CONCLUDING OBSERVATIONS

There is a clear and urgent need for a basin-wide approach to the environmental and resettlement and rehabilitation issues in the lower Narmada. This need, as well as the outline of the approach, is documented in the Bank's files. But what has emerged in the proposed Basin Development Project falls far short of what is necessary. We are especially concerned because the elements in the current proposal are unlikely properly to address the problems highlighted in the course of our review of Sardar Sarovar. There has not been an appropriate socioeconomic or environmental assessment. The needs and wishes of the people at risk, all of whom are tribal, have not been taken into account. Indeed, the hostility generated within the villages in the valley affected by the Projects, along with the failure of the current system to effectively implement previous agreements, makes it almost certain that the largest components of the proposed Basin Project will fail to meet their objectives.

The opportunity for sustainable development in the Narmada River valley is obvious. If this opportunity is to be seized with Bank assistance, we believe that the currently proposed Basin Development Project should be reconsidered, taking into account the findings of our review.

CONCLUSIONS

Men at Anjanvada, Madhya Pradesh, preparing food for a wedding feast.

Chapter 17

FINDINGS AND RECOMMENDATIONS

WE have completed an assessment of resettlement and environmental aspects of the Sardar Sarovar Projects. In this chapter we draw together the findings of our review, already explained in the preceding chapters, and set forth the recommendations which, in our judgment, are appropriate to these findings.

THE FINDINGS

Resettlement and Rehabilitation

- The Bank and India both failed to carry out adequate assessments of human impacts of the Sardar Sarovar Projects. Many of the difficulties that have beset implementation of the Projects have their origin in this failure.
- There was virtually no basis, in 1985, on which to determine what the impacts were that would have to be ameliorated. This led to an inadequate understanding of the nature and scale of resettlement.
- This inadequate understanding was compounded by a failure to consult the people potentially to be affected.
- Failure to consult the people has resulted in opposition to the Projects, on the part of potentially affected people, supported by activists. This opposition has created great obstacles to successful implementation.
- In drafting the terms and conditions of the 1985 credit and loan agreements, the Bank failed to take adequate account of the fact that a large proportion of those at risk from the development of the Sardar Sarovar Projects are tribal people. This meant that insufficient account was taken of the principles enshrined in the Bank's 1982 Operational Manual Statement outlining its policies regarding tribal people.

- In these and other ways, the Bank failed to follow the principles and policies it set out in 1980 and 1982. In addition, the Bank's overarching principle embodied in the 1985 credit and loan agreements by which resettlement and rehabilitation were to be judged, namely that oustees improve or at least regain their standard of living as quickly as possible, was not consistently advanced or insisted upon with sufficient force or commitment.
- The Bank failed to consider the effects of the Projects on people living downstream of the dam. We recommend that the Bank develop a policy to deal with the plight of persons affected downstream. They may not come within the rubric of resettlement, but their situation should be addressed.
- As a result of both the inadequate database and the failure to incorporate provisions of the Bank's policies in the 1985 credit and loan agreements, the provisions for resettlement and rehabilitation do not adequately address the real needs of those to be affected.
- In particular, the agreements allowed a distinction between "landed" and "landless" oustees which failed to recognize the realities of life in the submergence villages.
- Similarly, the rights of encroachers were not acknowledged. The only way of implementing resettlement policy, at least in the case of the Sardar Sarovar Projects, in a way that restores oustees' previous standard of living is by provision of adequate land. This is of special relevance to the oustees of Maharashtra and Madhya Pradesh.
- The people of the six villages affected by construction and development of Kevadia Colony were not appropriately and adequately compensated. The Bank failed to ensure that this be done as required by the 1985 agreements. We recommend that the Bank require India to provide land for the families of the six villages, with an adjustment for cash compensation received in the interim, as appropriate.
- Relocation and resettlement of the people of the rock-filled dyke villages was implemented in a way that meant that the Bank's overarching principle of resettlement and rehabilitation, i.e., that no one should suffer a fall in standard of living, was not likely to be achieved.
- The Bank failed to ensure that those affected by construction of the canal and irrigation system would be entitled to resettlement benefits.
- We recommend that the Bank should use its good offices to ensure that Gujarat provides resettlement benefits to canal-affected persons, especially those farmers who are rendered marginal or landless.
- The policies of the riparian states failed to anticipate the needs of major sons, and adopted what we regard as an unduly restrictive interpretation of the Tribunal award's provision for major sons. Maharashtra and Madhya Pradesh continue to maintain this interpretation and provide inadequate

benefits to major sons of landed families.

- In 1987-88 the Government of Gujarat expanded its resettlement and rehabilitation policies to provide two hectares of irrigable land to all oustees, including the landless, encroachers, and major sons. This represented a policy
package that came nearer than any thus far set out anywhere in India to establishing a basis for successful resettlement.
- Despite Gujarat's improved policy, Maharashtra and Madhya Pradesh continued to limit the provision of two hectares of land to "landed" oustees. This
means encroachers and major sons (including the major sons of landed
oustees) are not entitled to benefits in their own states that meet the Bank's
overarching principle of resettlement and rehabilitation. The proportion of
oustees thus vulnerable to a reduced standard of living is at least 60 per cent.
- The disparity between Gujarat's policy and the policies of Maharashtra and
Madhya Pradesh has meant that oustees' right to choose between relocation
in Gujarat and their own state has been rendered meaningless.
- Implementation of resettlement in Maharashtra has been limited by both
policy deficiencies and availability of irrigable land.
- Implementation of resettlement in Madhya Pradesh has been limited by policy deficiencies, inadequate institutional commitment, continuing failure of
consultation, and limited availability of suitable resettlement land.
- This state of affairs in Madhya Pradesh has produced a situation in which,
even if Madhya Pradesh were to adopt a policy with benefits equal to
Gujarat's, such a policy could not now be implemented, given the time necessary to meet the requirements of the Sardar Sarovar Projects.
- Resettlement of oustees in Gujarat has entailed a scattering of families and
villages among many different sites. This is in part a result of choices made
by oustees. It is also a result of inadequate land at resettlement sites to accommodate all oustees who wish to have land there. This has contributed to
some separation of families, especially in the case of oustees from the rock-
filled dyke villages.
- Gujarat is unlikely to be able to resettle a large proportion of oustees from
Maharashtra and Madhya Pradesh. Even if land were available for relocation sites, resettlement and rehabilitation at these sites presents major problems.
- The record of resettlement and rehabilitation in India, which has been unsat-
isfactory in virtually every project with a large resettlement component,
should reasonably have prompted the Bank to adopt a less flexible standard
for resettlement and rehabilitation of project-affected people. In this context,
the Bank's incremental strategy to obtain compliance, made explicit in 1989,
greatly undermines prospects for achieving successful resettlement and rehabilitation.

Environment

- Measures to anticipate and mitigate environmental impact were not properly considered in the design of the Projects because of a lack of basic data and consultation with the affected people.
- The Bank's appraisal took no account of the fact that environmental clearance in India was not forthcoming in 1983 from the Ministry of Environment and Forests because of insufficient information.
- Under the 1985 credit and loan agreements, the Bank required an environmental workplan to be developed by the end of 1985, later extended to 1989. It is still not available, resulting in a disjointed, piecemeal approach to environmental planning that is both inefficient and ineffective.
- In 1987 India's environmental clearance for the Projects was given, despite the fact that the information required prior to the Projects' clearance was unavailable. In order to overcome this deficiency, studies were to be conducted *pari passu* with construction. The clearance was conditional on completion of these basic studies by 1989. Most remain to be completed. We believe that the *pari passu* policy greatly undermines the prospects for achieving environmental protection.
- Significant discrepancies in the hydrological data and analyses indicate that the Sardar Sarovar Projects will not perform as planned either with or without the upstream Narmada Sagar Projects. A realistic operational analysis of the Projects upon which to base an impact assessment has not been done.
- The cumulative impacts of the Sardar Sarovar Projects together with the related upstream developments, especially the Narmada Sagar Projects, are very likely to be far reaching, yet they have not been studied.
- The afforestation and catchment area treatment programs proposed upstream are unlikely to succeed within the timetable of the Projects because of the lack of consultation with, and participation of, villagers in the affected areas.
- The compensatory afforestation approach being taken by Gujarat in Kutchch, if continued, will lead to a steady decline in the quality of forests. The practice of replanting marginal forest lands in substitution for better lands that will be submerged, means that the forests will be diminished in value.
- The impact associated with the backwater effect of sedimentation in the upper reaches of the reservoir has not been considered. Our assessment has concluded that it will be significant.
- The downstream ecological implications of dam construction have not been considered. Important but limited data have only recently begun to be collected. The downstream impacts are likely to be significant, including severe

losses to, if not the elimination of, the last important hilsa fishery in western India.

- There has been no comprehensive environmental assessment of the canal and water delivery system in the command area. Information we have gathered leads us to believe that there will be serious problems with waterlogging and salinity. We also found that many of the assumptions used in project design and for the development of mitigative measures are suspect.

- Despite the stated priority of delivery of drinking water, there were no plans available for review.

- The existing threat from malaria within the command area is serious. The Projects have been designed and executed without appropriate safeguards. The failure to adopt measures to reduce the likelihood of the spread of malaria illustrates the breakdown between assurances offered by the Bank and India and the reality on the ground. We recommend that the Bank use its good offices to ensure that preventive measures are taken as a matter of urgency to address the public health problems posed by water-borne diseases in the Projects area.

- The newly proposed Narmada Basin Development Project, although it appears to address some of the problems highlighted in our review, fails to address key issues, many of which are the same as have caused problems with the Sardar Sarovar Projects. Although some specific elements have merit, the Basin Development Project adopts a piecemeal approach, falling far short of the work that the Bank's own missions have said is needed for proper basin development. The implications of Narmada Sagar for basin development are overlooked.

- Bank requirements that the Basin Development Project not entail forced relocation and proceed on the basis of a participatory approach to forest management and catchment area treatment, as proposed, are laudable but unrealistic, given the hostility towards the Projects in the region and the time frames envisaged by the Projects.

THE BANK

We have made findings that reveal a failure to incorporate Bank policies into the 1985 credit and loan agreements and subsequent failure to require adherence to enforceable provisions of these agreements. Much of what has gone wrong with Sardar Sarovar Projects is the result of such failures over a range of resettlement and rehabilitation and environmental matters.

How did this happen?

It is apparent that there has been, and continues to be, deep concern among Bank officers and staff that India should have the means to enhance agricultural production. The Sardar Sarovar Projects were seen as offering enormous benefits, especially in terms of delivery of drinking water and irrigation. There developed an eagerness on the part of the Bank and India to get on with the job. Both, it seems, were prepared to ease, or even disregard, Bank policy and India's regulations and procedures dealing with resettlement and environmental protection in the hope of achieving the much-needed benefits.

Experience worldwide, in developed as well as developing countries, has shown that by factoring in and allowing for human and environmental considerations at the outset, projects can be substantially improved. To be effective, resettlement and environmental planning must be integrated into the design of projects; otherwise they become costly and burdensome add-ons.

These considerations lead to an examination of issues that focus on the Bank itself. Our work in conducting the independent review has encouraged us to make a number of observations which may be of value.

Embedded in the World Bank's operational directives is a resolve to establish *ex ante* project assessment. This requires an investment by the Bank of time and money and personnel with appropriate expertise, with on-the-ground studies and consultation as part of the planning of a project.

There should be a review of Bank procedures to ensure that the full reach of the Bank's policies is being implemented. The Bank should establish whether the problems we have found in the case of Sardar Sarovar are at issue in other projects in India and elsewhere. Our findings on this project may well indicate a need on the part of the Bank to strengthen quality control.

THE PROJECTS

The Terms of Reference provided that our assessment should include, as appropriate, recommendations for improvement of implementation. The absence of proper impact assessments and the paucity of undisputed data have limited our ability confidently to make project-specific recommendations of the kind that were contemplated. We have limited ourselves to recommendations with respect to the Kevadia villagers, the canal oustees, downstream policy, and the protection of public health, that should be carried through regardless of the fate of the Projects.

Our findings indicate that the Sardar Sarovar Projects are beset by profound difficulties. These difficulties have their genesis in the earliest phase of the Bank's involvement in the Projects, for they turn on the absence of an adequate database and failure to consult with the people whose lives and environment were and continue to be affected.

Lack of data meant that the Bank was not able, in the early 1980s, to appraise the Projects properly. No one is sure about the impacts of the reservoir and the canal on either people or the land. Without knowing what impacts were likely to be, we found it difficult to the point of impossibility to assess measures by which they might be mitigated; much of our work has therefore been devoted to gathering our own limited information base.

People who live in the villages and depend on the resources of the valley should have played a central part in determining the Projects' impact. Both their knowledge and their vulnerabilities are integral to any understanding of what is at issue. At the same time, failure to consult has fuelled intense opposition to the Projects which, as we have pointed out, has itself become a serious obstacle to design and implementation of mitigative measures.

These factors—absence of adequate data, failure of consultation, and hostility towards the Projects in the Narmada Valley—bear on every aspect of implementation. Our Terms of Reference invite us to recommend measures to improve implementation. It seems to us that the essential condition, the very starting point of any such recommendation, requires that these underlying difficulties be addressed.

But the underlying difficulties—the failures that reach back to the origin of the Projects—cannot be overcome by a patchwork of studies. The limited information base which we constructed is inadequate for the purpose. Nor is it a question of applying more intense pressure to Maharashtra and Madhya Pradesh in order to secure improved resettlement policies. As we say, the difficulties are profound. The Bank's incremental strategy and India's *pari passu* policy, adopted to deal with resettlement and environmental problems, have for the most part failed. A further application of the same strategy, albeit in a more determined or aggressive form, would also fail. As long as implementation continues in these ways, problems will be compounded rather than mitigated.

Absence of human and environmental assessment *ab initio* creates the impression that the demands of engineering carry far more weight in the Bank than the needs of the people to be affected or of the environment. The Bank's incremental strategy (and the Bank's concurrence in India's *pari passu* policy) strengthen this impression. Readiness to bear with non-compliance thereafter confirms it.

Decisions as to the future of the Sardar Sarovar Projects and the Bank's participation in them are within the exclusive domains of India and the Bank. But implementation of the Projects requires measures that go to the heart of the problems in which the resettlement and environmental components of the Sardar Sarovar Projects have become mired. We have been at pains in the section of this chapter summarizing our findings to demonstrate how those problems of human and environmental impact encompass all aspects of the Projects, including the uncertainties of hydrology, the upstream questions, the impact downstream, the command area issues, the health risks, the deficiencies in resettlement policy and implementation in each of the three states as well as the canal. None of these issues can be ignored.

It seems to us that the matters we have raised are fundamental. It would be prudent if the necessary studies were done and the data made available for informed decision-making before further construction takes place. Implementation requires that the Bank take a step back. Otherwise, the possibility of making sound decisions will be further compromised.

Little can be achieved while construction continues. What would a step back achieve? First, it would afford an opportunity to design the kinds of human and environmental impact studies that are still needed. Second, it would permit the assessment of the results of such studies, to see whether modifications of the Projects might be in order. Third, it would provide a chance to consider what resettlement and rehabilitation policies might meet the needs of the oustees, and how these could be implemented in a way that is consistent with the Bank's policies and principles as set out in its Operational Manuals and Directives.

Even though proponents describe Sardar Sarovar as the most studied and least implemented project in India, we do not agree. The Projects may well be the most talked about in India, but the fact is that their human and environmental consequences have not been studied, and their engineering, design, and operation would profit from further analysis.

There is a need to consider Sardar Sarovar in the social and environmental context of the Narmada valley as a whole, to consult, inform, and involve the people affected by the Projects throughout the Narmada valley, those affected in the command area, and those living downstream. The opposition, especially in the submergence area, has ripened into hostility. So long as this hostility endures, progress will be impossible except as a result of unacceptable means.

A way must be found to rebuild confidence, to demonstrate goodwill, and to send out an unambiguous message that the Bank continues to be committed to its principles and its policies.

REFLECTIONS

In the case of the Sardar Sarovar Projects, India has bound itself to meet standards for resettlement and rehabilitation more exacting than any it had agreed to in the past.

We do not expect perfect justice; in an imperfect world it cannot be obtained. There is no doubt that in the national interest, people can be required to resettle. However, India, in conformity with the development of international standards of human rights, has subscribed to certain minimum conditions that must be observed even when the national interest is involved. They reflect the inalienable human rights of the oustees. We believe that these norms must be adhered to.

Nor do we insist upon an unattainable standard in environmental impact assessment and mitigation. However, to construct the Sardar Sarovar Projects, India has availed itself of world-class engineering technology. Should it settle for less than adequate standards in the application of social and environmental science?

We are aware of the statement in the eleventh principle of the Rio Declaration presented to the 1992 United Nations Conference on Environment and Development:

> Standards applied by some countries may be inappropriate and of unwarranted economic and social cost to other countries, in particular developing countries.

But the environmental standards for the Sardar Sarovar Projects were established by India itself. On the resettlement side, standards were determined by the Narmada Water Disputes Tribunal and agreed to by India and the states in the credit and loan agreements.

We have felt obliged to illuminate what we think are flaws in the Sardar Sarovar Projects. It should not be thought that these would only be found in India or confined to the Sardar Sarovar Projects. The fragile assumptions which have supported this project can be found elsewhere. Failure to consider the human rights of the displaced and failure to consider environmental impacts occur in the development of megaprojects in both developed and developing countries.

If the human rights obligations identified by International Labor Organization Convention 107 and in Bank policy are acknowledged and respected, if the commitment to the environment is real, and if these are properly integrated into project design at the outset, more effective and equitable development will ensue. Some believe that these requirements make it more difficult, often more costly, to build megaprojects like Sardar Sarovar. This implies that human and environmental costs are to be heavily discounted in project planning and execution. But hard lessons from the past have taught us that this is unacceptable. In some cases it may be that alternatives to projects that cause compulsory relocation on a large scale or severe environmental impact may have to be sought.

We have found it difficult to separate our assessment of resettlement and rehabilitation and environmental protection from a consideration of the Sardar Sarovar Projects as a whole. The issues of human and environmental impact bear on virtually every aspect of large-scale development projects. Ecological realities must be acknowledged, and unless a project can be carried out in accordance with existing norms of human rights—norms espoused and endorsed by the Bank and many borrower countries—the project ought not to proceed.

The Bank must ensure that in projects it decides to support the principles giving priority to resettlement and environmental protection are faithfully observed. This is the only basis for truly sustainable development.

a) **TERMS OF REFERENCE**

INDIA—Implementation of Sardar Sarovar Projects
Assessment of Resettlement and Environmental Aspects

TERMS OF REFERENCE

The objective shall be to conduct an assessment of the implementation of the ongoing Sardar Sarovar Projects (SSP) (supported by IBRD/IDA Credits 1552 and Loan 2497) as regards:

> (a) the resettlement and rehabilitation (R&R) of the population displaced/affected by the construction of the SSP infrastructure and by the storage reservoir; and
> (b) the amelioration of the environmental impact of all aspects of the projects.

The assessment should include, as appropriate, any recommendations for improvement of project implementation in the above two areas.

The assessment shall take account of all covenants and understandings reached between Government of India GOI and IBRD/IDA in the loan/credit documents and other relevant agreements as well as:

> (a) the decisions of the Narmada Water Disputes Tribunal, which sanctioned the projects;
> (b) the environmental clearance decision of the GOI Ministry of Environment and Forests including subsequent decisions regarding release of forest lands for resettlement;

(c) union and state laws and directives relevant to the implementation of R&R in the three affected states Gujarat, Madhya
Pradesh and Maharashtra.

The assessment shall make reference to existing Bank operational directives
and guidelines with respect to project-related R&R and environmental assessments and safeguards, keeping in mind that several of these directives were
promulgated and/or amended after these loans/credits were approved in 1985.

In conducting the assessment, close liaison should be maintained with the
Government of India (Ministry of Water Resources, Ministry of Environment
and Forests, Ministry of Finance—Department of Economic Affairs, all in
New Delhi); the Narmada Control Authority (Indore, Madhya Pradesh); the
Government of Gujarat (Sardar Sarovar Narmada Nigam Ltd., Gandhinagar); the Government of Madhya Pradesh (Narmada Valley Development Authority, Bhopal); the Government of Maharashtra (Departments of
Forestry, Agriculture, Resettlement, Bombay); and the World Bank. In addition, the assessment should take into account the views of people affected by
the projects as well as local non-governmental organizations.

March 14, 1991

b) BIOGRAPHIES

THE HONORABLE BRADFORD MORSE

Mr. Morse is Chairman of the Independent Review. He is an American politi-
cian and administrator with a broad international reputation on development
issues.

Mr. Morse was admitted to the Bar in Massachusetts in 1948 and taught at
Boston University Law School from 1949 to 1953. The following year he became Special Counsel for the Senate Committee on Armed Services. He served
as Deputy Administrator of Veterans Affairs in the Eisenhower administration.

Mr. Morse was elected to the United States Congress in 1960. He served
until his resignation in 1972 to become Under-Secretary-General of the United
Nations, a position he held until 1976 when he became Administrator of the
United Nations Development Program. In addition to his other responsibilities, Mr. Morse organized the international famine relief effort for the ten Af-
rican countries that suffered the most severe drought in recorded history from

1984 through 1986.

Mr. Morse is a Member of the Board of the Georgetown University School of Foreign Service, and has served for 16 years as a Trustee of Boston University. He also serves on the Board of Directors of the Panos Foundation, the Population Crisis Committee, and the Save the Children Federation. He is a member of the Council of Foreign Relations, the American Academy of Diplomacy, and the Society for International Development.

Mr. Morse is a Distinguished Fellow of the United Institute of Peace and a Senior Fellow of the National Academy of Public Administration. He is the recipient of a number of decorations, including Officer de la Gran Cruz de la Orden de San Carlos de Colombia, Officier de l'Ordre Nationale du Niger, Grand Commandeur de l'Ordre du Lion de Senegal, Grand Officer of the Republic of Gambia, and Officer of the Grand Cordon of the Sacred Treasure of Japan. He has been the recipient of the American Society of Public Administration National Pubic Service award, the U.S. Presidential World Without Hunger Award, the North America Leadership Award, the F.D.R. Freedom From Want Award, the International Development Conference Humanitarian Award, the AMVETS Peace Award, and the Christian A. Herter Peace Award. Mr. Morse has also been awarded numerous honorary degrees.

THE HONORABLE THOMAS R. BERGER

Thomas R. Berger is Deputy Chairman of the Independent Review. He is a Canadian lawyer known internationally for his work on aboriginal, environmental, and human rights issues.

Mr. Berger graduated from the University of British Columbia in 1956 and practiced law in Vancouver until 1971. Mr. Berger was also active in politics, and served as a member of the Canadian Parliament from 1962 to 1963, and as a member of the British Columbia Legislative Assembly from 1966 to 1969, representing the New Democratic Party. In 1971, he was appointed to the Supreme Court of British Columbia. He served on the bench until 1983.

Mr. Berger has headed royal commissions of inquiry under each of Canada's three national political parties. In 1973-74, he undertook the British Columbia Commission on Family and Children's Law. From 1974 to 1977, he headed the Mackenzie Valley Pipeline Inquiry to determine the social, environmental, and economic impact of the proposed Arctic Gas pipeline to be built from Prudhoe Bay in Alaska down through the Mackenzie Valley in northwestern Canada. *Northern Frontier, Northern Homeland*, the report of the Inquiry, became the best-selling book ever published by the Government of Canada. For this work, Mr. Berger received a distinguished achievement award from the Sierra Club of North America in 1978, and was named an honorary member of the Engineering Institute of Canada in 1979. Mr. Berger headed a third royal commission in 1979 dealing with Indian and Inuit health programmes.

In 1981, Mr. Berger's intervention was instrumental in the including of aboriginal rights in the new Canadian Constitution. In the same year he wrote *Fragile Freedoms*, a study of human rights and dissent in Canada.

In April 1983, Mr. Berger was chosen by the Inuit Circumpolar Conference to head the Alaska Native Review Commission to consider the impact of the 1971 *Alaska Native Claims Settlement Act*. His report, *Village Journey*, was published in 1985 by Hill and Wang, New York.

Mr. Berger has received special calls to the bar in Alberta and in Manitoba. He holds honorary degrees from 12 universities. Since 1981, he has been a member of the International Commission of Jurists. He received the Order of Canada in 1990.

DONALD J. GAMBLE

Donald Gamble is the Chief of Staff and the senior environmental advisor for the Independent Review. He is an environmental policy and assessment specialist with wide experience in water development issues. He is Chairman of Resource Futures International (RFI) Inc. and the Advisor to the President of the Rawson Academy of Aquatic Science.

Mr. Gamble has a degree in civil engineering and a Master of Science in environment and resource studies. He practiced as a consulting engineer from 1970 to 1974 before moving to the Policy and Planning Division of Canada's Department of Indian Affairs and Northern Development in Ottawa. From there he joined the Mackenzie Valley Pipeline Inquiry as an engineering and environmental specialist. In 1978, he became the first Director of Policy Studies at the Canadian Arctic Resources Committee (CARC) where he headed the environmental and socioeconomic impact assessment programs. During this period, Mr. Gamble was also appointed for three successive terms to the Northwest Territories Water Board, a quasi-judicial regulatory agency established under the *Northern Inland Waters Act*. In 1983, he went to the United States as Chief of Staff for the commission examining problems associated with the implementation of the *Alaska Native Claims Settlement Act*. He return to Ottawa in 1986 to establish the national office for the Rawson Academy, a non-profit association of Canada's leading aquatic scientists and renewable resource professionals. He founded Resource Futures International (RFI) Inc. in 1989 to provide sustainable development expertise worldwide.

Mr. Gamble is a member of the Canadian Society of Environmental Biologists, the Canadian Water Resource Association, and the International

Association of Great Lakes Research. His publications have appeared in *Science*, the *Canadian Journal of Civil Engineering*, *Arctic*, and *The Geographical Magazine* (UK). He is on the Board of Directors of CARC, Organization and Management Services Company (OMSCO), and the Radha Foundation, and is the founding Vice-President of Cultural Horizons Inc.

HUGH BRODY

Hugh Brody is Senior Advisor, Resettlement and Rehabilitation Assessment, for the Independent Review. He is an internationally recognized anthropologist, author, and filmmaker. He is an Honorary Associate at the Scott Polar Research Institute at the University of Cambridge.

Hugh Brody was an undergraduate and postgraduate at the University of Oxford. He was the recipient of research awards from Trinity College, Oxford, and the Social Science Research Council of Great Britain. He taught philosophy at Queen's University in Belfast, and anthropology at the University of Cambridge and McGill University (Montreal).

Mr. Brody was a research officer with Canada's Department of Indian Affairs and Northern Development from 1972 to 1975, following which he was an anthropologist with responsibility for land use and occupancy studies in the Northwest Territories and Labrador. He was an adviser to the Mackenzie Valley Pipeline Inquiry in 1976 and 1977. From 1979 to 1981, Mr. Brody was co-ordinator of the assessment of impacts of the Alaska Highway Pipeline proposal. He has been an expert witness in public hearings and legal actions on the impacts of development and social change.

Mr. Brody's research projects include: social change in the west of Ireland, rural-urban migration and associated social pathologies, Inuit of the eastern Arctic, Dunneza of the Canadian Subarctic, and Gitksan and Wet'suwet'en of the north Pacific Coast. He has published extensively throughout his career. His publications include *Indians on Skid Row* (1970), *Inishkillane: Change and Decline in the West of Ireland* (1971), *The People's Land* (1975), *Maps and Dreams* (1981), *Nineteen Nineteen* (1986), *Living Arctic* (1987), and *Means of Escape* (1991). He has also written and directed anthropological films for British and Canadian television.